SAFEGUARDS AND ANTIDUMPING IN LATIN AMERICAN TRADE LIBERALIZATION

SAFEGUARDS AND ANTIDUMPING IN LATIN AMERICAN TRADE LIBERALIZATION

Fighting Fire with Fire

Edited by J. Michael Finger
and Julio J. Nogués

A copublication of Palgrave Macmillan
and the World Bank

1818 H Street NW
Washington, DC 20433
Telephone: 202-473-1000
Internet: www.worldbank.org
E-mail: feedback@worldbank.org

1 2 3 4 09 08 07 06

A copublication of The World Bank and Palgrave Macmillan.

Palgrave Macmillan
Houndmills, Basingstoke, Hampshire RG21 6XS and
175 Fifth Avenue, New York, NY 10010
Companies and representatives throughout the world

Palgrave Macmillan is the global academic imprint of the Palgrave Macmillan division of St. Martin's Press, LLC and of Palgrave Macmillan Ltd.

ISBN-10: 0-8213-6308-5 (softcover)
ISBN-10: 0-8213-6368-9 (hardcover)
ISBN-13: 978-0-8213-6308-9
eISBN-10: 0-8213-6309-3
eISBN-13: 978-0-8213-6309-6
DOI: 10.1596/978-0-8213-6308-9

Library of Congress Cataloging-in-Publication Data

Finger, J.M.
Safeguards and antidumping in Latin American trade liberalization : fighting fire with fire/ by J. Michael Finger and Julio J. Nogués
p. cm.
Includes bibliographical references and index.
ISBN-13: 978-0-8213-6308-9
ISBN-10: 0-8213-6308-5
1. Protectionism—Latin America. 2. Dumping (International trade)—Law and legislation Latin America. 3. Foreign trade regulation—Latin America. I. Nogués, Julio J. II. Title.
HF1770 5.F56 2005
382'.73'098—dc22
2005043682

Cover photos: Yuri Kozyrev/The World Bank; Royalty Free/Corbis.

CONTENTS

Figures

Tables

PREFACE

This book is about policy managers in national capitals, particularly those who created and used "trade defense" or "contingent protection" mechanisms to support unprecedented programs of trade liberalization. Although such mechanisms—safeguards and antidumping in particular—are often associated with international negotiations and trade relations between countries, this book is about the domestic management of trade policy. It is about the management of an agreement between government and domestic producers on what kind and what amount of international competition industry must face.

Many investigations of the use of trade defense instruments have been published in the recent past; a survey article by Professor Douglas Nelson of Tulane University (forthcoming) lists more than 200 references. But, as Professor Nelson points out, this research has been conducted in large part from the perspective of safeguards and antidumping being used as instruments for creating protection. That work focuses on the temptations to seek protection that these mechanisms arouse. The literature, he notes, sees trade defense as villain rather than as hero.

The work we report here comes from the more heroic perspective. This work focuses on how creation of these World Trade Organization–sanctioned mechanisms closed off other opportunities to seek protection and on how the mechanisms helped policy managers to introduce politically effective constraints on pressures that had overcome previous attempts at liberalization.

We also depart from the common perception that the existence of detailed international agreements and national codes on safeguards and on antidumping means that using these instruments is no more than a technical matter of "following the rules," an activity that demands no political or managerial skill. The experiences reviewed in this book show, however, that this perception is not correct.

Skillful management of these mechanisms has been crucial in defending and sustaining the liberalization programs.

Another motivation for organizing the study is a concern that attention to these matters has come too much from the perspective of Geneva negotiations and too little from the perspective of policy managers at home. The Geneva perspective is the mercantilist view of exports (good) versus imports (bad). Liberalization in the countries studied here has been based on a more sophisticated economics, an economics that recognizes the domestic gains that flow from increased competition from abroad and from increased access for domestic consumers and producers to imported goods. We want the book to bring forward the input of *domestic* policy managers, those left at home to organize domestic support and to face up to domestic opposition while the diplomats enjoyed the romance of international negotiations.

In Latin America, many political leaders have paid a high political and personal cost for having liberalized their economies. Additionally, they sustained the political costs of implementing international rules in a form that paid particular attention to ways in which they could most effectively discipline rather than defend the application of trade restrictions. Unsuccessful protection seekers were quick to point to industries in similar situations in the United States or in Europe that had received protection—within the WTO rules. Such comparisons have been the basis for intense criticism by some Latin American industrialists of what Latin American leaders put in place.

So far as the work has application to multilateral negotiations, the objective is to introduce the reality of developing country policy management—the issues policy managers in national capitals confront and the resource constraints they must accept. The experiences we review here show that the multilateral rules are supportive of liberalization, though we emphasize that the skill and courage of policy managers in using them is the difference between success and failure. We believe that the experiences of Latin America in using trade defense mechanisms as elements in their trade liberalization efforts should be considered by the Doha Round negotiators as examples of how the multilateral rules could be made even more supportive of liberalization. The usefulness of this experience will depend, however, on the negotiators' viewing these rules from the perspective of managing domestic pressures for and against liberalization rather than from the perspective of regulating the interests of exporters in one country versus competing producers in an importing country.

We emphasize that this study is not about who did or did not follow WTO rules. Such evaluation is the function of the WTO enforcement and dispute settlement process. We should point out, nevertheless, that the studies find a minimal involvement of the dispute settlement process. These countries have had problems staying within the rules no more often than the more traditional users of such mechanisms. Our studies ask how developing countries have effectively used these rules and how the rules might have been more supportive of what they wanted to do.

The concept "special and differential treatment" does not appear in this book. Our disposition has always been to consider Latin American experience, developing country experience, as part of the world's experience—not as secondary experience, and not as unique experience from which nothing can be learned that would improve policy management in the industrialized countries.

Reference

Nelson, Douglas R. Forthcoming. "The Political Economy of Antidumping: A Survey." *European Journal of Political Economy.*

ACKNOWLEDGMENTS

Because we wanted to give a voice to domestic policy managers, our first and most important task was to identify country authors who had been directly involved in the design and administration of trade defense mechanisms. After draft studies were completed, we brought the authors together for a workshop, hosted by the World Bank office in Buenos Aires. In addition to the country authors and the codirectors, a select group of Latin American trade economists made important contributions there: Julio Berlinski, Pablo Sanguinetti, and Diana Tussie. The workshop was a productive opportunity for each member of the group to learn from the other participants and for the authors to enjoy the benefit of comments and suggestions from all as to how to complete the studies. Pablo Sued served as note-taker; his analytical skill made his output particularly valuable.

Ms. Maria N. Gondell provided skilled administrative support, linking seamlessly the Latin American elements of arrangements with those managed from Washington, DC. The administrative staff of the Bank office in Buenos Aires likewise provided cheerful and able support.

We also acknowledge with gratitude the enthusiastic support for the project provided by Axel von Trotsenburg, director of the World Bank office in Buenos Aires. Likewise, without support and encouragement from Bernard Hoekman, Alan Winters, and Beata S. Javorcik of the World Bank's research staff in Washington, DC, the work could not have been completed.

Financial support was provided by the Bank-Netherlands Partnership. We acknowledge with gratitude not only the funds the Partnership provided but also the willingness of the Partnership to support promising work on the basis of sound but not overly detailed proposal and reporting documents.

This book is for Mary and Sylvina. Through it all they have kept their sense of adventure.

CONTRIBUTORS

Elías Baracat, professor, Universidad de CEMA, Buenos Aires; formerly president, International Trade Commission of Argentina

Josefina Camminati, attorney, Universidad Católica de Perú; formerly consultant to the legal vice ministerio comercio, the Peruvian Exporters Association

J. Michael Finger, lead economist (retired), World Bank; formerly Vernon F. Taylor Distinguished Professor, Trinity University, San Antonio, Texas

Jorge G. González, professor and chair, Department of Economics, Trinity University, San Antonio, Texas

Honorio Kume, research officer, Institute of Applied Economic Research, Rio de Janeiro, Brazil; professor, University of the State of Rio de Janeiro; formerly technical coordinator for Customs Tariffs for the Ministry of Finance, Economics, and Planning

Francisco Monge-Ariño, associate, Costa Rican High Technology Advisory Committee Foundation (CAATEC); graduate teaching assistant, Ohio State University, Dayton, Ohio; member, consultant, CAATEC; formerly director, Oficina Económica de la Cámara de Comercio de Costa Rica

Ricardo Monge-González, executive director, CAATEC; professor of International Trade at the Universidad Latina de Costa Rica

Julio J. Nogués, professor, School of Government, Universidad T. Di Tella, Buenos Aires, Argentina; formerly Undersecretary for International Trade; formerly commercial representative of Argentina in the United States

Guida Piani, research officer, Institute of Applied Economic Research, Rio de Janeiro, Brazil

Mauricio Reina, associate investigator, Fedesarrollo, Bogotá, Colombia; formerly vice minister of International Trade, Colombia

Luz Elena Reyes de la Torre, partner, SAI Consultores, S.C., Mexico City; formerly associate director-general, Unit of International Trade Practices

Sebastián Sáez, consultant; formerly alternate representative of Chile to the WTO

Raúl León Thorne, consultant on International Trade Negotiations; formerly member, Commission on Antidumping and Safeguards of the Instituto Nacional de Defensa de la Competencia y de la Protección de la Propiedad Intelectual

Richard Webb, director, Economic Research Center, University of San Martin de Porres, Lima, Peru; formerly president, Central Reserve Bank of Peru

Sandra Zuluaga, associate investigator, Fedesarrollo, Bogotá, Colombia; formerly adviser to the vice minister for International Trade of Colombia

ABBREVIATIONS AND ACRONYMS

ADC	Antidumping Code
ALADI	Asociación Latinoamericana de Intercambio
APRA	Alianza Popular Revolucionaria Americana (Peru)
ATC	Agreement on Textiles and Clothing (of WTO)
BCCH	Banco Central de Chile
CAATEC	Costa Rican High Technology Advisory Committee Foundation
CACEX	Foreign Trade Department, Bank of Brazil
CAMEX	Chamber of Foreign Trade (Brazil)
CCDC	Consultative Committee on Trade Defense (Brazil)
CCPCI	Consejo Consultivo de Prácticas Comerciales Internacionales (Advisory Council on International Trade Practices) (Mexico)
CDS	Commission for Control of Dumping and Subsidies (La Comisión de Fiscalización de Dumping y Subsidios) (Peru)
CEPR	Center for European Policy Research
CET	common external tariff
CETES	Certificados de la Tesoreria de la Federación (Mexico)
CNCE	Comisión Nacional de Comercio Exterior (National Foreign Trade Commission) (Mexico, Argentina)
CND	National Commission on Distortions
CNDP	National Commission for Price Distortions (Chile)
CPA	Customs Policy Commission (Brazil)
CTIC	Trade Exchange Technical Coordination (Brazil)
CTT	Tariff Technical Coordination (Brazil)
CVD	countervailing duty
DECEX	Foreign Trade Department (Brazil)

DECOM	Department of Commercial Defense (Brazil)
DEINTER	Department of International Negotiations (Brazil)
DEPOC	Department of Foreign Trade Policy (Brazil)
DGPCI	Dirección General de Prácticas Comerciales Internacionales (Mexico)
DIEMs	minimum specific import tariffs (derechos de importación específicos mínimos)
DOF	*Diario Oficial de la Federación* (Diary of the Federation) (Mexico)
DSB	Dispute Settlement Body (of WTO)
DTIC	Technical Department of Commercial Exchange (Brazil)
DTT	Tariff Technical Department (Brazil)
DUP	directly unproductive
EU	European Union
FINTRA	Fiduciaria de Inversiones Transitorias
FNE	Fiscal Nacional Económico (Chile)
FOB	free on board
FTAA	Free Trade Area of the Americas
GATT	General Agreement on Tariffs and Trade
GCE	External Commercial Affairs (Argentina)
GDP	gross domestic product
GPC	Georgia Pacific Corporation
IMF	International Monetary Fund
INCOMEX	Colombian Institute of Foreign Trade
Indecopi	Instituto Nacional de Defensa de la Competencia y de la Protección de la Propiedad Intelectual (National Institute for the Defense of Competition and the Protection of Intellectual Property) (Peru)
ITAM	Instituto Tecnológico Autónomo de México
Itintec	Technical Standards and Industrial Technological Research Institute (Peru)
ITC	International Trade Commission (United States)
MAC	Mechanism of administration of contingent duties (Colombia)
MCV	minimum customs value
MDIC	Ministry of Development, Industry, and Commerce (Brazil)
MEIC	Ministry of Economy, Industry, and Trade (Costa Rica)
Mercosur	Southern Cone Common Market, or Mercado Común del Sur
MFN	most-favored nation
MICT	Ministry of Industry, Trade, and Tourism (Brazil)
NAFTA	North American Free Trade Agreement
OECD	Organisation for Economic Co-operation and Development

PROPICE	Programa de Política Industrial y Comercio Exterior (Program for Industrial and Foreign Trade Policy) (Mexico)
RER	real exchange rate
SAC	Central American Tariff System
SECEX	Foreign Trade Secretariat (Brazil)
SECOFI	Secretaría de Comercio y Fomento Industrial (Mexico)
SHCP	Secretaría de Hacienda y Crédito Público (Secretariat for Finance and Public Credit) (Mexico)
SMEs	small and medium enterprises
TLC	tratado de libre comercio (free trade agreement) (Peru)
UGE	Gestión Comercial Externa (External Commercial Affairs)
UIA	Unión Industrial Argentina (Union of Argentine Industries)
UPCI	Unidad de Prácticas Comerciales Internacionales (Unit on International Trade Practices) (Mexico)
WTO	World Trade Organization

1

INTRODUCTION AND OVERVIEW

J. Michael Finger and Julio J. Nogués

This book is a report on success—success in trade liberalization and in the removal of trade barriers so as to integrate Latin American economies into the international economy. More particularly, this book is about how several Latin American governments created and managed safeguards and antidumping mechanisms as part of this liberalization.

The core of this book is a set of studies describing how seven Latin American countries—Argentina, Brazil, Chile, Colombia, Costa Rica, Mexico, and Peru—have used these trade instruments. Each country study was conducted by analysts from that country. Many of the analysts were high government officials during their country's liberalization, so they have hands-on experience with the construction and the management of these instruments.

Rather than ask the analysts to examine the technicalities of measuring dumping, injury, and so forth, we asked them to examine each country's use of these trade liberalization instruments as tools of policy management, for example,

- What role policy managers have seen for these instruments as part of a trade liberalization program,
- How the use of these instruments has contributed to maintaining a dynamic toward openness to international trade,
- Where these instruments have caused problems, and
- How policy managers have dealt with the problems.

Because safeguards and antidumping are instruments that, by their nature, impose import restrictions, identifying where policy managers have found discipline over application (for instance, within the economic content of the rules or through the deterrent effect of the information requirements imposed on petitioners and on the government) was of particular interest in the analyses.

In this overview, we provide our reflections on each country study.

Next, we review the overall use of trade defense measures and then go on to review several other cross-cutting issues. We compare the policy-making institutions of the seven countries, focusing on how World Trade Organization (WTO) rules for those mechanisms contributed to the liberalization effort and how those rules might be made even more supportive of the liberalization effort.

Reflections on the Country Studies

Even though many elements that we highlight in these reflections are present in more than one country's experiences, we have chosen the material in the reflections so that what we draw from one study overlaps minimally with what we draw from another, thus bringing out the comparative advantage lesson from each study. There is much more material in each country study than we have included in our reflections; the reflections should serve as an invitation to read the studies, not as a substitute for reading them.

Political Economy of Antidumping and Safeguards in Argentina, by Julio J. Nogués and Elías Baracat (Chapter 2)

In 1989, Argentina began a series of economic reforms that were revolutionary in speed, scope, and depth. Major sectors of the economy that were previously dominated by public enterprises were privatized, and foreign investment was put on an equal footing with domestic investment. All import licensing requirements were removed. Tariff rates that had averaged 40 percent in the mid-1980s fell to an average of 14 percent by the mid-1990s. On imports from within Mercosur (Mercado Común del Sur, or Southern Cone Common Market), most tariffs fell to zero by the mid-1990s. The adoption of GATT/WTO-sanctioned trade remedies—antidumping and safeguards mechanisms—was a small but significant part of the reform package.

In drafting the regulations and in creating the institutional mechanisms that would administer them, Argentina made a serious attempt to incorporate good economics into their structures and to establish discipline over their use. A presumption built into the mechanisms was that adhering to WTO requirements would strengthen the government's position in resisting domestic pressures for protection.

That presumption turned out to be false.

Imports increased sharply after the initial trade reforms, an increase resulting as much from setting the exchange rate at a level that proved in time to be unsustainable as from the removal of import restrictions. The business community subsequently applied pressures to use the instruments of protection that remained, particularly antidumping.

Antidumping The government's strategy was to delay decisions on antidumping initiations while the new regulatory and institutional frameworks were being completed. In a well-publicized speech to the business community in April 1992, Minister of Economy Domingo Cavallo was emphatic in announcing that the government would refrain from using antidumping measures until the price level had stabilized. The main policy objective at the time was to tame inflation, and the government considered import competition an important source of price discipline. Although the government received 135 petitions between 1988 and 1994, it opened only 69 investigations.

Complaints about the administration of the antidumping mechanism convinced the government that it should update that mechanism. The first step was to incorporate the Tokyo Round antidumping code into Argentine law. During the preparation of operational regulations for the antidumping mechanism, the Unión Industrial Argentina submitted a draft that more or less followed U.S. practice. The government, however, adopted a more liberal code that included several provisions that could serve as the basis for limiting use. (Such provisions are allowed, but not required, by the GATT code.) Among these provisions were

- A lesser duty rule that allows the government to limit antidumping duties to the level necessary to prevent injury when that level is below the observed margin of dumping,
- A method of imposing antidumping duties that makes it easy for exporters to know what price they must charge to avoid those duties, and
- A national interest clause that allows the government to deny antidumping measures, even when dumping and injury determinations are positive.

The second step in reforming the antidumping mechanism was to create a technically oriented commission to administer injury investigations—the Comisión Nacional de Comercio Exterior (CNCE). A major piece of evidence influencing the government's assessment of the need for a technically oriented commission was the finding from analysis of existing antidumping systems that the injury test provided more of an opportunity to apply discipline than did the determination of dumping. The legal definition of dumping differs so much from its intuitive or economic definition (pricing for export below home market price) that dumping in the legal sense has been found in virtually every investigation in every country that had antidumping regulations in place.

The CNCE, which was created in 1994, functions under the Ministry of Economy. To ensure their competence and their independence from the Commissioners, recruitment of the technical staff members was delegated to a private consulting company. Members of the technical staff prepare an injury report, and then the commissioners decide if the evidence supports a positive injury determination. The CNCE's decisions are made by a majority vote of its president and the four commissioners. Following an affirmative determination, the CNCE assesses the need for and recommends to the Minister of Economy the introduction of appropriate measures.

Contrary to what the government hoped to achieve, macroeconomic circumstances in Argentina overcame the capacity of WTO-sanctioned trade remedies and of the technical analysis supplied by the CNCE to discipline the application of trade restrictions. The trade liberalization policies and the overvaluation of the exchange rate led to a strong increase of imports, from less than US$5 billion in the late 1980s and early 1990s to more than US$30 billion in the late 1990s. With this increase in imports came large-scale displacement of domestic production. For the first time in several decades, the unemployment rate reached 10 percent in 1993, increasing to 20 percent by 1995.

After adopting the new antidumping regulations and creating the CNCE, Argentina became one of the world's most intense users of antidumping measures. From 1995 to 1999, Argentina applied 65 antidumping measures, exceeded only by the European Union (105), the United States (104), and South Africa (75).

Although the antidumping rules in the old *Código Aduanero* (customs code) had provided little discipline over when restrictions could be imposed, the rules had likewise provided minimal restraint on the government's discretion not to take action. Under the new rules with their deadlines and standards for content of a petition, the government could not indefinitely postpone the initiation of investigations. Moreover, in the distressed economic situation that existed in Argentina, many industries could meet the standards for relief. Sound technical analysis of the facts found that many industries were being injured by import competition and that, under the rules, were deserving of protection. The new mechanism provided minimal political leverage for the government to resist protectionist pressure. Particularly in 1999–2001, when the economy was in recession and the peso was severely overvalued, the government was unable to set aside the technical determinations. A high percentage of investigations ended with decisions to impose restrictions.

Safeguards In establishing a safeguard mechanism, the government attempted to follow the spirit as well as the letter of the WTO Safeguards Agreement. An industry that petitions for protection must present a plan for investment and structural reforms to demonstrate how it will overcome its competitive disadvantage. Moreover, the CNCE is authorized to take into account the requested actions' potential cost to consumers.

The CNCE turned down eight of the first nine safeguard petitions it received; through 2002, CNCE returned only three affirmative determinations. Consumer cost and the petitioner's not providing a convincing plan for recovery were often the basis for not initiating an investigation or for a negative determination. From the perspective of a protection seeker, the safeguard instrument became a less attractive alternative than the antidumping mechanism.

The positive side of the story is that the hard-won trade liberalization, in large part, has been maintained. Since devaluation, Argentina initiated 14 antidumping investigations in 2002, 1 in 2003, and 7 in the first half of 2004.

Lessons Discipline has come, in part, from the widespread realization that isolation is not an effective economic policy. As to Argentina's accepting the discipline of international rules, the economic content of the rules has not been a source of discipline. In a situation of macroeconomic balance, injury analysis separates the few from the many. In a situation of macroeconomic imbalance, the many are judged deserving of protection.

The most important lesson we draw from this study is that, in spite of Argentina's macroeconomic imbalance and its currency crisis, WTO rules did prevent the proliferation of protection instruments that has characterized previous crises in Argentina—a proliferation that, in the past, had made discipline impossible to maintain.

Antidumping and Safeguard Mechanisms: The Brazilian Experience, 1988–2003, by Honorio Kume and Guida Piani (Chapter 3)

By the late 1980s, the industrialization process of import substitution and recurrent exchange rate crises had led to the accumulation of many severe import controls in Brazil, such as lists of forbidden items, enterprise-specific limits on foreign purchases, and shipment-by-shipment authorizations for imports of steel and information technology products. Tariff rates were high, many surcharges were applied, and benchmark customs values could be applied if officials sensed there were irregularities in import prices. Exemptions from duties were available in some circumstances. Application of these restrictions and exceptions was done through processes that allowed wide discretion to government officials, with decisions often made at the sectoral level.

Reforms Although other Latin American countries have opened their economies rapidly, usually under the leadership of one administration, Brazil has conducted reform under several presidencies. In 1988 and 1989, the Sarney government was able to achieve some tariff reduction. In March 1990, shortly after coming to office, the Collor de Melo administration introduced a degree of flexibility to exchange-rate management, suspended the program for enterprise-specific limits on foreign purchases, and eliminated a number of special import regimes. The government also announced a tariff reform that by mid-1993 brought down the average rate on industrial products to 20 percent.

As in other Latin American countries, control of inflation was a major factor behind the decision to reduce import barriers. The Plan Real, initiated in July 1994 by the Franco administration and continued during most of the two terms of the Cardoso administration, had inflation as its most prominent target. (From 1964 to 1994, prices in Brazil had risen by 1 quadrillion percent, with 1 quadrillion being 10^{15}, or 1 million multiplied by 1 billion.) Fiscal and monetary reforms were the plan's most prominent elements, but the concern to discipline prices brought additional support for trade liberalization. Under the Plan Real, the Brazilian tariff average (unweighted) that was more than 50 percent ad valorem in 1987 declined to 11 percent by 1994.

By the end of 1994, the inflow of foreign capital attracted by the plan's privatization program brought substantial appreciation of the real exchange rate. This inflow of foreign capital, along with the accumulation of import liberalizations, brought a more than threefold increase of imports, and with this increase came intense pressure for protection from several sectors. Mercosur arrangements limited possible increases of tariff rates; even so, the average tariff rose by 1999 to almost 15 percent. The government applied safeguard actions on toys and textiles and, in some sectors, used administrative measures such as import deposit requirements or strict application of phytosanitary requirements to respond to protectionist pressures.

In 1999, the Brazilian currency, the real, was allowed to float freely; it quickly declined by more than 40 percent. Since then, tariff reduction has been renewed, and by the end of 2003, the average tariff was less than 11 percent.

Administering Institutions Policy formation in Brazil often requires an extended process of working toward consensus among a number of government agencies and the sectoral interests each represents. Administration of the antidumping, safeguards, and countervailing duties instruments reflects this approach to governance. Currently, investigations are conducted by the Department of Commercial Defense (DECOM) within the Ministry of Development, Industry, and Foreign Trade.

When DECOM's technical findings (dumping, injury, a causal link) are affirmative, the Brazilian Chamber of Foreign Trade (CAMEX) reaches a decision on trade defense measures by majority vote. CAMEX is an overview agency governed by a Council of Ministers. This council is composed of the ministers of Finance; Development, Industry and Foreign Trade; Foreign Affairs; Agriculture; and Planning and Budget, as well as the Civil Cabinet minister. The minister of Development, Industry and Foreign Trade presides.

Within CAMEX, protectionist and openness interests are balanced by the inclusion of both the ministries with sectoral interests and those with economywide interests. Those with sectoral interests are more inclined to view trade restrictions as support for jobs and production in Brazil. The Ministry of Finance's economywide responsibilities and its continuing concern about trade openness as a means to control inflation make it a major force in favor of disciplined use. Brazil's leadership position in international negotiations also comes into play. Brazil has a strong record in opposition to the unjustified use of antidumping and to its inclusion in regional arrangements.

The content of Brazil's antidumping (and other trade defense) regulations also reflects the Brazilian mode of conducting government affairs. In 1995, when Brazil modified its trade defense regulations to comply with the Uruguay Round agreements, it added several provisions that were allowed, but not mandated, by the agreements, for example,

- A national interest provision that would permit CAMEX not to impose a restriction when the trade defense investigation reached an affirmative determination, and
- A lesser duty rule that would allow an antidumping duty to be less than the dumping margin.

Experience Antidumping is by far the most frequently used commercial defense measure. From 1995 through June 2004, Brazil notified the WTO of 114 initiations and 59 measures. (Half of Brazil's antidumping cases ended without restrictive action, compared with less than 40 percent across all WTO members.) Steel, chemicals, and plastics are the most frequently affected sectors. During the same time period, Brazil has taken safeguard action in only two cases, against toys and against coconuts, and has not initiated a countervailing duty investigation since 1995. As in other Latin American countries that have created trade defense mechanisms as part of a trade liberalization program, Brazil has administered antidumping measures with attention to separating the effect of exposure to normal international competition from the effect of exposure to abnormal business practices. In half of Brazilian investigations, normal value—the value against which export price is compared to determine whether there is dumping—was estimated on the basis of international prices quoted in specialized publications or specialized information services.

Another outcome that the country study reports is a relatively high use of the lesser duty rule—the application of an antidumping measure that is smaller than the observed dumping margin. Overall, Brazilian antidumping duties have averaged about 60 percent of estimated dumping margins. The balancing of interests in CAMEX is largely a matter of the degree of protection provided. Of the 86 cases that the authors studied that did not lead to protective measures, only 2 cases came to that result because of a determination of other, overriding interests.

There is, however, a worrying finding. The Brazil study looks into one question on which the other studies did not concentrate: Have antidumping measures supported the monopoly power of domestic enterprises? The authors found that 41 percent of antidumping restrictions applied to a product for which there was only one domestic producer and 80 percent protected industries in which there were five or fewer Brazilian producers.

Lessons Since it was first established in the late 1980s, the Ministry of Development, Industry, and Foreign Trade has become more powerful in the administration of the antidumping mechanism while the Ministry of Finance has become less influential. The consensual nature of Brazil's decision-making process, however, mitigates against that change marking a significant shift toward the imposition of import restrictions. The Brazilian process demands consideration of many petitions, but it conditions petitioners to accept a relatively high rate of rejection. It also conditions the acceptance of a modified outcome, hence the high rate of application of duties that are lower than dumping margins.

Keeping Animal Spirits Asleep: The Case of Chile, by Sebastián Sáez (Chapter 4)

For a short period in the early days of its economic reform and liberalization program, Chile applied a number of contingent protection measures. Since 1995, however, Chile has imposed only six antidumping measures, six countervailing measures, and seven safeguard measures, none more than 12 months in length. As of December 2003, none remained in effect.

Among WTO members who use contingent protection instruments, Chile has perhaps the most tightly disciplined management of these instruments. That discipline stems from a prevailing politics that sees open trade policy as part of a reduction of government control over the economy—a transformation that enjoys wide support—and as an institutional structure that transforms this philosophy into a workable administrative system.

Chile's Economic Reforms Chile's trade opening was part of a broader macroeconomic stabilization process, and economic reforms, in turn, were part of a large-scale institutional transformation that encompassed the country's political regime and general economic framework, as well as the role of the state in the economy and in social policy.

Chile's reforms began in 1973, more than a decade earlier than those in other Latin American countries. By 1978, a tariff made up of widely varying rates that averaged more than 90 percent ad valorem had been replaced by a uniform 10 percent rate (with few exceptions). Other trade restrictions such as quotas, import prohibitions, and advance deposit requirements were eliminated.

Even with tariff rates reduced to 10 percent, the government had a skeptical attitude toward contingent protection and other mechanisms that would even temporarily suspend adjustment to the new trade regime.

Initial Experience By the early 1980s, however, the Chilean real exchange rate had notably appreciated, and many industries pressed for relief from import competition. The government viewed antidumping measures as having little economic rationale and the antidumping mechanism as being too easily captured by protectionist interests.

Safeguards, likewise, were seen as having questionable economic justification. Moreover, GATT rules required that any country that imposed a safeguard action must provide compensation—in the form of equivalent reduction of restrictions on other products—to principal-supplier exporting countries. If not, exporting countries would have the right to retaliate against, in this case, Chilean exports.

The government did, however, consider the correction of distortions a valid reason for intervention in the economy. (A distortion exists when the price of a product does not equal its cost of production in a competitive environment.) A foreign subsidy might therefore be a valid reason for trade protection.

In 1981, Chile created a Subsidies Commission within its central bank (BCCH, or Banco Central de Chile) and soon became an active user of antisubsidy measures. On the basis of a finding of the commission, the Minister of the Economy could impose tariff surcharges up to the 35 percent rate that was Chile's ceiling binding under the GATT. The commission could also recommend, and the minister could apply, minimum customs values for assessing duties.

Chile had signed the Tokyo Round subsidies code, but its commitment to a GATT ceiling binding of 35 percent allowed the latitude for tariff rate adjustments within that ceiling without the need for a code-complying finding of subsidy and injury. Chile took approximately 60 actions in the early 1980s. Most of these were against four countries—Argentina, Brazil, Peru, and Spain—and they led to considerable friction.

During the early 1980s, trade and current account deficits increased considerably, and the fixed exchange rate regime became unsustainable. In March 1983 Chile shifted to across-the-board measures to manage its trade situation, temporarily doubling its tariff rate and, most important, allowing the peso to float.

Administration of these trade policy mechanisms at the time was a compromise among the technicalities of the GATT subsidy code, the resources available to conduct investigations, and the economic objectives of the government. The resource demands for establishing a subsidy in accord with the demands of the GATT code meant that formal countervailing measures were taken infrequently. The GATT required that tariff surcharges be applied to all imports from all sources, independent of whether their prices were distorted. Hence, when the source of distortion-bearing imports provided a small share of Chile's imports, the remedy applied was usually a minimum customs value.

Current Instruments and Administration In 1989, the National Commission on Distortions (CND) succeeded the National Commission for Price Distortions (CNDP) through Imports, which had succeeded the original Subsidies Commission. The CND is responsible for investigations related to all aspects of safeguard, antidumping, and countervailing measures. The commission's members include

- One from the National Economic Prosecutor's Office, who chairs;
- Two from the BCCH;
- One each from the Ministries of Finance, Agriculture, Foreign Relations, and Economy; and
- One from the National Directorate of Customs.

The CND is served by a Technical Secretariat, which is lodged in and under the budget of the central bank. If the commission determines that the statutory requirements for action are met, it must adopt a resolution recommending the appropriate tariff surcharges. The resolution, along with the background information and conclusions of the investigation, are transmitted to the president of Chile, who makes a final decision through a decree of the Ministry of Finance. The discipline in the system comes from its structure, the statutory limits under which it operates, and, most important, strong public support in favor of an open economy.

Structural Sources of Discipline There are several structural sources of discipline over the use of trade defense measures, including the following:

- General interest agencies of government dominate the contingent protection process. The final decision is by the president. The only sectoral interest ministry with a seat on the CND is the Ministry of Agriculture. Agriculture is one of Chile's most trade-sensitive industries, and exceptional protection instruments have been designed for agricultural products.
- The CND is chaired by a representative of the National Economic Prosecutor's Office. That office is independent from any other governmental organization or service, particularly from the authorities and courts before which it fulfills its functions. It is responsible not only to see that competition law is enforced but also to actively promote competition in the Chilean economy.
- The Technical Secretariat of the CND is lodged in and under the budget of the BCCH, an institution that has little attachment to sectoral interests.
- A floating exchange rate regime has consistently avoided overvaluation of the peso since the early 1980s.
- A low uniform tariff (with few exceptions) implies that contingent protection measures create strong reactions from final producers and consumers.

Statutory Discipline There is statutory discipline over the use of trade defense measures as follows:

- Chilean law allows only tariff surcharges. Neither import quotas nor price undertakings can be used.
- The president cannot impose an action more restrictive than that recommended by the CND.
- The maximum length for which a measure may be imposed is one year. Extension requires an entirely new investigation, resolution, and decision.
- CND decisions are by majority of the votes cast. However, if the recommended surcharge will increase the tariff above the bound rate, the approval of three-quarters of the members of the commission is required.
- An antidumping or countervailing duty must not exceed the margin of distortion calculated by comparing the prices of dumped with nondumped (or subsidized with unsubsidized) imports. The objective is to remove the distortion to competition rather than to prevent displacement of domestic production.
- Consumers are recognized as interested parties. Regulations allow full participation during the course of an investigation by any person who may feel affected.

Widespread Support The structure of the contingent protection system described here is not one that carried over from the military regime. The laws that govern the use of contingent protection all date from the 1990s after the country returned to democratic government. The law that introduced safeguards is from 1999 when the Chilean Congress demanded it in exchange for supporting the reduction of the uniform tariff to 6 percent.

Lesson The trade regime has become a basic part of the new institutional structure of Chile's economy, and its stability and consistency toward openness have supported and been supported by the transition to democratic government. This support is the strongest source of discipline. The key lesson we draw from Chile's example is that, even in international trade, good economics, if skillfully managed, can be good politics.

Application of Safeguards and Antidumping Duties in Colombia, by Mauricio Reina and Sandra Zuluaga (Chapter 5)

During the second half of the past century, Colombia applied an industrialization strategy based on import substitution, as did most Latin American countries. While this strategy promoted some diversification of production, it also fostered concentrated property structures, high prices, low product quality, and few incentives for modernization. The high cost of imports made production based on foreign raw materials unsustainable.

Faced with this situation, the government implemented a trade liberalization policy that began at the end of the 1980s and was consolidated during the early 1990s. An import licensing arrangement that based import quotas largely on the volume of domestic production was abandoned, and the percentage of tariff positions subject to quantitative restrictions fell from 73 percent to 1 percent. The economy's nominal average tariff fell from near 100 percent to 11 percent, but escalation maintained high rates of effective protection for some processing activities. Colombia deepened its integration in the Andean Community, where most tariff rates have been reduced to zero, and concluded trade agreements with several countries, including Chile, Mexico, and the República Bolivariana de Venezuela. These trade reforms were accompanied by strong currency devaluations, and at the present time, the real rate of exchange is deemed to be close to its equilibrium level.

In the agricultural sector, the Andean Community countries maintain a system of variable levies that protect approximately 150 tariff positions for which the implicit average tariff is on the order of 60 percent. Reina and Zuluaga, authors of chapter 5, report that a good share of Colombia's agricultural sector has managed to remain outside the liberalization trends that began in 1990.

Part of the politics of liberalization was the establishment of legal antidumping and safeguard instruments to deal with the foreign competition previously neutralized by

TABLE 1.1 Colombia: Safeguard and Antidumping Investigations, 1990–June 2004

Category	Number completed	Restriction	
		Number	Percentage of number completed
Antidumping	37	23	62
Safeguard	34	25	74
WTO	11	10	91
Special	10	5	50
Andean	13	10	77

Source: Authors' tabulation from data in table 5.2.

the high overall level of protection. Table 1.1 lists instruments and reports their frequencies of use. (Colombia has undertaken no countervailing duty investigations.)

The normal safeguard mechanism follows the WTO Safeguards Agreement and is usually referred to as a WTO safeguard. A petitioner for a WTO safeguard action is subject to extensive WTO-based requirements to provide the information necessary to demonstrate injury or threat of injury. This information must be certified by a public accountant. In addition, the applicant must submit an adjustment program that lists the steps it will take to modernize and adapt to the new competitive conditions. Antidumping regulations were revised in 1995 to incorporate the discipline of the Uruguay Round agreements.

Larger enterprises in Colombia have begun using trade defense instruments, much as similar enterprises have done in other countries. Of the 37 antidumping cases that have been completed, 26 have been from the steel, chemicals, and petrochemicals industries. Throughout the world, these industries have been frequent petitioners for antidumping actions.

Other sectors, however, have not been satisfied with the usability of the safeguard and antidumping instruments. The experience of the textiles and apparel sector is illustrative. Even though tariffs on textile and apparel imports are relatively high (average 18 percent), trade liberalization produced a substantial increase of imports, and with the increase in imports came an increase in complaints about evasion of import duties (smuggling) and imports from Asia at very low prices. The sector soon became a user of the trade defense mechanisms: Three antidumping investigations and six safeguard investigations were undertaken on its behalf.

Preliminary measures as a result of these investigations brought a request from several Asian exporters for WTO consultations, but the matter was dropped when the measures expired and were not renewed. In 1997, the government, concerned that protection for the textile industry would disadvantage apparel producers, worked out an industry development plan with the industry that included temporary tariff reductions on capital goods and raw materials, stronger enforcement of smuggling controls, and modification of safeguard and antidumping procedures—within WTO Safeguards Agreement parameters—to expedite investigations and introduce flexibility into the criteria for application.

Experiences such as these made officials aware of the need for an instrument that imposes less stringent administrative and substantive standards. In response, the government in 1999 established a second safeguard mechanism, called a special safeguard, or safeguard by reason of disruption. This instrument allows an increase of the tariff rate up to the level of Colombia's WTO ceiling binding, an action that does not violate Colombia's obligations under the GATT and the WTO agreements. Thus, the investigation and determination do not have to meet the requirements of the WTO Safeguards Agreement for the increased import duty to be legal by WTO's standards. The special safeguard's standard—disruption—is interpreted as the existence of imports in unfair conditions such as low prices or an important increase of quantities. It does not require an adjustment plan, but this restriction can be in place for a maximum of two years and is not extendable. Chapter authors Reina and Zuluaga found in their interviews that the business community considers this instrument to be user-friendly.

The largest number of safeguard actions by Colombia has come under another form of safeguard—the provision in the Andean Community that allows for suspension of the benefits from the free trade area, imposing the tariff rate applicable to imports from outside the community. On a provisional basis, actions such as these may be taken unilaterally but cannot be retained without the approval of the Community Secretariat. The chapter authors learned from interviews that the secretariat review requires approximately four months to complete. The rules for this safeguard impose no limit on how long a measure—if approved—may be in place. Approval may, however, impose such a limit. Table 1.1 documents the popularity of the less stringent instruments.

Colombia has undertaken four investigations for Andean Community safeguards on agricultural products, with restrictions in place intermittently from 1996 through 2003. These measures became an issue within the Andean Community and led to the creation of a special arrangement in the Ministry of Agriculture to administer contingent duties.

While the worldwide statistics show one safeguard case for every 55 antidumping cases, the ratio for Colombia is nearly one to one. Moreover, 13 of 20 safeguard applications were not dependent on the Safeguards Agreement for their WTO legality.

Lesson In Colombia's case, we find that the substantive content of the WTO rules on trade defense instruments has not been sufficiently valuable to overcome the administrative demands that these instruments put on the government and the business community. Thus, Colombia's experience has involved a unique element—the development and use of safeguard instruments that impose lesser administrative demands. As to the use of these instruments to restrict trade, the number of restrictions is in line with the numbers observed for other countries in the study. Moreover, the instruments have limits on the level of protection that can be applied. A special safeguard cannot increase the tariff above Colombia's WTO bound rate, and an Andean Community safeguard cannot increase the level of protection above the rate applied to imports from outside the community.

Antidumping Policies and Safeguard Measures in the Context of Costa Rica's Economic Liberalization, by Ricardo Monge-González and Francisco Monge-Ariño (Chapter 6)

The Costa Rican economic crisis in the early 1980s sparked an extensive review of the country's situation. From this review came a decision to move away from the policies of import substitution that were then in place and, instead, to exploit the economy's comparative advantages in the international economy. Initially, the strategy was to provide higher fiscal incentives, intended to reduce the antiexport bias in its trade restrictions. Soon after this decision, the government introduced an important reduction of import barriers along with other structural reforms that increased the openness of the economy to foreign trade and capital flows. The government devalued the colón and adopted a flexible exchange-rate regime. Since the mid-1980s, the real exchange rate has been stable. The policy changes attracted considerable foreign investment.

Reforms in Costa Rica were complemented by the United States' Caribbean Basin Initiative of 1984. Under this initiative, a significant share of Costa Rican exports can enjoy zero tariffs in the United States.

Costa Rica's average most-favored nation (MFN) tariff by 2001 had fallen below 7 percent, though rates are considerably higher for agricultural products than for industrial products. As part of its market access commitments under the WTO Agreement on Agriculture, Costa Rica established tariff quotas for various agricultural products (for example, certain dairy and poultry products), and in almost all cases, the fill levels have been low. Moreover, Costa Rica has introduced several special safeguard measures based on the WTO Agreement on Agriculture.

Costa Rican exports, approximately US$1 billion in 1984, had expanded to US$6 billion by 2003. This export growth was accompanied by an important diversification away from coffee, bananas, sugar, and beef. Other products accounted for 39 percent of total exports in 1982, but grew to 87 percent of total exports by 2003. Meanwhile, the services sector, particularly tourism, became a significant earner of foreign exchange. At the macroeconomic level, increased trade contributed to overall gross domestic product (GDP) growth; with growth came reduced unemployment and a substantial reduction in the share of the population below the poverty line.

Regulations and Organization Costa Rican regulations on unfair trade practices have been reviewed and adapted to the agreements that were signed within the framework of the Uruguay Round. Costa Rica has also adopted the Regulations on Unfair Business Practices of the Central American Common Market, or Mercado Común Centroamericano, which provide for antidumping action by one member against exports from another member and for common action against exports from an outside country. Bilateral arrangements with Canada, Chile, the Dominican Republic, and Mexico recognize the rights of the parties to take antidumping action under the GATT and WTO agreements.

In 1995, to administer safeguard and unfair trade instruments, the government created an Office of Unfair Trade Practices and Safeguard Measures, reporting to the Ministry of Economy, Industry, and Trade, or MEIC). Because of relatively high operating costs in relation to the number of petitions, the government closed this office in 2000 and assigned its responsibilities to the Legal Office of the MEIC. Technical investigations are done by the Economics Department of the MEIC. Unlike the other countries included in this volume, Costa Rica has no specialized agency to administer antidumping and safeguard investigations.

Experience Costa Rica appears to be a country where industries dealing with import substitution, particularly in the manufacturing sector, have accepted the challenges of adopting an open economy model of development. Costa Rica's experience comprises eleven contingent protection cases: six antidumping petitions and five safeguard petitions.

Of the six antidumping complaints, two were dropped because the complainant did not submit the information required to support an investigation. No dumping or injury was found in two cases, and in one case, injury was found but attributed to causes other than imports. In the one case that reached an affirmative final determination, by the time the investigation was completed, imports had dropped virtually to zero. An antidumping duty of zero percent was imposed.

The outcome of one of these cases demonstrates the government's concern to promote competition. When a petitioner requested that an investigation be terminated because it had reached an agreement with the exporter, MEIC continued the investigation under its own initiative. MEIC completed the investigation, concluded that no import restriction was warranted, and then notified the Commission to Promote Competition so that it could investigate the arrangement between the parties involved. In another instance, the investigation revealed that the problem was underinvoicing and smuggling; the problem was handled through the appropriate legal institutions.

Of the five applications for safeguard action, only one has resulted in a restrictive measure being imposed. The National Cabuya Board applied in September 1995 for an investigation against imports of coarse fiber bags, used primarily to package coffee for export. The subsequent investigation did verify a substantial increase of imports of bags. It found also a substantial increase of coffee exports, but not one sufficient to explain the increase of imports of bags without a substantial displacement of Costa Rican production. The MEIC imposed a provisional measure, a duty increase to 140 percent, but asked the producers of bags for a commitment to improve and expand their capacity. When after six months domestic producers had not initiated that action, the provisional measure was withdrawn.

The few requests for protection that the government has been called on to manage are an obvious indication that the business community is an active partner in the new economic strategy. Though many Costa Rican enterprises began under the umbrella of the previous import substitution model many have succeeded in transforming themselves into exporters, including two enterprises that applied for antidumping protection a decade ago. Another indication is that, although the MEIC has issued a decree to establish a new office to specialize in unfair trade and safeguard matters, there has not been sufficient pressure from the business community for it to be created. Administration of matters such as these remains with the MEIC's Legal Office and Economics Department.

Lessons In Costa Rica as in Chile, the major element in the explanation of why antidumping and safeguard action has been minimal is that the business community is an active partner in the new economic strategy. (The fact that sensitive agricultural products remain highly protected should not be overlooked.) In this environment, the government is able to provide a strictly disciplined industrial policy. An industry actively seeking to achieve international levels of productivity and product quality will be supported, whereas an industry seeking protection from international competition will not. Also important is the record of good macroeconomic management by the government. The real exchange rate has been stable, and the rate of inflation has been low. There has been no challenge in Costa Rica to take on macroeconomic problems with microeconomic tools.

Antidumping and Safeguard Measures in the Political Economy of Liberalization: The Mexican Case, by Luz Elena Reyes de la Torre and Jorge G. González (Chapter 7)

Creating instruments of commercial defense was part of the bargain that the Mexican government struck with industry to win its support for opening the economy to international competition. At the same time, the government recognized that care must be taken to ensure that the commercial defense "monster" remained chained to the service of the trade liberalization program and did not develop a momentum of its own.

There was some risk that it would. Antidumping, at least in rhetoric, was intended to sort fair from unfair international competition. The government was aware that the instrument was tainted by its protectionist use in other countries, hence its reluctance to unquestioningly follow procedures as they had evolved in traditional users.

The Mexican case explains how the government developed operational techniques to sort unwanted competition from the competition that would serve their policy objectives: benefit consumers and stimulate the efficiency of the economy. The WTO rules' tolerance for import restrictions is more generous than is the concept that the Mexican government concluded would serve the national economic interest.

The Mexican case demonstrates the need for the technical capacity to operate commercial defenses correctly. It also demonstrates the need for skilled political management to take an emergency action that would save political support for trade liberalization without allowing that action to shift the central tendency of the system—in other words, to ensure that an exception remain an exception.

International Competition—Normal versus Abnormal Two examples illustrate how the Mexican government has made operational the concept of separating normal international competition from unfair or distorted competition. The first example involves diiodohydroxyquinoline, an ingredient in a medicine important in Mexico. It is produced only in Germany, India, and Mexico, and the Mexican producer who brought an antidumping case against the Indian producer is an affiliate of a German producer. The Indian market was at the time highly protected. Therefore, the home market price was considerably above the normal international price—the price that the Mexican government considered appropriate to distinguish normal international competition from dumping. The Mexican government's decision was to impose a duty of US$4.09 per kilo rather than the full dumping margin of US$15.56 per kilo. In its investigation, the government concluded that a duty equal to the full dumping margin would drive the Indian

TABLE 1.2 Mexico: Antidumping Duty Levels in Different Situations

Price comparison	Level of duty
Normal value = International price > Export price	Duty = Dumping margin
Normal value > International price > Export price	Duty = Difference between export price and international price
Export price = International price < Normal value	No antidumping duty. Injury, if observed, is from normal international competition

Source: Authors' interpretation of Mexican practice.

supplier out of the Mexican market and eliminate competition there. In such situations, Mexico applies the lesser duty rule.

In the second example, after conducting an investigation of imports of bond paper, the government concluded that the suppliers accused of dumping were doing so to meet the price set by more efficient suppliers. The government imposed no antidumping duty, the conclusion being that injury suffered by Mexican producers resulted from their having to compete with normal international competition rather than with dumping.

In the schema in table 1.2, the diiodohydroxyquinoline case would fall in the second row; the bond paper case, in the third. Only in the first situation described in the first row of the table would the Mexican government apply an antidumping duty.

Emergency Measures In mid-1993, the Mexican government was in a critical stage of its liberalization program. North American Free Trade Agreement (NAFTA) negotiations—ostensibly completed in 1992—had been reopened in early 1993 by the insistence of the new U.S. administration of President Bill Clinton that parallel agreements on labor and on the environment be included. The Mexican government had to maintain the national consensus needed to complete negotiation of the treaty and to gain its approval by its Congress.

By this time, Mexican trade barriers had been significantly reduced, and inflation had brought approximately 30 percent appreciation of the real exchange rate. Imports by 1992 were five times their level in 1987, an increase of more than 30 percent per year. Industry pressed hard for the government to keep its promise to apply antidumping measures to provide relief in this emergency situation. Were the government not to respond, it would risk loss of credibility for the system of contingent protection and, with it, the ongoing trade liberalization program.

The most focused pressure came from the Mexican steel industry. It was familiar with antidumping procedures, having been the target of U.S. and European measures several times. The industry presented a package of petitions that covered nearly all basic products and supplying countries. The Mexican government, however, was reluctant to act on these petitions. Use of antidumping measures by the U.S. government to protect its steel industry had played a major role in capture there of the instrument for protectionist purposes. Moreover, an increase of steel prices would be a burden on user industries and exporters.

At the same time, producers of a broad range of final goods—including clothing, toys, shoes, and electrical appliances—came forward with intense complaints about low-priced imports, particularly from China. These producers, however, were minimally organized and unfamiliar with antidumping procedures.

The government's strategy included immediate action on a range of final goods from China. As soon as the government self-initiated investigations on more than 3,000 tariff lines, it installed preliminary duties that ranged from 129 percent to more than 1,000 percent. (Because part of the discipline the government had built into its antidumping rules included strict standards on the information a petitioner must supply, it would have been time-consuming, perhaps impossible, for these producers to pull together a package of petitions.) Product coverage was carefully selected to exclude duties on any products used as inputs by Mexican producers. Moreover, China was not at the time a GATT contracting party; hence, Mexico's duties would violate its international commitments.

In contrast with their immediate action on the package of final goods, the government delayed action on petitions from the steel industry. Although most investigations were opened in 1993, the measures that were applied came near the end of 1995. In the interval, the government examined carefully where Mexican production could be expanded with minimal increase of cost to users. It also created a system of certificates of final use to exempt critical inputs from duties but, at the same time, ensure that these products did not substitute for products that Mexican producers could supply. The duties imposed were much lower than those imposed on final goods, mostly in the range of 30 to 50 percent ad valorem.

Mexico's 83 antidumping initiations in 1993 were more than the number for any other country. However, after devaluation of the peso in December 1994 relieved pressure for use of commercial defense measures, Mexico averaged 8 initiations per year from 1995 through June 2004, as compared with 40 by India, 37 by the United States, and 30 by the European Union. The emergency action was indeed an exception.

Lessons Creating and using contingent protection instruments has been a fundamental part of establishing the new open economy of Mexico. The political promise that the government made to industry at the beginning of Mexican liberalization was to provide relief from unfair competition while otherwise expecting Mexican industry to compete with the best in the world. The administrative unit and procedures established in Mexico show how the good sense of this promise can be translated into sound and impartial professional action. Mexican experience demonstrates that good policy management requires more than technical skill. The political acumen to judge when to emphasize the technical dimensions and when not to was critical.

Antidumping Mechanisms and Safeguards in Peru, by Richard Webb, Josefina Camminati, and Raúl León Thorne (Chapter 8)

Peru began its recent economic reforms in the face of a particularly severe economic and political crisis. Inflation raged in triple digits, and domestic production had fallen drastically. A collapse of public revenues brought severe reduction of public services, including courts, schools, and police. Increasing terrorism from Sendero Luminoso and Túpac Amaru groups added to the decline of public order. The multiple exchange rate system, along with high and distorted tariff rates, created effective rates of protection of more than 250 percent for some sectors and negative rates for others. Import prohibitions applied to 540 tariff lines that covered almost one-fourth of domestic production; another 534 tariff lines were subject to quantitative restrictions.

The trade reforms that began after Alberto Fujimori became president differed from previous reforms in several ways. In the election campaign of 1990, the liberal message—principally from unsuccessful candidate Mario Vargas Llosa—was no longer dismissed as a front for business interests. Liberalization was widely accepted as a way to advance the public interest, not simply as a desperate means to take on an economic crisis. (Fujimori had not campaigned on a liberal platform, but his practical perception of the emergency situation led him toward liberal policies.)

The government wanted to do more than just remove existing restrictions. It wanted to institutionalize trade policy decisions as well as install technical criteria and a unified evaluation system for protection requests. Previously, decisions on tariff rates, levels of quantitative restrictions, and import bans as well as decisions about which enterprises would receive tariff exemptions had been made by sector officials who operated with almost complete discretion. The lack of structure generated business uncertainty and permitted a high level of political interference.

Institutional Reform and Indecopi The centerpiece of institutional reform was the Indecopi (Instituto Nacional de Defensa de la Competencia y de la Protección de la Propiedad Intelectual, or National Institute for the Defense of Competition and the Protection of Intellectual Property). Indecopi was created in 1993 to administer the new economic rules and actively defend the market system against the lobby-based political erosions that had undermined previous reforms.

Indecopi is headed by a president and an Executive Board who are appointed by the president of Peru. The work of Indecopi is done by seven commissions—independent of one another—whose members are appointed by the Executive Board. The establishing regulation requires that each member be an experienced technical expert in the field that his or her commission will regulate. Each commission is served by a Technical Secretariat.

Role of the Indecopi Commissions The Indecopi commissions are the major public organs for maintaining a competitive market economy in Peru. The Commission on Technical Standards, for example, is responsible not only for maintaining systems of standards but also for ensuring that businesses do not use them to retard competition.

The Commission for Control of Dumping and Subsidies (CDS; La Comisión de Fiscalización de Dumping y Subsidios), which was created in 1991, was made a part of Indecopi when the latter was established. When the CDS was created, it incorporated the requirements of the relevant GATT codes; it has since incorporated the Uruguay Round agreements into its criteria and procedures. The CDS is the investigating and deciding agency on matters of antidumping and countervailing duties. On safeguards, however, the CDS conducts the investigation, but the decision rests with the Multisector Commission, which is made up of representatives of the Ministries of Economy and Finance, Industry, and Production for the sector on behalf of which the investigation was conducted.

The antidumping-safeguard procedural difference reflects a difference in the economics that lies between the two instruments. Dumping and subsidies are considered to be practices that create distortions to be evaluated against technical criteria. Under the economic philosophy of the system, a distortion merits correction; it creates an inequality between private and social costs and benefits. A safeguard action responds, however, to what is considered a political situation. Technical analysis is needed to gauge the extent of injury and to assure that it results from import competition. Nevertheless, the decision must balance the importance of the various effects that will follow from the proposed action on consumers, production, and employment, not only on the sector that petitioned for protection but also on other sectors and on other dimensions of the national interest such as the viability of the politics of openness. An industry that petitions for safeguard relief not only must document an increase of imports and consequent injury but also must submit (a) an adjustment plan and (b) an economic

TABLE 1.3 Outcomes of Peru's Antidumping Investigations, 1993–June 2004

	1993–2000	2001–June 2004
Number of investigations completed	32	25
Number of restrictive measures	11	18
Number closed without restrictive measures	21	4
Restrictive measures as percentage of investigations completed	34	82
Average number of definitive measures per year	1.4	4.5

Source: Indecopi (2005) Cuadro de los expedientes en trámite y resueltos por la Comisión de Dumping y Subsidios, Indecopi, Lima, which is available at http://www.indecopi.gob.pe/upload/cds/cuadros/estadoExpedientes.PDF (accessed April 2005); and tables 1.5 and 1.6.

report that quantifies the impact of the requested measure on final and intermediate consumers and on the public interest.

Outcome The CDS and the other Indecopi commissions have provided an example of how public decisions can be made in a transparent manner, in accord with objective, published criteria. They have won the confidence of the public as different from the traditional bureaucracy, both in the quality of their work and in the public's perception of whom they serve. The public media played an important role, publicizing commission decisions that favored consumers and commission efforts to facilitate the operations of small businesses.

As to the CDS in particular, in its early years, it established a pattern of disciplined procedure. As noted in table 1.3, from 1993 to 2000, the CDS imposed an average of only 1.4 antidumping measures per year. Moreover, standards for the content of a petition kept the number of investigations relatively low.

With the change in 2001 to the government of Alejandro Toledo (and already during the temporary government of Valentín Paniagua in 2000), the industrial lobby strove to identify the removal of import restrictions as being among the excesses of the Fujimori government and discredit the hard-line technical and independent approach to determining trade policy that the Indecopi and the CDS represent.

A safeguard petition on behalf of the textiles and clothing sector became an important vehicle for the pressure. The protection seekers opted for a safeguard petition because it offered greater possibility to minimize the technical input and bring trade union and other political pressures to bear. In the debate over whether to protect textiles and clothing producers, the major argument against restriction has been the damage to the Peruvian economy that retaliation from China would bring. This argument is being advanced by export industries, their trade unions, and the Embassy of China in Peru. As this country study was completed in August 2004, the option toward which the government was inclined was to shift from transitional safeguards against China (allowed under China's terms of accession to the WTO) to generalized safeguards.

The change of government also initiated a struggle to replace Indecopi's commissioners. The new commissioners have closer ties to industry, and they have focused on enterprise insolvency resulting from the 1997 banking crisis and have redirected resources toward issues of enterprise restructuring. Matters of market structure and free competition have received less attention.

As to decisions on trade issues, there has been an increase in the share and in the number of cases with restrictive outcomes. The numbers, however, are still low. Authors Webb, Camminati, and Thorne of the chapter on Peru report that, although decisions are now more influenced by the industrial sector, the technical quality of investigations has not been lost.

Lessons The positive lesson we draw from Peruvian experience is the example it provides of a unified, independent, and technically oriented decision structure. Peru's experience demonstrates that such an institution is not impervious to political pressure; however, the institution has maintained its technical integrity. Equally important, the idea of a unified decision structure rather than a sector-specific approach has prevailed.

Not all the political considerations that have entered into trade policy determinations have pushed in the protectionist direction. In the debate over whether to protect textiles and clothing producers, the major argument against restriction is the damage to the Peruvian economy that retaliation from exporters would bring. This argument is being advanced by export industries, their trade unions, and the embassies of exporting countries.

Scope and Background of the Reforms

Each of the reform experiences began in periods of macroeconomic crisis; hence, a major part of the dynamic behind them was to control inflation and restore macroeconomic balance. Microeconomic reforms included much more than removal of trade restrictions. Major sectors of the economy previously dominated by public enterprises were privatized; foreign investment rules were liberalized. In many countries, commercial legal codes were extensively revised, with new emphasis on creating and maintaining competition in domestic markets. With respect to trade policy, the application of extensive import restrictions during the second half of the last century had promoted some diversification of production. It also had fostered concentrated property structures, high prices, low product quality, and few incentives for modernization.

Trade liberalization was novel in speed, depth, and scope. Import licensing requirements and quantitative restrictions were almost entirely removed. Applied tariff rates that had averaged 50 percent or more in the 1970s and 1980s have fallen by three-fourths and, in Chile and Costa Rica, to well below 10 percent. Regional arrangements such as Mercosur, the Andean Community, the Central American Common Market, and NAFTA have been mechanisms for additional liberalization. (For example, two-thirds of Mexico's imports are from the United States and are thereby duty-free under NAFTA.) Separate protection regimes were maintained for agriculture in several countries, but import-sensitive manufactured goods were not excluded from the liberalization. There was no Multifiber Arrangement, no special arrangement for textiles and clothing among these countries.

In their economic histories, the seven countries in this volume had passed through several cycles of protection and openness. Although it is common to describe the periods of protection as application of a strategy for import substitution, swings toward protection are more accurately described as accumulations of political victories by protection- and subsidy-seeking interests—not as a coherent application of any particular economic strategy.[1] Many different import control instruments were in use: tariffs, surcharges, benchmark customs values, enterprise-specific limits on foreign purchases, and import prohibitions. Application of restrictions was done through processes that allowed wide discretion to government officials, with decisions often made at the sectoral level. Safeguards and antidumping—as GATT and WTO rules define them—were rarely used. With almost all tariff lines unbound through the GATT, WTO, or other international agreements, the international sanction that use of such instruments would have provided was not needed.

The reforms of the 1980s and 1990s took place as these countries increasingly saw the advantages of active participation in the GATT and WTO systems. At the Uruguay Round, they accepted ceilings on almost all tariff lines; hence, for any duty increase beyond these bindings, they would need the clearance that use of a GATT- or WTO-sanctioned instrument would provide. Moreover, there was widespread realization that, to prevent the eventual erosion of this round of liberalization, new institutions for managing trade policy would be needed—institutions that would help to control the emergence of many instruments and unify the application of the instruments into a policy process that would bring forward the economic logic of how openness would support economic development. The two sides of the issue reinforced each other: although the need for reform suggested the value of active WTO membership, active WTO membership required the use of approved instruments.

Thus, these liberalizations differed from past ones in more than their scope and depth. An important element was to institutionalize the changes that were made through the acceptance of GATT and WTO bindings and the adoption of WTO-sanctioned trade defense or contingent protection instruments.

Creating trade defense mechanisms was often part of the bargain to gain industry acceptance of liberalization. Industries find trade defense mechanisms attractive because a safeguard mechanism can slow the pace of liberalization where its impact turns out to be particularly severe. In principle, an antidumping mechanism will allow domestic industries to be exposed to normal international competition but, at the same time, be protected from unfair competition.

From the perspective of maintaining the momentum of liberalization, these mechanisms, once in place, should serve as a means to accommodate and isolate pressures that might otherwise grow into large-scale threats; they should allow the possibility of one step back to preserve two steps forward. In each country, trade liberalization did generate substantial increases of imports, hence the need for mechanisms to manage these pressures. Thus, maintaining an economically sensible trade policy was, in significant part, a matter of managing pressures for exceptions—for protection for a particular industry—so that the exceptions remained exceptions and the decision process reinforced, rather than undermined, the politics of liberalization.

An additional virtue of these mechanisms is that they would contribute to a shift of the culture of policy management that reform leaders wanted to advance: a shift to a culture of policy management based on facts of economic potential—unified, objective, and transparent mechanisms—from one based on relationships. Finally, trade regulations would form a part of the new regulatory structure intended to create a more competitive environment than existed before.

Trade Defense Use—The Overall Record

Trade defense mechanisms are instruments for imposing import restrictions rather than for removing them. Their creation raises the possibility of overuse: Have they been used so much as to substantially offset the liberalization that they were intended to promote?

With regard to applied tariff rates, table 1.4 presents the tariffs on industrial goods for seven countries: Argentina, Brazil, Chile, Colombia, Costa Rica, Mexico, and Peru.

The record of use of antidumping, countervailing duties, and safeguard investigations and measures since 1995 (as notified to the WTO) are presented in tables 1.5 through 1.8. Tables 1.5 and 1.6 list the numbers of antidumping investigations and

TABLE 1.4 Applied Tariff Rates on Industrial Goods for Selected Latin American Countries (most-favored nation rates, percentage ad valorem)

Country	Year	Simple average	Minimum rate	Maximum rate
Argentina	2003	15	0	35
Brazil	2003	14	0	35
Chile	2002	7	0	7
Colombia	2002	13	0	35
Costa Rica	2002	6	0	15
Mexico	2003	18	0	35
Peru	2000	13	12	20

Source: UNCTAD (United Nations Conference on Trade and Development) TRAINS database.

measures by the seven countries, as notified to the WTO. Countervailing duties have been minimally used; since 1996, only nine measures in total by the seven countries in the study (table 1.7). Safeguard actions have also been infrequent. Over the same period, Chile has notified the WTO of seven safeguard measures, three preliminary measures, and four definitive measures. All have been tariff measures at rates below 15 percent and in place for no longer than 12 months. No other country in the group has applied more than three safeguard measures.

Tables 1.5 and 1.6 list the numbers of antidumping investigations and measures notified by the seven countries. For the countries in this study, as for other WTO members, antidumping has been by far the most frequently used mechanism for managing pressures for exceptional protection,[2] Colombia's use of within-bindings safeguards being the only exception. Several of the countries studied were, for short periods, major users of trade defense measures. Chile, in the early 1980s, initiated more countervailing duty cases than any other GATT contracting party; Mexico, in 1993, initiated more antidumping investigations than any other contracting party. The country studies show, however, that these cases were truly emergency actions, coming at critical times in the trade liberalization process. Through the use of trade defense measures and other actions, governments were able to complete critical steps, and the rate of use dropped radically afterward.

Although trade defense measures are, in theory, intended to deal with other matters, these country studies show that an overvalued exchange rate often creates the conditions in which a safeguard or antidumping investigation will return an affirmative determination. The Argentine study provides an explicit demonstration.[3] Exchange rate overvaluation was part of the situations in Chile and Mexico mentioned in the above reflections, and the Brazil study also describes an incident in

TABLE 1.5 Antidumping Initiations as Notified to WTO, 1995–June 2004: Countries Included in the Study and Major Users

Initiations	1995	1996	1997	1998	1999	2000	2001
Argentina	27	22	14	8	23	45	26
Brazil	5	18	11	18	16	11	17
Chile	4	3	0	2	0	5	0
Colombia	4	1	1	6	2	3	6
Costa Rica	0	4	1	1	0	0	0
Mexico	4	4	6	12	11	7	5
Peru	2	7	2	3	8	1	8
Major users, for comparison							
United States	14	22	15	36	47	47	76
European Community	33	25	41	22	65	32	29
South Africa	16	33	23	41	16	21	6
India	6	21	13	27	65	41	79

TABLE 1.6 Antidumping Measures as Notified to WTO, 1995–June 2004

Measures	1995	1996	1997	1998	1999	2000	2001	2002
Argentina	13	20	11	12	9	15	15	24
Brazil	2	6	2	14	5	9	13	4
Chile	2	0	2	2	0	0	0	0
Colombia	1	1	1	0	6	2	0	0
Costa Rica	0	0	0	0	0	0	0	0
Mexico	16	4	7	7	7	7	3	4
Peru	2	1	2	0	3	4	1	6
Major users, for comparison								
United States	33	11	20	16	24	32	33	24
European Community	15	23	23	26	18	41	13	25
South Africa	0	8	18	14	35	13	5	15
India	7	2	8	22	22	57	38	64

TABLE 1.5 (*Continued*)

2002	2003	Jan.–June 2004	Totals	Per year 1995–June 2004	Per year 1995–2001	Per year 2002–June 2004
14	1	7	**187**	19.7	23.6	8.8
8	4	6	**114**	12.0	13.7	7.2
0	0	0	**14**	3.1	2.0	0.0
0	0	0	**23**	2.4	3.3	0.0
0	0	0	**6**	0.6	0.9	0.0
10	14	3	**76**	8.0	7.0	10.8
12	5	3	**51**	5.4	4.4	8.0
35	37	21	**350**	36.8	36.7	37.2
20	7	13	**287**	30.2	35.3	16.0
4	8	4	**172**	18.1	22.3	6.4
81	46	4	**383**	40.3	36.0	52.4

Source: WTO (2004); also in sources available at http://www.wto.org/english/tratop_e/adp_e/adp_stattab2_e.xls; http://www.wto.org/english/tratop_e/adp_e/adp_stattab7_e.xls (accessed April 2005).

TABLE 1.6 (*Continued*)

2003	Jan.–June 2004	Totals	Per year 1995–June 2004	Per year 1995–2001	Per year 2002–June 2004	Measures in place as of June 30, 2004
19	1	**139**	14.6	13.6	17.6	76
2	2	**59**	6.2	7.3	3.2	54
0	0	**6**	0.6	0.9	0.0	0
0	0	**11**	1.2	1.6	0.0	0
1	0	**1**	0.1	0.0	0.4	1
7	3	**65**	6.8	7.3	5.6	58
7	4	**30**	3.2	1.9	6.8	29
12	6	**211**	22.2	24.1	16.8	293
3	6	**193**	20.3	22.7	13.6	165
1	2	**111**	11.7	13.3	7.2	84
53	6	**279**	29.4	22.3	49.2	216

Source: WTO (2004); also in sources available at http://www.wto.org/english/tratop_e/adp_e/adp_stattab2_e.xls; http://www.wto.org/english/tratop_e/adp_e/adp_stattab7_e.xls (accessed April 2005).

TABLE 1.7 Countervailing Duty Initiations and Measures, 1995–June 2004

	1995	1996	1997	1998	1999	2000	2001
Initiations							
Argentina	1	1	1	0	0	0	0
Brazil	0	0	0	0	0	0	1
Chile	0	0	0	0	4	0	0
Costa Rica	0	0	0	0	0	0	0
Mexico	0	0	1	0	0	0	0
Peru	0	0	1	0	0	1	0
Measures							
Argentina	0	2	0	2	0	0	0
Brazil	5	0	0	0	0	0	0
Chile	0	0	0	0	0	2	0
Costa Rica	0	0	0	0	0	0	0
Mexico	7	0	0	0	0	0	0
Peru	1	0	0	0	0	0	1

which overvaluation brought intense pressure for import protection. The record shows, however, that when the exchange rate was appropriately adjusted, use of trade defenses quickly receded.

Rationale for Antidumping Mechanisms

The rationale for antidumping enforcement in Latin American countries tends to focus on the economic concept of distortion. A distortion exists when the price of a product does not equal its cost of production in a competitive environment. In modern economics, as opposed to the mercantilist economics from which the concept of dumping is drawn, the national economic interest, or economic welfare, would be higher if the distortion did not exist. A distortion thus justifies government intervention in the market.

When they established their procedures, Latin American governments were aware from analysis of antidumping systems in traditional users such as the United States and the European Union that dumping in its legal sense—even more than in its theoretical sense—did not identify circumstances in which government intervention would advance the national economic interest. Antidumping enforcement would use neither the exporter's home market price nor the constructed cost[4] as the measure of what price should be. Instead, the

TABLE 1.7 (*Continued*)

2002	2003	Jan.–June 2004	Totals 1995–June 2004	Per year 1995–June 2004	Per year 1996–June 2004	Measures in place as of June 30, 2004
0	1	0	4	0.4	0.4	n.a.
0	1	0	2	0.2	0.2	n.a.
0	0	0	4	0.4	0.5	n.a.
0	1	0	1	0.1		n.a.
0	1	0	2	0.2	0.2	n.a.
1	0	0	3	0.3	0.4	n.a.
0	0	0	4	0.4	0.5	3
0	0	0	5	0.5	0.0	0
0	0	0	2	0.2	0.2	0
0	0	1	1	0.1	0.1	0
0	0	0	7	0.7	0.0	1
0	1	0	3	0.3	0.2	1

Source: WTO (2004); also in sources available at http://www.wto.org/english/tratop_e/scm_e/scm_stattab2_e.xls; http://www.wto.org/english/tratop_e/scm_e/scm_stattab7_e.xls (accessed April 2005).

Note: n.a. = not applicable. Colombia has initiated no countervailing duty investigation. Comparative numbers for measures in place: United States 57, European Communities 18, and Canada 10.

price that enforcement attempted to reach would be the prevailing international price in competitive markets. Such interpretation followed the promise that governments had made to industry when they created the antidumping mechanisms; industry would be expected to adjust to normal international competition but would be protected from extraordinary situations.

The latitude provided by WTO rules allowed governments to accommodate at two levels the mismatch between the economic theory on which WTO rules were based and the concept that justified government intervention. At the level of antidumping investigation, WTO rules allow, in certain circumstances, the use of third-market price as the measure of normal value. An internationally competitive environment could be chosen as this third market. The more general basis for latitude is that the WTO rules do not demand that an antidumping duty be equal to the measured dumping margin. The duty cannot be larger, but it can be smaller, even zero. Latin American governments adopted the lesser duty rule, which, in theory, provides that the antidumping duty be set no higher than the level necessary to eliminate injury to domestic producers.

TABLE 1.8 Numbers of Safeguard Initiations and Other Safeguard Actions Notified to the WTO by Selected Latin American Countries, 1996–October 18, 2004

	1996	1997	1998	1999	2000	2001	2002	2003	Jan.–Oct. 18, 2004	1995–2000	2001–Oct. 18, 2004	1995–Oct. 18, 2004
Argentina												
Initiations	0	1	1	0	1	1	0	0	1	3	2	5
Preliminary measures	0	0	0	0	0	1	0	0	0	0	1	1
Definitive measures applied	0	1	0	0	1	1	0	0	0	2	1	3
Negative decision on definitive measures	0	0	0	0	0	0	0	0	0	0	0	0
Presumed negative	0	0	1	0	0	0	0	0	0	1	0	1
Ongoing	0	0	0	0	0	0	0	0	1	0	1	1
Brazil												
Initiations	1	0	0	0	0	1	1	0	0	1	2	3
Preliminary measures	1	0	0	0	0	0	1	0	0	1	1	2
Definitive measures applied	1	0	0	0	0	1	1	0	0	1	2	3
Negative decision on definitive measures	0	0	0	0	0	0	0	0	0	0	0	0
Presumed negative	0	0	0	0	0	0	0	0	0	0	0	0
Ongoing	0	0	0	0	0	0	0	0	0	0	0	0
Chile												
Initiations	0	0	0	1	4	2	3	0	0	5	5	10
Preliminary measures	0	0	0	1	2	0	0	0	0	3	0	3
Definitive measures applied	0	0	0	1	1	1	1	0	0	2	2	4
Negative decision on definitive measures	0	0	0	0	2	1	2	0	0	2	3	5

Presumed negative	0	0	0	0	1	0	0	0	0	1	0	1
Ongoing	0	0	0	0	0	0	0	0	0	0	0	0
Colombia												
Initiations	0	0	0	1	0	0	0	0	1	1	1	2
Preliminary measures	0	0	0	0	0	0	0	0	0	0	0	0
Definitive measures applied	0	0	0	0	0	0	0	0	0	0	0	0
Negative decision on definitive measures	0	0	0	1	0	0	0	0	0	1	0	1
Presumed negative	0	0	0	0	0	0	0	0	0	0	0	0
Ongoing	0	0	0	0	0	0	0	0	1	0	1	1
Costa Rica												
Initiations	0	0	0	0	1	0	0	0	0	1	0	1
Preliminary measures	0	0	0	0	1	0	0	0	0	1	0	1
Definitive measures applied	0	0	0	0	0	0	0	0	0	0	0	0
Negative decision on definitive measures	0	0	0	0	0	0	0	0	0	0	0	0
Presumed negative	0	0	0	0	1	0	0	0	0	1	0	1
Ongoing	0	0	0	0	0	0	0	0	0	0	0	0
Mexico												
Initiations	0	0	0	0	0	0	1	0	0	0	1	1
Preliminary measures	0	0	0	0	0	0	0	0	0	0	0	0
Definitive measures applied	0	0	0	0	0	0	0	0	0	0	0	0
Negative decision on definitive measures	0	0	0	0	0	0	0	0	0	0	0	0
Presumed negative	0	0	0	0	0	0	1	0	0	0	1	1
Ongoing	0	0	0	0	0	0	0	0	0	0	0	0

TABLE 1.8 Numbers of Safeguard Initiations and Other Safeguard Actions Notified to the WTO by Selected Latin American Countries, 1996–October 18, 2004 (*Continued*)

	1996	1997	1998	1999	2000	2001	2002	2003	Jan.–Oct. 18, 2004	1995–2000	2001–Oct. 18, 2004	1995–Oct. 18, 2004
Peru												
Initiations	0	0	0	0	0	0	0	0	1	0	1	1
Preliminary measures	0	0	0	0	0	0	0	0	0	0	0	0
Definitive measures applied	0	0	0	0	0	0	0	0	0	0	0	0
Negative decision on definitive measures	0	0	0	0	0	0	0	0	0	0	0	0
Presumed negative	0	0	0	0	0	0	0	0	0	0	0	0
Ongoing	0	0	0	0	0	0	0	0	1	0	1	1
Seven Countries												
Initiations	1	1	1	2	6	4	5	0	3	11	12	23
Preliminary measures	1	0	0	1	3	1	1	0	0	5	2	7
Definitive measures applied	1	1	0	1	2	3	2	0	0	5	5	10
Negative decision on definitive measures	0	0	0	1	2	1	2	0	0	3	3	6
Presumed negative	0	0	1	0	2	0	1	0	0	3	1	4
Ongoing	0	0	0	0	0	0	0	0	3	0	3	3

Source: Tabulated from information in WTO "Report [one per year for 2000–4] of the Committee on Safeguards to the Council for Trade in Goods."

Note: The actions are tabulated by the year in which each investigation was initiated. For example, if an Argentine investigation initiated in 1997 led to a definitive measure put in place in 1998, that definitive measure is included in the tabulation for 1997, not for 1998. The countries in the table all notified zero actions in 1995, which was the first year the WTO notification requirement was in force. The WTO reports no notification of measure taken or of termination for several investigations that have passed the WTO deadline for a final determination. We have labeled these "outcomes" as "presumed negative."

Although the lesser duty rule is sometimes described as being allowed by the WTO antidumping agreement, given that WTO members did not give up their sovereign right to set a lower duty by accepting the agreement, there is no need for a WTO rule to create that right. Within the rules, a WTO member can set an antidumping duty at any level determined with reference to any criterion the government considers appropriate—limited by the measured dumping margin. Because the rules for measuring the dumping margin are generous, once an affirmative determination is returned, the latitude is considerable.

Similarly, these countries included in their antidumping processes a national interest clause that allows the deciding agency to take no action or to modify action if the national interest would thereby be better served. Again, this action is a right not given up by accepting to abide by the WTO agreement; it is not a privilege granted by the agreement. The country studies explain additional criteria and limits governments included in their mechanisms.

Rationale for Safeguard Mechanisms

Though they have been infrequently used, safeguard regulations are in place in each of the seven countries. The Peru study provides a sharp example of the difference in philosophy behind safeguards and antidumping. Antidumping is a technical matter; a distortion compromises economic welfare (the national economic interest) and therefore should be corrected. A safeguard action responds to a political situation. Technical analysis is needed to gauge the extent of injury and assure that it results from import competition. The decision should, however, balance the importance of the various effects that will follow from the proposed action on consumers, production, and employment, not only in the sector that petitioned for protection but also in other sectors. The decision should also take into account other matters such as how action or inaction would affect the viability of the liberalization process and the possibility of retaliation by exporting countries. In Peru, an industry that petitions for safeguard relief not only must document an increase of imports and consequent injury but also must submit an adjustment plan and an economic report that quantifies the effect of the requested measure on final and intermediate consumers and on the public interest.

In practice, the most frequent users of safeguards have been Chile and Colombia. In Chile, increased import duties have been used on isolated occasions to provide short-term breathing space for domestic enterprises beset by competition from imports. Colombia's use of safeguards differs in that the most frequently used safeguard instrument avoids the procedural and substantive requirements of the WTO agreement by restraining restrictive action within the ceiling bindings the government has accepted at the WTO.

The Argentine experience is also illustrative. The trade commission there turned down eight of the first nine safeguard requests it received; the response by protection seekers was to apply for relief under antidumping regulations. In theory, antidumping applies only when an economic distortion can be identified, but in practice, its standards overlap considerably with the injury standard of safeguards. Moreover, when qualifying for antidumping relief, an industry need not meet the safeguard requirements to provide a workable recovery plan nor subject itself to review of how its protection will affect consumers or production in other sectors. Though different in theory, antidumping and safeguards have proven in practice to be quite fungible. In practice, the use of one versus the other is a matter of administrative or political convenience, not of the economics of the underlying situation.[5]

Decision-Making Bodies

Although each country's contingent protection processes have at their base a capacity to conduct investigations and reach determinations in accordance with the WTO rules, arrangements for deciding the restriction that will be imposed vary considerably. In antidumping cases, Argentina and Peru, for example, have created primarily technical mechanisms. The technical factors along with the independence and the analytical skills of the commission members are paramount. In contrast, Brazil entrusts the decision—once a technical determination is reached—to a vote by an overview board whose members come from a number of ministries that represent a diversity of interests. Colombia likewise entrusts the decision to an interministerial body, presided over by the country's president.

Chile has a system that controls application of contingent protection measures at several levels. At the administrative level, general interest government agencies dominate the commission that reviews technical determinations and prepares a recommendation for policy action. The commission is chaired by an official from the agency of government responsible for enforcing competition policy, and the final decision is made by the country's president. At the statutory level, only tariff surcharges may be applied, for no more than one year. A restriction that will increase the tariff above the bound rate requires approval of three fourths of the members of the commission. Moreover, consumers are recognized as interested parties.

No factor is more important to the disciplined use of contingent protection than the widespread support for the economic philosophy of openness. This point is made in each country study. The Chilean and Costa Rican studies particularly bring out the importance of deep constituent support for the economic philosophy of openness and constituent appreciation of the value of a competitive economy.

Costa Rica has no specialized agency to conduct contingent protection investigations. They are part of the normal workload of the legal and economics staffs of the trade ministry. The positive side of this arrangement is that a staff with more general responsibilities might remain more sensitive to general economic interests than a specialized staff. Because the technical work in an antidumping or safeguard investigation amounts in substance to document foreign unfairness and displacement of domestic production by imports, professionalism can take on a proprotection slant.[6]

It should be noted that Chile and Costa Rica have maintained relatively high protection for agriculture, and that they have a good record for macroeconomic stability, low inflation, and stable exchange rates. There has been no challenge to take on macroeconomic problems with trade instruments.

Sources of Discipline

After reviewing the country studies, we can look again at the question posed at the beginning of the section. Because safeguard and antidumping are instruments that, by their nature, impose import restrictions, where did policy managers find discipline over application? What helped promote acceptance of negative decisions?

The administrative content of WTO rules has made an invaluable contribution. A major source of erosion of previous liberalizations had been the tendency for instruments to proliferate, often controlled by different ministries and not unified by process or by criteria. Ministries most closely associated with industrial sectors were not counterbalanced by ministries with overreaching responsibilities or by consumer or import user interests. (In politics, concentrated interests have the advantage over more-dispersed interests, with that advantage being multiplied when decision making is at the sectoral level.) The WTO rules not only supported unification of process and criteria but also provided a template for objectivity, public notice of criteria, participation and access to information by interested parties, and publication of the legal and factual basis for decisions. They provided guidelines for objectivity, transparency, and accountability in public decision making, contributing not only to better trade policy but also to change of the policy management culture.

An important source of discipline has been the rigorous standard for the information that a protection-seeking industry was required to supply, both for initiation of an investigation and as evidence to support the impact of international competition on the industry. Peru also imposes an application fee, currently about US$925.

Effectiveness with respect to the continuance of liberalization has been a matter not only of the judicious application of WTO requirements but also of the skilled use of the discretion that WTO allows. In Mexico, the steel industry was familiar with WTO-based instruments, having been party to actions applied by the United States and the European Union against their exports. Other sectors found the administrative demands more formidable. When the survival of the liberalization program depended on such action, the Mexican government self-initiated investigations that involved smaller-scale producers of toys, clothing, and other consumer products. The combination of strict information requirements and the government's authority to self-initiate investigations provided a valuable degree of discretion. At the same time, the government used the discretion in its regulations to proceed more slowly with the investigation of the complaints by the steel industry and work out specific mechanisms to bring user interests into play.

In Colombia, the steel, chemicals, and petrochemicals industries adapted quickly to the information demands of the WTO-based system of trade defense. Sectors composed of smaller enterprises, however, found the requirements burdensome and, in time, convinced the government to create alternate trade defense mechanisms. Colombia's WTO bindings discipline the use of these instruments. The adoption of a unified mechanism for alternate instruments is another source of discipline.

The economic content of the WTO standards is another matter. Apart from the cost of demonstrating that the standards have been met, analysis of experience in other countries has shown that the standards required by the WTO agreements on safeguards and antidumping are generous in determining that petitioners are deserving of protection. Aware of this characteristic, the Latin American countries adopted their own additional bases for not taking action (for example, a national interest clause) or for limiting the degree of action that was taken (for example, a lesser duty rule). Latin American experiences confirm that the dumping and injury criteria required by WTO rules are generous. To keep the number and the degree of restrictions in check, the governments often had to depend on the discretionary authority they retained.[7] Rather than follow the rules creating political capital that governments could use to explain a negative response to a request for protection, governments had to use political capital otherwise gained to explain why protection was not given to a petitioner that the rules found to be deserving.

Recommendations for WTO Rules

The country studies in this book demonstrate that the WTO rules on safeguards and antidumping have proven to be essential and that the courage and skill of policy managers have proven to be indispensable in the sweeping trade liberalization that has taken place in Latin America trade policy over the past quarter century.

In this final section, we ask how the WTO rules could have been even more useful and more supportive of the liberalization that these countries set out to achieve. To be effective, a policy manager must master the technicalities, but we have found that the effective use of safeguards and antidumping mechanisms is as much art as science. In areas of economic policy in which the advice to "follow the rules" has perhaps been overemphasized, we will restrict ourselves to general observations; we leave the crafting of negotiating proposals to people with expertise in such work.

One might identify two objectives with respect to how international rules might shape domestic processes through which governments make decisions to impose protection. From perhaps an ideal perspective, one might hope that they would guide a country to identify those interventions that add more to the national economic interest than they take away. Eliminating distortions, in theory, follows from this perspective.

The experiences studied here show, however, that there are instances in which other considerations make it impossible to avoid what might be an economically unsound trade intervention. In those situations, good policy becomes a more pragmatic matter, a matter of managing interventions to maintain the momentum of liberalization and strengthen the politics of avoiding, rather than of imposing, such restrictions in the future.

The first objective is about economically good interventions versus economically bad; the second is—pragmatically speaking and over the long run—about fewer interventions rather than more. It is also about the number and form of interventions in the short run that, over the long run, will minimize opposition to liberalization.

The Rules Are Too Generous

Although the administrative dimensions of the rules have been supportive, the economic content has been less so. A key point that emerges from the country studies is that, from an economics perspective, WTO rules on safeguards and antidumping are too generous with respect to separating either good interventions from bad or fewer interventions from more. Although antidumping, in theory, is about interventions that make economic sense, in reality, WTO guidelines allow restrictions that amount to ordinary protection. Aware of this characteristic, Latin American governments attempted to make operational the economic concept of distortion. Qualitatively speaking, this concept would help them to separate trade interventions whose economics is good from interventions whose economics is bad. Sticking to the concept of distortion would also reduce the number of interventions that received sanction. At the same time, these governments introduced lesser duty rules and national interest clauses—additional bases not to restrict in instances in which the WTO rules would allow a restriction.

The safeguard mechanisms that the governments set up also included disciplines not mandated by WTO rules. WTO safeguard rules require only an investigation and determination of injury from imports, i.e. the cost that import competition imposes on competing domestic producers. They do not require that benefits to industrial users and to consumers likewise be taken into account. In the interest of reaching economically sensible safeguard decisions, Latin American governments supplemented their safeguard processes with requirements for an adjustment plan (and an economic report in the case of Peru) that quantifies the impact of the requested restriction on final and intermediate consumers and the public interest. The logic of the first of these is to assure that the protected industry will eventually be viable in an open economy and will not be a long-term burden on the rest of the economy. The logic of the second is that the imports that are an inconvenience for some domestic interests provide benefits for other domestic interests—lower-priced and state-of-the-art inputs for domestic producers and final goods for consumers.

Overcoming Conflicts Created by the Economic Content of the Rules

The overgenerosity of the economic content of the WTO rules leads to two points of conflict between the rules and the objective of defending liberalization:

- The case for protection has the weight of international obligation behind it, whereas the limits that governments included in their regulations do not.
- Technical analysis is expected—politically—to work in favor of liberalization, yet its economics is to make the case for protection and to document the costs that liberalization imposes on some domestic interests.

Latin American experience suggests a straightforward way to overcome these conflicts: mandate identification of the impact on users and consumers as well as the impact on competing domestic producers. The policy process would ask: Who in the domestic economy would benefit from the proposed import restriction, and who would lose? By how much?

The technicalities would be simple: recognize domestic users and consumers as interested parties, and require that the investigation determine the effect on them of the proposed restriction in parallel with its determination of injury from trade to the protection seeker. The effect of the restriction on users and consumers would be measured in the same dimensions as injury—for example, jobs lost because of higher costs and lower profits—the standard metric of effect. The existing rules of procedure would apply to the investigation of the costs of protection equally with that of the benefits. All interests would be treated the same in process and in concept.

Even in those instances in which the decision is to restrict imports, the process would bring forward the reasoning behind the liberalization, the benefits from openness. The limits that Latin American governments imposed on their use of trade defense measures would have been more effective against domestic pressures for protection if the reasons for minimizing use had had the force of international obligation behind them.[8]

Beyond making economic sense, such a safeguard process would be politically balanced. It takes into account the effect of trade on all interests in the country: those that benefit from liberalization and those who are burdened. This balance would not be a matter of the technical versus the political. The benefits to trade for user interests would be measured in the same business and economic terms as the costs to protection seekers.[9]

A shortcoming of this suggestion is that it would increase the cost of an investigation, and would impose administrative costs on potential victims of the restriction as well as on the potential beneficiaries. If, however, discipline over use were based on equal treatment of the costs of protection and its benefits rather than on the complexity of determining the benefits, then economies could be achieved without compromise to the viability of the information developed.

The balanced cost-benefit process would have to be applied in antidumping investigations as well as in safeguard investigations. The situations to which antidumping or safeguards can be applied overlap considerably. Because antidumping's popularity is not based on its unique identification of the existing business or economic situation, expanding the scope of the safeguard process would have the effect only of further increasing the use of antidumping in its place.

Other than modifying the technical dimensions of investigations to include the gains from trade, the alternative for reform is further manipulation of the technicalities of determining dumping or injury. That manipulation, illustrated by the proposals submitted at the Doha Negotiations, is not about matching the operational guidelines more closely with the economic concepts of dumping (predatory pricing) or externality—in theory, situations in which a trade intervention provides a net addition to the national economic interest. This struggle over technicalities, we contend, will have little effect on the quality or the quantity of import restrictions that are applied. There are sufficient technicalities that adding a few here, trimming a few there, will have no effect. Thinking, even tinkering within the box, is not likely to help. To support liberalization, the WTO rules should support identification of the benefits from liberalization.

Notes

1. Thirty years ago, Bela Balassa began the preface to his pathbreaking study, *The Structure of Protection in Developing Countries* (1971), by noting that a policy of import substitution was the rationale for the trade policies of many developing countries. He went on to point out that

> whatever the intrinsic merits of this policy, its application has rarely been based on a consistent program of action. Rather, the existing system of protection in many developing countries can be described as the historical result of actions taken at different times and for different reasons. These actions have been in response to the particular circumstances of the situation, and have often been conditioned by the demands of special interest groups. The authorities have generally assumed a permissive attitude toward requests for protection and failed to inquire into the impact of the measures applied on other industries and on the allocation of resources in the national economy. (xv)

2. Together, WTO members have initiated more than 2,500 antidumping investigations since 1995, compared with 174 countervailing duty investigations and 142 safeguard investigations.

3. Cross-country studies confirm that the business cycle influences the use of antidumping and other trade defenses. For example, see Leidy (1997) and Takacs (1981).

4. The WTO rules sanction constructed cost formulas that allow generous overstatement of what normal business accounting practices would determine.

5. Finger (2002) provides a general review of the point, drawing evidence from the evolution of use of GATT–WTO pressure-valve instruments since the GATT was first adopted.

6. For example, Boltuck and Litan (1991) document the biases in the administration of U.S. regulations.

7. Although the discretionary authority that countries retained and the political review processes that countries superimposed over technical determinations in a number of instances led to a reduced level of restriction, there were few instances in which no restriction was imposed after an affirmative determination.

8. Another conflict, perhaps more semantic than substantive, is between the national interest and the protection-seeking industry's interest. The protection seeker's interest is part of, not other than, the national interest. The effect of a trade restriction on the national interest, in concept, should include the cost of protection and those who bear this cost, along with the benefits and those who receive these benefits. A shortcoming of an injury investigation is that it does not give equal standing to all parts of the national interest.

9. The process could also be balanced in that users or consumer groups could petition for removal of an import restriction on the basis of the cost it imposed on them. History provides at least one example of a mechanism balanced in this way. Section 336 of the U.S. Tariff Act of 1930 empowered the U.S. president to increase or to decrease a tariff rate based on investigation by the U.S. Tariff Commission of the cost of producing the product in the United States compared with that cost in exporting countries. (The U.S. tariff would be set equal to the measured difference.) From 1931–41, the commission conducted investigations on 101 products. These investigations led to 29 tariff increases and 25 tariff reductions; in the other 47 instances, the rate was not changed.

References

Balassa, Bela. 1971. *The Structure of Protection in Developing Countries.* Baltimore, MD: Johns Hopkins University Press.

Boltuck, Richard, and Robert Litan, eds. 1991. *Down in the Dumps: Administration of the Unfair Trade Laws.* Washington, DC: Brookings.

Finger, J. Michael. 2002. "Safeguards: Making Sense of GATT/WTO Provisions Allowing for Import Restrictions." In *Development, Trade, and the WTO: A Handbook*, ed. Bernard Hoekman, Aaditya Mattoo, and Philip English, 195–205. Washington, DC: World Bank.

Leidy, Michael. 1997. "Macroeconomic Conditions and Pressures for Protection under Antidumping and Countervailing Duty Laws: Empirical Evidence from the U.S." *IMF Staff Papers* 44 (1): 132–44.

Takacs, Wendy. 1981. "Pressures for Protectionism: An Empirical Analysis." *Economic Inquiry* 27 (4): 687–93.

World Trade Organization (WTO). 2000–4. "Report of the Committee on Anti-Dumping Practices." (Document G/L/409 for 2000, Document G/L/494 for 2001, Document G/L/583 for 2002, Document G/L/651 for 2003, and Document G/L/707). Geneva: WTO.

2

POLITICAL ECONOMY OF ANTIDUMPING AND SAFEGUARDS IN ARGENTINA

Julio J. Nogués and Elías Baracat

Statistics from the World Trade Organization (WTO) indicate that, after implementing trade liberalization policies in the early 1990s, Argentina initiated a record number of antidumping investigations. This finding triggered criticisms by the media and professional economists, who say it indicates a protectionist bent. Is this interpretation correct? To what extent have antidumping and safeguard measures reversed trade liberalization policies?

This chapter makes clear that in drafting the regulations and creating the institutional mechanism that would administer them, Argentina made a serious attempt to minimize the risks of protectionism. Nevertheless, over time, changing domestic

We want to thank J. Michael Finger for his insightful comments to previous drafts of this paper, which have guided us in writing this chapter. Other comments—particularly those by Pablo Sanguinetti, Diana Tussie, and other participants at the seminar titled "Uso de Salvaguardias y Antidumping en América Latina" ("Use of Safeguards and Antidumping in Latin America"), which was held in Buenos Aires, May 24–25, 2004—also enriched the paper. Several public officials have been generous in taking time to meet with us and to assist as we prepare statistical information that has been used in several tables: Lic. Guillermo Feldman, undersecretary of Gestión Comercial Externa (External Commercial Affairs, or GCE), Elena Di Vico, president of the Comisión Nacional de Comercio Exterior (National Foreign Trade Commission, or CNCE); and Valeria Raiteri, national director of Competencia Desleal (Unfair Competition). Finally, we acknowledge the editorial work of María N. Gondell. All these contributions notwithstanding, we remain solely responsible for the contents and interpretations offered in this chapter.

and external circumstances, including macroeconomic imbalance and severe peso overvaluation, had significant effects on the number and outcome of antidumping investigations. Although the Argentine government attempted to use the discretion that existed in the institutional mechanism to refrain from protectionist responses, the tendency of the government's response to antidumping investigations under the recently adopted WTO rules was to acknowledge petitioners' right to protection rather than to refute it.

The major lesson drawn from this chapter's analysis is that the discipline behind the use of antidumping and safeguard mechanisms breaks down when the exchange rate is overvalued; in these circumstances, the tools of these mechanisms—for example, the injury test—lose their power to discriminate. If all petitioners suffer serious injury (as will be the case with an overvalued exchange rate), the basic metric of the WTO-sanctioned trade remedies—injury—loses its capacity to distinguish one industry from another and, therefore, its capacity to limit application. In this situation, the discipline inherent in WTO-based rules turns out to be more apparent than real.

To give the reader a better understanding of what happened in Argentina in the 1990s, this chapter provides an analysis of the changing circumstances surrounding the outcomes of antidumping and safeguard investigations in Argentina. First, the chapter describes the extent of trade liberalization measures that were implemented during the late 1980s and early 1990s and presents the changes that were specifically introduced to antidumping and safeguard legislation. Next, it offers a description of the important institutional reform that created an independent commission to administer the injury test using high technical standards. The chapter then presents an analysis of the outcomes of antidumping and safeguard investigations, followed by a summary of the main lessons the analysis provides with regard to the use of antidumping and safeguard mechanisms in the management of trade liberalization.

Trade Liberalization and Exchange Rate Policies

Starting in approximately 1988–89, Argentina undertook a massive program of reform and stabilization. The program's intention was to markedly reduce the role of government in the economy—to liberalize, privatize, deregulate, and open the economy to international competition in goods, services, and capital flows. The adoption of WTO-sanctioned trade policy instruments was a significant part—though only a part—of this program. Other instruments that Argentina had previously used to manage industry pressures for protection were eliminated. The government's objective was to develop instruments that would respond to industry pressures for exceptions to the ongoing process of trade liberalization but, at the same time, would control the application of trade restrictions to ensure that the momentum of reform was maintained, rather than reversed, as had been the case in previous attempts.

This trade liberalization program was essentially completed during the first half of the 1990s, and unlike the previous attempts and in spite of the serious crisis following devaluation in 2002, it has been sustained. The following sections summarize what we consider to have been some of the circumstances that shaped the outcome of antidumping and safeguard investigations, including (a) trade liberalization programs, both unilateral and under Mercosur (Mercado Común del Sur, or Southern Cone Common Market), (b) exchange rate policies, (c) recession and unemployment, and (d) trade performance.

Trade Liberalization Program

Starting in the late 1980s, trade liberalization policies resulted in a substantial reduction in average protection. Table 2.1 provides information on ad valorem tariffs and on the percentage of tariff lines covered with import licenses. The figures show high and increasing protection until 1987–88 and relatively fast decline

TABLE 2.1 Argentina: Ad Valorem Tariffs and Import Licenses, 1980–92

Year	Tariff rates, percentage ad valorem			Percentage of tariff lines with import licenses
	Maximum	Surcharge	Average	
1980	100	0	25	0
1981	75	0	29	0
1982	55	0	30	4
1983	55	0	30	15
1984	55	0	30	51
1985	55	10	32	52
1986	55	10	39	47
1987	50	15	39	51
1988	50	15	39	32
1989	30	0	18	0
1990	24	0	17	0
1991	35	0	12	0
1992	35	0	12	0

Source: Nogués (2001).

thereafter. In 1989, the dismantling of discretionary import licenses was completed, and average tariff protection declined from 39 percent in 1988 to 18 percent in 1989. In addition to these unilateral policies, in 1991, Argentina, Brazil, Paraguay, and Uruguay signed the Tratado de Asunción (Treaty of Asunción) that created the Mercosur. With some exceptions, the establishment of a common external tariff (CET) and the process of intraregional trade liberalization were completed in late 1994.[1]

With respect to export policies, the most significant changes were introduced to export taxes. Historically, Argentina deepened its isolation by imposing high export taxes on agricultural and agro-based products for which it has a strong comparative advantage. For example, in the mid-1980s, export tax collection represented more than 30 percent of total exports. From then on, these tax rates started to decline, and by 1992 export tax collection represented less than 2 percent of total exports.[2]

Exchange Rate Policies

In an attempt to tame inflation, in early 1991, the Argentine government legislated the convertibility regime that tied the peso to the U.S. dollar at par. After that, capital inflows financed excess demand and with residual inflation resulted in a severely overvalued peso. Toward the end of 2001, expectations of devaluation as signaled by the level of country risk increased rapidly, and a run against deposits in the banking system accelerated. In early 2002, the convertibility regime was abandoned, and a major devaluation process unfolded (de la Torre, Levi Yeyati, and Schmukler 1993).

Figure 2.1 shows the trend of the real exchange rate (RER) against the dollar.[3] The numbers indicate an important reduction of the average RER following the start of the convertibility regime in 1991. This overvaluation increased the challenges faced by domestic producers in adjusting to the trade liberalization program. During the second half of the 1990s, overvaluation was also a factor in slowing growth and in pushing the current account deficit to unsustainable levels; in the process, the high level of imports signaled to the antidumping and safeguard mechanisms the continued existence of injury or serious injury to domestic producers.

Growth, Crisis, and Unemployment

In addition to these negative circumstances, during the 1990s, Argentina was hit by several negative external shocks, including (a) the tequila effect that started in late 1994, (b) the Asian crisis in 1997, (c) the Russian default in 1998, and (d) the

FIGURE 2.1 Argentina: Real Exchange Rate, 1985–2002

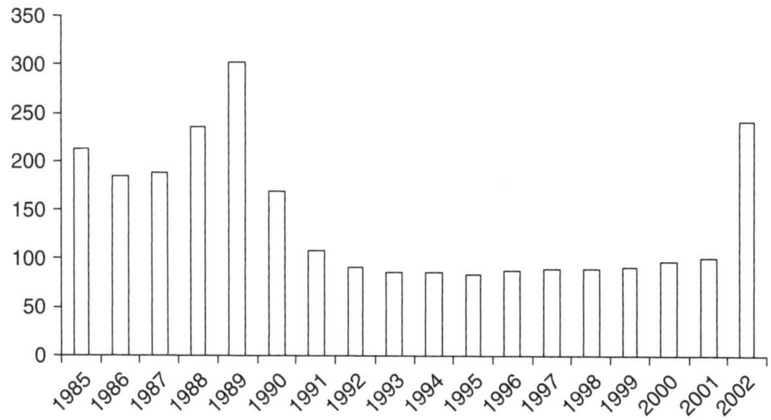

Source: Author's elaboration.
Note: The RER is estimated as the nominal exchange rate times the ratio of the U.S. cost-of-living index to the Argentine cost-of-living index.

decline of international commodity prices in the second half of the 1990s. In spite of these negative circumstances, the Argentine economy generally coped well and continued growing until mid-1998, but after that it entered into a prolonged period of recession that lasted until late 2002.[4] This recession was accentuated by Brazil's devaluation of early 1999.

During 2001 and under critical circumstances, a number of measures were attempted to avoid what by then was unavoidable—a major devaluation. In particular, the ad valorem tariffs on consumer goods increased to 35 percent, which was the maximum level that Argentina had bound during the Uruguay Round negotiations. This increase is indicative of the severe pressures that imports were putting on the trade regime and on the antidumping and safeguard mechanisms. In any case, these measures only delayed the severe devaluation that began in January 2002. During 2002, the economy collapsed when gross domestic product (GDP) declined by 10.9 percent.

After the devaluation, the Argentine government introduced three major policy changes to the trade regime. First, as imports declined rapidly, the government adjusted tariffs on consumption goods to return to the level of the Mercosur CET. Second, the government reintroduced high and escalated export taxes as a measure to finance its operations when it defaulted on its external debt. Finally, the government tightened foreign exchange controls. Devaluation was also accompanied by a reduced demand for antidumping and safeguard measures.

FIGURE 2.2 Argentina: Trade Flows

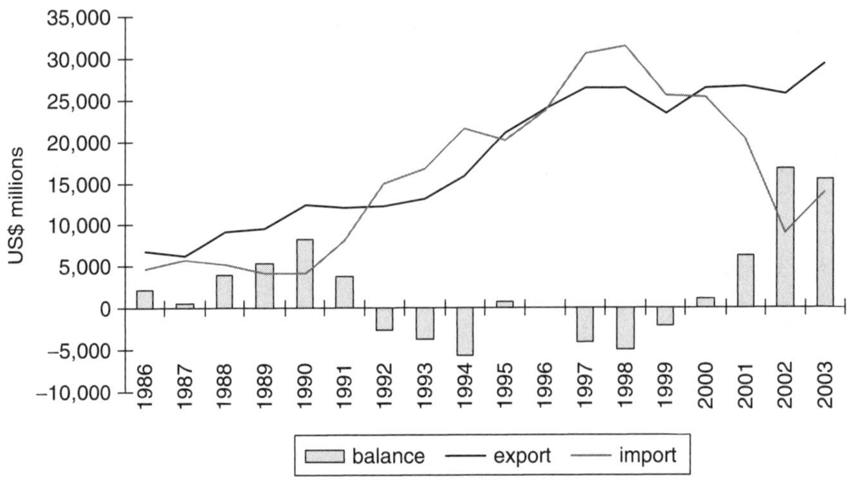

Source: Instituto Nacional de Estadisticas y Censos (INDEC) 2004.

Another important aspect of the macroeconomic scenario was the high rate of open unemployment. In 1993 and for the first time in many years, the unemployment rate surpassed 10 percent, reaching 20 percent in 1995 and declining thereafter to approximately 15 percent today.

Trade Performance

Trade liberalization policies resulted in an important increase in trade flows. Figure 2.2 shows that imports increased from less than US$5 billion in the late 1980s and early 1990s, to more than US$20 billion in 1994–95 and then to more than US$30 billion in the late 1990s. During this same period, exports increased from approximately US$6 billion to more than US$26 billion in the late 1990s. Not surprisingly, imports from Mercosur grew considerably more rapidly than those from other countries. Between 1990 and 2001, aggregate (including Mercosur) imports grew by 5 times while those from the Mercosur grew by 6.7 times. As indicated later in this chapter, the relatively fast growth of imports from Brazil spurred the demand for antidumping investigations against this country.

Summary of Trade Liberalization and Exchange Rate Policies

Argentina's trade liberalization policies of the early 1990s were significant, and with other important components of the reform program, they played a major role in changing the economic trends of the country. Until 2001–2 when trade policies were partially reversed, the Argentine economy experienced the longest period with an open trade regime that it had seen in several decades. Nevertheless, the severe overvaluation of the peso accelerated imports to unsustainable levels, and serious injury to domestic producers became generalized phenomena that would have obvious effects on the outcome of antidumping investigations (see section "Determinants of the Petitions and Outcomes of Antidumping Investigations").

Reform of Antidumping and Safeguard Legislation

The economic cabinet that came into power in early 1991 was concerned with the risks that, over time, the antidumping and safeguard mechanisms, along WTO guidelines, would be captured by powerful industries to the detriment of the trade liberalization program.[5] This cabinet also concluded that import competition played an important role in stabilization of the price level. Because Argentina was coming out of a period of high inflation, price stabilization was a paramount goal.[6]

Policy makers focused on two matters: the content of antidumping and safeguard legislation and the institutions that would administer the new regulations. In this section, we start with a brief discussion of factors that prompted the demand to update antidumping and safeguard legislation. We then discuss the political economy forces that shaped the contents of the domestic regulations.

External and Domestic Pressures for the Reform of Legislation

Under increasing competitive pressures, the previously discussed trade liberalization program lacked what domestic groups regarded as an effective mechanism for providing relief to industries that were injured by imports. Although by the early 1990s Argentina had been a General Agreement on Tariffs and Trade (GATT) contracting party for several years, it was not a signatory of the Tokyo Codes on antidumping and countervailing measures (GATT 1986). This situation created problems for both export- and import-competing industries.

On the export side, the major problem was countervailing measure investigations initiated in the United States. U.S. legislation did not apply the injury test to imports from countries that were not signatories to countervailing measures code. In this environment, Argentina's subsidized exports faced high risks of being countervailed (Finger and Nogués 1987).[7] To eliminate this source of uncertainty, Argentina negotiated with the United States and in 1991 signed a bilateral agreement by which Argentina would dismantle its export subsidies in exchange for the United States' granting the benefits of the injury test.[8]

On the import side, the Argentine government saw the GATT rules as a means of introducing discipline over the possibility that antidumping measures would reverse the momentum of liberalization. The government interpreted the existing antidumping regulations as excessively protectionist and as being in conflict with the multilateral rules toward which the government wanted to move. For example, according to the old Código Aduanero (customs code), a margin of dumping above 15 percent was sufficient evidence to conclude that the domestic industry was being injured. Domestic producers also complained that the regulations in the Código Aduanero provided too much discretion, and the producers demanded a more effective instrument.

Until the late 1980s, the existing antidumping mechanism created no problems because antidumping measures had hardly ever been demanded in Argentina's decades-old closed economy.[9] Imports were restrained through other means. This situation changed when imports began growing rapidly (see figure 2.2) and the business community put pressure on the government to implement import relief measures.

Political Economy of Antidumping and Safeguard Legislation

Increased pressure to use an antidumping mechanism that the government viewed as inconsistent with GATT obligations led the Argentine government to decide that it had to update its antidumping and countervailing measure legislation. The first step was the passage of Law 24,176 in September 1992 that incorporated the Tokyo Codes and Decree 2,121 of 1994 that included operational guidelines. The second step was the creation of the Comisión Nacional de Comercio Exterior (National Foreign Trade Commission, or CNCE) in 1994, which we discuss in the next section.

The government's drafting of operational guidelines to administer the new GATT-consistent antidumping investigations created a debate between the government and a group of powerful import-competing industries. After passage of Law 24,176, the government hired a prominent lawyer who was based in Washington, DC, to draft relatively liberal antidumping regulations. In parallel, the Unión Industrial Argentina (Union of Argentine Industries, or UIA), which represents relatively protected manufacturing enterprises, also proposed antidumping regulations to the government (UIA 1992). Some enterprises represented by the UIA had been the target of U.S. investigations; therefore, they were well aware of the highly protectionist nature of U.S. antidumping legislation.

Decree 766 of 1994, which created the CNCE and the operating regulations in Decree 2,121 of 1994, indicates that the government favored relatively liberal regulations compared with the more protectionist alternative of adopting U.S.-like regulations supported by the UIA. Examples of the more liberal regulations include the following:

- *Lesser duty.* Argentina's legislation offers the freedom to apply lesser duty, or antidumping measures that are sufficient to eliminate injury even if they are lower than the margin of dumping. The principle of lesser duty was established by Decree 766 of 1994, which, in its article 16, states that "En el análisis y recomendación de las medidas, la Comisión deberá orientarse con el criterio de contrarrestar el daño y deberá evitar la utilización de la normativa con fines proteccionistas." ("In its analysis and recommendation of measures the Commission should orient itself toward the elimination of injury and should avoid the use of the mechanism toward protectionist objectives.")
- *Type of measure.* Unlike other countries where antidumping measures are expressed as an ad valorem duty and are paid by all imports from the target enterprise or country, Argentina determines a minimum free on board (FOB) export price below which specific duties are applied to reach the threshold level. Imports carrying FOB prices above the specified level pay no antidumping duties.[10]
- *Prospective methodology.* Unlike the United States where measures are applied retrospectively—a methodology that creates high business uncertainty to exporters (Finger and Murray 1993)—Argentina applies measures prospectively from the date that the preliminary or final decisions are published.
- *Duration.* Initially, Argentina's antidumping measures were usually applied for short periods of two to three years.
- *Competition authority.* Government officials managing antidumping investigations have the right to consult the competition authority to evaluate the likely effect of antidumping measures.
- *National interest.* Measures decided by the Ministry of Economy (Ministerio de Economía) can take into account "la política general de comercio y al interés público"("the general interests of trade policy and the public interest") (article 30 of Decree 1,326, 1998). Article 30 opens the possibility to deny antidumping measures in spite of final positive dumping and injury determinations. This clause has been used only once.

Safeguard Measures

Before passing Law 24,425 (in 1994) that adopted the Uruguay Round agreements, Argentina had not issued regulations for safeguards under article XIX of GATT. Again, the country's decades-old closed economy was the main reason for the lack of demand for these measures. Another reason was that, unlike antidumping measures, the country's exports had not been affected by safeguard measures; therefore, neither the business community nor the government was knowledgeable about safeguard mechanisms. Even after passage of Law 24,425, it took nearly two years before safeguard regulations were issued by Decree 1,059 of September 1996. Therefore, during the crucial years while the economy was adjusting to the trade liberalization program, Argentina operated without a formal safeguard regime. It should also be noted that Mercosur was created without a safeguard mechanism, and its ban on the use of these measures continues today.[11]

Summary of Reforms to Antidumping and Safeguard Legislation

During the early 1990s and in spite of opposition from some interest groups, the Argentine government was successful in passing relatively liberal antidumping legislation. Shortly after issuing Decree 2,121 of 1994 that contains operating regulations, the Congress approved Law 24,425 that contains WTO's (1996) publication *The Results of the Uruguay Round of Multilateral Trade Negotiations*. Since then, only one reform to the antidumping regulations has been implemented, through Decree 1,326 of 1998, which includes procedural modifications of no substance. As we argue in a following section, "Determinants of the Petitions and Outcomes of Antidumping Investigations," after pressures from the business community, the government drafted regulations during 2001 that replicated some of the worst characteristics of the U.S. legislation. The devaluation followed by strong growth in 2003 reduced the demand for antidumping measures and for changes in the antidumping regulations. Therefore, the draft changes were never implemented.

Creation of the CNCE

After passing Law 24,176 (in 1992) that adopted the Tokyo Codes, the government began assessing alternative ways of administering the new legislation. The government, convinced that discipline over the use of antidumping measures would have to come from the injury test, looked for a workable way to structure and administer such a test. After surveying experiences in other countries, the government concluded that the execution of an injury investigation would have to be entrusted to an independent commission. This section summarizes the history of the process behind this decision.

Role of Injury

In the early 1990s, one major influence in the government's assessment of the creation of the CNCE was the conclusion reached by authors such as Finger and Murray (1993, p. 250) that the "patterns of petitions and of results suggests strongly that injury to U.S. producers ... by import competition is what the antidumping and countervailing law are about." The findings reported in Finger and Murray's (1993) paper and in other articles indicated quite clearly that, although it is relatively easy to play with the numbers to find a positive margin of dumping, the same is not always the case for injury, particularly when, as in the United States, it is evaluated by an independent agency such as the International Trade Commission (ITC). For example, these authors concluded that of 100 petitions that end with a formal determination, 56 cases would not result in a final antidumping or countervailing duty order, and of those 56 cases, 48 would end with a negative injury determination rather than a negative dumping determination. Such findings were a central element in convincing the government that an agency that could replicate this performance would add an element of restraint to antidumping investigations.

Obstacles to Creating an Independent Agency

The fact that a technical evaluation of injury was the major consideration that prompted the creation of the CNCE implied that Argentina would adopt a two-track mechanism: the margins of subsidy and dumping would be assessed by the Secretariat of Industry and Trade (Secretaría de Industria y Comercio),[12] whereas injury would be assessed by the CNCE.

Early in the process, a major obstacle to creating an independent office became evident. Independence required passing a law, but the economic cabinet concluded that any submission to Congress had no chance of passage. The cabinet also feared that congressional debate could undermine and change the relatively liberal regulations that it was proposing. Therefore, the CNCE was created by Decree 766 of 1994. In its formal statement, this decree indicates a strong mandate to protect the interests of consumers:[13] "en la administración de los instrumentos de política comercial contra prácticas de comercio desleal y las referidas a las medidas de salvaguardia deben buscarse los máximos niveles de eficiencia y transparencia a fin de asegurar que los precios pagados por los consumidores no excedan los que se hubieran observado bajo condiciones de competencia normal en el mercado internacional" ("administration of the instruments of commercial policy against unfair competitive practices and of safeguard regulations must seek to achieve maximum levels of transparency and efficiency in order to ensure that prices paid by consumers do not exceed those observed under normal conditions of international competition").

The CNCE's main goal was to undertake injury investigations using high technical standards and to issue binding decisions. Whenever the CNCE reaches a preliminary or final negative determination, the investigation is closed and the possibility of applying measures no longer exists.

Decision-Making Mechanism

As does the Secretariat of Industry and Trade, the CNCE functions under the Ministry of Economy, and its determinations are made by a majority vote of its president and four commissioners. Essentially, the process has two steps: (a) members of the technical staff prepare an injury report, and (b) the members of the CNCE board decide whether the evidence supports a positive determination.[14] When this decision-making mechanism was adopted, the thought was that rent-seeking entrepreneurs would approach an independent commission with greater care than they would approach a decision maker who was more directly subject to political pressures.

Staffing and Budget

In the creation of the CNCE, achieving technical excellence was an important goal. Except for the president and the commissioners who are political appointees, the responsibility for its staffing was delegated to a private consulting company specializing in the recruitment of qualified personnel. The comments gathered on this experience indicate that this strategy has had good results.[15] Injury investigations have been done professionally, and the exporting countries have had no serious objections with the work undertaken by the CNCE.

However, over the years, successive fiscal adjustments have diminished public sector wages with clearly negative implications for employment profiles. As an example, starting in early 2002 and for more than two years, public officials could earn no more than Arg$3,000, or approximately US$1,000, per month; this requirement applied to the president of Argentina, as well as to the president and members of the CNCE. Given this constraint, the public sector lost valuable human resources.[16]

Summary of CNCE's Creation

After passage of Law 24,176 that adopted the Tokyo Codes, the Argentine government began assessing alternative ways of administering this new legislation. In the end, it determined that an independent agency that would undertake injury investigations was important to add some degree of economic meaning to antidumping measures. The country created the CNCE at approximately the same time that it adopted the Uruguay Round agreements. Consequently, the question of interest has become: How successful has the CNCE been in disentangling those requests that deserved protection from those that did not?

Determinants of the Petitions and Outcomes of Antidumping Investigations

The preceding two sections described how Argentina approved liberal antidumping legislation and created a technically oriented institution to manage injury investigations. Statistical information indicates that, after these reforms, a high number of antidumping investigations took place and, as we shall see, an increasing share of them ended with positive injury determinations. What went wrong?

This section argues that, while the economy was growing, the antidumping mechanism was able to sort out deserving petitioners from undeserving petitioners. However, while the economy was experiencing recession and peso overvaluation, an increased share of CNCE technical reports indicated that imports were inflicting serious injury to domestic producers.

To provide a sharper picture of what happened, this section discusses (a) the effect of political determination and economic cycles on the demand for antidumping measures, (b) the country incidence and coverage of antidumping measures, (c) the overvaluation and the incidence of injury determinations, (d) the dumping determinations and antidumping measures, and (e) the mounting pressures to replicate a U.S.-like antidumping mechanism. The section ends with a brief summary that attempts to unify the picture.

Effect of Political Determination and Economic Cycles

Between the late 1980s, when trade liberalization measures started to be implemented, and 1994, Argentina administered antidumping measures under the guidelines of the Código Aduanero. According to the 1994 annual report of the CNCE (CNCE 1994, p. 75), from 1988 to 1994 the government received 135 antidumping petitions for which 69 investigations were initiated and, of those 69, 19 had measures applied. These numbers indicate that trade liberalization was accompanied by an important increase in the demand for antidumping protection, but the political determination of the government remained in favor of openness.[17]

The strategy of the government during the initial years of the trade liberalization program was to delay decisions on antidumping investigations while the new regulatory and institutional frameworks were being completed. The Código Aduanero regulations that were used to process the early petitions had no time limits for the different steps of antidumping investigations (including opening an investigation), so the government retained important degrees of discretion. Former Minister Cavallo often reiterated that the government would be very careful in the use of antidumping measures until the price level had stabilized. During those days, the taming of inflation was a major policy objective, and the government considered that import competition had an important role to play in attaining it.

Furthermore, during the early years of the CNCE's operation, the relatively high incidence of negative determinations is likely to have reduced the number of frivolous petitions. Political determination in favor of openness and a technically oriented CNCE defined an environment where ex ante an antidumping petition had a high likelihood of ending in a negative determination. Another factor reducing the demand for antidumping protection was the time and money a petitioner would have to expend to present and defend an investigation with a low likelihood of providing positive returns.[18]

The CNCE began operating in January 1995, and between 1995 and early 2004, it completed 111 investigations, or 166 when each country of origin of imports is considered a different case. In this relatively brief experience, a first point to note is the cyclical behavior of the number of new investigations: The number of initiations increased during recession years; however, this number declined during growth years. Figure 2.3 shows that a relatively high number of 25

FIGURE 2.3 Argentina: Antidumping Initiations and GDP Growth, 1995–2003

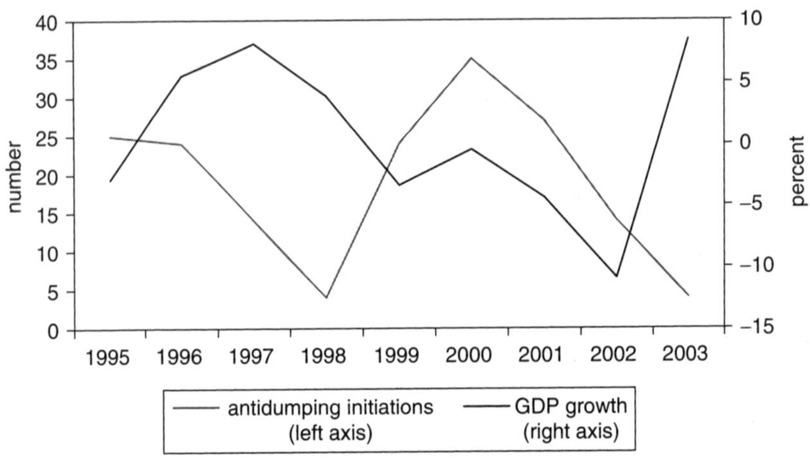

Source: Figure data from the CNCE and INDEC (Instituto Nacional de Estadísticas y Censos).

investigations were initiated during the crisis year of 1995 (the tequila effect). As the economy regained strong growth from 1995 until mid-1998, initiations declined drastically and reached only four cases in 1998. After that, with four consecutive years of negative growth, initiations increased to an average of 25 per year—79 percent higher than the average number during the growth years from 1996 to 1998.[19] Finally, after the devaluation in early 2002 and strong growth in 2003, the number of initiations declined to 14 in 2002 and 4 in 2003.

Winners and Losers of the Antidumping Mechanism

Table 2.2 presents the incidence of antidumping investigations by requesting industries for the period 1995–2004. The steel and steel products industry has demanded one-third of all cases, and the chemical industry has one-eighth. As discussed in the earlier section "Reform of Antidumping and Safeguard Legislation,"

TABLE 2.2 Argentina: Antidumping Investigations by Requesting Industries, 1995–2004

Industry	Number of investigations	Investigations with positive injury determinations (%)[a]
Steel & steel products	36	94
Chemicals	14	43
Others	13	77
Consumer durables	11	100
Electrical equipment	9	56
Plastic & plastic products	6	83
Processed food	6	33
Textiles & textile products	5	100
Machinery & nonelectrical equipment	4	75
Wood & paper products	4	75
Rubber & rubber products	3	33
Total	111	77

Source: Author's elaboration of CNCE data.

Note: Negative preliminary injury determinations are taken as negative cases and undertakings as positive determinations. Of the 26 negative outcomes, 10 were decided at the preliminary stage, 15 at the final stage, and 1 on the basis of the national interest.

a. In six cases, the final determination was negative in some parts and positive in others. In this table, we have counted these as a positive determination. If we had these outcomes as negative, the percentage of positive determinations would have declined to 70 percent.

TABLE 2.3 Argentina: Antidumping Investigations by Target Country, 1995–2004

Country/region	Number
Brazil	31
China	34
European Union	42
United States	9
Others	50
Total cases	166

Source: Authors' elaboration of CNCE.
Note: In this table, each is taken as a case. One case against the EU has been taken as a single case.

one hypothesis explaining the high incidence of antidumping cases requested by the steel and steel products industry is that, during the 1980s, this industry had been hit by several investigations, particularly in the United States (Nogués 1991). As a consequence, this industry was more alert to how antidumping could be used for obtaining import relief than other industries.[20] The last column of table 2.2 presents the percentage of cases with a positive injury finding. Although 94 percent of the steel cases ended with a positive determination, only 43 percent of the chemical cases did so. Overall, table 2.2 shows that 77 percent of all investigations ended with a positive injury determination, a figure that is higher than what has been estimated for other countries including the United States (Irwin 2002) and Mexico (Francois and Niels 2003)

Table 2.3 shows that, at the country level, China and Brazil have been the hardest hit by Argentina's antidumping investigations, with 34 and 31 cases, respectively, for the period 1995–2004. The high incidence of cases against Brazil can be explained by the regional liberalization in the Mercosur and by the absence of a safeguard mechanism for fine-tuning intraregional trade flows. This explanation implies that import relief measures can be provided only by antidumping measures or by other obscure nontariff barriers.[21]

Table 2.4 presents two indicators of the importance of antidumping: (a) the percentage of imports covered as a share of total imports, and (b) the value of apparent consumption affected as a share of value added by the manufacturing sector.[22] As in other studies, the first indicator shows relatively low values, which is not surprising given that the objective of antidumping measures is to reduce imports. Still, the rapidly increasing trend of positive injury determinations after 1995 is evidence of an antidumping system that is moving closer to the needs of petitioners.

TABLE 2.4 Argentina: Coverage of Antidumping Measures, percent

Year	Import coverage[a]	Output coverage[b]
1995	0.10	0.50
1996	0.30	1.50
1997	0.80	4.30
1998	0.70	4.50
1999	1.10	6.40
2000	1.30	7.90
2001	1.80	6.20
2002	2.10	4.10
2003	1.60	5.90

Source: Authors' elaboration of CNCE and INDEC data.

a. Of total imports, the percentage of imports under initiated investigations.

b. The percentage of manufacturing value added, in sectors for which antidumping investigations were initiated.

The second indicator better captures the economic importance of antidumping protection on the domestic economy. It shows the share of output (value added) of the manufacturing sector protected by antidumping measures (CNCE 1994 and other annual reports). This indicator also shows an increasing trend from less than 1 percent in 1995 to approximately 6 percent in 2003.

Overvaluation and the Incidence of Injury Determinations

The CNCE appears to have met the goals of its original designers: its injury analysis has been driven by objective economic factors, and there are no precedents indicating that foreign exporters have had serious objections to its work. Therefore, we take its findings as a good approximation of the extent of injury suffered by the domestic economy.

The analysis presented in the earlier section "Trade Liberalization and Exchange Rate Policies" and the time trends of initiations shown in figure 2.3 suggest several hypotheses. First, currency overvaluation-cum-recession increased the likelihood of injury that should show in increasing shares of positive determinations. Second, peso devaluation in early 2002 and strong growth in 2003 should have relaxed the demand for antidumping and safeguard measures. Finally, given the efforts in designing liberal regulations and creating technically oriented institutions, a relatively high number of negative injury determinations should have characterized the functioning of Argentina's

TABLE 2.5 Argentina: Injury Determinations in Antidumping Investigations, 1995–2004

Years	Determination[a]	Preliminary	Final[b]
1995–98	Positive	18	21
	Negative	7	14
	Percentage negative	28.0	40.0
1999–2004	Positive	45	64
	Negative	2	3
	Percentage negative	4.5	4.5
1999–2001	Positive	20	31
	Negative	2	1
	Percentage negative	10.0	3.2
2002–3	Positive	25	33
	Negative	0	2
	Percentage negative	0	6.1
1995–2004	Positive	63	85
	Negative	9	17
	Percentage negative	12.5	16.7

Source: Authors' elaboration of CNCE data.

Note: Undertakings are assumed to be final positive determinations; there were two undertakings during 1995–98, and four during 1995–2004. In investigations arriving at mixed results, we have assumed that the determination is positive. Revisions are counted as individual cases.

a. Cases included in each period are determined according to the year when the final determination was published.

b. The case decided on national interest (Decree 69 of 2001) is taken as a final negative determination.

antidumping mechanism. The statistical analysis that follows will test these hypotheses.

Table 2.5 shows the outcome of antidumping investigations between 1995 and 2004. The evidence indicates that between 1995 and 1998 when the Argentine economy was growing strongly, the share of negative injury determinations by the CNCE was relatively high, but during the following years, this share declined. Our hypothesis is that the continued overvaluation of the peso and the prolonged recession between late 1998 and 2002 increased the likelihood that technical reports prepared under WTO antidumping guidelines would show in an increasing share of positive injury determinations. The figures in the table indicate that although the 2002 devaluation and 2003 growth reduced the number of petitions and initiations (see figure 2.3), they had no effect on negative injury determinations.[23] One hypothesis is that the investigations that were concluded during this period were still affected from injury attributed to imports in previous years. Finally, the incidence of negative injury determinations under the CNCE has not been higher than that observed in other countries that have independent commissions like the United States (Irwin 2002) or that have centralized systems like Mexico (Francois and Niels 2003)

The new investigations under WTO regulations differed from the previous investigations under Código Aduanero regulations in one important sense: degree of discretion. The new regulations took away much of the discretion that was in the old system, including whether and when to open an investigation. Under the system that prevailed until 1994, the government received 135 antidumping petitions, of which only 69 cases were investigated. These numbers show that, at least in part, the exploitation of the discretion in the old system kept the number of investigations relatively low;[24] strong growth during the early 1990s and political determination in favor of openness were the other important factors.[25]

Dumping Determinations and Antidumping Measures

In most cases, the UGE has arrived at positive determinations on dumping; therefore, this stage of the investigation has generally not worked as a filter for antidumping petitions. It should be said that the UGE lacks resources to verify, in situ, the prices offered by exporters, which has been a problem in some decisions on dumping margins, particularly after a 2001 WTO ruling against Argentina in a ceramic tile case.[26] In any event, this ruling has made the UGE more careful in the use of information on prices provided by both the petitioners and the exporters.

The stringency of antidumping barriers is a tricky issue to assess because imports can be shifted to sources other than countries against which measures have been imposed. On the one hand, an antidumping duty can be very high, but if the source of imports can be substituted, the protectionist effect may not be that serious. On the other hand, antidumping duties can be relatively low but if barriers are imposed against all major suppliers, these measures are likely to be unavoidably costly.[27]

Keeping this tricky issue in mind, we offer brief comments on some characteristics of Argentina's antidumping measures. First, with respect to the methodology used to assess the margin of dumping, in the majority of cases, investigations have estimated normal values from domestic market prices.[28] The most significant exception has been cases against China, where normal values have been estimated from domestic prices in surrogate market economies. It is also of interest to note that normal values from cost-based estimates have been used in only one case: laminated steel products imported from Kazakhstan and Romania.

A second issue of interest to note is that the duration of antidumping measures has been increasing. From the initial years until approximately 1998, this duration was relatively short, usually two to three years. More recently, the normal duration has been extended, and now it is not uncommon to find measures being imposed for five years (Nogués and Baracat 2005, statistical appendix).

A third topic refers to the nature of the antidumping measure. We mentioned before that, during the initial years of operation of the system, the usual measure was the determination of a reference FOB export price; when the price of imports is lower than this reference, a specific duty would close the gap. Imports with invoice prices above the regulated FOB price paid no duties. More recently, however, the system has moved closer to one in which the dumping margin is transformed to an equivalent ad valorem duty that is paid by all imports from the target country or enterprise, which is closer to the U.S. system.

The analysis presented above indicates that a lesser duty was a characteristic of the liberal approach that prevailed when Argentina's antidumping mechanism was designed in the early 1990s. It is of interest to note that, contrary to our expectations, the information presented in table 2.6 indicates that during the initial years of the antidumping mechanism (1995–98), the concept of lesser duty was applied in relatively few cases: only 3 of 16 determinations. That proportion contrasts with the 22 lesser duty cases out of 78 determinations after 1998, when the economy was mostly in recession. This contrast indicates how the degrees of freedom allowed by WTO rules can be used to lessen protectionist impacts of antidumping measures even in situations of severe recession.

TABLE 2.6 Argentina: Antidumping Measures

Period	Number of dumping cases with antidumping duties applied	Number with full dumping margin imposed	Number with lesser duty rule applied	Average dumping margin, percentage ad valorem
1995–98	16	13	3	315
1999–2003	78	56	22	251
1995–2003	94	69	25	267

Source: Authors' elaboration of CNCE data.

Note: The end points of the different periods are defined by the dates when the final measures were announced. For several cases, we lacked information on dumping margins, therefore calculated the averages from the cases for which data were available.

Table 2.6 also presents estimates of the average dumping margins in ad valorem equivalents. Because Argentina has usually determined minimum FOB export prices below which specific antidumping duties are applied, the rates on which we based these calculations correspond to maximum values; when export prices are above the minimum, no specific antidumping duties are applied (see the section "Reform of Antidumping and Safeguard Legislation"). This fact and the fact that Argentina has often applied lesser duties implies that the numbers in table 2.6 could be well above the antidumping duties actually applied. Therefore, we take these numbers more as an indication of dumping margins than of the stringency of antidumping measures. With this thought in mind, we first note that the estimates for the 1995–2003 period show unusually high dumping margins. Second, and more surprising to us, is that the breakdown of this period into the high-growth and low-growth years (1995–98 and 1999–2003, respectively) reveals that the presence of high dumping margins has been a persistent characteristic and not one that has been particularly acute in bad times.[29]

In sum, Argentina has not resorted to what is generally considered to be the most subjective and protectionist methodology for estimating normal values, namely cost-based estimates. It is also important to note that in over 20 percent of the cases included in this study, the antidumping measure has been a lesser duty, which was the case even during the recessionary years between 1999 and 2002. The WTO rules indicated injury, but the Argentine government still applied some of the liberal dimensions of its legislation.

Another example was the application of the national interest clause in one case decided in 2003—imports of Glifosato from China.[30] It would be an error to conclude from this example that Argentina's antidumping mechanism is relatively lenient. The fact of the matter is that after its initial years, the system has evolved toward one that has provided higher levels of protection through, among other things, extending the duration of the measures and changing the nature of the antidumping barrier. But the most important factor indicating a protectionist trend—an increasing share of positive injury determinations—was not the effect of an administration that changed its objectives, but mainly the effect of the application of multilateral rules that, under Argentina's economic situation, clearly signaled the existence of injury.

Overvaluation and Pressure to Shift to U.S.-Like Antidumping Legislation

A proposal for reforming antidumping regulations is contained in Decree 1,088 of 2001. The protracted recession that had started in late 1998 and the important overvaluation discussed in the section "Trade Liberalization and Exchange Rate

Policies" were major factors pushing entrepreneurs to seek legislation that was more protectionist. The pressures were also exacerbated by the highly publicized and politicized U.S. antidumping and countervailing duty (CVD) measures against honey imports from Argentina.[31] This investigation had ramifications for many honey-producing provinces and for thousands of beekeepers; both groups faced serious problems in meeting the information requirements and deadlines established by the U.S. Department of Commerce (Nogués 2003).[32]

Decree 1,088 was drafted in this atmosphere of recession, currency overvaluation, and animosity. Under these unfavorable circumstances, the same Ministry of Economy that had signed Decrees 766 (creation of CNCE), and 2,121 (liberal antidumping regulations) in 1994, concluded in 2001 that it made little sense to continue implementing antidumping regulations that provided foreigners and, in particular, the United States more lenient treatment than what Argentina's exporters were receiving abroad. The natural reaction was to adopt U.S.-like regulations—such as those included in Decree 1,088—including (a) shorter time periods of the different stages of antidumping and CVD investigations, particularly in the opening stage, and (b) the adoption of retroactive provisional measures and retrospective final antidumping and countervailing duties.[33]

Although article 71 of Decree 1,088 stated that it would become legally binding on January 1, 2002, it never did. In late December 2001, amid a major economic and social crisis, the president of Argentina resigned, and in early 2002, a new president was sworn in. As shown in figure 2.1, by then, the devaluation process had been set in motion, and the RER had started its path of accelerated climbing. Later in 2003, strong growth resumed. Under these conditions, the pressures for reform lessened, and the new economic team concluded that the time for implementing the changes of Decree 1,088 had not arrived. Now the expectation is that this decree most likely will never be implemented.[34]

Summary of Determinants of the Petitions and Outcomes of Antidumping Investigations

During the early years of the reform movement, when the country had not yet signed the Tokyo Codes, what was not in the books—for example, no time limits for deciding on the opening of investigations, political determination against accepting protectionist demands, processing costs, and high likelihood of negative injury determinations—was of great importance for dismissing frivolous petitions for antidumping measures. In late 1994 when the government put into effect the new WTO antidumping regulations, it lost much of the discretion that it had under earlier antidumping legislation. For example, it could no longer decide to delay the initiation of investigations with as much freedom as it used to have. As a consequence, since 1995 but particularly after 1998, most petitions for antidumping measures have ended in formal investigations.

Having opted for the adoption of multilateral rules, the government searched for ways of preventing antidumping and safeguard mechanisms from being co-opted by special interests. Toward this end, it passed liberal antidumping legislation and created the CNCE to administer injury reports in antidumping, countervailing measure, and safeguard investigations. The government believed that managing injury investigations on a technical basis—within the regulations established by WTO—was the key to maintaining discipline over use.

At the technical level, Argentina's experience with conducting injury tests was a success and the CNCE did a professional job. On the dumping side, the ceramic tiles case points more to the lack of resources available for measuring dumping margins than to a lack of professionalism. Argentina's management of pressures for protection on a technical basis was, however, less successful. Delicate macroeconomic problems exceeded the capacity of the antidumping mechanism to distinguish likely deserving from undeserving petitions; in the situation that existed, dumping and injury reports tended to document the petitioner's right to protection than to refute it. Mercosur, where safeguards are banned, heightened pressure on the antidumping mechanism; relief from imports coming from Brazil has been provided essentially through antidumping measures. Under these conditions, the technical standard tended to support restriction, and increasingly the antidumping mechanism became a reliable instrument for petitioners. It is of interest to note that, even during the recession years, in several instances the government resorted to the liberal aspects of the legislation, for example, the implementation of lesser duties, to graduate the protectionist effects of antidumping measures.

Throughout the 1995–2004 experience, the evidence indicates that, in terms of the share of negative determinations, Argentina's antidumping mechanism has not delivered less protection than those in other countries that either are administered by independent commissions like the United States or are centralized antidumping mechanisms like Mexico. The experience of Argentina is successful across a significant dimension: in spite of the weight of negative circumstances, there has been a resolve of successive governments to hold the line against import restrictions. Also, today there are far fewer and more transparent trade restrictions in place than there had been in previous restructurings of the exchange rate, when trade liberalization measures were fully reverted by resorting to higher tariffs and several obscure and arbitrary instruments (Nogués 1986).

Finally, a visible attempt at eroding the mechanism came only in 2001 after more than three consecutive years of recession and currency overvaluation. Tensions under these circumstances were heightened by the honey case that illustrated how other WTO members like the United States used the multilateral rules to provide more effective antidumping protection than Argentina did. Nevertheless, after the 2002 devaluation and 2003 growth experience, demands for more protectionist regulations and antidumping measures have lessened significantly, and apparently neither the government nor the private sector continues to push for the adoption of U.S.-like regulations. We take this trend as another indication of a determination to hold the line.

Use of Safeguards

With respect to the use of safeguards for fine-tuning the trade liberalization program, the experience of Argentina can be summarized as quite unsuccessful. Before the Uruguay Round agreements came into effect, the country could restrict imports at ease, and no safeguard regulations were necessary. That situation explains why—during the initial years of the trade liberalization program—the government increased barriers at the border to facilitate adjustment of some industries like footwear, textiles, and clothing. This freedom to fine-tune the trade liberalization program came to an end when the Uruguay Round agreements began to be enforced in 1995, and successive adverse WTO Panel Reports reduced the margins for using safeguard measures (Baracat and Nogués forthcoming).

For these industries, the safeguard instrument that was used was the so-called minimum specific import tariffs (derechos de importación específicos mínimos, or DIEMs).[35] The equivalent ad valorem tariffs of the DIEMs was often above 35 percent, so when the Uruguay Round came into effect in 1995, trading partners requested Argentina to reduce them in line with the maximum tariff that the country had set in these negotiations. After consultations ended with negative results, trading partners initiated a case in the WTO Dispute Settlement Body (DSB).

In the following discussion, we comment on the experience with safeguards under article XIX of GATT and the WTO Safeguards Agreement, as well as with the textile safeguards under the WTO Agreement on Textiles and Clothing (ATC).

Safeguards under Article XIX of GATT and the WTO Safeguards Agreement

Table 2.7 shows that there have been 13 petitions under the Safeguards Agreement, of which 7 were turned down by the CNCE before initiation, 1 was withdrawn by the petitioner, 1 was returned to the petitioner on the basis of insufficient information, and 4 resulted in the opening of investigations. Safeguard measures were introduced in three of the four investigations: footwear, canned peaches, and small motorcycles. In the fourth case, the toy industry, the CNCE determined at the end of the investigation that safeguards were not applicable.

TABLE 2.7 Argentina: Outcome Petitions under the Safeguards Agreement

Year of Petition	Product	Notes
1996	Footwear	Positive injury determination
1997	Toys	No investigation initiated
1997	Bicycle tires	No investigation initiated
1997	Ham	Withdrawn by petitioner
1997	Toys	Final negative determination
1997	Camping gear	No investigation initiated
1997	Cardboard	No investigation initiated
1999	Tires	No investigation initiated
2000	Electronic converters	No investigation initiated
2000	Small motorcycles	Positive injury determination
2000	Canned peaches	Positive injury determination
2001	Nuts and bolts	Turned down for not submitting information of the sort and in the form required
2002	Wheat gluten	No investigation initiated

Source: CNCE (http://www.mecon.gov.ar/cnce).

Information gathered during our research indicates some of the factors that help readers to understand why so few safeguards were processed by the CNCE. The list of factors includes the following: (a) the injury test in safeguard cases is more demanding than in antidumping cases; (b) the domestic industry has to be able to show that it can overcome its competitive disadvantages by implementing a plan of structural reforms (for instance, in the cases of toys, cardboard, and bicycle tires, the evidence was not strong enough to argue that these requirements could be met); (c) in some cases, the domestic industry accounted for only a small fraction of the market, with most of the apparent consumption being supplied by imports (for example, in the toy sector, this factor was included in the assessment of the CNCE); (d) the fact that safeguards are closely watched by the WTO implies that a careful evaluation of possible demands for trade compensation has to be undertaken (for example, when an industry like camping gear was considered to be able to reconvert without safeguards, the CNCE turned down the petition); and (e) the WTO dispute in one of the first safeguard cases processed by the CNCE (footwear), raised fears that other cases could follow.

Of the three industries where Argentina adopted safeguard measures—footwear, canned peaches, and small motorcycles—two were taken to the WTO DSB. Footwear was the most visible case, and on the basis of particular interpretations of WTO regulations, the DSB issued a decision against Argentina (Baracat and Nogués

2005). Argentina also lost the dispute against its measures in favor of the canned peach industry.

The evidence from Argentina's experience with safeguards under article XIX of GATT and the WTO Safeguards Agreement suggests that the government tried to operate safeguards as an economic instrument to facilitate the adjustment of industries damaged by increased imports, but in successive cases lost in WTO disputes, the safeguards acted as a barrier. This barrier has been interpreted by Sykes's (2003)[36] argument that the WTO dispute settlement process never found a thread of economic reasoning on which to build its interpretations against safeguards. This interpretation helps in understanding the outcome of the WTO dispute in the footwear case (Baracat and Nogués forthcoming).

Textile and Clothing Safeguards

Since 1993, the textile and clothing industry had also benefited from the DIEMs' equivalent ad valorem duties, which were in many cases above 35 percent. When the Uruguay Round agreements came into force in 1995, several trading partners noted the inconsistency with Argentina's obligations. In response, the Argentine government attempted to provide protection on the basis of the transitional safeguard measures contemplated in the ATC.

Table 2.8 shows the seven petitions for safeguards under this agreement. The CNCE found evidence of serious injury in only three cases: cotton textiles, polyester fibers, and polyester textiles. The other cases were turned down either because the request had not satisfied the procedural requirements or simply because the information contained in the petitions indicated that the supporting evidence was too weak to merit these measures.

TABLE 2.8 Argentina: Petitions for Safeguards under the ATC Agreement

Year of petition	Product	Notes
1998	Cotton textiles	Positive injury determination
1998	Polyester fibers	Positive injury determination
1998	Polyester textiles	Turned down
1998	Polyester textiles	Positive injury determination
1998	Rugs	Turned down
1998	Fine textiles	Turned down
1998	Wool and synthetic fiber pullovers	Turned down

Source: CNCE.

To understand the outcome of these safeguards, one needs to remember that the ATC seeks to dismantle the protection system under the Multifiber Agreements. If one keeps that note in mind, the measures regulated by article 6 of the ATC are transitional safeguards that should be allowed only in exceptional and well-justified cases. Under these requirements, the WTO Textile Monitoring Body, which clears those measures, has taken a restrictive view. Thus, Argentina had to dismantle practically all measures it had imposed.

As was the case with the footwear industry, Argentina's textile producers were hard hit by the trade liberalization-cum-currency overvaluation. In addition, the condition of lower wages in Brazil was another negative external factor for this industry. In the end, textile producers had to face the full burden of adjustment as they were stripped of the possibility of receiving import relief measures regulated by the WTO.[37]

Summary of Use of Safeguards

Argentina's experience with safeguard investigations shows that, in assessing the safeguard petitions, the government followed a cautious economic approach. The CNCE took the leading role in turning down 13 of the 20 petitions for safeguard protection under article XIX of the GATT and article 6 of the WTO ATC. In spite of this careful approach, of the three cases that received safeguard protection under article XIX of the GATT and the WTO Safeguards Agreement, two cases—footwear and canned peaches—were turned down by the WTO DSB. Likewise, the WTO Textile Monitoring Body turned down almost all transitional safeguard measures that Argentina had introduced to ease the adjustment process of textile producers. In short, the trade liberalization program was implemented under a system of regional and multilateral rules that practically made no room for the use of safeguards. We believe this development is a serious drawback that is likely to create a backlash against future liberalization attempts.[38]

Also, Argentina appears to be a clear example where the frustrations with safeguards have shifted demands for contingent protection to antidumping measures. We doubt that this result is the type of outcome that negotiators were seeking when they drafted the WTO antidumping and safeguard agreements. We also doubt that this system of multilateral rules will be the one to facilitate future trade liberalization attempts.

Lessons from This Chapter's Analysis

Argentina's trade liberalization policies of the early 1990s were significant and, together with other important components of the reform program, played a major role in changing the economic trends of the country. Until 2001–2 when trade policies were only partially reversed, the economy experienced the longest period with an open trade regime that it has seen in several decades. In relation to the previous experience, it is during these years when the demand and supply for antidumping and safeguard measures increased considerably. Our objective in this final section is to summarize the main lessons from our analysis of the factors that determined the use of such measures.

Liberalization and Contingent Protection

Unlike previous attempts, the trade liberalization policies that started to be implemented in the late 1980s have withstood the test of time, and in some cases, as in the 2001–3 period, turbulent times from which the country is only now emerging. Our conclusion is that, along the adjustment process, antidumping and safeguard measures offered some import relief, but unlike past attempts, the latest trade liberalization policies have been only partially reversed by these or other measures. Our lesson here is that the country has realized that isolation is not good economic policy and has accepted international discipline over trade policy even though some multilateral rules do not make economic sense.

Currency Overvaluation and Contingent Protection

A misaligned exchange rate will make it impossible to sustain a technical approach to antidumping and safeguard investigations that calibrate on degree of displacement. In a situation of macrobalance, injury analysis separates the few from the many; in a situation of imbalance, the many are judged as deserving of protection. Argentina made an explicit and careful attempt to isolate its trade remedies from protectionist interests through liberal rules and professional analysis. In 2001, after more than two years of recession and currency overvaluation, policy makers stretched the limits of the trade regime by increasing the tariff rates for consumer goods to the maximum allowed under its WTO obligations. This same situation that increased imports beyond sustainable levels resulted in the CNCE's indicating that an increasing number of industries were suffering serious injury. Following the devaluation of 2002 and strong growth in 2003, the number of antidumping and safeguard initiations declined significantly, and now these instruments are functioning in an environment where they can better distinguish the petitions for protection.

Flexibility of WTO-Based Antidumping Regulations

Important inputs of time and resources were invested to ensure that the antidumping legislation would dismiss frivolous petitions for protection. In spite of these efforts, the lesson from Argentina's experience indicates the tremendous flexibility that WTO-based antidumping regulations have for adapting to political and economic cycles. Argentina maintained a technical approach to antidumping investigations, but as the economy worsened, the mechanism delivered information signaling the need for increasing protection, which happened without a single change to the regulations. Argentina adopted several of the more liberal options allowed by the WTO rules, and although these provisions did not prevent implementation of measures, liberal provisions such as lesser duties resulted in lower antidumping barriers.

Political Economy Implications of Multilateral Safeguard Regulations

Essentially during and following the implementation of the trade liberalization program, Argentina functioned without a safeguard mechanism. Because of the high standards required for their application and the lack of an economic basis in the jurisprudence that has been established by the WTO DSB, safeguards under article XIX of the GATT and the WTO Safeguards Agreement, as well as the transitional textile safeguards under the WTO ATC were nearly useless to the business community. The tentative lesson is that the political economy of these high safeguard standards may, in the medium term work (a) against further trade liberalization programs, (b) in favor of the establishment of more obscure barriers, or (c) in both ways.

It is of interest to compare the WTO rules on safeguards with the WTO rules for the special agricultural safeguards demanded by industrial countries when they accepted tariffs being added to nontariff measures under the Agreement on Agriculture (WTO 1996). This adding of tariffs had practically no liberalization in it (Anderson 1996), and still, special agricultural safeguards were necessary to persuade the agricultural interest groups of the Organisation for Economic Co-operation and Development (OECD) countries to accept the shift of policy instruments. The big difference is that, unlike article XIX of the GATT safeguards, the special agricultural safeguards have automatic trigger mechanisms.

Antidumping and Safeguards in the Mercosur

Given the ban on safeguards for intra-Mercosur trade, policy makers and the business community have resorted to antidumping and other more obscure forms of nontariff barriers (Berlinski 2001). Argentina's experience indicates that it made no reserves for its sensitive industries either in the Uruguay Round or in the Mercosur negotiations. Because of this situation, the government continues to face demands for import relief from relatively labor-intensive sectors. Because the

Brazilian industry has sufficient industrial capacity to overwhelm Argentine producers, under Mercosur's trade regulations, Brazil has a privileged position. The lesson here is that Argentina should have made reserves in the Mercosur, negotiated a special regional safeguard as the Andean Community has, or both (Reina 2004). The current situation has created, and will continue to create, friction and, what is worse, will result in the establishment of ad hoc measures such as voluntary export restraints.

Political Determination and the Demand for Antidumping Protection

Another lesson refers to factors having negative effects on the number of antidumping petitions. In addition to the obvious factors such as the legal costs and time involved in an investigation, other factors—such as the political decision to not process antidumping petitions while the economy was still under high inflation in the early 1990s and the unbounded time that officials had to open an investigation under the previous regulations—had negative effects on the demand for antidumping measures. Although it is impossible to determine with precision how many companies or industries considered submitting a petition and in the end decided against doing so, it is of interest to note that approximately 50 percent of all potential petitions were finally not submitted. This incident is a clear example of the role that perceptions play in the business community with respect to policy preferences and political determination that favor the government's openness during the initial years of the trade liberalization program.

Resource Constraints

The administrative and institutional reforms that were implemented to administer the WTO antidumping and safeguard regulations demanded an important investment in human and financial resources. In spite of this demand, the CNCE's operating budget has often been insufficient to do the job as expected. For example, because of insufficient funds, in situ verifications of dumping margins have been undertaken in only a handful of cases. Likewise, in the creation of the CNCE, the government was careful in the qualifications required for staff appointments. Nevertheless, the CNCE and the UGE have not always been successful in offering wages attractive enough to retain staff members nor have they consistently met training and infrastructure needs, including information technology. These factors can eventually undermine the capacity to maintain a technical approach in the investigations.

Notes

1. Some industries such as steel, textiles, and footwear benefited from a prolonged period of tariff dismantling that lasted until the end of 1998. The Mercosur common external tariff is escalated (highest rates for manufactured goods and lowest rates for fuels), and the average rate during recent years has been approximately 14 percent (ALADI 2002).

2. The policy of essentially no taxes on exports continued until the devaluation of 2002 when export taxes were reimposed. In the early 1990s, financial subsidies granted to noncompetitive manufactured exports were also dismantled (Nogués 2001). As discussed in the next section, this dismantling allowed Argentina to sign a subsidy-countervailing agreement with the United States, with clear gains to domestic exporters.

3. The RER is estimated as the nominal exchange rate times the ratio of the U.S. cost-of-living index to the Argentine cost-of-living index.

4. Starting in 1990, Argentina's economy recorded the following growth rates (stated as percentages): 1990, –2.4; 1991, 12.7; 1992, 11.9; 1993, 5.9; 1994, 5.8; 1995, –2.9; 1996, 5.5; 1997, 8.1; 1998, 3.9; 1999, –3.4; 2000, –0.5; 2001, –4.4; 2002, –10.9; and 2003, 8.4 (Cuentas Nacionales, Ministerio de Economía, 2004).

5. In a speech delivered in April 2002, former Minister Cavallo, alerted to the dangers of antidumping measures, asserted that "behind several antidumping petitions, there are people who would like to return to a closed economy, so that each one of us who live in this country would have to pay higher prices." (Archivos del Ministerio de Economía, April 2002, p. 437).

6. The average annual inflation rates in 1989 and 1990, as measured by the cost-of-living index, were 3,080 percent and 2,314 percent, respectively.

7. During the 1980s, the United States countervailed several imports from Argentina, including leather clothing, leather footwear, textile and clothing, steel pipes and several other steel items, petroleum tubes, and wool (Nogués 1991).

8. Compliance with this agreement resulted in a significant reduction in the number of U.S. countervailing cases against Argentina.

9. Some antidumping measures were implemented in the late 1970s and early 1980s when the peso was also highly overvalued. Initially, these measures were adopted under Law 21,388 of 1978, Régimen de Aplicación de Derechos Antidumping Compensatorios y Móviles. Later, this law was merged in the 1981 Código Aduanero, under which the initial antidumping cases of the 1990s were processed.

10. Very recently, in some cases, Argentina has begun to establish ad valorem antidumping duties.

11. This resistance to create a Mercosur safeguard measure reflects more the position of Brazil than that of other Mercosur member countries. During Mercosur's initial years, there were some temporary exemptions to the intraregional trade liberalization program, and some industries also benefited with longer phase-in periods. Nevertheless, these transitional safeguards were mostly ad hoc.

12. Over the years, the Secretariat of Industry and Trade has changed names several times depending on its changing mandate. At the time of writing this chapter, its name is Secretaría de Industria, Comercio y de la Pequeña y Mediana Empresa.

13. A decree can be overturned by another decree whereas changing a law requires congressional debate.

14. Consensus has not been the common denominator of these votes.

15. Commissioners can be removed only by executive power. Also, board and staff members are required to follow behavioral procedures. Decree 766 of 1994 stipulates that failure to comply with this requirement can trigger removal of the staff member who violates it.

16. As will be indicated in the section "Determinants of the Petitions and Outcomes of Antidumping Investigations," unlike the CNCE, budget constraints have weakened the capacity of the undersecretary of Gestión Comercial Externa (UGE) to complete accurate dumping investigations. For example, the UGE has lacked resources to undertake in situ verifications of prices.

17. After 1998, 22 additional cases of the 69 investigations that were opened between 1988 and 1994 ended with measures.

18. By some accounts of key informants, perhaps as much as 50 percent of potential petitions decided against submission. By the estimate of one informed observer during the years of convertibility, the processing of an antidumping investigation could cost firms approximately US$60,000 in legal fees. This sum was and still is well beyond the means of all small and several medium enterprises.

19. Other factors that pushed up the number of investigations during the recession years were (a) revisions of earlier cases in which measures had normally been imposed for two years and (b) the end of the phase-in period of Mercosur in early 1999, during which safeguards were not allowed.

20. This explanation accounts for only part of the story. The high incidence of the steel cases is accounted for not only by what is known as "big steel" such as cold- and hot-rolled laminated products but also by several smaller industries such as locks and bathroom faucets that had not been under antidumping attacks in the earlier years.

21. According to the annual reports of the CNCE (CNCE 2004), during 1995–2003, Brazil's share of imports covered with antidumping measures was 40 percent whereas Brazil's share in the number of antidumping investigations was 19 percent (see table 2.3).

22. In both cases, imports affected include the sum of the value of imports under antidumping measures and under investigations. Imports under investigation are included because market conditions are likely to be affected from the very moment that an antidumping investigation is requested (for example, see Prusa 1992). An earlier estimate of the import coverage indicator is presented in Sanguinetti and Salustro (1999).

23. Some industries receiving antidumping protection after devaluation include tires, flat steel and iron products, laminated steel, chemical products, faucets, air conditioning equipment, and so forth.

24. Nevertheless, it is relevant to note that, on initiations, the CNCE retained authority to administer article 5.3 of the Antidumping Agreement, stating that "the authorities shall examine the accuracy and adequacy of the evidence provided in the application to determine whether there is sufficient evidence to justify the initiation of an investigation" (WTO, p. 176). Key informants have indicated that, until 1998, an important share of petitions did not pass the standards set by the CNCE to administer this article.

25. As discussed in the next section, until the late 1990s when WTO rulings against Argentina were published, the textiles and footwear industries received safeguard protection. Those measures also lessened the demand for antidumping protection.

26. In the case of Argentina—Medidas Antidumping Definitivas Aplicadas a las Importaciones de Baldosas de Cerámica para el Suelo Procedentes de Italia, Italy explained that some Italian firms had presented confidential price information together with nonconfidential summaries so that the UGE could determine dumping margins at the firm level. Italy argued that, when the UGE decided not to use the information provided in those summaries, Argentina violated article 6 of the Antidumping Agreement. WTO concluded that "Argentina actuó de manera incompatible con el párrafo 8 del artículo 6 y con el Anexo II del Acuerdo Antidumping al descartar en gran parte la información presentada por los exportadores para la determinación del valor normal y del precio de exportación, sin informar a los exportadores de las razones del rechazo" (In discarding the major part of the information presented by exporters for determination of normal value and export price, without informing exporters of the reason for this rejection, Argentina acted in a manner incompatible with paragraph 8 and article 6 and with Annex II of the antidumping agreement). Note that lacking resources to verify information can put a government in a bind. If the government rejects the information supplied by the petitioner, the government is in political trouble at home and perhaps caught up in judicial appeal. If the government rejects the information supplied by the exporter, then the government is in trouble in the WTO. We credit this comment to J. Michael Finger.

27. In general, we believe that competitive imports have remained free of antidumping duties; therefore, importers have been able to substitute country of origin at a cost. However, in cases such as those relating to "big steel," information indicates that a chain of successive investigations has affected imports of hot- and cold-rolled laminated plates from several of the biggest suppliers. In most instances, antidumping investigations of these imports have been opened in response to protectionist measures (safeguards and antidumping barriers) applied by industrial countries that have depressed world steel prices.

28. The source of information on prices has usually been journals or data that has been either gathered by commercial attachés or directly provided by the exporters.

29. To complete the picture, we have calculated from information on the entire list of case outcomes (Nogués and Baracat 2005) that the average minimum margin of dumping is 109 percent. Again, for the reasons explained in the text, this number is not an indication of the extent of antidumping duties. In addition to the factors mentioned there, we have been informed that the UGE has found some cases or enterprises not to be dumping.

30. Glifosato is an herbicide developed by Monsanto, which in combination with genetically modified seeds accounts for an important share of increasing agricultural productivity observed in recent years. Here, the final dumping and injury determinations were positive, but the case was closed without antidumping measures. The political economy behind this decision had to do with two important factors. First, China has become a major importer of several agricultural products from Argentina, especially soybeans, which use Glifosato. The second factor has to do with a forceful domestic agricultural lobby indicating that a wrong would be done if antidumping measures were to be implemented against these imports.

31. Antidumping measures were also requested against imports from China. At the peak of the tensions, a significant number of beekeepers gathered at Plaza de Mayo to demonstrate against the U.S. investigation.

32. A request by the minister of Economy to the U.S. Secretary of Commerce to soften the antidumping measures had a negative response on the basis that these are decisions taken at a technical, not a political, level (Nogués 2003).

33. In a newspaper article commenting on the reform, the former Secretary of Foreign Trade Debora Giorgi makes an interesting comment on the retroactive measures: "La posibilidad de aplicación retrospectiva de los derechos finales garantiza a la industria nacional que la protección contra la práctica desleal pueda retrotraerse hasta la apertura de la investigación" (The possibility of retrospective application of final antidumping measures guarantees the national industry that protection against the unfair practice may be dated from the opening of the investigation) (Giorgi 2001).

34. One hypothesis is that the existing regulations have proved to be capable of supplying the protection that is demanded by the least competitive industries.

35. DIEMs are minimum specific duties defined for the target products. These duties are applied whenever they are higher than the collections from the ad valorem tariffs. The regulations established that the DIEMs would not be charged whenever they were lower than the duties collected through ad valorem tariffs. It is also of interest to note that the resolutions that were established to implement the DIEMs acknowledged the plans and actions by the protected industries to invest and reconvert. Therefore, the objective behind these barriers was similar to those sought by safeguard measures.

36. "In the absence of any coherent theory as to when safeguards should be allowed, it is absurd to expect WTO members to produce a 'reasoned and adequate' explanation as to how their measures are in compliance with the law" (Sykes 2003).

37. The evidence from the media indicates that this industry has regrouped to resist any further liberalization proposals. In this regard, the absence of a workable safeguard instrument has had negative long-run effects.

38. We also note from table 2.7 that, after 2000, there have been only two new petitions for safeguards under article XIX of the GATT. We consider this observation to be an indication that the business community has given up its expectations that it can rely on this instrument.

References

Anderson, Kym. 1996. *Strengthening the Global Trading System: From GATT to WTO*. Adelaide, Australia: Centre for International Economic Studies, University of Adelaide.

Asociación Latinoamericana de Intercambio (ALADI). 2002. "Probable impacto que tendrían los acuerdos con la Unión Europea en el comercio intrarregional y en el comercio de los países miembros con los países de Europa." ALADI/SEC/Estudio 149. Montevideo, Uruguay: ALADI.

Baracat, Elias, and Julio Nogués. Forthcoming. "WTO Safeguards and Trade Liberalization: Lessons from the Argentine Footwear Case." *Journal of World Investment and Trade*.

Berlinski, Julio. "El efecto en el comercio exterior y bienestar de lñas restricciones no Arancelarias en el Mercosur: El caso de las exportaciones argentinas de arroz y productos lácteos al Brasil." Serie de Estudios en Finanzas Públicas. La Plata, Argentina: Universidad Nacional de la Plata. Available at http://www.depeco.econo.unlp.edu.ar/mfinpub/estufp13.pdf.
Comisión Nacional de Comercio Exterior (CNCE). 1994–2004. *Informe Anual.* Buenos Aires: CNCE. Available at http://www.mecon.gov.ar/cnce/informes_anuales.
de la Torre, Augusto, Eduardo Levi Yeyati, and Sergio Schmukler. 2003. "Living and Dying with Hard Pegs: The Rise and Fall of Argentina's Currency Board." Policy Research Working Paper No. 2980, World Bank, Washington, DC. In *Antidumping—How It Works and Who Gets Hurt,* ed. J. Michael Finger. Ann Arbor: University of Michigan.
Finger, J. Michael, and Tracy Murray. 1993. "Policing Unfair Imports: The U.S. Example." In *Antidumping: How It Works and Who Gets Hurt,* ed. J. Michael Finger, 241–54. Ann Arbor: University of Michigan Press
Finger, J. Michael, and Julio J. Nogués. 1987. "International Control of Subsidies and Countervailing Duties." *World Bank Economic Review* 1 (September): 337–55.
Francois, Joseph, and Gunnar Niels. 2003. "Business Cycles, the Current Account, and Administered Protection in Mexico." Center for European Policy Research (CEPR) Discussion Paper Series 3981, CEPR, London.
General Agreement on Tariffs and Trade (GATT). 1986. *The Tokyo Round Agreements.* Geneva: GATT.
Giorgi, Debora. 2001. "Acerca del nuevo decreto antidumping y antisubvenciones." *La Nación,* September 11, 2001.
Irwin, Douglas. 2002. *Free Trade under Fire.* Princeton, NJ: Princeton University Press.
Nogués, Julio J. 1986. "The Nature of Argentina's Policy Reforms during 1976–1981." Staff Working Paper 765, World Bank, Washington, DC.
———. 1991. "Less Than Fair Value Trade Cases against Latin American Countries." *The World Economy* 24 (December): 61–77.
———. 2001. "La institucionalización de la globalización." In *La globalización, la Argentina, y cada uno de nosotros,* ed. Juan De Pablo, Julio J. Nogués, and Rudiger Dornbusch, 105–239. Buenos Aires: Consejo Empresario Argentino.
———. 2003. "U.S. Contingent Protection Measures against Honey Imports: Regulations, Development, and the Doha Round." World Bank Staff Working Paper 3088, World Bank, Washington, DC.
Nogués, Julio J., and Elías Baracat. 2005. "Political Economy of Antidumping and Safeguards in Argentina." Policy Research Working Papers Series No. 3587, World Bank, Washington, DC.
Prusa, Thomas. 1992. "Why Are So Many Antidumping Petitions Withdrawn?" *Journal of International Economics* 33: 1–20.
Reina, Mauricio, and Sandra Zuloaga. 2005. "Application of Safeguards and Anti-dumping Duties in Colombia." Policy Research Working Paper No. 3608, World Bank, Washington, DC.
Sanguinetti, Pablo, and Marina Salustro. 1999. "Mercosur y el sesgo regional de la política comercial: Aranceles y barreras no tarifarias." Unpublished document, Universidad Di Tella, Buenos Aires, Argentina. Available at http://www.utdt.edu/~sanguine/Mercosur.pdf.
Sykes, Alan. 2003. "The Safeguard Mess: A Critique of WTO Jurisprudence." *World Trade Review* 2 (3): 261–95.
Unión Industrial Argentina (UIA). 1992. "Proyecto de decreto reglamentario a la ley 24176." Unpublished document. Buenos Aires: UIA.
World Trade Organization (WTO). 1996. *The Results of the Uruguay Round of Multilateral Trade Negotiations.* Geneva: WTO.

79-107

F13
519 024

3

ANTIDUMPING AND SAFEGUARD MECHANISMS: THE BRAZILIAN EXPERIENCE, 1988–2003

Honorio Kume and Guida Piani

In the late 1980s, the import substitution industrialization process together with recurrent exchange rate crises led Brazil to implement an import policy pursuant to which only those goods without an equivalent domestic product or those necessary to satisfy an unexpected spike in demand were allowed entry. This policy comprised high customs tariffs, discretionary controls (such as a list of forbidden items and an annual maximum limit for foreign purchases by enterprise). Special tax schemes subjecting a substantial portion of imported goods to tariff rebates or outright exemption.

From 1988 onward, Brazil adopted an import policy with the goal of fostering more efficient allocation of resources through foreign competition. In 1987, to minimize potential political pressure before implementing this new policy, Brazil introduced a law that put into force agreements on antidumping, subsidies, and countervailing duties, thus developing a new protection mechanism for domestic industries.

Together with a gradual import liberalization process, Brazil began implementing trade defense instruments to provide temporary relief to certain sectors when they were affected by foreign competition. Efficient and judicious management of these mechanisms was essential not only to support any activity affected by unfair trade

The authors acknowledge Leane Naidin and attendees at the seminar "Use of Safeguards and Antidumping in Latin America" organized by J. Michael Finger and Julio J. Nogués, with the support of the World Bank, May 23–25, 2004, in Buenos Aires. We are especially grateful to Julio Berlinski, Julio J. Nogués, and J. Michael Finger for their comments.

practices but also to ensure the continuity of the trade liberalization program. In sum, the government was faced with the challenge of implementing a system to protect its national interests that would also be compatible with garnering the political support needed to enhance the openness of the Brazilian economy (Finger 1998).

The enforcement of antidumping mechanisms is subject to the rules of the Agreement on Implementation of Article VI of the General Agreement on Tariffs and Trade (GATT 1994) of the World Trade Organization (WTO), which require proof of the dumping practice, determination of injury on the production of the equivalent domestic products, and establishment of a causal relationship between the dumped imports and the injury to the domestic industry. The use of safeguard measures, as specified in article XIX of the GATT (Emergency Action on Imports of Particular Goods), involves stricter requirements to prove injury (serious injury). Brazilian practice also requires a commitment by the domestic industry to improve its competitiveness. Notwithstanding the technical and objective language of the WTO agreements, any assessment with respect to these requirements is open to a high degree of subjectivity, turning the antidumping and safeguard mechanisms into such a strong protection instrument that they may even contradict trade liberalization.

The purpose of this chapter is to assess the Brazilian experience with the use of antidumping and safeguard mechanisms in a context of trade liberalization and macroeconomic stability programs. This chapter includes an introduction and three sections. The first section reviews the main changes introduced to the import policy of Brazil between 1988 and 2003, divided into four different stages. The second section describes the legal system and the institutional and administrative agencies concerned with the enforcement of antidumping and safeguard mechanisms in Brazil from 1987 until 2003. It also describes the evolution of the claims filed during this period and evaluates their main results in relation to the import liberalization target. The final section summarizes the main conclusions and makes policy recommendations in light of the Brazilian experience.

The Import Policy in Brazil, 1987–2003

Overview

In 1987, after decades of import substitution policies and recurrent exchange rate crises that had affected the Brazilian economy, Brazilian import policy exhibited the following basic characteristics (Kume, Piani, and Souza 2003):

- A tariff structure based, with few exceptions, on the rates established in 1957,[1] during the initial phase of the Brazilian import substitution process
- Generalized water in the tariff or tariff redundancy

- Several additional taxes such as the tax on financial operations (IOF[2]), the port improvement tax (TMP), and the freight surcharge for renovation of the merchant maritime fleet (AFRMM)
- Wide use of nontariff barriers such as a list of products with suspended import licenses, specific authorizations required before the entry of certain products (for the steel and information technology industries), and annual import quotas allocated to each importing business
- Forty-two special tax regimes favoring the rebate or exemption of import duties

Hence, the reformulation of the import policy involved first a tariff restructuring process to equalize tariff rates with the difference between domestic and foreign prices, thus eliminating water in the tariff. Second, it involved necessarily eliminating special tax regimes, with the exception of those intended to favor previously selected activities. After that stage, nontariff barriers would become useless and, thus, could be removed without any significant effect on domestic production and currency outlays. Finally, during the last stage, after understanding of the resulting protection structure became clear, tariffs could again gradually be reduced to foster greater production efficiency. In general, the changes introduced in the import policy between 1988 and 1993 followed that pattern.

Next, we break down the main characteristics of Brazil's import policy into four periods.

The 1988–89 Period In this first stage, two tariff reforms were introduced, in June 1988 and September 1989 with the purposes, respectively, of eliminating water in the nominal tariff and of eliminating the special tax regimes (with the exception of those related to international agreements, export activities—drawback, regional development projects, and the Manaus free trade zone) as well as other taxes such as the IOF, the TMP, and the AFRMM.

Because of pressure by certain groups whose privileges would be undermined, the government decided to implement a less comprehensive reform: it lowered tariffs to a lesser degree than originally planned, kept a high degree of tariff redundancy, dismantled both the IOF and the TMP, and only partially removed special import regimes. Nontariff barriers, at the time under the purview of CACEX (the foreign trade department of Banco do Brasil) and probably a more efficient tool to restrict imports, were not modified. In short, these reforms did not eradicate most special taxes, but they did succeed in introducing some rationality in the tariff structure, though without significantly modifying the degree of protection for domestic industries (Kume 1988).

The 1990–93 Period In March 1990, after the new government was inaugurated, new measures were adopted that dramatically changed Brazilian foreign trade policy. The exchange rate became flexible and imports were liberalized by eliminating the list of products with revoked import licenses and the special import duty regimes—with the exception of drawback, the free trade area of Manaus (intended to benefit its goods), and goods imported under international agreements. In July 1990, company quotas that were in force were suspended. With the removal of the major administrative controls, customs tariffs became the leading instrument to protect domestic industries.

A few months later, the government announced a tariff reform that entailed a four-year tariff phaseout for all products, at the end of which a modal tariff of 20 percent, with a 0 to 40 percent tariff range, would be attained. For industrial activity, the effective tariff rate was set at approximately 20 percent, to be applied from January 1994. Indeed, the two last stages of the tariff phaseout schedule were actually moved ahead by six months.

The 1994–98 Period After the launching of the Real Plan in July 1994, the trade liberalization process was reinforced because of the need to impose greater discipline on domestic prices of importable goods. In the same spirit, a lowering of import duty rates was announced as a result of the application of the Mercosur (Southern Cone Common Market) common external tariff.

Changes introduced in 1994 can then be summarized as follows (Kume 1998):

- Lowering of tariff rates to 0 percent or 2 percent, especially for inputs and some consumer goods with a relatively important effect on the price index.
- Early adoption of the Mercosur common external tariff in September 1994,[3] previously scheduled for adoption in January 1995. (In general, whenever a tariff was expected to increase because it was lower than the agreed tariff for the Mercosur, the lower rate was maintained.)

By the time tariff reductions entered into force in September 1994, the upward trend of imports was already evident; in fact, it had started in the beginning of 1993. In addition, the increase in foreign capital inflows induced by the launching of the Real Plan provoked a substantial exchange rate appreciation. Thus, if on the one hand, tariffs were considered an important factor to ensure price stability—basically in the early stages of the stabilization program—then on the other hand, the unbalanced external trade accounts led domestic industries to face quite intense pressure from foreign competition, without an adequate adjustment time after the 1991–93 liberalization period.

In fact, the widening of trade deficits in the last two months of 1994—an event not seen since January 1987—together with the capital outflows resulting from the Mexican crisis in late 1994, raised concerns with respect to the risk of continuously financing high current account deficits. Furthermore, the substantial tariff reduction applied specially on cars and electronic goods, simultaneously with a strong appreciation of the exchange rate, increased the industrial sector's exposure to foreign competition, thus generating protectionist pressures, which had been dormant since the beginning of trade liberalization in the late 1980s.

During the first half of 1995, the government decided—with a view to satisfying the demands for a higher level of protection and favoring a more balanced trade—to increase the tariff rates for cars,[4] motorcycles, bicycles, tractors, electronic goods, fabrics, and sport shoes, which were the main items accountable for spikes in import growth. At the same time, to prevent abusive domestic price increases, the tariff rates on a series of inputs were lowered.

Because of the loss of autonomy in tariff policy management resulting from membership in the Mercosur bloc, the government had to include most of those products in the National List of Exemptions for the Mercosur. Furthermore, Mercosur member countries were allowed to draw up a new list of products with rates fixed at higher or lower levels than those of the common external tariff for a one-year term.

With the exception of the above-mentioned cases, the Mercosur common external tariff blocked the introduction of other changes in the tariff structure. Nevertheless, the Brazilian government again resorted to administrative measures to restrict imports, namely cash payment requirements (deposits made at the Central Bank) for imports financed over less than a year, compliance with phytosanitary requirements, licensing of imports for a long list of products, and implementation of safeguards for the import of textiles and toys.

Finally, in November 1997, the government introduced a temporary tariff increase of 3 percent, capital goods excepted. This measure was to be reversed later through a phaseout schedule of 0.5 percent per year.

The 1999–2003 Period In January 1999, after a strong speculative attack against the Brazilian currency and after a quick attempt to implement a controlled currency devaluation, the government decided to adopt a floating exchange rate system, which led to an actual devaluation of 43.6 percent in that year. The previously fixed exchange rate that had tethered inflation was successfully replaced by inflation targets, thus avoiding inflationary spikes. The adoption of this new exchange rate regime made it once again feasible to adopt a more stable import policy, though with some sectoral problems of competitiveness that were solved through trade defense instruments.

In early 1999, the first 0.5 percent rebate scheduled to gradually compensate for the 3 percent rate increase in late 1997 was applied. The remaining 2.5 percent was eliminated in 2001 and 2003.

FIGURE 3.1 Indexes of Import Volumes, Real Exchange Rate, Real GDP, and Average Nominal Tariff Rate for the 1987–2003 Period (base year 1987 = 100)

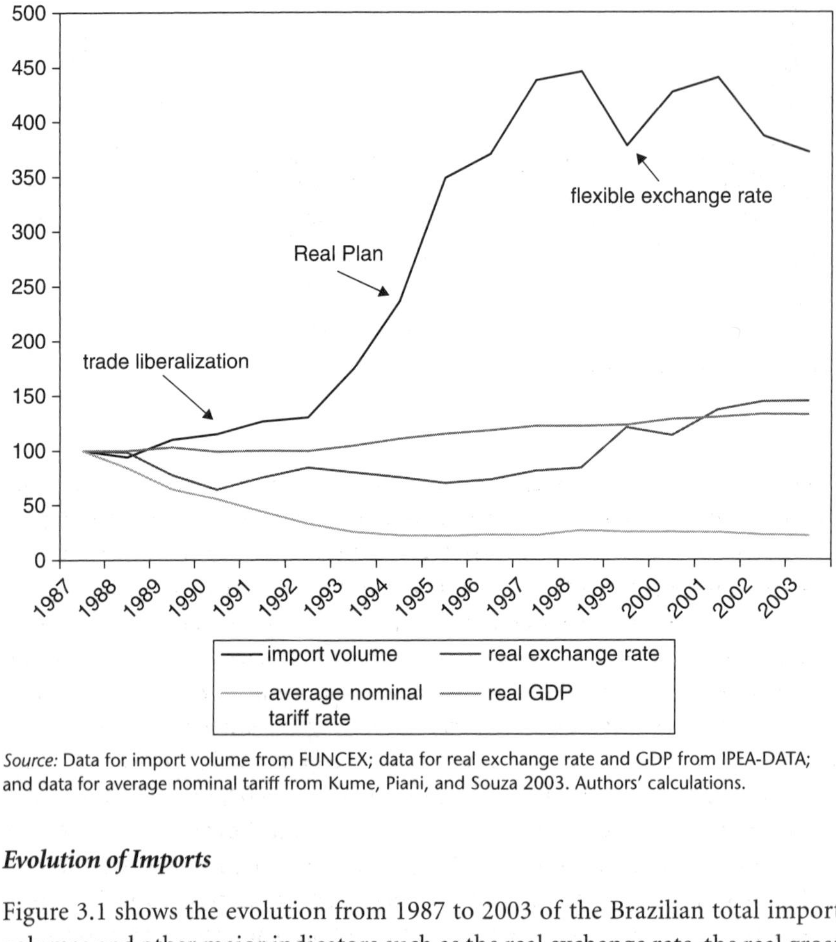

Source: Data for import volume from FUNCEX; data for real exchange rate and GDP from IPEA-DATA; and data for average nominal tariff from Kume, Piani, and Souza 2003. Authors' calculations.

Evolution of Imports

Figure 3.1 shows the evolution from 1987 to 2003 of the Brazilian total import volumes and other major indicators such as the real exchange rate, the real gross domestic product (GDP), and the average nominal tariff rate. In the 1987–98 period, one clearly observes a strong expansion in import volumes, though annual growth rates varied significantly in subperiods. Between 1987 and 1992, the average annual variation was 5.4 percent because of the initial effects of trade liberalization, which were dampened, however, by two currency devaluations (in 1991 and 1992) and by stagnating economic activity. In 1993–95, the annual growth rate reached 21.8 percent as a result of additional rebates in import tariffs, exchange rate appreciation, and GDP expansion, these last two events having occurred as a result of the implementation of the Real Plan. During the

FIGURE 3.2 Brazil: Ratio of Import to Domestic Production Values for Certain Products, 1990 and 2002 (percent)

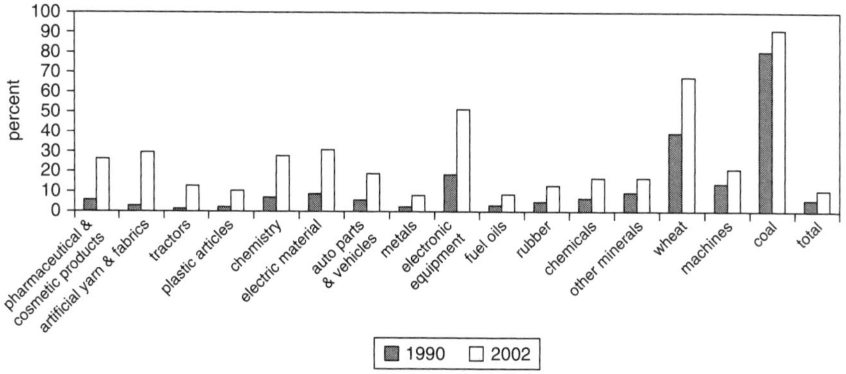

Source: IBGE 1990, 2002; authors' calculations.

1996–99 subperiod, the control on imports together with the decline in economic activity reduced the annual variation rate of foreign purchases to 8.5 percent. Finally, after changes were introduced in the exchange rate regime, imports showed a downward trend with a negative annual variation of 3.5 percent.

Figure 3.2 identifies the products that, between 1990 and 2002, underwent a variation above the general average for import rates, measured in terms of the ratio of import to domestic production values. This group encompasses the major enterprises that had demanded trade defense measures—among others, manufacturers of artificial yarn and fabrics whose share of imports in domestic production rose from 2.9 percent in 1990 to 29.6 percent in 2002; pharmaceutical and cosmetic products, from 7.1 to 27.9 percent; chemical products, from 6.7 to 16.7 percent; rubber, from 4.9 to 13.1 percent; plastic products, from 2.2 to 10.4 percent; and metals, from 2.5 to 8.2 percent. Other sectors such as electronics as well as vehicles and auto parts were given additional protection through an increase in tariffs.

The Brazilian Antidumping and Safeguard System

Legal, Institutional, and Operational Aspects

Until 1988, Brazil had two instruments to fight dumping, and these tools enabled the fiscal value of imported goods to be changed to increase import duties. The first, known as the *minimum customs tariff*, was established by the Tariff Act of 1957 and could be applied whenever the foreign price was difficult to estimate or when there were signs of dumping; the second, known as the *benchmark price*, was introduced in 1970 and was applied whenever price differences were detected among goods imported from several countries to the detriment of domestic production.

Although somewhat similar to the GATT Antidumping Agreement, the administrative procedures adopted to implement the Brazilian protective measures were not entirely consistent with the GATT rules. Therefore, at the enactment of the Customs Valuation Agreement in 1986, the Brazilian government committed itself to phasing out such mechanisms by July 1988 (Naidin 1998).

In January 1987, Brazil passed national legislation ratifying the Agreement on Implementation of Article VI of the GATT (Antidumping Agreement) and the Agreement on Interpretation and Application of Articles VI, XVI, and XXIII of the GATT (Subsidies and Countervailing Duties). The implementation of both agreements and the power to set antidumping and countervailing duties were entrusted to the Customs Policy Commission (CPA), under the purview of the Ministry of Finance.

The CPA, an agency chaired by an executive secretary appointed by the minister of finance, was in charge of conducting investigations and preparing technical reports to be submitted to a group made up of six representatives of economic-related ministries, seven officials of other governmental agencies, and three representatives of the private sector. Thus, the CPA was commissioned with the task of laying down the rules governing administrative proceedings for the measures provided for in the previously mentioned agreements. The legal instrument that was created, to all practical ends, provides formulas and procedures to initiate, conduct, and report findings involving antidumping or subsidies.[5]

However, in this period during which the Brazilian economy was highly protected against foreign competition, the most important agency for implementing foreign trade policy was CACEX, under Banco do Brasil,[6] in charge of issuing export and import documents—a crucial factor, indeed, in all foreign trade transactions—and financing exports. Through these administrative mechanisms, CACEX had imports under its total control until the late 1980s.

In 1990, at the beginning of President Collor's administration, an administrative reform gave birth to the Ministry of Economy, Finance, and Planning, thus merging three former ministries, those of Finance, of Planning, and of Industry and Trade. This new ministry included an Executive Secretariat, ranked as a vice ministry, and four secretariats, among which was the National Economic Secretariat with jurisdiction over the Foreign Trade Department (DECEX). In turn, DECEX supervised the Tariff Technical Coordination (CTT, the former CPA) and the Trade Exchange Technical Coordination (CTIC, the former CACEX), which retained the same attributes as before. This restructuring was viewed as an essential condition for carrying out a more liberal trade policy, which implied reducing the role of the CTIC and strengthening the role of the CTT.

In October 1993, President Itamar Franco created the Ministry of Industry, Trade, and Tourism (MICT), under which the Foreign Trade Secretariat (SECEX)[7] operated in close association with the former coordinating agencies, now raised to the rank of departments: the Tariff Technical Department (DTT) and the Technical Department of Commercial Exchange (DTIC). Because any issue related to changes in import duties was within the purview of the Ministry of Finance, as set forth in the federal constitution, all technical decisions made by the DTT and approved by the SECEX had to be submitted for the consideration and approval of the Ministry of Finance. The lack of a coordinated trade policy was thus made more profound because the Ministry of Finance was more concerned with using tariff policy as a tool for stabilizing domestic prices whereas the MICT was focused on maintaining a higher level of protection for domestic manufacturers.

In 1995, Fernando Henrique Cardoso's administration created the Brazilian Chamber of Foreign Trade (CAMEX), made up of representatives from six ministries.[8] The MICT and the SECEX were left unchanged while the three previous departments were restructured into four: the Foreign Trade Department (DECEX), which in practice undertook the activities of the former DTIC; the Department of International Negotiations (DEINTER), which engaged in negotiations such as those with Mercosur and the WTO as well as those about any change introduced in import duty rates; the Department of Commercial Defense (DECOM), which was concerned with implementing antidumping proceedings; and last, the Department of Foreign Trade Policy (DEPOC).

The creation of a special department in charge of commercial defense issues is to be underscored because it reflects how significant these instruments came to be for Brazilian trade policy. The officials appointed for this new department were former DTT and DTIC members.

These new changes did not resolve problems arising from conflicting powers. The Ministry of Finance had to approve any legal action related to changes[9] in "ex" tariffs[10] (exceptions to the tariff nomenclature). However, the decisions on trade defense (technically analyzed by the DECOM, under the MICT) had to be made not only by the ministers of industry and trade and tourism but also by the minister of finance.

A Consultative Committee on Trade Defense (CCDC) was created to confer credibility on DECOM and DEINTER; it was made up of representatives of governmental agencies such as the Ministries of Finance, Budget and Planning, Foreign Affairs, Agriculture, and the Executive Secretariat of the Chamber of Foreign Trade. The CCDC, chaired by the secretary for Foreign Trade, was empowered to review dumping and subsidy-related investigations and, when particularly summoned for it, also safeguard-related investigations.

In March 1995, Brazil implemented the Antidumping Agreement of the Uruguay Round. As expected, this legislation was in line with the WTO Agreement. To mitigate the private sector's dissatisfaction with the delays in the analysis of the claims already submitted and to give more credibility to the trade defense instruments, the government set maximum terms for the decision-making process: 20 days to determine whether the request for a procedure included all the relevant information, 30 days to decide to initiate the investigation, and 360 days to reach a final determination (this term could be extended, under exceptional circumstances, to 540 days).

Another law strongly supported by domestic industries[11] was also enacted: the retroactive imposition of final antidumping duties on dumped imported goods when those goods had reached consumers within 90 days before the application of preliminary antidumping measures, provided the corrective effect of antidumping duties might be otherwise seriously impaired (for example, when injury results from a growing volume of goods imported at dumping prices during a relatively short period of time).[12]

In contrast, to minimize the protectionist bias in the managing of antidumping laws, the government explicitly included two issues that were not provided for in the WTO Antidumping Agreement. The first issue—the determination of injury—was a recommendation to exclude the trade liberalization effects on domestic prices so long as those effects were caused by reasons other than dumped imports.

The second issue referred to exceptional circumstances, such as the inclusion of the "national interest" clause,[13] whereby even if dumping and injury were determined, the relevant authorities may decide either to interrupt the application of a specified duty or to apply a (presumably lower) rate different from the recommended one.

Brazil introduced its first decree on safeguard measures in May 1995 and entrusted the MICT and the Ministry of Finance with the decision-making process. As expected, the decree followed WTO's rules in the field. Later on, in July 1998, Brazil implemented Mercosur regulations on safeguard measures to be applied to imports from third countries. Finally, in October 2001, the president of Brazil entrusted CAMEX with the power to establish antidumping and countervailing duties and adopt safeguard measures. CAMEX, presided over by the Ministry of Development, Industry, and Commerce (MDIC), was made up of five more ministries whose mission was to discuss trade defense measures and reach a decision by the majority of its members.[14]

From the institutional point of view, this new restructuring substantially weakened the Ministry of Finance's role in the antidumping and safeguard decision-making processes. Its voting power was reduced to one of six votes.

This weakening of the Ministry of Finance in favor of the more protectionist-oriented Ministry of Industry, Trade, and Tourism apparently had no significant consequences on the implementation of the antidumping, subsidy, and safeguard measures, but it certainly was a gateway to greater pressures by the often opposing interests of some policy makers, on the one hand, and certain local production sectors, on the other. Likewise, the government agencies created to replace the CPA were, or seemed to be, increasingly weaker until creation of the current DECOM.

Indeed, with the creation of the DECOM in 1995, Brazil had a governmental agency exclusively devoted to conducting antidumping, subsidy, and safeguard procedures as well as international negotiations on those issues. Notwithstanding increases since the creation of the agency, the continuing shortage of human and financial resources seemed to be a limiting factor in its activities.[15]

Table 3.1 bears out this difficulty in securing adequate resources. The data show the number of antidumping investigations[16] and the number of on-the-spot verifications conducted to determine injury (for domestic firms) and dumping (for foreign producers). In almost all determinations of injury, domestic producers were visited. However, for determinations of dumping, the number of on-the-spot verifications conducted on the exporting firms' premises to verify domestic and export prices is still limited. Therefore, for dumping determination purposes, the DECOM still acts based on the data supplied by businesses and on the price information available in specialized journals.

TABLE 3.1 Brazil: Number and Percentage of Investigations with On-the-Spot Verifications for Injury and Dumping Determinations

Year	Number of investigations	Injury	Percentage of injury investigations	Dumping	Percentage of dumping investigations
1996	7	2	28.6	1	14.3
1997	10	7	70.0	0	0.0
1998	10	9	90.0	3	30.0
1999	5	3	60.0	0	0.0
2000	7	6	85.7	1	14.3
2001	8	7	87.5	1	12.5
2002	11	10	90.9	2	18.2

Source: MDIC (2003); authors' calculations.

Brazilian Experience with Antidumping and Safeguard Measures

According to the notifications submitted to the WTO Committee on Antidumping Practices, Brazil[17] was ranked eighth among the countries that had resorted the most to antidumping measures between 1995 and 2002, after India, the United States, the European Union, Argentina, South Africa, Australia, and Canada (see table 3.2). Brazil, together with India, Argentina, South Africa, China, the Republic of Korea, and Turkey, is one of the countries that began seriously adopting antidumping measures in the 1990s. The case of India is worth mentioning because it largely outperformed other countries with a longer tradition in the use of such legal instruments.

China is the main target in antidumping cases (with 232 actions against it), followed by the Republic of Korea (92); Taiwan, China (75); the United States (69); Japan (68); the Russian Federation (66); Thailand (58); Brazil (54); and India (48). Brazil's position in the ranking is influenced by measures adopted by

TABLE 3.2 Number of Antidumping Cases Initiated between 1995 and 2002—Main Countries (from highest total number to lowest)

Country/bloc	1995	1996	1997	1998	1999	2000	2001	2002	Total
India	6	21	13	27	65	41	79	80	332
United States	14	22	15	36	47	47	76	35	292
EU	33	25	41	22	65	32	29	20	267
Argentina	27	22	14	8	24	45	26	14	180
South Africa	16	33	23	41	16	21	6	4	160
Australia	5	17	42	13	24	15	23	16	155
Canada	11	5	14	8	18	21	25	5	107
Brazil	5	18	11	18	16	11	17	9	105
Mexico	4	4	6	12	11	7	5	10	59
China	0	0	0	0	0	6	14	30	50
Korea, Rep. of	4	13	15	3	6	2	4	9	56
Turkey	0	0	4	1	8	7	15	17	52
Subtotal of countries shown	125	180	198	189	300	255	319	249	1,815
Total of all countries	157	224	243	256	356	294	366	309	2,205

Source: WTO AD Initiations (http://www.wto.org/english/tratop_e/adp_e/adp_stattab2_e.xls); authors' calculations.

Argentina, its main partner in Mercosur. If measures adopted by Argentina (26) and Uruguay (1) were to be excluded, then Brazil would be ranked 14th among the exporting countries most affected by antidumping measures.

The production sectors most affected internationally by antidumping measures between 1995 and 2002 were metals (31.6 percent of the total measures), chemical products (18.6 percent), and plastics (12.2 percent). The same trend holds true in Brazil where the chemical industry, followed by the metal and plastic sectors, accounts for 73.4 percent of all the measures adopted in that period.

Last, according to Zanardi (2003), who evaluated more comprehensively the use of antidumping measures—based on data from the semiannual notifications submitted by WTO member countries and on a specific survey for nonmember countries between 1981 and 2001—considering all the antidumping investigations initiated by the European Union, the United States, Canada, and Australia, the proportions of final affirmative determinations for those countries were, respectively, 73.7 percent, 59.3 percent, 58.4 percent, and 41 percent. In the countries that started resorting to this instrument in the 1990s (such as India, Korea, Mexico, and Turkey), affirmative determinations amount to 71.9 percent, 65.1 percent, 65.0 percent, and 52.5 percent, respectively. In Brazil, almost half of the proceedings (49.6 percent) end up with a final affirmative determination.

Brazil is ranked 15th in safeguard measures notified in the same 1981–2001 period, having resorted to them only twice (toys and coconut), lagging behind the United States (12); Czechoslovakia, or Czech Republic after 1992 (10); Jordan (9); Chile (8); and República Bolivariana de Venezuela (6). Total safeguard actions for the main countries involved have increased substantially since 1998, rising from 11 in 1998 to 34 in 2002 (see table 3.3). However, the number of cases involving safeguard actions is still much lower than those involving antidumping measures.

Antidumping in Brazil Even though Brazil implemented the antidumping as well as the subsidies and countervailing duties agreements as of 1987, the country did not need to resort to those measures given the high tariffs and nontariff protection that prevailed at the time. For this reason, until 1989, only one case was opened and concluded, resulting with the imposition of antidumping duties on bicycle chains imported from the former Soviet Union, former Czechoslovakia, India, and China.

The demand for protection through the adoption of measures against "unfair trade" increased after trade was liberalized, especially after the tariff phaseout process, which was initiated in February 1991 and concluded ahead of schedule in July 1993. Table 3.4 shows that, during the first year of the implementation of the

TABLE 3.3 Countries Initiating the Largest Numbers of Safeguard Cases (from highest total number to lowest)

Country	1995	1996	1997	1998	1999	2000	2001	2002	1995–2002
India			1	5	4	2		3	15
United States	1	2	1	1	2	5			12
Czech Republic					1	2	2	5	10
Jordan						1		8	9
Chile					1	3	2	2	8
Venezuela, R. B. de						3		3	6
Bulgaria						1	2	2	5
Argentina			1	1		1	1		4
Korea, Rep. of	1	2			1				4
Poland						1		3	4
Egypt, Arab Rep. of				1	1	1			3
Slovak Republic					1	1		1	3
El Salvador						3			3
Japan						3			3
Brazil		1					1		2
Subtotal of countries shown	2	5	3	8	11	27	8	27	91
Total of all countries	2	5	3	11	13	28	11	34	107

Source: WTO (1998, 1999, 2000, 2001, 2002, and 2003a); authors' calculations.

tariff phaseout schedule (1991), Brazil initiated 13 investigations (counted on the basis of product-country pairs); it implemented 8 during the second year of the phaseout and 27 in 1993. In 1994, the number of cases dropped to 10 and then to 5 in the following year, involving only one product (iron-chromium) and the countries of former Yugoslavia.[18]

Table 3.4 also shows that Brazil—just like other major users—resorts most often to antidumping measures (215 in total) and less often to antisubsidy measures (24) and safeguard measures (only 2). Reviews of antidumping investigations started in 1997 and have involved 35 cases. During the 1996–99 period (1997 excepted), the number of measures adopted shows an upward trend, giving rise to 27 cases in 1999 (see figure 3.3). This increase resulted from the currency appreciation that took place at the beginning of the Real Plan during the second half of 1994, which had a strong impact during the whole period.[19]

TABLE 3.4 Number of Antidumping, Antisubsidy, and Safeguard Cases Initiated by Brazil, 1987–2003

Year	Dumping	Dumping review	Subsidies	Safeguards
1987	0	0	0	0
1988	2	0	0	0
1989	2	0	0	0
1990	2	0	0	0
1991	13	0	2	0
1992	8	0	13	0
1993	27	0	1	0
1994	10	0	7	0
1995	5	0	0	0
1996	16	0	0	1
1997	15	7	0	0
1998	23	2	0	0
1999	27	3	0	1
2000	10	2	0	0
2001	19	1	1	1
2002	16	8	0	0
2003	20	12	0	0
Total	215	35	24	3

Source: MDIC (2003); authors' calculations.
Note: The number of antidumping and antisubsidy cases is based on a product-country pair. European Union countries were considered individually; therefore, results differ from official statistics. Safeguard measures, instead, are counted by product.

In 2000, again in a flexible exchange rate context, the number of antidumping measures dropped substantially; if the cases under review are excluded, this downward trend is even more noticeable.[20] All applications for review requesting the renewal of antidumping duties in force had every chance of being accepted.

With respect to the cases with final positive determinations (that is, where measures were approved), figure 3.4 shows that during the period under study, only in five years[21]—1988, 1989, 1990, 1992, and 1995—were all cases concluded with affirmative determinations. In general terms, a greater acceptance is observed in the 1993–99 period (save for 1995) whereas fewer approvals occurred in the following years, precisely when a flexible exchange rate system was in place again. Given the differences among the measures adopted, it is impossible to ascertain whether the government tried to counteract the effects of currency appreciation on certain sectors by resorting to antidumping duties.

FIGURE 3.3 Number of Antidumping Cases in Brazil, 1988–2003

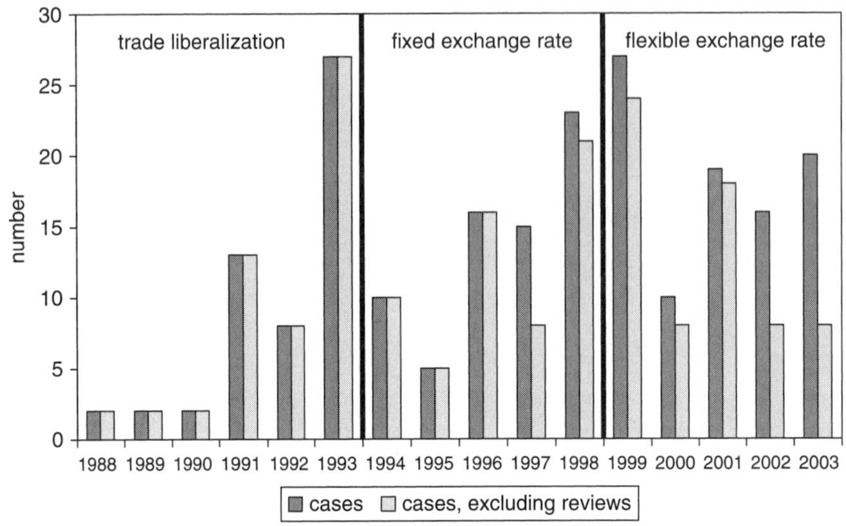

Source: MDIC (2003); authors' calculations.

FIGURE 3.4 Share of Approved Antidumping Cases in Brazil, 1988–2002

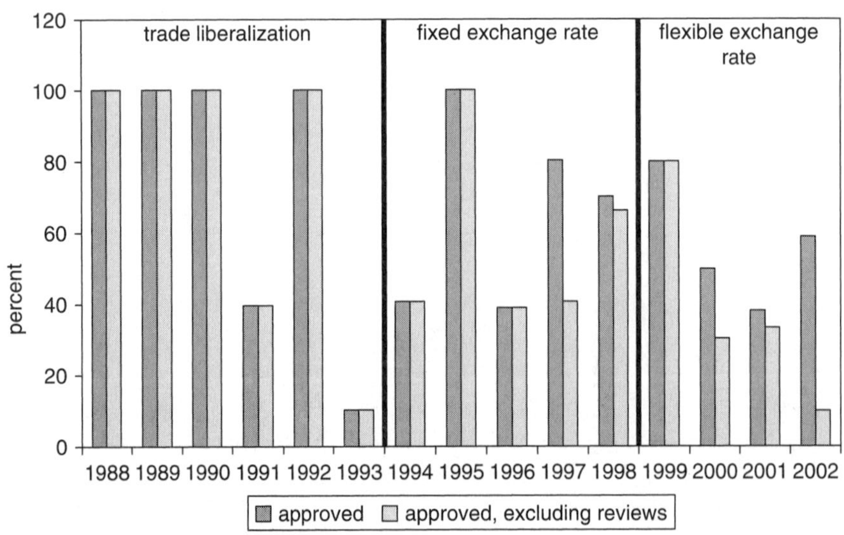

Source: MDIC (2003); authors' calculations.

Note: Accepted cases were those concluded with a final positive determination of dumping and injury.

Table 3.5 shows the distribution of antidumping actions and their final determinations per group of products, divided according to categories of use. Notably, of 193 cases, 107 (55.4 percent) resulted in an affirmative determination, 102 of which were settled through antidumping duties and 5 through price undertakings, while the other 86 (44.6 percent) resulted in no restriction.[22]

Raw materials, especially chemicals, metals, and plastics, stand out among the other categories on the list; these three subcategories account for 55.9 percent of the total number of antidumping investigations opened in Brazil between 1988 and 2002. Chemicals and plastics can be described as products subject to structural or long-term dumping, based on international price discrimination, and they benefit from a policy intended to maximize profits for a group of enterprises to increase the capacity use of their manufacturing plants. In large producing countries such as the United States and some European countries, the production scale is very large and their domestic sales cannot absorb total production volumes. Domestic sales are ruled by contracts[23] in which prices can be higher than marginal costs; in foreign markets, prices and marginal costs are equalized.

In the sector of base metals and articles thereof, steel and metal products such as iron-chromium stand out. It is common practice to sell abroad at prices lower than those charged in the domestic market, which is protected by tariffs.

Cases with affirmative determinations involving consumer goods—both durable and nondurable (soft goods)—prevail, their degree of acceptance amounting to 83.3 percent and 78.3 percent, respectively.[24] Thus, even though the actions related to steel, chemicals, and plastic products are more numerous, the percentage of those actions reaching affirmative final determinations is lower than the average.

The countries most affected by the antidumping investigations initiated by Brazil are the United States (29 cases), followed by China (25) and India (11) (see table 3.6). Unlike the situation in Argentina, where a large share of antidumping investigations have involved imports from Mercosur partners, only five of Brazil's cases involved Mercosur countries: Argentina (3) and Uruguay (2). Nevertheless, even though the United States is the exporter most frequently involved in Brazilian antidumping investigations, affirmative final determinations were made in only 34.5 percent of the cases, a percentage much lower than the overall ratio of 52.8 percent and lower than the rate of restrictive outcomes in cases against China and India (80 percent and 63.6 percent, respectively).

It is widely recognized that adopting certain methods may lead to a more protectionist approach to the use of antidumping measures. In particular, the choice of the normal value is a crucial issue in the determination of a greater (or smaller) dumping margin. Table 3.7 lists some specific indicators. Note that in 41.4 percent of accepted cases for Brazil, preliminary duties were applied, mainly

TABLE 3.5 Brazil: Antidumping Cases by Group of Products, 1988–2002

Category of use	Cases undertaken		Cases ending with application of antidumping duties		Cases ending with price undertakings		Cases ending without restrictive action	
	Total number for product category	Number for product category as percentage of total cases	Number	Percentage for product category	Number	Percentage for product category	Number	Percentage for product category
1. Consumer durables	**6**	**3.1**	**5**	**83.3**	**0**	**0.0**	**1**	**16.7**
2. Soft goods	**23**	**11.9**	**18**	**78.3**	**2**	**8.7**	**3**	**13.0**
2.1 Food	20	10.4	16	80.0	2	10.0	2	10.0
2.2 Other	3	1.6	2	66.7	0	0.0	1	33.3
3. Raw materials	**154**	**79.8**	**71**	**46.1**	**3**	**1.9**	**80**	**51.9**
3.1 Food	5	2.6	0	0.0	0	0.0	5	100.0
3.2 Rubber	10	5.2	7	70.0	0	0.0	3	30.0
3.3 Pharmaceuticals	12	6.2	4	33.3	2	16.7	6	50.0
3.4 Metals	44	22.8	22	50.0	0	0.0	22	50.0
3.5 Plastics	19	9.8	8	42.1	0	0.0	11	57.9
3.6 Nonmetal minerals	6	3.1	4	66.7	0	0.0	2	33.3
3.7 Paper	1	0.5	0	0.0	1	100.0	0	0.0
3.8 Chemicals	45	23.3	20	44.4	0	0.0	25	55.6
3.9 Textiles	12	6.2	6	50.0	0	0.0	6	50.0
4. Spares & components	**10**	**5.2**	**8**	**80.0**	**0**	**0.0**	**2**	**20.0**
Total	193	100.0	102	52.8	5	2.6	86	44.6

Source: MDIC (2003); Aduaneiras (1996, 1997, 1998, 1999, 2000, 2001, 2002, and 2003); authors' calculations.

TABLE 3.6 Number of Antidumping Cases in Brazil with Final Determinations, Grouped by Exporting Country or Bloc (from highest number of cases to lowest)

Exporting country/bloc	Total no. of cases	Cases resulting in antidumping duties		Cases resulting in price undertakings		Cases resulting in no restrictive action	
		Number	Percentage	Number	Percentage	Number	Percentage
United States	29	10	34.5	1	3.4	18	62.1
China	25	20	80.0	0	0.0	5	20.0
India	11	7	63.6	0	0.0	4	36.4
Russian Federation	8	4	50.0	0	0.0	4	50.0
South Africa	6	4	66.7	0	0.0	2	33.3
Germany	6	4	66.7	0	0.0	2	33.3
United Kingdom	6	4	66.7	0	0.0	2	33.3
Mexico	5	4	80.0	0	0.0	1	20.0
Ukraine	5	2	40.0	0	0.0	3	60.0
Bangladesh	4	2	50.0	0	0.0	2	50.0
Japan	4	2	50.0	0	0.0	1	25.0
Korea, Rep. of	4	1	25.0	0	0.0	3	75.0
Spain	4	2	50.0	0	0.0	2	50.0
France	5	3	60.0	1	20.0	1	20.0
Argentina	3	1	33.3	1	33.3	1	33.3
Canada	3	1	33.3	0	0.0	2	66.7
Kazakhstan	3	2	66.7	0	0.0	1	33.3
Chile	3	1	33.3	1	33.3	1	33.3
Subtotal	134	74	55.2	4	3.0	55	41.0
Other countries not shown	59	28	47.5	1	1.7	30	50.8
Total	193	102	52.8	5	2.6	85	44.0

Source: MDIC (2003); Aduaneiras (1996, 1997, 1998, 1999, 2000, 2001, 2002, and 2003); authors' calculations.

Note: In the actions against the European Union, only member countries exporting to the Brazilian market were included. In the case of the former Soviet Union, such a detailed breakdown was not possible.

on consumer goods. In general, using the constructed-value method to estimate the normal value rather than using the price in the exporting country or in third countries allows for greater discretion. In fact, in 57.9 percent of cases, this method was applied. Nonetheless, in many cases, the constructed value was estimated on the basis of international prices quoted in specialized publications, especially for inputs and commodities. This approach usually leads to prices

TABLE 3.7 Antidumping Cases for Brazil: Preliminary Duty Rates, Normal Value Method, and Antidumping Duty as Percentage of Estimated Dumping Margin

Product categorys	Average preliminary duty rate (percentage)	Method used to determine normal value								Applied antidumping duty as a percentage of estimated dumping antidumping
		Domestic price in exporting country		Third country price		Constructed value		Method not known		
		Number	Percentage	Number	Percentage	Number	Percentage	Number	Percentage	
1. Durable goods	**80.0**	**0**	**0.0**	**3**	**60.0**	**2**	**40.0**	**0**	**0.0**	**55.8**
2. Soft goods	**25.0**	**0**	**0.0**	**3**	**15.0**	**17**	**85.0**	**0**	**0.0**	**48.1**
3. Raw materials	**44.9**	**28**	**37.8**	**6**	**8.1**	**38**	**51.4**	**2**	**27.0**	**65.4**
3.1 Rubber	42.9	0	0.0	0	0.0	7	100.0	0	0.0	66.7
3.2 Pharma-ceuticals	18.7	2	33.1	2	33.3	2	33.3	0	0.0	44.4
3.3 Metals	72.7	2	9.1	1	4.5	19	86.4	0	0.0	74.7
3.4 Plastics	50.0	6	75.0	0	0.0	2	25.0	0	0.0	65.8
3.5 Nonmetal minerals	0.0	2	50.0	0	0.0	2	50.0	0	0.0	24.8
3.6 Paper	0.0	1	100.0	0	0.0	0	0.0	0	0.0	n.a.
3.7 Chemicals	25.0	9	45.0	3	15.0	6	30.0	0	10.0	64.1
3.8 Textiles	83.3	6	100.0	0	0.0	0	0.0	0	0.0	64.8
4. Spares and components	**12.5**	**1**	**12.5**	**2**	**25.0**	**5**	**32.5**	**0**	**0.0**	**85.3**
Total	**41.4**	**29**	**27.6**	**14**	**13.3**	**62**	**59.0**	**2**	**1.9**	**61.3**

Source: Aduaneiras (1996, 1997, 1998, 1999, 2000, 2001, 2002, and 2003); authors' calculations.

Note: n.a. = not applicable. According to WTO rules, three methodologies can be used to estimate normal value: domestic price, third country price, and constructed value. ADD/DM measures the ratio between the antidumping duty applied and the dumping margin.

TABLE 3.8 Brazil: Cases Ended without a Restrictive Outcome, Classified by Motives

Description	No. of cases	Percentage of cases
No injury	30	34.9
No dumping	21	24.4
No causation	9	10.5
Government interest	2	2.3
Requested by petitioner	7	8.1
Other support measures provided	8	9.3
Other	9	10.5
Total	86	100.0

Source: Aduaneiras (1996, 1997, 1998, 1999, 2000, 2001, 2002, and 2003); authors' calculations.

lower than the domestic ones. The last column in table 3.7 shows that Brazil systematically applies an antidumping duty lower than the relative dumping margin—that is, a rate barely enough to remedy the injury—as recommended in the Antidumping Agreement; on average, the ratio between the antidumping duty and the dumping margin is 61.3 percent.

Table 3.8 shows the reasons given for negative determinations in some antidumping investigations. In view of the experience of other countries such as the United States (Finger and Murray 1993; Niels 2000), the "no injury" determinations (approximately 34.9 percent of the cases) were dismissed because no injury resulting from dumping was found whereas the "no dumping" determinations (24.4 percent of all actions) were dismissed because dumping could not be shown. As a result of direct government intervention, two cases were turned down to avoid an effect on domestic prices. In another eight cases, other measures were adopted to protect the affected industries.

To find out whether the antidumping measures adopted had been used to support the monopoly power of domestic enterprises, we distributed the cases into groups according to the number of manufacturing companies (see table 3.9): a single firm (monopoly), two to five (oligopoly), and six or more (competition). Given the highly concentrated industrial market structure, the majority of actions involved the first two categories of firms. Nonetheless, for those two categories, the proportion of accepted cases (82.4 percent) is almost equivalent to that of the rejected ones (88.4 percent).

Finally, we examined whether the application of antidumping duties had undergone any change in the four subperiods for which the import policy was

TABLE 3.9 Brazil: Distribution of Antidumping Cases with a Final Determination, by Number of Domestic Firms

Determination	1 firm		2 to 5 firms		6 or more firms		Total no. of cases
	No. of cases	Percentage of total no.	No. of cases	Percentage of total no.	No. of cases	Percentage of total no.	
Antidumping duty imposed	42	41.2	42	41.2	18	17.6	102
Price undertaking	2	40.0	0	0.0	3	60.0	5
Not restrictive outcome	49	57.0	27	31.4	10	11.6	86
Total	93	48.2	69	35.8	31	16.1	193

Source: Aduaneiras (1996, 1997, 1998, 1999, 2000, 2001, 2002, and 2003); authors' calculations.

analyzed by analyzing four indicators: the number of actions, the percentage of actions resulting in affirmative determinations, the average length of the investigation conducted (the number of days from filing date until final determination), and the antidumping duties and dumping margin ratios (see table 3.10). The 1994-98 period witnessed a substantial increase in the percentage of accepted cases. However, on average, the investigations were increasingly protracted, and the ratio between antidumping duties and dumping margins decreased in each subperiod following the first. This finding reveals that establishing time frames for analyzing disputes, as prescribed in 1995 by special law, failed to accelerate the

TABLE 3.10 Brazil: Antidumping Cases and Selected Indicators, by Subperiods

Subperiod	No. of cases	Antidumping duty applied	Percentage with antidumping duty applied	Average duration (days)	Antidumping duty applied as percentage of estimated dumping margin (average)
1988–89	4	4	100.0	213	—
1990–93	50	18	36.0	292	83.1
1994–98	69	43	62.3	440	68.1
1999–2002	70	42	60.0	480	47.1
Total	193	107	55.4	422	61.3

Source: Aduaneiras (1996, 1997, 1998, 1999, 2000, 2001, 2002, and 2003); authors' calculations.

Note: — = not available.

course of investigations and that a more moderate approach prevailed in the application of antidumping duties during the periods under study.

Safeguards in Brazil The new Safeguard Agreement was implemented for the first time in June 1996 when the Consultative Committee for Commercial Defense adopted a provisional safeguard measure increasing import duties on toys by 50 percent, which was added to the common external tariff of 20 percent.

Until modification of the conditions for applying safeguard measures during the Uruguay Round, the majority of GATT members had avoided using such measures. GATT article XIX permitted safeguard measures to protect any domestic industry injured or threatened by increased quantities of an imported good. However, this provision was not used because of the difficulties encountered in negotiating compensation for the affected countries and because of the fear of retaliation. Instead, less transparent measures such as voluntary export-restraint agreements became common. The Uruguay Round agreement on safeguards was intended to make the safeguards instrument more practical while at the same time introducing stricter conditions on its application. Thus, even though the new Safeguard Agreement constitutes a waiver of the need to offer compensation during the first three years that the safeguard measure is in force, it sets forth clear time frames for the application, or any extension thereof, of safeguard measures. It also requires that all measures be liberalized year by year if the period of application is longer than one year.

Given the advantages introduced by the new agreement, Brazil took provisional safeguard measures[25] after a preliminary determination found that the increase of toy imports was causing (or threatening to cause) severe injury to the domestic industry. Preliminary measures may be applied for a maximum period of 200 days. In Brazil, in the case of toys, they took the form of an increase in import duties that was added to the Mercosur common external tariff.[26]

The Brazilian toy industry had retained its high level of tariff protection during the trade liberalization program, on the grounds that seasonal imports occurred between July and September every year. Thus, the tariff rates applied to toys were kept at 65 percent until September 1992, then lowered to 55 percent between October 1992 and July 1993, when they were reduced to 40 percent until March 1994. They were then lowered to 20 percent, though only for three months. The industry requested a tariff increase to 30 percent for the June-September period, which was accepted.

The Brazilian government officially notified the WTO in late 1996 of its decision to extend the enforcement of safeguards for three more years. It established a phaseout schedule, by which the tariff rate should converge to the 20 percent level agreed among Mercosur's partners in 2000 (see table 3.11).

TABLE 3.11 Safeguard Measures in Brazil, 1996–2003

Restriction applied, final determination							
Year	Case	Percentage tariff rate, preliminary measure	Form of restriction	Year 1	Year 2	Year 3	Year 4
1996	Toys	70	Tariff (%)	63	49	35	20
1999	Toys (review)	n.a.	Tariff (%)	34	33	32	31
2001	Coconut	—	Quota (tons)	3.957	4.155	4.353	4.551
2003	Toys (extension)	n.a.	Tariff (%)	30			

Source: MDIC (2003); Aduaneiras (1996, 1997, 1998, 1999, 2000, 2001, 2002, and 2003); authors' calculations.

Note: n.a. = not applicable; — = not available.

In 1999, the toy industry filed a new request for the extension of the safeguard measure. Once accepted, additional tariffs were reimposed for a four-year term, though at much lower rates.

In 2001, coconut producers, protected by a countervailing duty in force until August 2000, filed a petition for the adoption of a safeguard measure, a request that was accepted in mid-2002 by imposing an import quota.

Finally, toy manufacturers requested that the safeguard measure be extended for one more year, and the application was granted in late 2003. A 10 percent tariff added to the common external tariff of 20 percent was thus imposed.

Conclusions

This chapter analyzes the relationship between Brazil's import liberalization policy and the antidumping and safeguard system from 1998 to 2003. The time span was divided, for methodological reasons, into four intervals: 1988–89, 1990–93, 1994–98, and 1999–2003.

The first two years (1988–89) correspond to the period in which the antidumping system was first implemented, in the context of an import substitution policy based on very high tariffs and a widespread use of nontariff barriers. These two factors made the use of antidumping measures unnecessary.

The next subperiod (1990–93) corresponds to a new federal administration (Collor), whose goal was to dismantle the existing protectionist structure. In fact, most import-related administrative prohibitions and restrictions were removed and a tariff phaseout schedule was successfully implemented. However, macroeconomic instability led to low economic growth rates and currency overvaluation, the exchange rate having been adjusted twice (in late 1991 and 1992). Thus, the implementation of a competitive, or free market, policy, which—according to economic theory—should be offset by a currency devaluation, was concomitant with a negative domestic situation, encouraging the search for protectionist measures through the use of antidumping mechanisms.

The first two years of the third subperiod (1994–98) coincide with the launching of the Real Plan, during which the fight against inflation was subordinated to currency overvaluation, a situation that remained unchanged until the end of this subperiod. The economic growth in 1994–95, together with an overvalued currency, led to growing trade deficits that were curtailed by increasing tariff rates on electronic goods and the automotive industry. Applications for investigations filed by other industries—such as the chemical and metal sectors—increased substantially until 1999 (except for 1995).

The last subperiod (1999–2003) began with a strong currency devaluation and was marked, in general, by low economic growth rates. Antidumping mechanisms start progressively losing their meaning, especially when the results of the reviewed cases are not taken into consideration.

In short, the events throughout these years reveal that the search for increased protection through antidumping measures is not related exclusively to the trade liberalization process, but is related to a combination of that process with a currency misalignment and Brazil's economic growth cycles.

With respect to the evaluation of the institutional aspects of the system and the implementation of the Antidumping Agreement negotiated at the Uruguay Round, the constant changes introduced in the organizational structure of governmental agencies responsible for implementing antidumping measures did much to disrupt any attempt at organizing the system properly. From 1993, when antidumping responsibility was under the purview of the Ministry of Finance, power was steadily shifted to the Ministry of Development, Industry, and Commerce, a fact that did not add to the credibility of the agency in charge of conducting investigations and making decisions. By its nature an antidumping action affects different groups—domestic producers, importers, and exporters—and, quite often, governmental policy. A feature of all antidumping systems in the world is their tendency to give top priority to the demands of domestic producers to the detriment of consumers and general economic welfare. Therefore, the technical finding in any action is even more biased when it is subject to review by a government agency with close links to local producers that is therefore more sensitive to their demands for protection.

In addition to the series of institutional and administrative changes that put in danger a well-functioning antidumping system, this study identified another issue worthy of concern: the high percentage of review cases accepting requests for time extensions. Given the limited human and financial resources available, the agency engaged in investigations (DECOM) is very likely to accept most requests for review filed with it.

On the positive side, if the Brazilian antidumping system is compared with that of other countries such as the United States, the Republic of Korea, the European Union, and India, it stands out for its lower percentage of cases with final positive determinations and for its stricter adherence to the important recommendation of the Antidumping Agreement that antidumping duties smaller than the relative dumping margins be adopted. As this chapter has shown, throughout the 1990s this systematic approach led to ratios between the antidumping duties and the dumping margins that were quite lower than one and increasingly so. Such a limited use contrasts positively with the usual practice in other countries such as the United States, which favors the adoption of the total dumping margin. Results show that the Brazilian government succeeded in adequately handling the protectionist pressures exerted through requests for trade defense in an environment of macroeconomic difficulties that led the Brazilian economy to a higher exposure to international competition, with the exception of certain sectors such as the toy industry.

Despite the sensible moderation exercised by Brazil in estimating antidumping duties, Finger's caveat—voiced in 1993 and 2000—is still meaningful: although a need exists for a reform in the antidumping system, reform should not be sought in the details of the agreement. Rather, such reform should entail *less* antidumping. To this end, investigations should not restrict themselves to the effect of competition of imported goods on the domestic production of a like good (a specific interest) but should focus on its effects on the national economic interest, which comprises other economic actors such as other producers and end consumers.

Notes

1. Surcharges established since mid-1974, during the first oil crisis, were removed in late 1984, after numerous extensions.

2. This abbreviation and those following, as well as all other abbreviations and acronyms in this chapter representing Brazilian agencies, are from the Portuguese.

3. The Mercosur common external tariff introduced rates slightly lower than those in force in the Brazilian tariff structure.

4. The government also applied quotas to car imports, which were later removed because of their condemnation by the WTO. Thereafter, a series of incentives for the automotive sector was implemented.

5. From the very beginning, the agency responsible for conducting dumping and subsidy investigations in Brazil was the same body responsible for determining injury to domestic industries.

6. Even though Banco do Brasil operated under the purview of the Ministry of Finance, the director of the CACEX was appointed by the President of the Republic.

7. The DECEX, then renamed SECEX, reported directly to the MICT.

8. CAMEX was expected to act as a center for working out the foreign trade policy guidelines and as a forum for resolving the main disputes between supporters of free trade measures and those who backed more protectionist ideas.

9. In 1995, after the common external tariff came into force, tariff changes came to be decided by the Common Market Group of Mercosur and implemented in Brazil through a presidential decree.

10. "Ex" tariffs were created in 1990 in Brazil so that capital goods and raw materials that were not locally produced could be imported at a 0 percent tariff rate, and they were kept in force with the common external tariff.

11. The Brazilian private sector has always supported the U.S. antidumping system because of its celerity in the initiation of proceedings as well as the possibility of applying duties retroactively and of imposing duties equivalent to the dumping margin.

12. The retroactive duty was never applied.

13. For example, if the application of the antidumping duty would harm the politics of stabilization of prices, the measure would not be applied.

14. To facilitate the decision-making process, CAMEX created a technical committee made up of a representative of each member ministry that would make decisions on the report submitted by SECEX.

15. DECOM is not allocated a separate appropriation.

16. In this context, investigation means an action involving one product and all the countries concerned; when conducting on-the-spot investigations for the purpose of determining injury, the country of origin of the imported good is irrelevant.

17. For comparison purposes, the number of investigations quoted is that reported by Brazil to the WTO Antidumping Committee.

18. The reasons for such an abrupt drop in 1995 are not clear. Perhaps the increase in GDP is a partial explanation because, in this year, the second-highest growth rate of 4.2 percent is recorded.

19. In spite of the changes introduced in the exchange rate system in January 1999, it is possible that claims already submitted, based on data of previous periods, did not consider the devaluation as permanent.

20. A more rigorous assessment would require conducting econometric tests such as those by Leidy (1997), Knetter and Prusa (2000), Francois and Niels (2003), and Irwin (2004).

21. The fact that all the requests submitted in the first three years—1988, 1989, and 1990—were accepted does not bear the same significance as in 1992 and 1995 because in the first three years of antidumping implementation in Brazil, few requests were made for investigations.

22. A price undertaking is considered a restrictive outcome.

23. Sales based on contracts guarantee ongoing supply, even in times of shortage. Conversely, domestic buyers are ready to pay a higher price than that of the international market when supply is insufficient to satisfy their demand.

24. For durable consumer goods, China is the only exporting country involved in all investigations. For nondurables, of 18 actions accepted, 10 refer to milk imported from the European Union countries where it is subsidized, thus lowering its export price. In the rest of the cases, China is the only exporting country involved.

25. The domestic producers of toys filed a request for the adoption of safeguard measures in mid-1995. The preliminary duty was introduced one year later.

26. Final safeguard measures can be taken by increasing import duty rates or by introducing nonselective quantitative restrictions. Under normal conditions, the maximum period of application is four years and, regardless of the circumstances, the total period of application cannot exceed eight years.

References

Aduaneiras. 1996. Coletânea de Leis de Comércio Exterior. São Paulo: Aduaneiras.

———. 1997. Coletânea de Leis de Comércio Exterior. São Paulo: Aduaneiras.

———. 1998. Coletânea de Leis de Comércio Exterior. São Paulo: Aduaneiras.

———. 1999. Coletânea de Leis de Comércio Exterior. São Paulo: Aduaneiras.

———. 2000. Coletânea de Leis de Comércio Exterior. São Paulo: Aduaneiras.

———. 2001. Coletânea de Leis de Comércio Exterior. São Paulo: Aduaneiras.

———. 2002. Coletânea de Leis de Comércio Exterior. São Paulo: Aduaneiras.

———. 2003. Coletânea de Leis de Comércio Exterior. São Paulo: Aduaneiras.

Finger, J. Michael. 1993. "Reform." In *Antidumping—How It Works and Who Gets Hurt*, ed. J. Michael Finger, 57–79. Ann Arbor: University of Michigan.

———. 1998. "GATT Experience with Safeguards: Making Economic and Political Sense of the Possibilities That the GATT Allows to Restrict Imports." Policy Research Working Paper 2000, World Bank, Washington, DC.

Finger, J. Michael, and T. Murray. 1993. "Antidumping and Countervailing Duty Enforcement in the United States." In *Antidumping—How It Works and Who Gets Hurt*, ed. J. Michael Finger, 241–54. Ann Arbor: University of Michigan.

Francois, Joseph, and Gunnar Niels. 2003. "Business Cycles, the Current Account, and Administered Protection in México." Discussion Papers 03-054-2. Amsterdam: Tinbergen Institute.

FUNCEX (Fundação Centro de Estudos de Comércio Exterior). *Base de Dados FUNCEX*. Rio de Janeiro: FUNCEX. http://www.funcex.com.br.

General Agreement on Tariff and Trade. 1994. *Agreement on the Implementation of Article VI of General Agreement on Tariff and Trade—GATT Antidumping Code, Tokyo Round*. Geneva: GATT.

IBGE (Instituto Brasileiro de Geografia e Estatística). 1990. *Contas Nacionais do Brasil*. Rio de Janeiro: IBGE. http://www.ibge.org.br.

———. 2002. *Contas Nacionais do Brasil*. Rio de Janeiro: IBGE. http://www.ibge.org.br.

IPEA-DATA (Instituto de Pesquisa Econômica e Aplicada–DATA). *Base de Dados Macroeconômicos e Regionais*. Rio de Janeiro: IPEA. http://www.ipeadata.org.br.

Irwin, Douglas A. 2004. "The Rise in U.S. Antidumping Actions in Historical Perspective." NBER Working Paper 10582. National Bureau of Economic Research, Cambridge, MA.

Knetter, Michael M., and Thomas J. Prusa. 2000. "Macroeconomic Factors and Antidumping Filings: Evidence from Four Countries." NBER Working Paper 8010, National Bureau of Economic Research, Cambridge, MA.

Kume, Honorio. 1988. "A reforma aduaneira proposta pela CPA: um primeiro passo para a formulação de uma política tarifária." *Revista Brasileira de Comércio Exterior* 3 (15): 14–25.

———. 1998. "A política de importação no Plano Real e a estrutura de proteção efetiva." In *A Economia Brasileira em Perspectiva—1998*, ed. IPEA, 147–69. Rio de Janeiro: IPEA.

Kume, Honorio, Guida Piani, and Carlos F. B. Souza. 2003. "A política brasileira de importação no período 1987–1998: Descrição e avaliação." In *A abertura comercial brasileira nos anos 1990: impactos sobre emprego e salário*, ed. Carlos H. Corseuil and Honorio Kume, 9–37. Rio de Janeiro: MTE and IPEA.

Leidy, Michael P. 1997. "Macroeconomic Conditions and Pressures for Protection under Antidumping and Countervailing Duty Laws: Empirical Evidence from the United States." *IMF Staff Papers* 44 (1): 132–44.

MDIC (Ministério de Desenvolvimento, Indústria e Comércio Exterior). 2003. Relatório DECOM (Departamento de Defesa Comercial) number 7. Brasília: MDIC.

Naidin, Leane C. 1998. "Dumping e antidumping no Brasil: evolução da regulamentação, aplicação e efeitos sobre o comércio." PhD diss., Instituto de Economia, Universidade Federal do Rio de Janeiro.

Niels, Gunnar. 2000. "What Is Antidumping Policy Really About?" *Journal of Economic Surveys* 14 (4): 467–92.

WTO (World Trade Organization). 1994. *Agreement on Implementation of Article VI of the General Agreement on Tariffs and Trade (Antidumping): Final Act of the Uruguay Round*. Geneva: WTO. http://www.wto.org.

———. 1998. *Report of the Committee on Safeguards*. Geneva: WTO. http://www.wto.org.

———. 1999. *Report of the Committee on Safeguards*. Geneva: WTO. http://www.wto.org.

———. 2000. *Report of the Committee on Safeguards*. Geneva: WTO. http://www.wto.org.

———. 2001. *Report of the Committee on Safeguards*. Geneva: WTO. http://www.wto.org.

———. 2002. *Report of the Committee on Safeguards*. Geneva: WTO. http://www.wto.org.

———. 2003a. *Report of the Committee on Safeguards*. Geneva: WTO. http://www.wto.org.

———. 2003b. *Antidumping Initiations by Reporting Member*. Geneva: WTO. http://www.wto.org.

Zanardi, Maurizio. 2003. *Antidumping: What Are the Numbers?* Glasgow, Scotland: Department of Economics, University of Glasgow.

4

KEEPING ANIMAL SPIRITS ASLEEP: THE CASE OF CHILE

Sebastián Sáez

The multilateral trading system has defined the instruments that the members of the World Trade Organization (WTO) can adopt, under certain conditions, to correct distortions (subsidies and dumping practices) on imported goods and to prevent the damage that a sudden increase of imports may cause. These instruments have been part of trade regimes since the end of the 19th century and the beginning of the 20th century.

The thesis presented in this chapter is that the political economy of contingent trade protection demands at least an institutional regime that will significantly reduce the possibility that these instruments will be captured by private interests or by proponents within the government of the import substitution philosophy that the reformers want to set aside. At the same time, under certain conditions, experience indicates that these instruments can be a useful tool to support economic opening, because they offer society mechanisms that can temporarily alleviate or facilitate the adjustment that a sector may need in the transition to the new context of economic liberalization.

This chapter examines the origin, the evolution, and the operation of the institutions responsible for adopting safeguard measures and antidumping duties in Chile.

The author would like to acknowledge J. Michael Finger and Julio J. Nogués for their invitation to participate in this project. The author would also like to acknowledge the comments of Diana Tussie and the participants of the seminar in which a preliminary version of this paper was discussed. During the preparation of this paper, the author received useful comments from several experts—in particular from Juan S. Araya, Alvaro Espinoza, and Ambassador Alejandro Jara—who intently and patiently read the paper and made suggestions that contributed to improve it. Evelyn Caserio collaborated in the research of basic and statistical background data. As is usual, all errors or omissions are the author's sole responsibility.

The first section studies the evolution of legislation and the creation of administering agencies from 1981 to the present. The second section examines the measures adopted and the sectors that have benefited from them. The third section reviews and analyzes Chile's experience, and the fourth pulls together conclusions from this experience and examines proposals for improvement.

Development of Chilean Legislation on Unfair Competition

For a number of reasons, Chile's trade policy reform process differs from that of other Latin American countries. In the first place, the process started at the end of 1973 in Chile, earlier than in the rest of the region. Hence, Chile's reforms have a degree of maturity that contributes to the stability of trade policy and the continuous opening process that the economy has experienced in the context of democracy. Second, these reforms took place in the context of a military regime that did not need to seek support to enforce its policies. Moreover, it did not give the public any explanation for the negative consequences that reforms had at the beginning. Therefore, it was not necessary to create instruments that would temporarily alleviate the effects of the reform or to establish mechanisms that would promote a gradual adjustment to the new conditions. In the third place, the Chilean trade reform is characterized by its wide scale and speed. In fact, as figure 4.1 shows, in June 1979 tariffs that had averaged over 90 percent in 1974 were reduced to a uniform 10 percent level. Additionally, the currency exchange was fixed for nearly three years from June 1979 to mid-1982, a period during which economic policy adopted the monetary approach to the balance of payments. All this change took place in a context in which the set of trade policy instruments in force in September 1973 was disassembled at the same time as tariffs were reduced (quotas, prohibitions, and advance deposits, among others). Moreover, trade opening took place and was a key piece in the macroeconomic stabilization process launched by authorities. Finally, it is important to take into account that Chile's trade reform process is part of a larger, integrated, institutional transformation process, which encompassed diverse aspects of Chilean society such as its political regime, the role of the state in the economy, the general economic framework, and social policies as they developed throughout the 20th century.

Although in 1973 protection was initially very high, at the end of the unilateral liberalization process, when the tariff level reached 10 percent, introducing contingent protection instruments to support the adopted policy could have been justified. Nevertheless, such instruments were introduced only during the great economic crisis of 1982.

FIGURE 4.1 Chile: Tariffs and Real Exchange Rate, 1973–2003

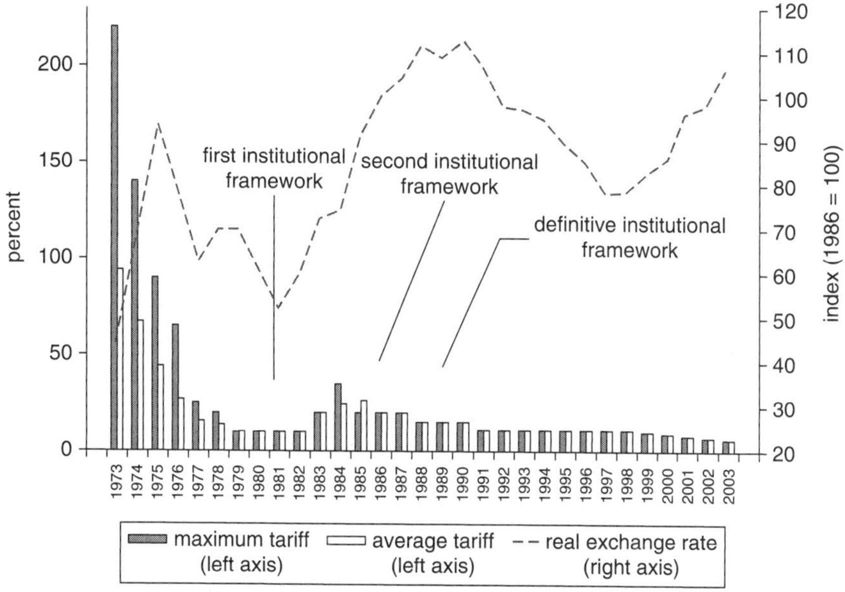

Source: Tariffs: French-Davis (1980); Meller (1996); author's analysis. Real exchange rate provided by R. French-Davis, following calculus methodologies described in French-Davis (2003).

In the framework of the trade negotiations of the Tokyo Round, Chile signed the General Agreement on Tariffs and Trade (GATT) Subsidy Code because the existence of subsidized imports was considered to be the only situation that justified a temporary restriction in favor of the domestic industry. Conversely, the economic rationale of safeguard measures was less sustainable. Besides, in their original form, these measures contemplated compensations for the countries affected by them, which discouraged their application. Finally, it was considered that in an open economy antidumping duties could lead to protectionist measures that would favor sectors that might feel affected by the opening and could have political influence to get protection. Moreover, in the evaluation of Chilean authorities, GATT regulations on antidumping were too permissive; they would allow import restrictions that did not have a sound economic basis.

In October 1981, the Subsidies Commission was created and installed in Chile's central bank (Banco Central de Chile, or BCCH). Its role was to initiate, conduct, and conclude investigations on subsidized imports and to submit its conclusions to the Ministry of Finance, which could use them to adopt compensatory adjustments. These adjustments took the form of tariff surcharges, which consisted of an increase in the tariff up to the maximum level of 35 percent consolidated by Chile in the

TABLE 4.1 Chile: Development of Legislation, 1981–2000

Year	GATT and WTO legislation	Domestic legislation	Responsible entity	Instruments
1981	Subsidies Code, Tokyo Round, and GATT 1947	Decree 742	BCCH	Compensatory adjustments, MCVs, and surcharges
1986	Subsidies Code, Tokyo Round, and GATT 1947	Law 18,525	BCCH	Compensatory adjustments, MCVs, and surcharges
1989	Subsidies Code, Tokyo Round, and GATT 1947	Laws 18,840 and 18,908	CNDP	Compensatory adjustments, MCVs, and surcharges
1992	Subsidies Code, Tokyo Round, and GATT 1947	Law 19,155	CNDP	Compensatory adjustments, MCVs, surcharges, and antidumping duties
1995	WTO Uruguay Round agreements and Chile's tariff bindings	Law 19,383	CNDP	Compensatory adjustments, MCVs, surcharges, and antidumping duties
1999	WTO Uruguay Round agreements and Chile's tariff bindings	Law 19,612	CNDP	Safeguards, antidumping duties, and compensatory adjustments

Source: *Diario Oficial*, several issues.

Note: In 1999, both MCVs and surcharges were removed from Chilean legislation.

Tokyo Round. Likewise, the commission was entitled to recommend the adoption of minimum customs values (MCVs).

At the end of 1985, in an attempt to increase the commission's representativeness, the composition of the Subsidies Commission was modified to include members from the Ministries of Economy and Foreign Affairs, the National Customs Service, and the antitrust authority (Fiscal Nacional Económico, or FNE). The BCCH continued to chair the commission (see table 4.1). In 1986, Law 18,525 was passed. This law created the National Commission for Investigations on Import Price Distortions (Comisión Nacional Encargada de Investigar la Existencia de Distorsiones en el Precio de las Mercaderías Importadas),[1] which became known as the National Commission for Price Distortions (CNDP). The CNDP coexisted with the Subsidies Commission, which was based in the BCCH and, as mentioned, investigated applications against subsidies. The CNDP, however, had a wider scope of action because it focused on price distortions. Finally, with the promulgation of Law 18,840 in 1989, the constitutional organic law of the BCCH (which established the substantive provisions over this institution and implemented the autonomy set forth in the constitution of 1980), and Law 18,908 of January 1990, both commissions were merged. An important change introduced was the faculty to initiate an investigation without having received a written application by or on behalf of a domestic industry.

The CNDP was thus constituted in the general terms as it operates at present, by two representatives from the BCCH, one representative from the Ministry of Finance, one representative from the Ministry of Economy, one representative from the Ministry of Foreign Affairs, the director of the National Customs Service, and the head of FNE, who chairs it.[2] In 1995, by means of a law, a representative from the Ministry of Agriculture also joined the commission. The Technical Secretariat of the CNDP, which is in charge of conducting investigations on price distortions, is based in the BCCH.

At the beginning of the 1990s, authorities foresaw that, in the context of the Uruguay Round and the possibility of Chile's subscribing to the Customs Valuation Code or a successive agreement, MCVs could not continue to be applied to correct price distortions. Moreover, in a context in which continuous trade opening was foreseen—through unilateral liberalization or trade agreements—this instrument and the tariff surcharges would disappear as contingent protection.

Therefore, Law 19,155 of August 13, 1992, entitled the CNDP to recommend that authorities adopt antidumping duties and discontinue practices with less adequate instruments such as surcharges and MCVs. This modification was opposed by orthodox economists, who, from a theoretical standpoint, correctly argued that in an open economy such as Chile's it would be impossible for a company to practice dumping because the country would not be able to permanently hold a leading market position and would experience midterm losses if it kept this strategy. However, there were sectors that considered it very difficult to continue with the liberalization process if properly regulated escape clauses subject to disciplines to control the application of this type of measures were not contemplated.

Finally, Law 19,612, which was approved on May 31, 1999, made it possible for the president of Chile to adopt safeguard measures in compliance with article XIX of GATT and the corresponding WTO agreement on the basis of a report from the CNDP. The legislation incorporated the form of adopting safeguard measures in compliance with the provisions of some bilateral agreements signed by Chile. At the same time, the possibility of adopting surcharges in the terms contemplated by the original law and MCVs was eliminated.

Application of Measures over Time

As figure 4.2 indicates, the first version of the CNDP was very active. According to the data available for the period between October 1981 and December 1985, 155 applications were submitted to the commission, an investigation was conducted

Figure 4.2 Chile: Applications Submitted and Investigations Initiated, 1981–2002

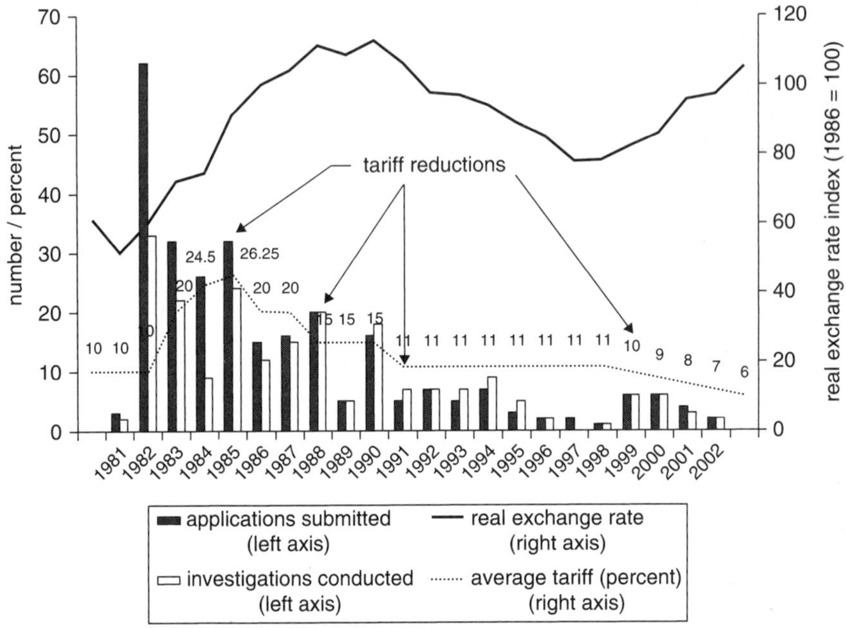

Source: BCCH (http://www.cndp.cl); figure 4.1 above.

for 90 cases (58 percent), and definitive measures were adopted for 47 cases investigated (52 percent of these cases, or 30 percent of the applications originally submitted (see figure 4.2 and Finger 1987). Of the measures adopted, 76 percent were tariff surcharges and 22 percent were MCVs. Concerning the sectors protected, the textile sector was predominant, with 37 percent of the measures (all of them surcharges), followed by electrical products (8 percent) and metal-mechanics (7 percent), (see table 4.2).[3]

In the 1981–90 period, the difficulties generated by the requirements of the GATT Code—especially the requirement of the existence of a subsidy—and the fear of retaliation from the trade partners affected by Chile's measures explain why the instrument that was most frequently used by authorities was the tariff surcharge.[4] Because Chile's GATT tariff commitment was a ceiling binding of 35 percent, Chile could increase the tariff on any product up to that level without offending its GATT obligations.[5] The tariff surcharge instrument provided for such action only after an investigation determined the existence of injury or threat thereof to the affected Chilean industry. The same requirement applied to the adoption of MCVs.

TABLE 4.2 Chile: Definitive Measures of the National Commission for Price Distortions and Sectors Affected

Sector	Tariff surcharges			Minimum customs values			Countervailing duties		Antidumping duties	
	1981–87	1986–89	1990–2002[a]	1981–87	1986–89	1990–2002[b]	1981–87	1986–1989	1990–2002	1990–2002[c]
Agriculture	0	0	5	1	0	1	0	0	1	1
Food products	3	0	1	3	0	0	0	0	0	0
Electrical, mechanical, or fuel products	5	0	0	0	1	1	0	0	1	0
Capital goods	0	0	0	0	0	0	0	0	0	0
Leather and shoes	1	0	0	0	0	0	0	0	0	1
Forestry, paper, and wood	0	0	0	0	0	0	0	0	0	0
Dairy products	3	3	2	1	2	4	0	0	2	0
Metals and metal-mechanics	4	0	1	0	3	1	0	0	0	2
Mining	2	0	0	0	0	0	0	0	0	0
Tires, rubber, and plastics	1	4	1	1	3	1	0	0	0	0
Fishing	1	0	0	0	0	0	0	0	0	0
Chemicals	2	1	0	5	0	0	0	0	0	2
Textiles	22	6	4	0	14	8	0	0	2	0
Glass and ceramics	3	0	0	1	0	0	1	0	0	0
Total	47	14	14	12	23	16	1	0	6	6

Source: BCCH; CNDP Secretaría Técnica (2003); http://www.cndp.cl

Note: In 2003, there were no investigations and no measures of any kind were adopted.

a. From 1999, surcharges correspond to safeguard measures. The former system of surcharges up to a 35 percent level was eliminated.

b. From 1999, MCVs were removed from Chilean legislation.

c. Before 1992, antidumping duties were not applied.

From the point of view of compensating for distortions, the surcharges were inefficient, because they affected imports independently of their origin and regardless of whether their prices were distorted. Another problem was that when measures were applied to intermediate goods, the effective protection of the final good was reduced.

In the 1986–92 period, tariff surcharges were applied in 41 percent of the investigations that concluded with recommendations, MCVs in 53 percent, and countervailing duties in just 6 percent (http://www.cndp.cl). Except for one case, it is worth noting, however, that countervailing duties were in large part applied only between 1990 and 1992. The use of MCVs was aimed to "punish" imports whose prices were more "distorted." Thus, the goal was to soften the impact of protection, as MCVs were applied independently of origin and affected mainly those imports whose prices were more "distorted" or, in other words, lower. During that period, a sensitive reduction in the number of applications submitted to the CNDP occurred, although the number of applications and investigations increased as tariffs were lowered (in 1985 and 1988). Thus, the measures served as a temporary deviation from the liberalization policy. They supported the opening, because they gave an option to the sectors that were more sensitive or reluctant to embrace this policy. With the return of democracy in 1990 came the expectation that in the new political context authorities would be more inclined to grant protection. The authorities, however, did not do so; after a small increase in 1990, the numbers of investigations and of measures both fell to levels below those observed in the nondemocratic period (see figure 4.2).

Concerning the sectors that resorted to these instruments, the predominant ones continued to be textiles (with 55 percent of the measures adopted), dairy products (10 percent), metals and metal-mechanics (10 percent), and electrical products (7 percent) (see table 4.2). In the period from 1993, when this type of measure was introduced, to 1997, only six antidumping duties were adopted, but more recently, between 1998 and 2003, no new measures have been implemented. Between 1993 and 1998, tariff surcharges were not adopted. In 1993 and 1994, there were only four MCVs and only one countervailing duty. Between 1999 and 2003, seven safeguard measures were adopted. Since 2002, only one application has been submitted for safeguards against fructose imports, and there have not been any new investigations. In sum, during the 1990s and in recent years, the CNDP faced relatively lower levels of activity.

It is useful to try to understand which variables explain the evolution of the investigations performed by the commission. For that purpose, a simple econometric regression has been undertaken in which the dependent variable is a logarithm of the applications submitted (LAPPLICATIONS) and the independent variables are a constant, the logarithm of the gross domestic product (LGDP) and the real exchange rate (LRER) of the previous period. A dummy variable (DU99) was included from 1999 to 2002, when the safeguard legislation was introduced, to capture any possible change in policy from the moment the legislation was modified.

(4.1) LAPPLICATIONS = 57.70391 – 1.147683 LRER (–1) – 3.007096 LGDP (1) + 1.069985 DU99
(10.03122) (–2.213121) (–8.459161) (3.199322)

DW = 2.485215
$R^2 = 0.859129$
R^2 adjusted = 0.834270

As the results of the regression reflect, the number of applications submitted is a function of GDP, and the RER lagged one year. The elasticity of the previous year's GDP is 3, and the elasticity of the RER is 1.14; both are statistically significant. The positive sign of the dummy variable indicates that the introduction of safeguards created expectations of a change of regime. This finding is reflected in the number of applications submitted after the legislation was approved (12 applications in 1999). However, this finding is not validated by the behavior of the CNDP, which adopted five safeguard measures between 1999 and 2000.

(4.2) LINITIATED = 48.45148 – 2.711487 LGDP (1) – 0.211594 LRER (1) + 0.724832 DU 99
(6.152791) (–5.562588) (–0.299738) (1.654273)

DW = 1.680560
$R^2 = 0.713528$
R^2 adjusted = 0.665783

The exercise was also performed using initiations as the dependent variable (LINITIATED). In that case, the RER is not a relevant variable, but GDP behavior of the previous year does help to explain the number of investigations initiated. In relation to the behavior of the CNDP, this result can indicate that the expectations of those who seek protection because of the appreciation of the RER are not validated. The dummy variable continues to be significant, which again indicates an expectation that the commission would change its policy. Specifically, once the legislation was approved, the CNDP tended to initiate investigations in response to an important fraction of the applications, and on three occasions (out of the total 15 initiated from 1990 to 2002), it initiated investigations itself, thus validating a possible change of policy. Nevertheless, this expectation was frustrated by the low number of measures adopted.

Experiences with Investigations and Applications of Measures

When an industry files an application for an investigation against an alleged price distortion on imported merchandise, the first response of the CNDP is to acknowledge receipt of the application. If the CNDP evaluates the application as satisfying the minimum criteria, the CNDP must then undertake an investigation. The commission is to publish the initiation date of the investigation and its subject matter in the *Official Bulletin* (*Diario Oficial*) within five working days after the application is submitted. The commission has to receive the background data that the interested parties want to submit, and it must request the necessary reports within 30 days after the application is published. On request from the interested parties and before presenting its conclusions, the commission is to hold a public hearing.

The CNDP is entitled to carry out ex officio investigations when the data available justify such an investigation. In those cases, the procedure is the same as for cases initiated through an application. The stages in the investigations and their development are in accordance with the general guidelines of WTO agreements (see table 4.3). It is the president of the country, through the minister of finance, who finally determines the products that will be subject to measures, the magnitude of the restriction that will be applied, and the duration of the measure.[6] The president has the discretion to set aside the CNDP's recommendation and impose no restriction. If, however, the president adopts a measure, it cannot be more restrictive than the one recommended by the commission. For example, if the commission recommends that a 10 percent antidumping duty be adopted, the president is entitled to apply a lower duty or one equal to 10 percent. Likewise, a measure can be extended for an additional year, without a limit of years, provided a *previous* de novo investigation is conducted by the CNDP to recommend maintaining the measure or modifying it. The request for renewal must be made by one of the interested parties in the case of safeguards, or it can be a decision of the commission in the case of dumping and subsidies. In the latter case, the request for renewal triggers an ex officio investigation.

The law that created the CNDP has been modified to incorporate the WTO agreements; new measures were added (safeguards) and others were eliminated (surcharges and MCVs). However, the concept that the commission is in charge of investigating price distortions on imports and that it is also responsible for safeguards, subsidies, and dumping investigations has been kept. The question arises whether there are other distortions on the prices of merchandise sold on international markets besides those mentioned here that the commission should be responsible for investigating. Likewise, the coexistence of the terminology of the original law, including its time frames, and of decrees that regulate the operation of the commission and have not been updated with the provisions of WTO

TABLE 4.3 Chile: Investigation Procedure and Stages

Investigation stages	Time frame	
	Antidumping	Safeguards
Submission of application or request		
Dumping/subsidy application form		
Safeguard request form		
Acceptance of application		
Investigation process		
Initiation of investigation and time frames	One year, maximum 18 months in exceptional cases, from the date of publication in the *Diario Oficial* of the notification of initiation	90 days from the date of publication in the *Diario Oficial* of the notification of initiation
Notification to parties	15 days to make comments or observations	Immediately after taking a measure
Receipt of evidence	30 days	30 days
Access to information related to the investigation	Once initiation of an investigation is notified, the CNDP makes available to all interested parties the complete text of the public version of the application	
Hearings	The CNDP fixes the date, time, and venue of the hearings and notifies interested parties in writing. The latter must communicate their intention to attend in writing before the third working day before the hearing.	The date, time, and venue of the hearing must be included in the notice of initiation of investigation that is published in the *Diario Oficial*.
In situ visits	When an investigation is initiated the authorities of the exporting member countries and all companies known to be interested in carrying out in situ investigations must be informed.	
Technical report		
Public notice of determinations	The CNDP gives public notice of all preliminary or definitive determinations, positive or negative, and of the termination of an investigation without a determination.	

(Continued on the next page.)

TABLE 4.3 (*Continued*)

Investigation stages	Time frame	
	Antidumping	Safeguards
Measures		
Recommendation of provisional measures	60 days from the date of publication in the *Diario Oficial* of the notification of initiation	60 days from the date of publication in the *Diario Oficial* of the notification of initiation
Recommendation of definitive measures	At completion of the investigation. Measures become effective as of the date notification is given in the *Diario Oficial.*	
Provisional measures	Can be in place a maximum of 4 months or, in exceptional circumstances, 6 months	Can be in place a maximum of 200 days
Definitive measures	Can be in place a maximum of 1 year. According to current norms, the measure cannot be higher than the distortion margin.	Can be in place a maximum of 1 year if provisional measures have not been applied. If provisional measures have been applied, the 1 year limit includes the time that provisional measures were in place.
Extension of definitive measures	Measures can be extended after a new request is made and a new investigation is completed.	Measures can be extended for a maximum of 1 year. The request for extension must be made at least 30 days before the expiration of the original measures.

Source: Author's tabulation from Chile law 18.525, Normas Sobre Importación de Mercancías al País; available at http://www.sice.oas.org/antidumping/legislation/chile/19612_s.asp#18525.

agreements—the ones that should prevail when investigations are conducted—could bring about some ambiguity and confusion.

A point that draws one's attention when studying the Chilean legislation is the double role that the BCCH plays. In fact, the BCCH acts as a member of the

CNDP with two representatives (25 percent of the members) and at the same time is responsible for the CNDP's Technical Secretariat. In the latter capacity, the BCCH is in charge of conducting investigations and submitting to the commission a report in which all the evidence gathered is analyzed. This double role has been maintained since the Chilean system was created. In 1989, when the organic constitutional law of the BCCH, which gave legal expression to the constitutional norm that established its autonomy, was passed, the role of the BCCH as the Technical Secretariat of the CNDP was maintained even though the BCCH was giving up almost all its functions in trade policy.

Two reasons can explain that decision. In the first place, there was a concern that the new democratic regime would be very sensitive to pressures from sectors that would demand trade protection.[7] Conversely, the BCCH would be less acquiescent and would maintain a technical approach to investigations. Its weight in the commission provided a balance that supported an exclusively technical approach. In the second place, there was a budgetary issue, because transferring the functions of the Technical Secretariat to another public entity implied the need to provide the new entity with the means and the technical training to perform this function. At present, the Technical Secretariat has sufficient budget to conduct investigations initiated by the commission through applications or ex officio, because it is part of the functional structure of the BCCH. This budget allows the Technical Secretariat to pay higher market remunerations than the public sector; to hire additional full- or part-time professionals when needed; to commission external studies, which have not been necessary so far; to carry out in situ visits; and, in general, to access all the local and international statistical information that is necessary to conduct an investigation.

The Technical Secretariat is formed by a small group of professionals who are in charge of conducting investigations. These professionals also have other roles inside the Department of Trade Policy of the BCCH, which reports to the Department of International Exchanges and Trade Policy. The work of the secretariat is defined as exclusively technical, low profile, and protected by the global institutionality of the BCCH. Thus, the political and public pressures that in many cases are exercised during investigations fall mainly on the members of the commission, particularly on the representatives of ministries, who adopt recommendations on the basis of the investigations performed by the Technical Secretariat. However, the law does not prevent commission members from contributing additional evidence in the course of the investigation or during deliberations.

One of the functions of the Technical Secretariat is to explain to the interested parties the legal requirements of the WTO and of local laws that must be fulfilled to initiate and conduct an investigation. Another is to analyze the evidence provided by the parties and to gather all the necessary information to prepare the technical report that is submitted to the CNDP. The Technical Secretariat is also responsible for compliance with all the legal requirements of the WTO and Chilean legislation. The Technical Secretariat does not perform dissemination activities of its work, although it participates in seminars and other activities to which its members are invited to discuss aspects of Chilean law and of international legislation of general interest. Throughout the years, the autonomy of the BCCH has been consolidated, and its credibility in conducting monetary and exchange rate policies has been strengthened. Consequently, there have not been serious proposals to move the secretariat out of this institution.

Application of Antidumping Duties

Since the legislation on antidumping measures was introduced, the CNDP has recommended and the president has adopted antidumping measures on just six occasions, of which two correspond to extensions of existing measures (see table 4.4). Chilean legislation takes the provisions of the WTO agreement, which are "fully incorporated in [our] national legislation, and are therefore Chilean law in each and every part."[8]

Both Chilean legislation and the practice followed in investigations so far have maintained stricter and more restrictive criteria than those contemplated in the corresponding WTO agreements and in most member country legislation. In fact, measures have a duration of one year and can only be extended through a previous de novo investigation. Furthermore, in the investigations that have been conducted so far, the following parameters have been applied[9]:

- The measure recommended to correct dumping takes into consideration the injury margin instead of the dumping margin.
- The injury margin is calculated, in general, on the basis of the prices of other competitors and not on the basis of domestic prices.[10]
- In the calculation of dumping margins on the basis of the domestic price of imports in the country of origin, sales below cost price are not excluded, which reduces the dumping margin.
- The investigation is not always carried out against all imports from the origin reported in the application, but only against imports from the companies reported, although there are only some examples of this criterion.
- The approach applied favors the determination of the causal relationship between the existence of dumping and the damage instead of analyzing simple correlations (one-track versus two-track approach).
- Neither anticircumvention nor retroactive measures are applied.

Nevertheless, the current practice used to assess the dumping cases could be modified by the CNDP itself. Consequently, in a favorable atmosphere, this instrument

TABLE 4.4 Chile: Antidumping Duties, 1992–2002

Diario Oficial initiation date	Name of product	Rate of duty (%)	Country of origin	Incidence (country/ total)[a,b]	*Diario Oficial* definitive measure date	Measure effective date	Measure termination date	Measure duration
November 18, 1993	Phthalic anhydride	7.0	Venezuela, R. B. de	86%	May 11, 1994	May 11, 1994	May 11, 1995	12 months
March 12, 1994	Phthalic anhydride	7.0	Venezuela, R. B. de	47%	September 6, 1994	September 6, 1994	May 11, 1995	9 months
December 19, 1994	Wheat flour	7.0	Argentina	95%	May 5, 1995	May 5, 1995	May 5, 1996	12 months
February 9, 1995	Shoes	10.0	China	64021900: 30% 64029900: 49% 64039900: 23% 64039190: 47%	June 21, 1995	June 21, 1995	June 21, 1996	12 months
October 16, 1996	Hot-rolled steel rolls, for thicknesses smaller than 1.8 mm	9.0	Russian Federation	72082500: 100% 72082600: 94% 72082700: 15% 72083700: 50% 72083800: 64%	April 24, 1997	April 24, 1997	April 24, 1998	12 months
			Ukraine	72083900: 36% 72083700: 6% 72083800: 4% 72083900: 0.2%				
May 5, 1998	Hot-rolled steel rolls, for thicknesses smaller than 1.8 mm	9.0	Russian Federation	72082500: 0% 72082600: 0% 72082700: 0% 72083700: 18%	October 24, 1998	October 24, 1998	October 24, 1999	12 months
			Ukraine	72083800: 7% 72083900: 8% 72082600: 14% 72082700: 15% 72083700: 1.1% 72083800: 17% 72083900: 1.7%				

Source: Technical Secretariat, BCCH.

a. Imports from country of origin over total imports for the investigation year.

b. The 8-digit numbers are the import product codes for the products to which measures were applied.

could become a tool with a protectionist orientation. Therefore, it is necessary to seek mechanisms to ensure that the actual practice is consolidated. Even though it is not possible to establish full guarantees that a restrictive approach will be maintained, the role played by the leadership of the economic authorities responsible for conducting trade policy is important to maintain the actual orientation of this instrument.

In the context of its bilateral trade negotiations, Chile has sought to eliminate the application of antidumping measures because the government has considered such measures a protection mechanism rather than an instrument that will correct dumping practices (Finger 1993; Peña 2001). In the framework of the existing free trade agreement with Canada, both countries have agreed to eliminate antidumping measures in reciprocal trade. Likewise, the free trade agreement with the European Free Trade Area eliminates the application of antidumping duties. However, those measures have not been replaced by the application of legislation on competition, as some authors propose. Nevertheless, concerning the application of antidumping measures to third countries, both parties have the ability to follow the procedures established by their legislation. In other words, criteria on the application of legislation have not been harmonized, which is an advantage because it allows the continuation of a more restricted approach for the application of measures, instead of introducing complex and difficult procedures that are not related to the economic rationale of the instrument (Peña 2001).

Application of Safeguard Measures

After Chile signed the Economic Complementation Agreement with Mercosur (Southern Cone Common Market, or Mercado Común del Sur) and the free trade agreement with Canada, a debate arose on the trade diversion effects of these two agreements, given the country's relatively high most-favored-nation rates. The executive proposed reducing the uniform applied rate from 11 percent to 6 percent over a period of five years. As part of its negotiation with the Chilean legislature, the executive agreed that the legislation to adopt safeguard measures in compliance with article XIX of GATT 1994 and the WTO Safeguards Agreement would be submitted.

The situation tends to favor the hypothesis that, in the case of Chile, safeguard measures, as well as the measures used in the 1980s, have complemented and supported the tariff reduction that took place in the second half of the 1990s. In other words, unilateral tariff reductions are accepted as long as there are protections for contingencies. The same happens in the trade negotiation processes in which temporary alleviation mechanisms are introduced.

With the adoption of safeguard legislation, the possibility of applying surcharges, which are subject to less strict disciplines, below the WTO bound tariff level and the possibility of applying MCVs were eliminated. Finally, in agreement with the provisions of the treaties negotiated by Chile, the application of safeguards (bilateral or multilateral) was regulated.

The approved legislation is restrictively applied with respect to the provisions of article XIX and the WTO Safeguards Agreement. When the recommended safeguard measure surpasses the WTO 25 percent bound tariff, approval by the CNDP requires a special quorum equivalent to three-fourths of the members of the commission. Additionally, safeguard measures can only be ad valorem tariffs, and the legislation does not contemplate the application of quotas or specific duties. Likewise, safeguard measures can be in force for a maximum of one year, including the effective period of provisional measures. Safeguard measures can be extended for an additional year provided a previous de novo investigation requested by the interested party accredits that the requirements of the Safeguards Agreement are fulfilled. In the case of an extension, a gradual dismantling schedule is established, unless there are exceptional circumstances properly qualified by the commission. Requesting the renewal of safeguards on a given product requires that no measures have been applied for a period of two years.[11] This limitation is not explicitly established in the law that authorized the application of safeguards, but it is derived from the provisions of the WTO Safeguards Agreement. Situations such as these, which are not explicitly contemplated in the law, are a source of confusion when one is evaluating the framework of application of measures in Chile.

Furthermore, the bilateral agreements have established other limitations to the application of these measures, which add exceptions to them. Thus, safeguards have become more complex in terms of their application, administration, and surveillance, and they are less effective.

Table 4.5 shows some of the rules on measures.[12] The first rule refers to temporary bilateral safeguards that exclusively affect trade between the parties and are normally applied during the liberalization period. Once the tariff elimination program concludes, they cannot be applied except with the authorization of the affected party. A second category of safeguards introduced in treaties is aimed at addressing the situation of more politically sensitive sectors. In particular, these rules have applied to the agricultural and textile sectors, where the Chilean counterpart has demanded the safeguards. For both sectors, countries must follow certain rules before applying a measure,[13] and there are limits on the types of measures they may apply. Normally, only tariffs may be applied, and the rate of such tariffs must be set at the lowest level in force between the time when the liberalization program started and the time when the safeguard was adopted. Moreover, compensation equivalent to the trade affected by the safeguard must be offered.

TABLE 4.5 Chile: Global Safeguards and Bilateral Agreements

	Bilateral safeguard provisions[a]				WTO safeguard provisions	
Agreement	Period	Sectors	Investigation	Compensation	Includes	Contents
Canada	Temporary[b]	General, textile	Yes	Yes	Yes	Any party that applies an emergency measure in agreement with article XIX of GATT 1994 and the WTO Safeguards Agreement will exclude imported goods from the other party from the measure, unless (a) imports from the other party represent a substantial share in total imports and (b) imports from the other party will significantly contribute to the serious damage or damage threat caused by such imports.
Mexico	Temporary[b]	General	Yes	Yes	Yes	The same as Canada, except that the measures applied to such goods will solely and exclusively consist of tariff measures, and the increase of the tariff rate for the original good must not exceed the lowest of (a) the most-favored-nation customs tariff applied when the measure is adopted and (b) the most-favored-nation customs tariff applied the day before the effective date of the treaty.
Mercosur	Permanent	General	Yes	Yes	No	
Peru	Temporary[b]	General	Yes	No	Yes	The best treatment granted by the parties.
Korea, Rep. of	Yes	Not specified	Not specified	Not specified	Yes	The parties maintain their rights and obligations in virtue of article XIX of GATT and the WTO Safeguards Agreement. The actions undertaken in agreement with article XIX of GATT and the Safeguards Agreement are not subject to chapter 19 of the present treaty
United States	Temporary	General, agriculture (automatic), and textile	Yes	Yes	Yes	The parties will not impose a safeguard measure to a good that is subject to a measure that the party has imposed by virtue of article XIX of GATT 1994 and the Safeguards Agreement. Neither will a party be able to maintain a safeguard measure on a good that might be subject to a safeguard article that the party imposes by virtue of XIX of GATT 1994 and the Safeguards Agreement.
European Union	Yes	Agriculture (automatic)	No	Yes	Yes	The suspension right referred to in paragraph 2 of article 8 of the WTO Safeguards Agreement will not be exercised between the parties during the first 18 months in which a safeguard measure is in force on condition that the measure has been adopted as the result of a rise in imports in absolute terms and that the measure is in compliance with the provisions of the WTO Safeguards Agreement.

Source: Direcon, Ministry of Foreign Affairs, http://www.direcon.cl.

a. The bilateral treaties listed contemplate a bilateral safeguard; have provisions for the application of WTO safeguards, including individualized elements such as investigation requirements and compensation; or both.

b. At the end of the transition period, an emergency bilateral measure can be adopted to address cases of serious damage or threat of damage to a national industry.

Finally, the terms and conditions necessary to exempt one of the parties from the application of WTO safeguard measures must be considered. Such an exemption has the effect of decreasing the effectiveness of the measure because it generates incentives to divert trade toward the partner that the measure does not affect. At the same time, however, it benefits exporters who are exempted from the measures.

Therefore, in the safeguards regime applied by Chile, measures have a rather limited effect, because of both the general regime and the provisions negotiated in bilateral treaties. On the one hand, the goal of the regime is to provide temporary relief rather than long-term industrial policy. (Two years would not be long enough for an industry to design and apply major economic adjustments.) On the other hand, the legislation gives a strong signal to industries that suffer more permanent structural problems, in the sense that they will not be able to resort to this type of relief to promote an adjustment. Chile's legislation offers more adequate alternatives, such as direct support to displaced workers. In the long run, however, this situation could result in political problems.

In the 1999–2002 period, seven safeguard measures were adopted (table 4.6). The traditional agricultural sector was the main user of the measures, which have been successfully questioned by Argentina and other trading partners in the context of the WTO. These questions led to the creation of a dispute settlement panel to analyze the safeguard measures that Chile applied to wheat imports.[14]

In this case, the WTO panel ruled against Chile, as it considered that Chile had acted in a way that was incompatible with the country's obligations (a) by not providing the relevant minutes of the sessions held by the CNDP in an adequate means so that they could be considered a "published" report; (b) because the commission failed to prove the existence of an unexpected development of circumstances and because the report did not include grounded findings and conclusions on this matter; (c) because the commission failed to prove the similarity or direct competition of products manufactured by the domestic industry and, therefore, did not identify the domestic industry; (d) because contrary to the WTO rules, the commission did not prove the increase in imports of products subject to safeguard measures; (e) because the commission did not prove the existence of a threat of serious injury; (f) because the commission failed to prove a causal relation; and (g) because the commission did not make sure that the measures were limited to what was necessary to prevent or repair the damage and facilitate the readjustment. In sum, the safeguard measures were not based on the requirements of article XIX of GATT 1994 and the WTO Safeguards Agreement.

This experience shows that even when safeguard measures are applied in a more restrictive way than contemplated by the WTO agreement, this practice does not guarantee that the requirements of the agreement are fulfilled. It is not enough to maintain a restricted safeguards regime to ensure adequate use of measures.

TABLE 4.6 Chile: Safeguard Investigations, 1999–2003

Diario Oficial initiation date	Name of product	Measure rate (%)	Country of origin	*Diario Oficial* definitive measure date	Measure effective date	Measure termination date	Measure duration
September 9, 1999[a]	Wheat, flour, sugar, and vegetable oils	Variable	All	January 22, 2000	January 22, 2000	November 26, 2000	10 months
February 9, 2000	Synthetic fiber socks	13	All	November 8, 2000	November 8, 2000	April 27, 2001	4 months
November 4, 2000	Wheat, flour, sugar, and vegetable oils[b]	Variable	All	November 25, 2000	November 25, 2000	November 27, 2001	12 months
June 21, 2000	Powdered and liquid ultra heat treatment milk	12	All	January 10, 2001	January 10, 2001	July 13, 2001	6 months
April 19, 2001	Synthetic fiber socks[c]	6	All[d]	April 30, 2001	April 30, 2001	October 31, 2001	6 months
April 5, 2002	Steel products: hot-rolled steel and wire rod rolls and sheets	10	All[d]	July 16, 2002	July 16, 2002	July 16, 2003	12 months
June 8, 2002	Remaining fructose and fructose syrups, with a fructose content over the dry product higher than 50% in weight	14	All[d]	November 19, 2002	November 19, 2002	February 14, 2003	3 months

Source: BCCH; http://www.cndp.cl.

a. From this investigation the initiation dates correspond to safeguard measures.

b. Safeguard extension dated January 22, 2000. For wheat and wheat flour, the measure was terminated by Directive 244 exempted (Diario Oficial, July 27, 2001), and for vegetable oils, by Directive 559 exempted, (Diario Oficial, November 20, 2001).

c. Safeguard extension dated November 8, 2000.

d. Except imports from Canada, Mexico, and Peru.

Another interesting case refers to the investigation of safeguards for steel imports. These safeguards were requested in the context of the adoption of safeguard measures by the United States and the adoption or threat of adoption of similar measures by the international community. Although measures were exclusively adopted for three types of specific products, included in five tariff items, the application made by the Chilean industry, requesting measures for 17 product categories classified in 21 items, was rejected. In this case, the opposition of steel product consumers resulted in a decision to moderate the pressure for measures in favor of the industry because it showed the negative impact that the measures would have on the exports of manufactured products and, consequently, on labor.

Review and Evaluation of the Chilean Institutional Framework

The context in which the CNDP was created in 1981 and the type of measures adopted by this entity support the idea that the objective of the commission was to alleviate the political pressures generated by the difficult economic situation rather than to correct problems originated by the "price distortions of goods." In the second half of the 1980s, the commission supported the liberalization process that started in 1985.

During the 1990s and until the present day, this philosophy has been maintained. The legislation has undergone modifications to adjust the instruments used to support the economic opening and international commitments. However, the use of these instruments has developed to target alleged distortions. The law has maintained the criterion that measures should be effective for only one year and that their renewal entails a de novo investigation procedure, which implies an important cost for the applicant. That limitation is also a signal, because the protection offered by this legislation is considered to be and essentially is temporary, and exceptional treatments are limited in time and in the types of instruments.

From the point of view of the operation of the commission, the entry into effect of the WTO meant having to follow the WTO's procedures in accordance with the requirements of the antidumping agreement and, once safeguard legislation was adopted, the corresponding WTO agreement.

Over time, the commission has refined the procedures it follows in performing its duties. Its analytical methodology has been enhanced to fulfill the requirements of WTO agreements, including hearing and transparency procedures. Additionally, the commission's actions and decisions are subject to the review requirements of WTO committees, to the notification requirements of the agreements, and to the reviews of the Trade Policy Review Mechanism. This oversight has been an important source of discipline over the procedures and decisions of the commission.

Since formal safeguard legislation was passed, the measures adopted have been the subject of consultations—and even of a panel—that have been requested by the affected WTO members. These events represent an important disciplinary element for the commission and have been helpful to the commission as it has sought to refine its own procedures. The commission has recently adopted measures to increase transparency and access to information. However, it has not been possible to prove the practical scope of these modifications, because there have been no new investigations.

Chilean legislation is quite conservative, especially if compared with international practice. However, its application has not been free of criticism, and it is necessary to seek mechanisms that combine limitations set forth in the law and self-imposed limitations that can change under pressure.

Some sectors consider that the commission has not been sufficiently active. They would like the government to take a more decisive initiative to protect the industry without their having to incur the costs of submitting applications. Additionally, these sectors consider the procedures of the commission very slow; they feel that the commission reacts late, when the damage is already done. This criticism has sometimes been taken up by political groups linked to the agricultural and textile sectors, which have lobbied for a more active performance of the commission in favor of the sectors affected by what they feel is unfair competition.

However, both private sector representatives and academic economists consider the safeguards and unfair competition systems to be mechanisms that favor protectionist sectors, which, sheltered by these situations, seek to elude the demands generated by economic liberalization.

Although protectionist interests that wish to avoid external competition can capture these mechanisms (as in the case of much international legislation), the Chilean experience shows that, under certain circumstances, the mechanisms have supported the liberalization process. The crisis that took place at the beginning of the 1980s put the existing model in serious difficulty, so a more pragmatic approach was followed to conduct trade policy (Meller 1996). In this context, creating a mechanism to temporarily alleviate the strong demands for protection was a necessary step to continue pursuing the strategic goal of economic liberalization. In fact, from 1985, an economic team orientated toward liberalization resumed the tariff reduction process. In March 1985, tariffs were uniformly reduced to 30 percent, and in June of the same year, only three months later, they were again reduced to 20 percent. Finally, in January 1988, tariffs were reduced to 15 percent. However, even though the tariff reduction affected all sectors equally, a selective and temporary protection was established for politically sensitive sectors—especially for some agricultural products, textiles, and shoes, through the Subsidies Commission and CNDP and probably also through other less known means. Thus, this mechanism had a supporting role for the second liberalization process, which started in 1985.[15] This situation coincides with the arguments of Fischer and Prusa (1999) and Fischer and Osorio (2004), in the sense that, in the context of negotiations between two or more countries, safeguard or unfair competition clauses contribute to a more profound opening than would be achieved without these mechanisms and can even increase social welfare under certain conditions. In the context of a unilateral opening process, such as the one that prevailed in Chile, the possibility of selectively resorting to temporary protection had the same role.

In the 1990s, in the context of a democratic regime subject to periodic elections and the usual pressures of the system, maintaining an open economy rendered it more necessary to have a mechanism of this nature, which could grant some limited flexibility to conducting economic policy—more so when the system is subject to national and international rules that allow the authority to base its decisions on them.

How was Chile able to maintain this policy approach under a democratic regime in spite of having undergone a strong economic deceleration process since 1998? The Chilean institutional framework for safeguards and unfair competition is part of a more general economic institutional framework. In fact, as Bauer (1998) points out, the constitution of 1980 contains a set of economic principles. An important example is that the legal initiative to establish or modify any tax belongs to the executive branch. Consequently, members of the legislature cannot of their own initiative take action in this area. This provision does not prevent the legislative branch from influencing—or seeking to influence—tax or tariff matters; as we have seen, safeguards legislation arises from a negotiation between both branches. But it implies that the leadership of the economic authority in customs tariffs matters, supported by constitutional provisions, is key to maintaining the orientation of trade policy.

A second element that has contributed to Chile's ability to maintain its policy approach is the existence of a relatively strong consensus on the global benefits of the economic reforms adopted since 1973. There is, in both the business and political sectors, a favorable environment for economic policies that promote liberalization, although there are specific initiatives against it. This favorable environment has not prevented certain sectors, such as the traditional agriculture sector and, to a lesser degree, the textile and steel industries, from receiving support for their demands for more protection from certain political sectors, although so far those demands have been limited.

However, there is scope to improve the Chilean institutional framework and grant it a higher level of autonomy and transparency. For example, at present the

CNDP is constituted of a majority of governmental representatives or members appointed by political authorities. Although in practice this composition does not mean that the commission will adopt an active protectionist approach, there is no guarantee that it will not do so in the future or that it will be immune to pressure from interest groups. In fact, there are diverse mechanisms through which interested parties seek to exert pressure to influence decisions, such as organized demonstrations and even lobbying activities.

Therefore, it is relevant to consider modifying the composition of the commission to include representatives appointed by a mechanism that will ensure a higher level of autonomy. There is little international experience, however, for such a mechanism, and, therefore, it is important to analyze why this mechanism is normally under government control. Such a proposal poses the problem of securing a form of financing so that the commission could have autonomy, not only in the appointment of its members but also in its operation. An aspect that must be assessed when considering a higher level of independence is the effect that this type of measure could have on international relations. As was explained previously, when the CNDP started operating, Chile suffered threats of trade retaliation if it adopted trade defense measures. Therefore, it is also necessary to assess how to adequately manage the international dimension of the possibility of greater autonomy for the institution, especially regarding safeguard mechanisms.

An additional aspect refers to the requirement that administrative measures linked to definitive determinations are to undergo (a) reviews by courts or arbitration, (b) judiciary or administrative procedures, and (c) the review of determinations contemplated by the WTO Antidumping Agreement. In this respect, there are, at present, several mechanisms in Chile by means of which the decisions of the commission can be reviewed. In the first place, one of the roles of the Comptroller General of the Republic (Contraloria General de la República) is to control the administrative acts of the executive branch. A second option is "recourse to protection," an option that is widely used to protect the "economic public order" established by the constitution with respect to private economic rights. This mechanism allows any person who feels that his or her economic rights are not respected by the state or by other private agents to request an immediate judiciary review. The submission of this request must be immediately reviewed by the corresponding appellate court and is used to prevent or correct economic damage (see Bauer 1998).

However, this review mechanism could be improved by means of a specialized review body such as the recently created Competition Court. This option would give more support to the decisions adopted by the president with respect to the recommendations of the commission. Moreover, it would protect against lobbying actions or other forms of pressure that could be used and that are aimed at influencing the decisions of the executive. Furthermore, the actual composition of the commission could remain unaltered, because it would not be necessary to grant the CNDP the higher levels of independence proposed before.

Additionally, the commission could introduce additional transparency into its operations. Since the WTO panel issued its conclusions, the CNDP has worked to correct its procedures. The commission has increased the amount of information it makes available to the public on its findings and on the grounds for its conclusions. The opportunity for interested parties to comment during the investigation process on the accuracy and on the relevance of information has also improved. However, there is still scope for change. For example, the Report of the Technical Secretariat could be made public if the sections that the interested parties would consider confidential were removed. Together with the minutes of the commission, which record the findings and the grounds for decisions, the report could be used to help the CNDP function more effectively and to clarify better how it ponders the different evidence.

Finally, the commission could have a wider approach to review of applications. At present, a mandatory review of the effect of measures on domestic market competition and on consumers or users of the product who are subject to the measures is not incorporated in the respective WTO agreements or in Chilean legislation. Although such a review can be considered, at present there is no obligation for one, and, therefore, it is again subject to the criterion of the commission. If we take into account that in many cases where measures have been requested the applicant has important market power (for example, the sugar, steel, and matches sectors), these considerations are particularly relevant.

The improvements proposed are always limited by the political context of democratic regimes, and when we want to improve an instrument of this nature, efforts often result in a worse situation. Once more the leadership role played by economic authorities is key to assess the need and opportunity to introduce these improvements.

Notes

1. Before the enactment of Law 18,525, article 186 of Law 16,464 delegated the faculty to suspend, reduce, or raise customs duties to the president of Chile. From the entry into effect of the constitution of 1980, which established the legal reserve principle, the duty (both the rate and the substantial elements that determine it) must be established by law, and this action cannot be delegated to the administrative authority.

2. FNE is in charge of investigating actions against market competition and of submitting its findings to the relevant authorities.

3. These numbers refer to the 1981–87 period. (See BCCH, CNDP Secretaría Técnica 2003 and http://www.cndp.cl.)

4. In fact, in some cases there were Latin American countries that expressed their intention to adopt disguised restrictions if Chile adopted countervailing duties against their exports, because they considered that such a measure would lead developed countries to react against them.

5. Chilean regulations provide that a 3 percent, 5 percent, 8 percent, 10 percent, 12 percent, 15 percent, 18 percent, or 20 percent ad valorem surcharge may be established.

6. According to the Chilean constitution, duties can be established or modified only by means of a law proposed by the executive branch and approved by the parliament. In this case, articles 9 and 11 of Law 18,525 establish the duties and the requirements that must be fulfilled for their application. The responsibility of the president is only to confirm compliance with these requirements through a supreme decree after having received a favorable report from the CNDP.

7. In fact, the number of applications submitted in 1990 proves that there was an expectation in this sense.

8. Responses given by the government of Chile before the WTO (WTO 2002; WTO Committee on Anti-Dumping Practices, Committee on Subsidies and Countervailing Measures 1995).

9. See Peña (2001) for an analysis of the practical application of the provisions of the Antidumping Agreement in Chilean legislation.

10. The technical criterion applied is the "nondumped import price method." The best information available has not been frequently used, and so far, the possibility of negotiating price agreements has not been applied either.

11. After the two-year period, a countervailing or antidumping duty can be requested for a product subject to safeguard measures, provided that the requirements established by the law are fulfilled.

12. In bilateral trade negotiations, there is tension about safeguard disciplines. On the one hand, there is interest in supporting a sector that could be affected by the opening. On the other hand, there is also interest in defending the exporters who will be affected by the adoption of safeguard measures. The instrument and the compensation clause can provide the construction of a politically acceptable balance.

13. In some agreements, there are agricultural safeguards that automatically apply. For example, in the case of the Chile–United States free trade agreement, safeguards automatically apply to specific products.

14. The panel analyzed two different matters: (a) the price band system that is applied to wheat, wheat flour, and vegetable oil imports and (b) the safeguard measures that benefited those products (WTO 2002).

15. The first liberalization process started in 1973.

References

Bauer, Carl J. 1998. "Derecho y economía en la Constitución de 1980," *Perspectivas* 2 (1): 23–47.

BCCH (Banco Central de Chile), CNDP Secretaría Técnica. 2003. *Estadisticas y antecedentes sobre investigaciones.* http://www.cndp.cl/interior_estadis_indicecuadros.asp.

Finger, J. Michael. 1987. "Antidumping and Antisubsidy Measures." In *The Uruguay Round: A Handbook for the Multilateral Trade Negotiations*, ed. J. Michael. Finger and Andrej Olechowski, 153–61. Washington, DC: World Bank.

———. ed. 1993. *Antidumping: How It Works and Who Gets Hurt.* Ann Arbor: University of Michigan Press.

Fischer, Ronald D., and Manuel Osorio. 2004. "Why Do We Need Antidumping Rules?" http://www.dii.uchile.cl/~cea/pags/publicaciones/index.html.

Fischer, Ronald D., and Thomas J. Prusa. 1999. "Contingent Protection as Better Insurance." http://www.dii.uchile.cl/~cea/pags/publicaciones/index.html or http://www.nber.org/papers/w6933.

French-Davis, Ricardo. 1980. "Liberalización de importaciones: La experiencia chilena." *Colección Estudios de Cieplan* 4 (November): 17–51.

———. 2003. *Entre el neoliberalismo y el crecimiento con equidad: Tres décadas de política económica en Chile.* 3rd ed. Santiago: Dolmen Ediciones.

Meller, Patricio. 1996. *Un siglo de economía política chilena (1890–1990).* Santiago: Editorial Andrés Bello.

Peña, Gloria. 2001. "Las prácticas desleales en los procesos de integración del continente americano: La experiencia chilena." In *Las prácticas desleales de comercio en el proceso de integración comercial en el continente americano: La experiencia de América del Norte y Chile*, ed. Sergio López-Ayllón and Gustavo Vega Cánovas, 24–57. Mexico City: Biblioteca Jurídica Virtual. http://www.bibliojuridica.org/libros/1/33/5.pdf.

WTO (World Trade Organization) 2002. "Chile—Price Band System and Safeguard Measures Relating to Certain Agricultural Products—Report of the Panel." WT/DS207/R, Geneva, WTO.

WTO (World Trade Organization) Committee on Anti-Dumping Practices, Committee on Subsidies and Countervailing Measures. 1995. "Replies to Questions Posed by Australia, Canada, European Communities, Hong Kong, and Venezuela Concerning the Notification of Chilean Laws and Regulations." G/ADP/W/156, Geneva, WTO.

5

APPLICATION OF SAFEGUARDS AND ANTIDUMPING DUTIES IN COLOMBIA

Mauricio Reina and Sandra Zuluaga

In some major respects, Colombia's recent experience in applying safeguards and antidumping duties differs from international trends. On the one hand, the number of investigations that Colombia has conducted is substantially lower than that recorded in most of the hemisphere's large- and medium-sized countries.[1] On the other hand, although the trend toward using antidumping more frequently than safeguards is growing around the world, no such trend is observed in Colombia.

Several factors could explain the distinctive features of Colombia's experience: the relative ignorance of the private sector regarding the meaning and scope of the instruments, the little discretion the government has shown in their use, and the stability and robustness of the institutions linked to the investigations and the decision-making process. Also, the interviews conducted in the preparation of this chapter show that there is an official awareness of the importance of preserving the competitiveness of production chains to improve the country's performance in international markets.

This chapter seeks to analyze the evolution of the application of safeguards and antidumping duties in Colombia since the beginning of the 1990s as well as to explain their determining factors and the role these instruments have played in the country's trade policy. The first section summarizes the recent evolution of Colombia's trade policy, the framework within which the above-mentioned instruments were developed. The second section contains an evaluation of the

This chapter has taken into account the points of view of numerous Colombian government officials and private sector representatives. We are grateful for their opinions.

background and the current status of legislation related to safeguards and antidumping duties. The third section analyzes the various safeguards and antidumping investigations carried out since 1990 and discusses some case studies. The fourth section deals with aspects related to the political economy of the application of such instruments. Finally, the fifth section presents some conclusions.

The Recent Evolution of Trade Policy

Like most Latin American countries during the second half of the last century, Colombia applied an industrialization strategy based on import substitution. Although this policy promoted the diversification of the productive structure, by the end of the 1980s, the protectionist strategy had been exhausted. The closed economy had fostered concentrated property structures, high prices, low product quality, and few incentives for innovation. At the same time, the high cost of imports made production based on foreign raw materials more expensive, thus generating an antiexport bias in the economy.

Faced with this economic situation, the government implemented a trade liberalization policy that began at the end of the 1980s, was consolidated at the beginning of the 1990s, and extended into the regional integration processes. These initiatives not only reduced the level of protection of the economy but also created a new role for private agents in the formulation of trade policy. Although protectionism favored the development of a lobbying culture among businesspeople to adjust policy decisions toward their interests, liberalization significantly reduced the space for that sort of lobbying.

The Opening of Trade

The liberalization policy comprised the elimination of quantitative restrictions to imports, the reduction of tariffs and number of tariff levels, the reduction of the number of procedures required for foreign trade, and a series of institutional reforms (Hommes, Montenegro, and Roda 1994).[2] The measures taken at the beginning of the 1990s reduced the percentage of tariff positions subject to quantitative restrictions from 73 percent to 1 percent while the economy's nominal average tariff fell from levels close to 100 percent to 11.1 percent, and the effective protection was set at 26.2 percent (see figure 5.1).

In the context of the new trade policy, the agricultural sector received special treatment. The distortions of the international markets led to the design of a variable tariff arrangement for a sizable number of products (namely, price bands). With the price band mechanism, tariffs are automatically increased when international prices fall below a certain level. By the same token, tariffs are reduced when

FIGURE 5.1 Colombia: Average Tariff, 1986–2002

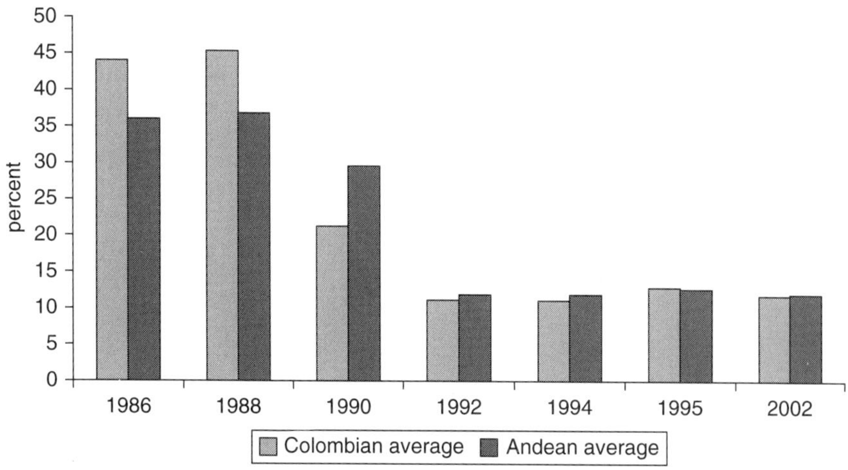

Source: Echavarría and Gamboa (2001); UNCTAD TRAINS database.

international prices increase above a given level. The price band mechanism was harmonized at the Andean level, and it currently covers 13 main products and close to 150 tariff positions of derivative or substitute products.[3]

Although the original objective of the Andean System of Bands was to insulate regional economies from the fluctuations of international agricultural prices, the design of the instrument had a protectionist bias that was soon apparent. In fact, the average tariff applied to the products that were part of the Andean system reached levels close to 60 percent in the last few years. Although Colombian authorities justified this situation based on the argument that this protection is a way to deal with the subsidies of developed countries, several papers have shown that the protection generated by price bands exceeded the level of distortion generated by the subsidies (Norton and Balcázar 2003). Thus, a good share of Colombia's agricultural sector has managed to remain outside the liberalization trends that began in 1990.

Finally, it should be mentioned that these trade reforms took place in a context of strong currency devaluations that persisted almost uninterrupted until the end of 1997 (see figure 5.2). Since the beginning of 1999, there have been corrections to this trend and it is currently deemed that the real rate of exchange is close to its equilibrium level. However, as will be seen later, in certain periods the drop in the real exchange rate did not result in increased applications for antidumping duties and safeguards.

FIGURE 5.2 Colombia: Real Exchange Rate Index

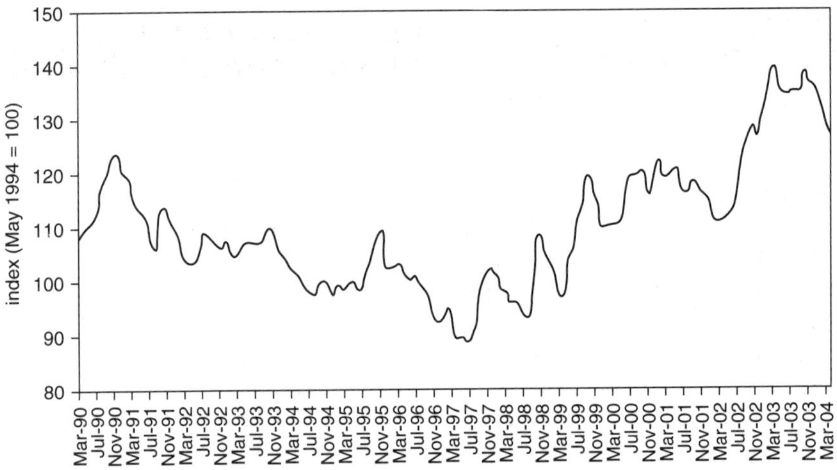

Source: Banco de la República.

Regional Negotiations

In addition to the tariff reduction adopted between 1990 and 1991, the main factor that transformed Colombia's tariff structure was the negotiations leading to greater regional integration. In that area, the most significant processes were the strengthening of the Andean integration, the negotiation with Mexico in the framework of the Group of Three, and the signing of an agreement with Chile. Of these processes, the one with the greatest effect on Colombia's tariff structure was the strengthening of Andean integration (Reina, Zuluaga, and Gamboa 1996).

In December 1991, the heads of the Andean countries signed the Barahona Act, which reiterated the purpose of establishing a regional free trade area and a common external tariff. These objectives were almost totally met. In 1992, the Andean Free Trade Area became effective, and República Bolivariana de Venezuela and Colombia established a common external tariff. At the end of the same year, Peru suspended the liberalization program and decided to maintain significant exceptions to regional free trade. On their part, República Bolivariana de Venezuela, Colombia, and Ecuador moved forward in harmonizing their tariffs, though in an imperfect manner, because the latter invoked its condition of country with a lower level of relative development to maintain a tariff below that of its partners for several products.

During the mid-1990s, Colombia negotiated agreements with Chile and Mexico that involved a lesser scope than the Andean integration. The agreement with

TABLE 5.1 Preferential Tariffs Granted by Colombia: Liberalization Levels

Countries	Preferential tariffs granted by Colombia
Argentina	Average tariff: 10.7%
Bolivia	Free trade
Brazil	Average tariff: 10.6%
Canada	11.7%
Chile	91% of tariff items excepted from duties in 1999
Costa Rica	11.7%
Ecuador	Free trade
El Salvador	11.7%
Guatemala	11.7%
Honduras	11.7%
Mexico	Average tariff: 4.9%
Nicaragua	11.7%
Peru	List of preferences
United States	11.7%
Venezuela, R. B. de	Free trade
Average MFN tariff level	11.7%

Source: Reina and Zuluaga (2001).

Chile became effective in January 1994, and it is restricted to liberalizing trade in goods. The agreement with Mexico was negotiated in the framework of the Treaty of the Group of Three and comprises, besides the liberalization of goods, agreements on the so-called new generation issues: services, intellectual property, government procurement, investment, and dispute resolution, among others. Table 5.1 shows the preferential tariff levels granted by Colombia to some countries under the signed regional agreements.

As a result of the regional integration process, the geographical distribution of Colombia's trade flows was partially modified. Between 1989 and 2003, the share of Colombian exports going to the Andean Community countries increased significantly. The share of Colombian exports going to other countries in the hemisphere such as those of Central America and Mexico also increased. During the same period, imports to Colombia from Andean countries and Mexico also increased their share, at the expense of those from the United States, the European Union, and Japan.

Main Institutional Reforms

The Ministry of Foreign Trade, currently the Ministry of Trade, Industry, and Tourism, was created in 1991, taking over the policies that previously had been the responsibility of the Ministry of Economic Development. The Ministry of Foreign Trade's major functions include controlling the enforcement of foreign trade policies and procedures as well as formulating and executing regional negotiation strategies.

As a result of the reforms introduced in 1991, the Colombian Institute of Foreign Trade (Incomex) became responsible for the prevention and investigation of unfair trade practices. The institute's deputy director of unfair practices filled the void that existed before liberalization when there was no specific agency in charge of issues such as dumping and underinvoicing of imports. Then, in 2003, the deputy director of trade practices in the Ministry of Trade, Industry, and Tourism took on the responsibility for investigating unfair trade practices. The deputy director is currently the investigating authority in cases of dumping, subsidies, and safeguards and is charged with investigating the merits of applications, carrying out investigations, and making the pertinent recommendations to decision makers.

Evolution of Antidumping and Safeguard Rules

The commercial opening that took place in Colombia at the beginning of the 1990s required the development of legal instruments to deal with the foreign competition that previously had been neutralized through protectionist policies. Although Colombia had joined the General Agreement on Tariffs and Trade (GATT) in 1981, the development of general safeguard rules was limited. By contrast, within the framework of the Andean Group, the application of trade preferences of greater magnitude caused Andean safeguards to be used.[4]

The design of antidumping mechanisms in Colombia dates to the beginning of the trade liberalization in the late 1980s, whereas the rules on safeguards were implemented in 1994. Thus, the first two antidumping rules (Decrees 1500 and 2444 of 1990) show the traces of a protectionist approach. Law 7 of 1991 provided the basis for reform, Decree 150 of 1993 implemented reform of antidumping rules, and Decree 809 of 1994 implemented Colombia's first safeguard rules.

Background of Antidumping Legislation

Antidumping legislation was devised as a complement to the trade liberalization process and was first regulated by Decree 1500 of 1990. The instrument was presented to the producers as an option to confront unfair trade practices, with the intent of reducing their concerns about imports. This first norm established that imposing antidumping duties would respond to the public interest with preventive or corrective purposes.[5] The causes were limited to serious injury or threat of serious injury to production in Colombia. Decree 1500 was replaced by Decree 2440 of

1990, which made some adjustments in the deadlines for different stages of investigations and introduced the concept of injury by reason of massive imports.

In 1993, as a result of the antidumping discussion in the GATT context, a new decree was passed incorporating the refinements that had been consolidated in the multilateral scenario on evidence of injury and threat of injury as well as on investigation procedures. This decree changed once again the setup of the Trade Practices Committee thus allowing them to adjust the new institutional arrangements for foreign trade expressed in Law 7 of 1991. In addition to the director of Incomex, the agency responsible for the investigations, the members of the committee included a delegate of the Senior Foreign Trade Council (Consejo Superior de Comercio Exterior), an adviser to the same council, the vice minister of trade, and the vice ministers of the sectors related to the investigation.[6] This rule established that, before making its recommendation to the Foreign Trade Ministry, the committee must take into consideration the opinion of the superintendent of Trade and Industry, who is responsible for safeguarding the rights of consumers.

Decree 150 of 1993 was repealed by Decree 299 of 1995 that incorporates the progress of the Uruguay Round into Colombia's legislation. The most important changes include limiting the duration of duties to a maximum of five years, with the possibility of reviewing the duties one year after their effectiveness. The process of adjustment to the multilateral arrangements was completed with Decree 991 of 1998, the rule currently in force. For the first time in Colombia, this measure introduced specific antidumping legislation; the previous decrees had regulated dumping and subsidies jointly.

Current Antidumping Regulations

Decree 991 of 1998 regulates the application of antidumping duties for both World Trade Organization (WTO) member countries and nonmember countries. In the case of investigations of non-WTO members, the sectoral representation of domestic production requires a lower percentage to request an investigation. It is also possible to apply provisional duties to these countries from the beginning of the investigation.

Causes for the Application of Duties Colombia's antidumping legislation considers the following three elements required by the Multilateral Trade System for the application of antidumping measures: (a) the existence of dumping or price differentials between the exporter's domestic market and the destination market; (b) injury, or the threat of injury or of significantly retarding the establishment of a branch of domestic production; and (c) a causal relationship between the dumping and the above situations that may be faced by domestic production.

The legislation in force is almost a copy of the multilateral agreement. As such, the legislation maintains the flexibility that the Antidumping Agreement affords to investigating authorities. The Colombian Authority may select the methodology to calculate the normal value (that is, the price that is used as a benchmark to compare with the price of exports). Similarly, the authority may suggest the level of antidumping duty anywhere within the dumping margin it determines; there in no rule limiting that duty to the amount needed to prevent the injury caused to domestic production. (However, note that the regulations for the calculation of the duties do contemplate the need to consider the effect of the measures on the domestic market and on the domestic prices of the product.) Colombian rules for the determination of injury or threat of injury likewise preserve the flexibility the WTO agreement provides. On how to determine material retardation of the establishment of a branch of domestic production, Columbian regulations provide that the factors to be reviewed include feasibility studies, loans negotiated, and machinery purchase agreements leading to new projects or the expansion of existing plants, as well as evidence indicating whether the domestic market is being adequately and sufficiently supplied.

Evidence to Be Submitted Colombia's legislation replicates the multilateral requirements for the information to initiate an antidumping investigation. It requires that the product be identified within the specifics of Colombia's statistical nomenclature. Furthermore, the legislation requires submission of evidence not only on price behavior (the differential between home and export prices) but also on the effects of this dumping on Colombian production. Besides the need to submit the respective evidence of all the required information,[7] the requirements to open an investigation also consider the possibility of conducting verification visits to the applicants, a practice that is not widespread and that in some countries is limited to exporters.

Procedures, Instances, and Time Frames The technical elements of the antidumping process are handled by the deputy director of trade practices of the Ministry of Trade, Industry, and Tourism. Technical findings are reported to the Committee on Trade Practices (Comité de Prácticas Comerciales).[8] This committee determines if the conditions required for a restrictive action have been demonstrated and makes the final recommendation on the action (if any) that will be taken. The superintendent of Trade and Industry is involved in the decision on a possible price agreement, the final outcome of the investigation, and the review of the antidumping measures established.

The maximum time to carry out and conclude an investigation is eight months, counted from its initiation. The deputy director of trade practices has 20 business days to evaluate the investigation application. Once the investigation has been opened, questionnaires have to be remitted to the interested parties, who have 40 calendar days to answer them. The deputy director of trade practices has 65 calendar days from the beginning of the investigation to make a preliminary decision and establish provisional duties, as may be the case. Once a preliminary determination has been adopted, the deputy director of trade practices may obtain evidence, make verification visits, and conduct hearings with the parties. In total, the deputy director has three months to submit a final report to the Trade Practices Committee, counted from the preliminary determination. The committee issues an opinion that has to be circulated to the interested parties, who have 10 calendar days to make their comments. Subsequently, the committee has 10 calendar days to review comments and produce an opinion for the minister who, in turn, has 7 calendar days to adopt a decision.

Duration of the Measures Antidumping duties can be maintained for five years, extendable for equal successive periods, provided that the investigating authority determines, through investigation, that removal of the duties would likely lead to continuation or recurrence of dumping and injury.

Background of the Legislation on Safeguards

Colombia's safeguard legislation dates back to 1994 when the process of economic liberalization had already been consolidated. Safeguard rules stemmed, on the one hand, from the need to respond to the demands of the private sector for instruments to exercise an industrial policy and, on the other hand, to comply with the requirements derived from Colombia's membership in the WTO. The legislation, enacted by Decree 809 of 1994, applied both to tariff changes not in violation of multilateral commitments and to tariffs that exceeded the tariff levels consolidated before the WTO.

The regulations establish serious injury as a cause, defining it as an important and significant deterioration in the situation of one branch of national production, and require demonstration of a causal relationship between the increased imports and the injury. The application is to be filed with Incomex, as investigating authority, which reports to the Customs and Tariff Affairs Committee (Comité de Asuntos Aduaneros y Arancelarios). This committee, in turn, makes a recommendation to the Senior Foreign Trade Council, which is responsible for assessing the measure and providing an opinion to the government on its application.[9]

In addition to this regulation, Decree 2657 of 1994 was passed, applying specifically to countries with which Colombia has signed no agreements and which are not members of the WTO that impose regulations in addition to those mandated by multilateral (WTO) agreements. It provides for the application of a restriction without proof of injury or threat of injury by WTO standards. Such action, however, is limited to the discretion that Colombia holds within the ceiling tariff bindings the country has made through the WTO. Subsequently, certain limits were set to the application of provisional measures under this regulation, and a procedure was established to impose measures to countries with which Colombia has signed trade agreements.[10]

Decree 809 of 1994 was repealed in 1998 by Decree 152, which enacted legislation for WTO member countries in accordance with multilateral arrangements where the causes are serious injury or threat of serious injury. This legislation is currently in force for problems with imports from WTO member countries.

Additionally, in 1999, Decree 1407 regulated the "special safeguard," or "safeguard by reason of disruption," which applies to imports of any origin. However, when the investigation involves imports from a WTO member country, the requested tariff increase may not exceed the rate bound that Colombia agreed to at the Uruguay Round.[11] The conditions for restrictive action are less strict under this "special safeguard" procedure than under the "WTO safeguard" procedure.[12]

Current Regulations on Safeguards

The above overview shows the existence of several types of safeguard measures in Colombian legislation. On the one hand, those safeguard measures that are applicable to imports from WTO member countries include three categories: those applicable to agricultural and farm products, transition measures applicable to textiles and apparel in light of the WTO's agreement for that sector, and those applicable to the remaining products.

On the other hand, measures applicable to non-WTO member countries and the special safeguard, or safeguard by reason of disruption, allow for the increase of import duties above the Common External Tariff of the Andean Community, which applies to any country as long as the measures do not exceed the WTO consolidated tariff levels. Additionally, other safeguards apply to products that have been the object of tariff liberalization in the framework of Regional Integration Agreements, for example, the Andean safeguards, the safeguard in the Agreement of the Group of Three, and the safeguard of the agreement between Colombia and Chile.

This chapter focuses on the analysis of the safeguard for WTO member countries (Decree 152 of 1998) and the special safeguard (Decree 1407 of 1999). The former may be characterized as a safeguard by reason of injury and the latter as a safeguard by reason of disruption.

WTO Safeguard This section reviews the elements of the WTO safeguard procedure.

Causes for Measures The WTO safeguard (Decree 152 of 1998) requires imports of the affected products to have increased, whether in absolute terms or as compared with domestic production of like goods, and in conditions that cause or threaten to cause serious injury to a branch of domestic production. It also established that the investigation should prove a causal relationship between injury or the threat of injury and the increase in imports.

Evidence to Be Submitted The regulations require submitting financial and accounting information, signed by a public accountant, on the industry corresponding to the product to be investigated. They also require submitting information on the objectives that the applicant firm will attain within the so-called adjustment program, which refers to the adoption of modernization programs to increase competitiveness and adapt to the new competitive conditions.

Procedures, Instances, and Terms An investigation related to a safeguard by reason of injury lasts approximately 127 days in the technical instance, during which the Customs and Tariff Affairs Committee and the Senior Foreign Trade Council make their decisions. The former has 15 business days to review the technical report and make a recommendation to the latter. If the recommendation is positive, the Ministry of Trade is asked to conduct consultations with exporting country governments. Finally, the Senior Foreign Trade Council determines what action, if any, will be taken. The regulations allow the Senior Foreign Trade Council to request consultations with exporters even if the recommendation from the Customs and Tariff Affairs Committee is negative. Without a positive determination, of course, the Senior Foreign Trade Council cannot authorize restrictive action.

Terms of the Safeguard Measures Safeguard measures have a maximum term of four years, extendable for another four.

Special Safeguard Decree The decree regulating the special safeguard defines it as a "special procedure to impose safeguard measures."[13] This mechanism is not strictly a safeguard according to WTO parameters. The measure that is applied is a tariff increase (a) above the rate Colombia has in force (usually the common external tariff agreed with the Andean countries), but (b) for WTO member countries, it may not exceed the tariff level bound at the WTO. Because it is limited to action within Colombia's bound rates, this instrument has not been notified to the WTO as a safeguard.

The special safeguard differs in several ways from the general legislation established in 1998. First, the cause to invoke this rule is that an important proportion of a domestic production branch has suffered or could suffer a disruption by reason of an increase in imports or imports occurring in unfair conditions such as low prices or large quantities.[14] Second, the rule does not require an adjustment program to be submitted by the applicant firm.

Third, the rule shortens the period of investigation. It establishes that the deputy director of trade practices will have 20 business days to produce recommendations to the Customs and Tariff Affairs Committee, compared with 25 days under Decree 152 of 1998. In addition, all necessary visits and evidence must be completed within this 20-day term. The Customs and Tariff Affairs Committee has 5 business days to make its technical report and submit it to the Senior Foreign Trade Council, compared with 15 days under Decree 152 of 1998. Finally, the safeguard measures by reason of disruption are limited to the imposition of a duty, can remain in force only for two years, and are not extendable.

In summary, Colombia's legislation on dumping and safeguards follows the guidelines developed by the WTO at the multilateral level. However, two aspects of these regulations stand out because of their analytical interest. The first relates to the fact that there are two different decision-making instances for the application of duties and for the adoption of safeguard measures. The general modification of the tariff that a safeguard implies must have the approval of the instance studying tariff policy (Customs and Tariff Affairs Committee) and the president of the Republic. In contrast, a tariff modification resulting from a process of defense against unfair competition is the responsibility of the minister of trade.

The second factor relates to the special safeguard, which is not strictly a safeguard but a mechanism that makes it possible to increase tariffs above the Andean commitments without infringing WTO rules and that gives the government greater flexibility in the decision-making process.

Analysis of Dumping and Safeguard Investigations in Colombia

The first dumping and safeguards investigations in Colombia date back to the end of the 1990s and mid-1994, in coincidence with the implementation of each of the laws on these matters. Between 1990 and 2004, 37 dumping investigations took place in Colombia (an average of 2.6 cases per year) whereas 34 safeguards-related investigations took place between 1994 and 2004 (3.4 cases per year). The safeguard investigations that have been undertaken have been in large part about imports from within the Andean Community. During this period, 12 investigations were conducted in the Andean zone, whereas the investigations carried out within the framework of the WTO and for the special safeguard amount to 11 and 10 cases, respectively (see table 5.2). If the Andean safeguards were excluded, the yearly average would drop to 2.1 investigations per year.[15]

TABLE 5.2 Colombia: Investigations Conducted, 1990–2004

Type of investigation	Number of Investigations			Percentages				
	Conducted	No duties or measures imposed	In process	Conducted	No Imposition	In process	No imposition/ conducted	In process/ conducted
Dumping	37	14	4	52.1	60.9	44.4	37.8	10.8
Safeguard[a]	34	9	5	47.9	39.1	55.6	26.5	14.7
WTO	11	1	2	15.5	4.3	22.2	9.1	18.2
Special safeguard	10	5	2	14.1	21.7	22.2	50.0	20.0
Andean	12	3	0	16.9	13.0	0.0	25.0	0.0
AEC 24	1	0	1	1.4	0.0	11.1	0.0	100.0
Total	71	23	9	100.0	100.0	100.0	32.4	12.7

Source: Author calculations based on Ministry of Trade, Industry, and Tourism statistics. http://www.mincomercio.gov.c/VBeContent/documentos/operaciones/Practicas/estadisticasinvestigacione.

a. The information on safeguards is broken down in accordance with the existing legislation: Decree 152/98 for WTO member countries; Decree 1407/99 for all the so-called special safeguard countries; Andean rules; AEC 24, which is the agreement between Colombia and Chile within the framework of ALADI, using ALADI's Resolution No. 70.

Independent from whether the Andean safeguards are included in the calculation, Colombia has undertaken relatively more safeguard investigations and relatively fewer antidumping investigations than other countries. According to Finger (2002), between 1983 and 1993, an annual average of three safeguard measures were reported to the GATT, whereas the yearly average of antidumping cases was 164. Although the worldwide statistic is one safeguard case for every 55 cases of dumping per year, the ratio for Colombia is almost 1 to 1.

Evolution of Investigations, 1990–2004

Between 1990 and 2004, there were a total of 71 dumping and safeguard investigations in Colombia. Of these, 37 were dumping investigations and 34 were safeguard investigations. Of the latter, 17 percent were Andean safeguards, 14 percent special safeguards, and 15 percent WTO safeguards (see table 5.2).

In 23 cases out of the total 71 investigations conducted in the above period, no duties or measures were levied. A breakdown of the figures shows that 61 percent of the investigations where no duties were imposed correspond to dumping cases, compared with 39 percent for safeguard cases. Among the various classes of safeguards, the special safeguard accounts for the highest number of cases where no measures were applied, followed by the Andean safeguard. As of July 2004, 9 of the 71 investigations conducted were in process (4 cases of dumping and 5 of safeguards), of which 2 were submitted under the WTO rules and 2 under the special safeguard.

The highest number of antidumping applications was submitted in 1998 whereas more safeguard applications were filed in 2001. It may be noted that no relationship seems to exist between the use of the instruments and the evolution of the exchange rate; the highest number of applications was submitted during the period of greatest devaluation. What does seem evident is that the introduction of a more flexible instrument such as the special safeguard generated a demand for this type of commercial defense (see figure 5.3).

Finally, two aspects related to safeguard investigations can be highlighted. On the one hand, the figures evidence a greater use of the special safeguard as compared with the WTO safeguard. In the 10 years of existence of the WTO safeguard, an average of one investigation per year has taken place, whereas between 1999 and 2004, an average of two investigations per year have occurred under the special safeguard. The preference for this last type of instrument could be the result of less stringent requirements to prove the disruption and shorter periods of investigation and decision making than those contemplated in the WTO safeguard.

In sum, between 1990 and 2004, Colombia has made relatively equal use of the antidumping and safeguard arrangements. To a great extent, this trend is the

FIGURE 5.3 Colombia: Number of Dumping and Safeguard Investigations and Real Exchange Rate

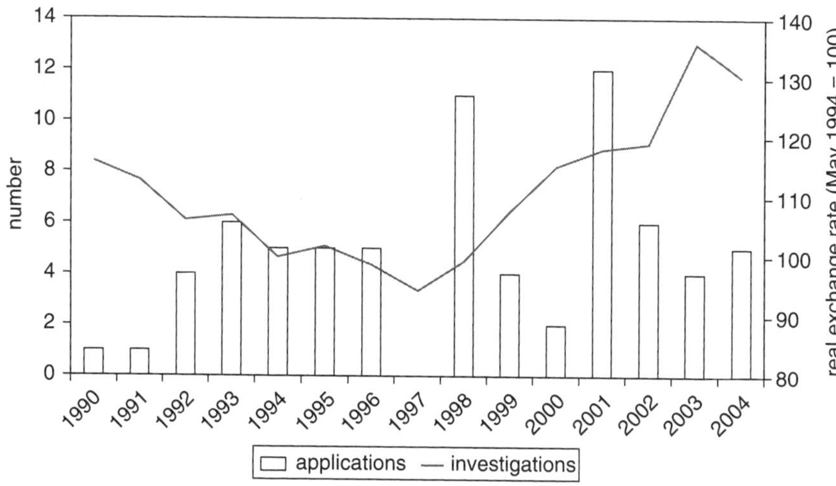

Source: Ministry of Trade, Industry, and Tourism Statistics on Dumping and Safeguards, http://www.mincomercio.gov.co/VBeContent/documentos/operaciones/Practicas/estadisticasinvestigaciones; Banco de la República, Revista Mensual, Statistics.

result of the recurrent use of the Andean safeguard, although if it is excluded from the statistics, an important number of safeguard investigations still remain.[16] Note that the proportion of investigations not resulting in the levying of duties or measures has been higher in the case of dumping investigations. Additionally, with the adoption of the special safeguard in 1999, the conditions were created for an increase in the number of applications linked to this type of measure.

Sectors Applying for Investigation

Out of the total investigations conducted between 1990 and 2004, 17 percent corresponded to agricultural products, understood as the summation of agriculture and agricultural industry products, and 83 percent corresponded to industrial products (see table 5.3). The agricultural sector made greater use of the safeguard mechanism as compared with antidumping measures. Of the total investigations conducted for agricultural products, 25 percent were for dumping and 75 percent for safeguards, and of the later percentage, three-fifths corresponded to Andean measures.

Of the dumping investigations, 92 percent focused on industrial products and only 8 percent corresponded to agricultural ones. In the case of safeguards, 26.5 percent corresponded to agricultural products and the remaining 73.5 percent to industrial goods. The case of the Andean safeguard stands out to

TABLE 5.3 Colombia: Investigations by Sector, 1990–2004

	Number of investigations					
	Conducted		No duty or measures imposed		No imposition/ conducted	
Mechanism	Agricultural	Industrial	Agricultural	Industrial	Agricultural	Industrial
Dumping	3	34	3	11	100.0	32.4
Safeguard	9	25	0	9	0.0	36.0
WTO	1	10	0	1	0.0	10.0
Special	0	10	0	5	n.a.	50.0
Andean	7	5	0	3	0.0	60.0
AEC24	1	0	0	0	0.0	n.a.
Total	**12**	**59**	**3**	**20**	**25.0**	**33.9**
	Percentage breakdown of total investigations					
	Conducted		**No duty or measures imposed**			
Mechanism	**Agricultural**	**Industrial**	**Agricultural**	**Industrial**		
Dumping	25.0	57.6	1.0	55.0		
Safeguard	75.0	42.4	0.0	45.0		
WTO	8.3	16.9	0.0	5.0		
Special	0.0	16.9	0.0	25.0		
Andean	58.3	8.5	0.0	15.0		
AEC24	8.3	0.0	0.0	0.0		
Total	**100.0**	**100.0**	**1.0**	**100.0**		
	Percentage breakdown per mechanism					
	Conducted		**No duty or measures imposed**			
Mechanism	**Agricultural**	**Industrial**	**Agricultural**	**Industrial**		
Dumping	8.1	91.9	21.4	78.6		
Safeguard	26.5	73.5	0.0	100.0		
WTO	9.1	90.9	0.0	100.0		
Special	0.0	100.0	0.0	100.0		
Andean	58.3	41.7	0.0	15.0		
AEC24	100.0	0.0				
Total	**16.9**	**83.1**	**13.0**	**87.0**		

Source: Author calculations based on Ministry of Trade, Industry, and Tourism Statistics on Dumping and Safeguards, http://www.mincomercio.gov.co/VBeContent/documentos/operaciones/Practicas/estadisticasinvestigacione.

Note: n.a. = not applicable.

TABLE 5.4 Colombia: Dumping Investigations by Sector, 1990–2004

Sectors	Number of investigations		Percentage breakdown		Without duties/ total conducted
	Conducted	Without duties	Conducted	Without duties	
Agricultural products	3	3	8.1	21.4	100.0
Chemicals	10	2	27.0	14.3	20.0
Petrochemicals	7	1	18.9	7.1	14.3
Tires	2	2	5.4	14.3	100.0
Textiles	3	3	8.1	21.4	100.0
Tableware and crockery or china	2	0	5.4	0.0	0.0
Iron & steel products	9	2	24.3	14.3	22.2
Stationary batteries	1	1	2.7	7.1	100.0
Total	**37**	**14**	**100.0**	**100.0**	**37.8**

Source: Author calculations based on Ministry of Trade, Industry, and Tourism Statistics on Dumping and Safeguards http://www.mincomercio.gov.co/VBeContent/documentos/operaciones/Practicas/estadisticasinvestigaciones.

the extent that 58 percent of the investigations conducted refer to agricultural products. The investigations under the special safeguard relate only to industrial products.

Another interesting result is that all the investigations for dumping of agricultural products have ended with no duties being imposed whereas, in the case of industrial products, duties were denied in 32 percent of the cases. In the case of safeguards, it may be noted that all the investigations conducted for agricultural products have ended with the levying of measures whereas 36 percent of the investigations for industrial products have resulted in no measures being imposed.

A more detailed breakdown of the sectors that have requested the application of antidumping duties shows that chemicals, iron and steel products, and petrochemicals represent almost 70 percent of the investigations (see table 5.4).[17]

As for safeguards, the breakdown by sector is different according to the type of instrument (see table 5.5). Most of the investigations under the WTO safeguard were made for textiles and apparel, and home appliances. Besides these two sectors, special safeguard investigations focus on chemicals and petrochemicals. In the case of the Andean safeguard, almost 60 percent of the cases are agricultural and focus on two products: rice and vegetable oils.

TABLE 5.5 Colombia: Safeguard Dumping Investigations by Sector, 1990–2004

Type of safeguard	Number of investigations		Percentage breakdown		Without measures/ conducted
	Conducted	Without measures	Conducted	Without measures	
WTO Safeguards					
Rice	1	0	9.1	0.0	0.0
Shoes	1	0	9.1	0.0	0.0
Textiles and apparel	6	0	54.5	0.0	0.0
Home appliances	2	0	18.2	0.0	0.0
Taxis	1	1	9.1	100.0	100.0
Total	**11**	**1**	**100.0**	**100.0**	**9.1**
Special safeguard					
Chemicals and petrochemicals	3	1	30.0	20.0	33.3
Textiles and apparel	3	2	30.0	40.0	66.7
Chains	1	0	10.0	0.0	0.0
Home appliances	3	2	30.0	40.0	66.7
Total	**10**	**5**	**100.0**	**100.0**	**50.0**
Andean community					
Agricultural products	7	0	58.4	0.0	0.0
Extra-neutral alcohol	1	1	8.3	33.3	100.0
Polypropylene bags	2	1	16.7	33.3	50.0
Triplex and particle boards	1	0	8.3	0.0	0.0
Iron & steel products	1	1	8.3	33.3	100.0
Total	**12**	**3**	**100.0**	**100.0**	**25.0**
AEC 24 ALADI					
Agricultural products	1	0			
Total	**34**	**9**			**26.5**

Source: Author calculations based on Ministry of Trade, Industry, and Tourism Statistics on Dumping and Safeguards http://www.mincomercio.gov.co/VBeContent/documentos/operaciones/Practicas/estadisticasinvestigaciones.

Note: Agricultural products appearing in the Andean safeguard are rice and refined vegetable oils.

In sum, most of the dumping and safeguards investigations have involved industrial products. In addition, the investigations on agricultural products have mainly concentrated on safeguards, and in those few cases in which the application of antidumping duties were requested for this sector, they were denied. Finally, textiles, apparel, iron and steel products, and chemicals and petrochemicals are the sectors requesting more investigations, which is consistent with international patterns. In effect, data for dumping investigations in the Western Hemisphere show that these investigations tend to concentrate on chemicals, plastics, paper, textiles, and basic metals (Tavares de Araujo, Macario, and Steinfatt 2001).

Two Case Studies

An analysis of the previous sections provides interesting insights by looking into two sectors more deeply. The first sector is the agricultural sector, from which rice was selected for this analysis because of the persistence over time of the measures to protect it against imports. This case illustrates the difficulty of managing the liberalization process when political considerations seem to prevail over technical ones.

The second sector is the textile-apparel sector, which reveals the problems that are created in a production chain when inputs become more expensive because of the application of duties or safeguard measures. In this case, the government's decisions privileged the defense of the competitiveness of the productive chain.

Rice Rice stands out as one of the agricultural products with the highest number of investigation applications, both for dumping and safeguards. However, it should be noted that the commercial defenses imposed during the period under analysis were almost exclusively concentrated in the Andean market and suspended the benefits derived from the Andean free trade area.

Sector Evolution Rice represents approximately 12 percent of Colombia's cultivated area; it is the third most important crop in terms of extension, after coffee and corn, and represents 6 percent of the agricultural production (Ministerio de Agricultura 2002). This product is covered by the price band system whereby the average ad valorem tariff between 1995 and 2003 was about 40 percent.

According to 1999 data, the country has about 34,000 rice production units and a milling industry that employs approximately 5,000 people. The milling industry has an advanced level of technological development when compared with countries such as the United States, Brazil, and República Bolivariana de Venezuela. In 2001, Colombia was ranked 23rd in world rice production and third in the Free Trade Area of the Americas (FTAA) after the United States and Brazil. Yields per hectare are above the international average, with 4.9 tons as compared with a world average of 3.9.

The trade balance of rice had a deficit throughout almost all the 1990s. During the decade, the imports of rice mainly originated from three countries: Ecuador, the United States, and República Bolivariana de Venezuela. Ecuador and República Bolivariana de Venezuela's share of imports are 43 percent and 21 percent, respectively, and the United States and the Asian countries have shares of 21 percent and 13 percent, respectively.

Use of Trade Defenses Rice stands out, together with refined oils, for concentrating most of the investigation applications involving agricultural products, both on grounds of dumping and safeguards. In the meetings for this project that were held with officials and former officials of the Ministry of Trade, there was a consensus on the strong political pressure that historically characterized the investigations involving rice. It is important to note that, in the case of the applications for safeguards filed within the framework of the Andean Community, the government acted on its own initiative on two occasions.

The political sensitivity of rice imports shows in the number of investigations that have involved this product. Three antidumping investigations involving agricultural products were conducted since 1990. One of these, concerning rice from Vietnam, was completed in 1994, and the application of duties was denied. Almost simultaneously producers submitted a safeguard application motivated by the imports of the product from Vietnam; this investigation ended with the levying of a tariff-type measure that was to be reviewed in mid-1995.

Later, there were four safeguards investigations relating to imports of rice within the framework of the Andean Community. As a result of these, imports were suspended for the period January 1996 through May 1998. Restrictions were imposed again in 2002 and in 2003. Note that the Andean safeguard establishes neither a maximum period of application of a measure nor a limit to the extensions. Given the composition of the countries that supply rice to Colombia, the regulation of Andean imports affects a high percentage of the imports.

As expected, this measure has generated an ongoing issue in the Andean Community (especially with Ecuador), taking into account that Colombia is the main producer of rice in the Andean region, followed by Peru and Ecuador. In 2004, the Ministry of Agriculture implemented the mechanism of administration of contingent duties (MAC, for the Spanish-language acronym) for some agricultural products—rice among them—and it is therefore expected that the recurrent application of safeguards for this product in the Andean market will be abandoned.[18]

Textiles and Apparel The textiles-apparel sector is interesting to the extent that its representatives—together with those of the agricultural sector—have been particularly critical of the trade liberalization policy. This characteristic could help explain why, when analyzing trade defense instruments, this sector turns out to be among those that have applied for more measures and into which the government has conducted several investigations on its own initiative. However, the government denied the imposition of duties and the adoption of safeguard measures when pertinent.

Sector Evolution The textiles sector represents close to 6 percent of the industrial production and the apparel sector, approximately 3 percent, and together they constitute one of the sectors with the highest average tariffs in Colombia. Although the most-favored-nation (MFN) average tariff is close to 11 percent, the average duty for the textiles and apparel sector is 18 percent. The textiles sector shows a high concentration in a small number of firms while the apparel sector is particularly atomized.

The economic opening of the early 1990s had an important impact on these two sectors, especially on textiles, because of the growing penetration of imports in a context in which not all of the links in the production chain had a good competitive position. Colombia's textiles and apparel industry had been characterized by a low penetration of imports in the period before trade liberalization. By 1990, apparel's penetration of imports was 3.2 percent and that of textiles was 4.4 percent, with some exceptions in certain subsectors of manufactured textile products other than apparel. By the end of the 1990s, this indicator had increased to almost 30 percent in textiles and close to 10 percent in apparel.

At the time of the opening, the cotton textile industry faced high labor costs and heavy indebtedness as a result of an investment program leading to modernization and the reduction of labor costs. However, the companies in the subsector of woven products presented more advantageous competitive conditions in terms of low labor costs, low debt burden, and vertical disintegration and were able to respond more rapidly to the changes in domestic and external demand. In the synthetic fibers sector, trade liberalization caused the closure of most of the existing companies, which were multinational and adopted strategies of regional relocation. Only one company (ENKA) survived the opening, in part because it continued enjoying the tariff advantages derived from the Andean market.

In the case of apparel, it is difficult to identify a distinctive behavior pattern, given the heterogeneity of the sector. However, it can be noted that, during the 1990s, apparel firms that competed in the high-volume and low-price market were particularly hit whereas those dedicated to maquila processes or to those that manufacture low to medium volumes at medium to high prices, both for the domestic and international markets, succeeded in surviving.

At the beginning of the 1990s, the whole production chain suffered the impact of a strong unfair competition generated by smuggling, which was caused by the circumstantial exports of Asian products at very low prices and which affected all the countries in the region. This situation led to considerable financial losses and, in some cases, resulted in the closing down or bankruptcy of firms, especially in the textiles sector.

The difficult circumstances faced by the sector during the 1990s did not lead to the adoption of a particular commercial and industrial policy by the authorities. However, the sector was included within the competitiveness policy applied by the government between 1994 and 1998.[19]

In 1997, the government signed competitiveness agreements pursuant to the commercial and industrial policy with the textiles and apparel sector. In the commercial field, those agreements resulted in temporary tariff reductions for the import of capital goods and raw materials, a stronger enforcement of smuggling controls, and the modification of the legislation with respect to safeguards and antidumping to expedite investigations and introduce flexibility in the application criteria. However, as seen in the section on the evolution of the regulations of these instruments, the government did not deviate from the multilateral arrangements in this respect. Only in the case of the special safeguard might the government have been responsive to the private sector's demands as reflected in the competitiveness agreement, but it should be noted that this instrument is not a safeguard in the strict sense of the word. Besides, almost all the applications made by the sector for the imposition of this instrument were denied.

Use of Trade Defenses Since 1990, there have been three dumping investigations and nine investigations to apply safeguard measures to products of the textiles-apparel sector in Colombia. The textiles and apparel sector is not among those that have requested more antidumping measures, but—together with the agricultural sector—it is included in the group that has requested more safeguard measures.

In no case did the applications for dumping result in the imposition of duties, whereas in only two of the nine safeguard investigations was the adoption of measures denied. The two denied safeguard measures were submitted through the special safeguard mechanism, and the six applications filed for the WTO safeguard, including the transition facility of the Textiles and Apparel Agreement, ended with the imposition of measures.

As mentioned above, two elements are of interest for this analysis. First is the fact that two of the safeguard applications (those for polyester fibers and texturized yarns) that were denied in 2001 included a clear recommendation to the Foreign Trade Ministry to begin a dumping investigation on its own initiative, which ended without duties being levied. Second is that this sector is one in which there was an objection to the safeguard measures applied within the WTO framework, in particular by Asian economies such as Thailand and Taiwan, China, but the objection did not go beyond a regular proceeding, by the end of which the measures had expired.

FIGURE 5.4 Colombia: Textile and Apparel Imports

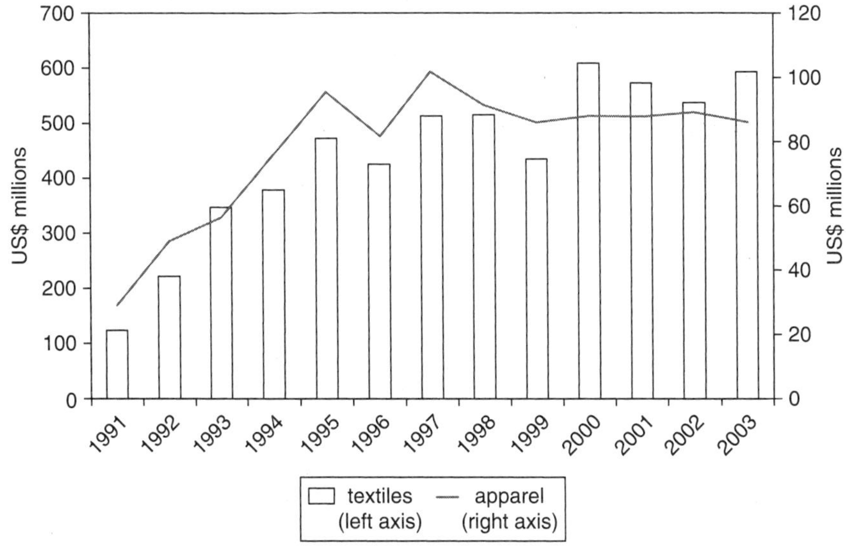

Source: Dirección de Impuestos y Aduanas Nacionales (National Office of Tax and Customs) Statistics of Imports.

The conclusions on the effect of the measures are not obvious. Textiles and apparel imports grew at a declining rate until the middle of the 1990s and at a lower-than-average level during the second half of the decade. However, these disappointing growth rates are difficult to explain based exclusively on the use of commercial defense mechanisms because, from 1996, the economy suffered a sharp drop in growth. Finally, the amounts of both textile and apparel imports have not dropped to preliberalization levels (see figure 5.4).

A review of the investigations bore out evidence of the government's concern to act on behalf of the whole production chain. The case of synthetic yarns and fibers illustrates their condition as raw materials. Although for the decision makers it was clear that the survival of the production lines of a firm with a long history in the country was at stake, no safeguard measures were applied, there was an unsuccessful dumping investigation, and the government simply promoted an agreement of the production chain to purchase polyester granules, another product of the same company.

Political Economy and the Use of Safeguards and Antidumping Measures in Colombia

A review of the investigations conducted in the last few years by Colombia's authorities to impose safeguard and antidumping measures reveals that there has not been a bias in favor of using one of the two instruments. Between 1990 and

2004, 37 investigations into alleged cases of dumping and 34 to assess the imposition of safeguards were initiated.[20] Duties were imposed in 59 percent of the investigations for safeguards, and similar results were achieved in 51 percent of the cases of alleged dumping.

The pattern of use of safeguards and antidumping measures seems to respond to several factors. On the one hand, the design of the various instruments and the requirements for their imposition makes some safeguards easier to apply than others. On the other hand, although the institutional structure that is related to the decision-making process seems to have maintained a political space for the emergence of protectionist inclinations of the government of the day, this type of discretion seems not to have been used excessively. Finally, the profile of those who apply for the investigations (in terms of size, economic sector, and so forth.) also seems to play a role in the relative use of the instruments.

The Role of the Instruments

As already mentioned, the evolution of Colombia's *antidumping legislation* has followed two routes. First, each new legal instrument related to antidumping has sought to better adapt to the multilateral regulations provided by the WTO. Second, through time, there is a clear tendency to make procedures more expeditious, always within the multilateral guidelines.

The case of *safeguards legislation* has a different feature, to the extent that, in the last few years the authorities not only passed instruments according to the evolution of the multilateral arrangements, which offer little margin for discretion, but also have designed and implemented a more lax mechanism. Consequently, the instruments are not a safeguard in the strict sense of the word but have an equivalent relief effect for the private sector within the margin of maneuverability granted by the multilateral framework for tariff policy. A review of the circumstances under which these instruments were designed and the way they have been used leads us to assert that the use of the special safeguard is more accessible to the private sector and offers greater discretion to the authorities than antidumping instruments.

The first safeguard instrument, enacted by Decree 809 of 1994, was the result of an initiative by the government designed to offer a lifesaver to sectors that, at the time, were under hardship because of the greater competition generated by the commercial opening. However, this initiative had more of a political than practical meaning because the conditions imposed for application prevented this initiative's massive use. The instrument was modified to adapt to WTO rules by Decree 152 of 1998, which remains in force.

The use of safeguards applicable to WTO member countries was partially limited because of their strict requirements; however, three other types of instruments offer greater flexibility. The first of these is a safeguard that applies to countries that are not members of the WTO and that is used when the requirements for investigation are less strict and authorities have greater discretion.[21]

The second is the special safeguard procedure. Although this instrument does not allow for the increase of tariffs above the levels consolidated before the WTO, it has been very useful for authorities because it allows them to increase tariff levels above the Andean Common External Tariff, thus becoming an important relief measure for the private sector.

The interviews conducted for this chapter show that the enactment of the special safeguard sought to offer a more flexible mechanism to respond to protection requests by the private sector. A review of the requirements of the instrument seems to confirm this finding because it introduces the concept of *disruption*, defined as an increase in imports or the existence of imports in unfair conditions such as low prices or important quantities, a concept less demanding than that of *injury*.

The requirements to demonstrate a disruption are much more vague and lax than those corresponding to the demonstration of injury. The relative use of the special safeguard seems to show that the private sector perceives it as a user-friendly instrument; since 1999, there have been 10 special safeguards investigations, a figure similar to the 11 investigations that were conducted since 1994 for WTO-consistent safeguards.

The third instrument that has made it possible to channel the demand of the private sector with greater flexibility than the WTO-consistent safeguard is the safeguard applicable among Andean countries. This safeguard is an important relief mechanism for the private sector to the extent that it makes it possible to suspend the benefits of the free trade area of the Andean region, which is the source of a significant portion of the imports of some products.

The Andean safeguard has three conditions that facilitate its use: (a) its application does not demand compensation to the countries affected by the measure; (b) it makes use of the concept of disruption, which, as already noted, is more lax than that of injury; and (c) the Andean regulations consider the levying of provisional duties while the Andean Community Secretariat makes a determination on each case. This circumstance guarantees a minimum of four months of protection, even in those cases in which the measure is considered to be unwarranted. The fact that 12 out of the 34 investigations that were initiated based on safeguard applications corresponded to the Andean regulations shows the relative importance of the instrument to respond to the demands of the private sector.

The Role of Institutions

It is possible to identify three instances in the investigation and decision-making processes with respect to safeguard and antidumping measures applications. The first instance is responsible for carrying out the investigation processes, and it has always reported hierarchically to the Ministry of Foreign Trade.

When the investigations have been conducted, the deputy director of Trade Practices formulates a recommendation and submits the case to the second instance, at the vice ministerial level. In the case of investigations into alleged dumping, this second instance is the Unfair Practices Committee whereas, in the case of investigations linked to safeguards, it is the Customs and Tariff Affairs Committee. Both committees are chaired by the foreign trade vice minister and, with slight variations, have the vice ministers of the economic areas as members.

The third instance making the final determination in the case of dumping investigations is the minister of foreign trade. In general terms, there were no cases of a minister making a decision that opposed the recommendations of the Unfair Practices Committee, which stresses the importance of rigorous investigations and subsequent discussions among the vice ministers of the economic area. The instance making the final decision in applications linked to safeguard investigations is the Senior Foreign Trade Council, which has the ministers of the economic areas as members and is chaired by the president of the republic, which may deviate from the recommendations of the Customs and Tariff Affairs Committee. It is worthwhile noting that the Ministry of Agriculture usually undertakes the defense of the applications filed by this sector, which is not the case with the investigations requested by the industrial sector. With a few exceptions, this council has operated with formal rigor and usually its decisions have had solid foundations.

The interviews conducted for this chapter revealed that the work of the officials responsible for the investigations complies with the regulatory requirements and is not usually interfered with by political pressures from senior government levels, which does not mean that officials are fully protected from those sorts of pressures. At the same time, the discussions of the vice ministers usually balance technical and political criteria. Although such behavior is the general rule, there have been some minor exceptions that coincide with periods in which the government had suffered a political setback and sought to remedy it by granting preferential treatment to some representatives of the private sector. However, these temporary exceptions have not eroded the institutionality of the processes. In an interview with a government official, an interesting hypothesis emerged in this sense. In his judgment, the fact that the majority of the applications for investigation involved raw materials made it very difficult to take measures for the benefit of a specific group because the dynamics of liberalization made evident the need to preserve the competitiveness of production chains to improve their insertion in international markets.

The analysis of the institutional operation in the cases of dumping and safeguards shows that, with the above-mentioned exceptions, the officials responsible for the investigation usually work in a serious and independent manner, and their recommendations are assessed by the vice minister, who brings together both technical and political criteria. The general opinion of those interviewed is that technical rigor has prevailed and that the recommendations are generally adopted by the Minister or Senior Foreign Trade Council, as may be the case. According to this diagnosis, although authorities do have a margin for political considerations to prevail over technical criteria, this behavior has not dominated in Colombia.

There is, however, one instance in which the government's or the minister's inclination toward greater or lesser protection became effective. It lies in the ability to modify the instruments and their procedures within the boundaries permitted by multilateral regulations. The issuance of the special safeguard in 1999 is a case in point to the extent that it opened up the possibility of a more discretionary and expeditious protection in response to requests from the private sector. In other words, in some cases, by adjusting the rules, the authorities have sought to attain the flexibility and discretion that are not afforded by the investigation and decision-making processes.

Finally, it cannot be asserted that the relatively little use of the antidumping and safeguard instruments in Colombia stems from a lack of resources. Although the deputy director of Trade Practices has a staff of 10, including administrative officials, those interviewed estimate that the staffing is qualified and sufficient to process the applications that are filed. In the opinion of the current deputy director of Trade Practices, having more staff would make it possible to investigate cases more in depth and would reduce the workload per official but would in no case determine the adoption of a greater number of measures or reduce the time. Additionally, although the budget is limited, resources have always been found to make on-site verifications and collect first-hand information.

The Role of the Applicants and the Affected Counterparts

The sectors having requested more dumping investigations are, in order, chemicals, iron and steel, and oil by-products. The sectors that have requested more investigations for the application of safeguards have been textiles, apparel, agricultural products (through the Andean safeguard), chemicals, and petrochemicals. Note that most of these sectors coincide with the majority of the dumping and safeguard investigations in the world.

According to the interviews conducted for this chapter, the bulk of the private sector is ignorant of the use and meaning of the antidumping instruments and safeguards. The exception is usually found in large companies or in those that have traditionally been involved in foreign trade. In fact, the interviews show that, with few exceptions, the companies that usually request an investigation for the imposition of antidumping measures and safeguards are those that have enough resources to pay a law firm. Similarly, investigation applications usually come from relatively concentrated sectors in which it is easier for the interested parties to reach an agreement to demonstrate that an important proportion of a branch of domestic production has been affected.

Although hiring a law firm is not required to file an application for investigation, most of the applicant firms usually prefer it. The competent authorities offer step-by-step procedural guidelines for firms to apply for an investigation directly, an assistance that has been used in some instances. However, in most cases, either the applying companies do not have sufficient staff to take care of the case directly or they believe that law firms have an expertise that is worthwhile using. Also, it is clear that by hiring a law firm, interested parties acquire not only the technical expertise to file the application but also the potential of lobbying for the corresponding follow-up, sometimes at the most senior level.

The preference for hiring law firms reinforces the trend for most applications to come from the largest companies. It is worthwhile noting that, although rates vary, the cost of hiring a law firm to apply for an investigation may range from US$50,000 to $75,000 for the whole process. Importantly, the authorities or former officials consulted for this chapter indicated that there is no bias in favor of applications filed by law firms.

Several respondents pointed out that the applicants for investigations do not have a bias in favor of safeguards or antidumping mechanisms and that they choose to request one or the other depending on the case they believe can be established. However, experts who have closely followed several cases pointed out that firms tend to perceive that it is more feasible to build a solid case by way of the safeguards because the information required is of a domestic nature and more readily obtainable than that about international prices or costs required for a dumping case. This perception is probably reinforced by the greater flexibility of instruments such as the special safeguard or the Andean safeguard mentioned above.

An analysis of the role played by the affected parties in an antidumping or safeguards investigation shows a mixed result. On the one hand, the technicians responsible for the investigations always comply with the requirement of consultation with the parties affected in the process. On the other hand, the respondents pointed out that the role of the counterparts is limited because they have a period of time in which to prepare their arguments that is shorter than the one available to the applicants because the latter are already preparing their allegations before the submittal of the application.

The relative lack of knowledge on the instruments and their operation also limits the potential reaction of the counterparts because, in many cases, they become intimidated when they learn that the authorities are conducting an investigation and prefer not to engage in the debate. In the case of dumping investigations, this situation usually results in the party that is the importer of the goods choosing to change the supplying country to avoid the problems they believe may be derived from the investigation.

The stakeholder absent in dumping and safeguard investigations is the consumer. Colombia does not have strong consumer associations to make their positions felt in the large national economic debates, let alone in a specialized investigation. The only exception in this sense is the sporadic presence of the superintendent of Trade and Industry at the vice ministerial instance that analyzes the recommendations of the deputy director of Trade Practices. This superintendency is responsible for conducting the investigations related to anticompetitive practices and usually has consumer interests very much in mind. However, the superintendency does not always attend the vice ministerial meetings, and when it does, it has the right only to speak, not to vote.

Conclusions

Colombia's experience with the use of antidumping duties and safeguards shows that (a) the government has not resorted to this option to satisfy the demands of the economic agents looking for greater protection and (b) the number of applications that are filed is low when compared with international standards.

This trend can be explained by the private sector's relative ignorance with respect to the instruments as well as by the stability and soundness demonstrated by the institutional arrangements connected with the investigations and the decision-making process, even if they are not independent agencies within the government's structure.

The interviews and the cases analyzed in this chapter show that the dynamics of the trade liberalization process in the country created awareness of the importance of preserving the competitiveness of production chains to improve their insertion in the international markets. This fact has placed the government at a complex crossroads at the time of restricting access of cheap raw materials, which helps explain the stability and prudence in the institutions associated with the process of commercial defense. However, the agricultural sector seems to lie beyond this logic, and to the extent allowed by the instruments, the domestic market has often been closed, at least for Andean competition. The case of rice is illustrative in this respect.

Notes

1. For example, Tavares de Araujo, Macario, and Steinfatt (2001) compare Colombia's 35 antidumping investigations with countries in the Free Trade Area of the Americas (FTAA) zone between 1987 and 2000, including 782 in the United States, 302 in Canada, and 233 in Mexico.

2. Before the liberalization, imports were controlled through a prior licensing arrangement, and import quotas were granted taking into account criteria mainly associated with the volumes of domestic production.

3. The main products covered by the Andean system of price bands are meats, vegetable oils, wheat, dairy products, corn, rice, soja, and sugar, as well as their derivatives and substitutes.

4. The Cartagena Agreement, which gave rise to the creation of the Andean Group, contemplates four types of safeguards: sectorwide, per product, by reason of exchange rate, and another related to balance of payment crises. Between 1980 and 1990, the Andean countries invoked safeguard clauses more than 30 times. Approval for the measure was granted in a little more than 20 occasions, in most of which the safeguard invoked was related to the exchange rate.

5. The concept of public interest makes reference to the obligation of taking into account, in the decision making process, all parties that may be potentially affected by the enforcement of a measure. This obligation gives the decision maker a margin to deviate from eminently technical criteria.

6. The Senior Foreign Trade Council is a national government advisory organization on all aspects related to the country's foreign trade and its members are the president of the republic (who chairs it), the ministers of the economic area, the head of the National Planning Department, the manager of the central bank, the director of customs, the advisers to the Senior Council and the president of the Foreign Trade Bank (Banco de Comercio Exterior). The last three have no voting rights.

7. Required information includes indicators such as the actual and potential drop in sales, profits, production volume, market share, and volume of imports at dumped prices.

8. The members of this committee are the deputy director of trade practices of the Ministry of Trade, a delegate of the Senior Foreign Trade Council, an adviser to said the Senior Foreign Trade Council, the vice minister of trade (who chairs the committee), and the vice ministers of the sectors connected with the investigation.

9. The members of the Customs and Tariff Affairs Committee are the vice minister of trade (who chairs it), the vice ministers of the economic area, the deputy chief of the National Planning Department, the director of customs, and the advisers to the Senior Foreign Trade Council. In 1998, it was established that, to assess safeguards, the superintendent of trade and industry would be invited to provide an opinion on the measure.

10. Decrees 2038 and 2259 of 1996.

11. For example, if Colombia has bound its tariff rate on machinery at 35 percent but in practice applies a rate of 15 percent, the country may—without violating WTO obligations—raise the tariff rate it applies up to 35 percent.

12. Decree 2681 of 2001.

13. Decree 1407 of 1999.

14. Decree 1407 of 1999.

15. As seen in the second section of this chapter, the special safeguard is not strictly a safeguard but, rather, an arrangement that allows for tariff measures to be levied up to the level consolidated in the WTO and that is higher than the tariffs applied under the Andean Common External Tariff.

16. The application of the Andean safeguard contributes to making the number of safeguard cases not much lower than those of dumping. However, if the Andean investigations are subtracted, the percentage of safeguard cases is still 37 percent of the total, as compared with 63 percent linked to dumping.

17. In most sectors, the investigations have concentrated on a few products. The cases of dumping in the chemical sector focus on orthophosphoric acid, ethyl acetate, and fertilizers; in the petrochemical sector, polypropylene and suspension-type polyvinyl chloride. The agricultural products are corn by-products, poultry, and rice. In textiles, the investigated products are denim, polyester fiber, and

texturized yarns. In iron and steel, the products are steel bars, chrome plated sheets, iron or steel wire rods, billets, tin sheet, and hot-rolled steel.

18. The MAC works as an imports management instrument subject to the absorption of the national harvest.

19. The competitiveness policy was based on the joint work of the government and the private sector to improve some cross-cutting issues that affect the performance of the economic sectors. These factors include regulations, transport, infrastructure, human resources qualifications, and raw materials import costs.

20. As already explained and as will be analyzed in further detail later, the cases of safeguards include those of the special safeguard, which in a strict sense does not constitute a safeguard from the WTO's perspective, but has played an important role in granting protection to various sectors.

21. This safeguard was regulated by Decree 2657 of 1994 and later by Decree 1407 of 1999.

References

Echavarría, Juan José, and Cristina Gamboa. 2001. "Colombia y Venezuela: Reformas de política comercial y ajustes institucionales después de la Ronda de Uruguay." *Coyuntura Económica* 21 (3–4): 159–92.

Finger, J. Michael. 2002. "Safeguards: Making Sense of GATT/WTO Provisions Allowing for Import Restrictions." In *Development, Trade and the WTO: A Handbook*, ed. Bernard Hoekman, Aaditya Mattoo, and Philip English, 195–205. Washington, DC: World Bank.

Hommes, Rudolf, Armando Montenegro, and Pablo Roda. 1994. *Una apertura hacia el futuro*. Bogotá: Ministry of Finance and Public Credit and National Planning Department.

Ministerio de Agricultura. 2002. "Características y estructura de la cadena de arroz en Colombia." Observatorio de competitividad agrocadenas, Colombia.

Norton, Roger D., and Alvaro Balcázar. 2003. "A Study of Colombia's Agricultural and Rural Competitiveness." Unpublished document, United Nations Food and Agriculture Organization, World Bank, and United States Agency for International Development.

Reina, Mauricio, and Sandra Zuluaga. 2001. "Lineamientos para una estrategia de negociación de Colombia en Acceso a Mercados en el ALCA." Unpublished paper, Ministry of Trade, Industry, and Tourism, Bogotá.

Reina, Mauricio, Sandra Zuluaga, and Cristina Gamboa. 1996. "El Grupo de los Tres y el Grupo Andino." In Las *Américas: Integración económica en perspectiva*, 169–91. Bogotá: National Planning Department and Inter-American Development Bank.

Tavares de Araujo, José Jr., Carla Macario, and Karsten Steinfatt. 2001. "Antidumping in the Americas." OAS Trade Unit Studies, Organization of American States, Washington, DC.

6

ANTIDUMPING POLICIES AND SAFEGUARD MEASURES IN THE CONTEXT OF COSTA RICA'S ECONOMIC LIBERALIZATION

Ricardo Monge-González
and Francisco Monge-Ariño

After the economic crisis of the beginning of the 1980s, the government of Costa Rica decided to abandon its import-substitution strategy and move toward integration with the world economy by means of a gradual process of economic liberalization. During the same period, the country joined international organizations such as the World Trade Organization (WTO) to have the necessary legal instruments to defend its commercial interests worldwide. As part of agreements and commitments such as these memberships, Costa Rica began an important institutional transformation in the field of foreign trade, creating institutions to safeguard the rights of its businesses (producers, exporters, and importers) and citizens in commercial matters.

Two decades after the start of the economic liberalization process, Costa Rica has faced unfair trade practices or has had to apply safeguard measures because of substantial increases of imports that are negatively affecting its productive sector. Of interest was also the idea to analyze the degree to which those sectors that benefited from the previous import-substitution model and that have been facing increased foreign competition with the elimination of tariff and nontariff barriers to imports and have attempted to make use of the mechanisms of protection against unfair practices as a new protectionist instrument.

The chapter is organized into an introduction, four main sections, and a section with conclusions. The first of the main sections explains the reasons for the adoption of the new model of economic development based on economic liberalization during the mid-1980s, the manner in which this new model has been implemented, and the performance of Costa Rica's economy during these two decades that the new model has been in effect. The second and third main sections discuss the legal and institutional arrangements established by Costa Rica to process complaints about unfair practices and petitions for safeguard applications. The fourth main section contains an individual analysis of each of the cases brought before the Ministry of Finance, Trade, and Industry by Costa Rica's productive sectors. Finally, the section on conclusions summarizes the main findings of the study and their economic policy implications.

Economic Liberalization: From Import Substitution to Export Promotion

What Motivated the Liberalization of the Economy?

During the 1980s, many events contributed to causing the deepest economic crisis in Costa Rica's recent history—a crisis that, according to González (1989), resulted from a combination of both structural and short-term factors and made it necessary to review the development strategy the country had pursued. The structural determinants of the crisis reflected a contradiction between the country's main characteristics (small domestic market, relative abundance of highly specialized labor, and natural resources) and the policies adopted as part of the import-substitution strategy. The commercial policies generated distortions of relative prices, leading to an antiexport bias, as well as a reduction in the well-being of domestic consumers and the efficiency of domestic production (Taylor 1984; Monge and Corrales 1988). The short-term drivers of the crisis include, most important, the oil crisis and the coffee boom after the mid-1970s, followed by the unfortunate domestic policies adopted in response to these events and the international inflation and recession during the end of the 1970s and beginning of the 1980s (González 1984).

The major macroeconomic indicators deteriorated rapidly between 1981 and 1982. Inflation reached 80 percent per year, the open unemployment rate amounted to 9 percent of the working force, gross domestic product (GDP) fell 10 percent in a single year, the colón was sharply devalued compared with the U.S. dollar, and the fiscal deficit increased significantly (Lizano 1992). Thus, those who benefited from the import-substitution model and those who did not perceived the need for a change of strategy. This situation fostered the adoption of a new economic development scheme, the so-called "economic liberalization model," which has not yet become fully effective in Costa Rica to this day.[1]

What Was the Economic Liberalization Model, and How Was It Implemented?

The economic liberalization model, adopted by Costa Rica after the second half of the 1980s, pursues a greater integration of Costa Rica's economy with the world economy. The goals included making Costa Rica's economy more competitive in international markets by reducing protection for those activities that compete against imports and by eliminating the distortions in the domestic markets for goods and factors, all of which directly reduced unproductive profit-seeking activities (Bhagwati 1982, 1991); downsizing and modernizing the government so that it would not hinder the growth of the private sector but, instead, would facilitate its development; granting compensatory subsidies and other incentives to nontraditional exports, on a temporary basis, to compensate for the antiexport bias generated by the import-substitution model; and adopting stable macroeconomic policies that would be consistent with the economic liberalization model (Edwards 1990; IMF 1998; Mesalles 1998) and, thus, would promote foreign investment by means of incentives of a fiscal nature.[2]

The Response of Costa Rica's Economy to Economic Liberalization: A Long-Term Vision

Although several studies show individual positive outcomes for Costa Rica's economy during the period of economic liberalization,[3] a comprehensive vision of the economy's performance during the period under analysis is not available. This section addresses that comprehensive vision by describing the behavior of Costa Rica's economy during the last two decades (1983–2003), with a focus on trade, employment, and poverty, and by providing a long-term view of the results achieved with the economy's liberalization.

First, it should be noted that, although Costa Rica eliminated most of its tariff and nontariff protectionism, the process was carried out gradually. As figure 6.1 shows, since 1986, trade flows responded rapidly when the first tariff reduction and simplification of the protectionist system took effect. Imports began growing in an important and sustained manner and so did exports, the latter as a response of the export sector to the reduction of the antiexport bias that was generated by the import-substitution model (liberalization of imports and subsidies to exports).

It is important to note that, in 1984, in parallel with economic liberalization, Costa Rica's export products began enjoying free access to the U.S. market (zero tariffs on almost all agricultural and manufacturing products), thanks to the Caribbean Basin Initiative. Not surprisingly, the U.S. market has grown in importance as a major destination for Costa Rica's exports, from 26 percent in 1982 to

FIGURE 6.1 Costa Rica: Exports, Imports, and Average Tariff, 1982–2003

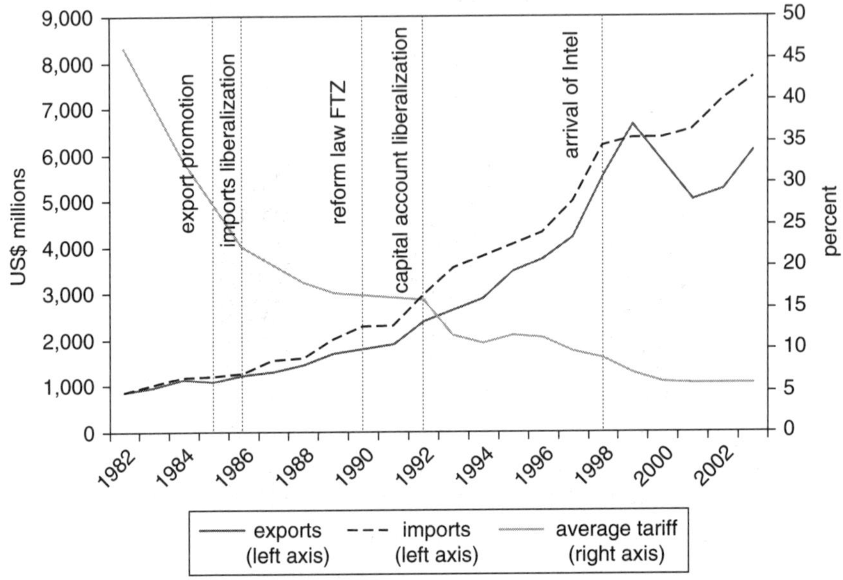

Source: Prepared by the authors using data from Banco Central de Costa Rica.

Note: "Reform Law FTZ" refers to a comprehensive set of amendments introduced to the law that regulates the operation of free trade zones in the country, while "Arrival of Intel" refers to the establishment of Intel's first two microchip assembly plants located in Costa Rica.

38 percent in 1992 and to 46.5 percent in 2003 (see figure 6.2). In part, this growth was the result of a significant increase in foreign investment flows such as those that occurred with the establishment of companies such as Componentes Intel in 1998.

The good export performance and the higher foreign direct investment, together with a correct foreign exchange policy, have resulted in a relatively satisfactory result in the trade account. Although the current account deficit is higher at present in absolute terms, as a share of the economy, the deficit has tended to decrease (see figure 6.3).

The decreased trade deficit is an important result because opponents of the liberalization process had forecast that, as a consequence of import liberalization, the trade balance would be wrecked. Thus, the performance of Costa Rica's economy during the last two decades demonstrates the profound economic understanding of the designers of the reform (in taking into account general, and not merely partial, equilibrium effects) when designing and implementing the process of economic liberalization. In fact, because of the prudent management of the fiscal, monetary, and exchange policies, Costa Rica has been able to guarantee a

FIGURE 6.2 Costa Rica: Evolution of Share of Destination Countries for Main Exports

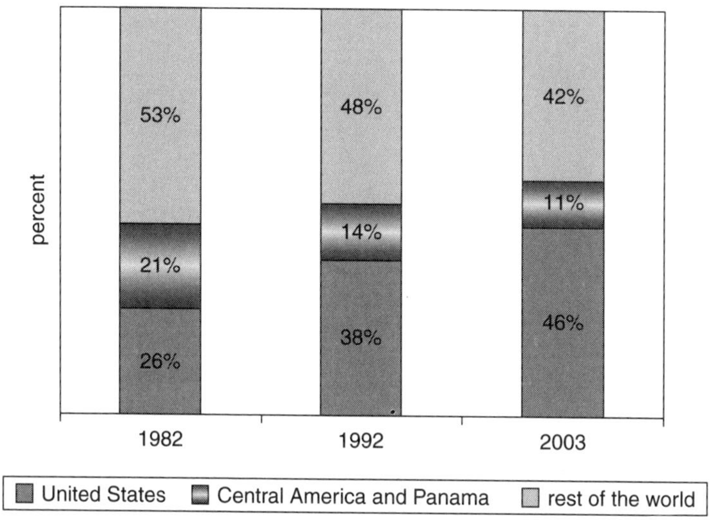

Source: Prepared by the authors using data from PROCOMER.

neutral rate of exchange for its export sector (as measured by the real effective exchange rate index) and extremely low inflation levels (see figure 6.4).

Attempts have been made to minimize the role of Costa Rica's businesspeople in the liberalization of the economy by pointing out that the increase of exports in Costa Rica is mainly associated with the foreign sales of the multinational companies that have taken advantage of the free trade zones. The truth is that, although multinational companies are currently an important source of wealth for the country—by generating new and better jobs and transfers of technology to domestic businesses, among other positive effects—the results shown in the previous figures stress the importance of the liberalization in achieving a better allocation of the resources of Costa Rica's economy whereas the arrival of multinational companies took place only since the second half of the 1990s.[4]

The sustained growth of foreign direct investment in Costa Rica is another positive outcome of economic liberalization, especially as proof of the confidence of foreign investors in the new development model (see figure 6.5). Foreign direct investment has become not only an important source of jobs but also a major destination market for the products manufactured by domestic microenterprises, as well as small and medium enterprises (SMEs), turning them into indirect exporters (Monge, Rosales, and Arce 2004).

FIGURE 6.3 Costa Rica: Current Account Deficit, 1983–2003

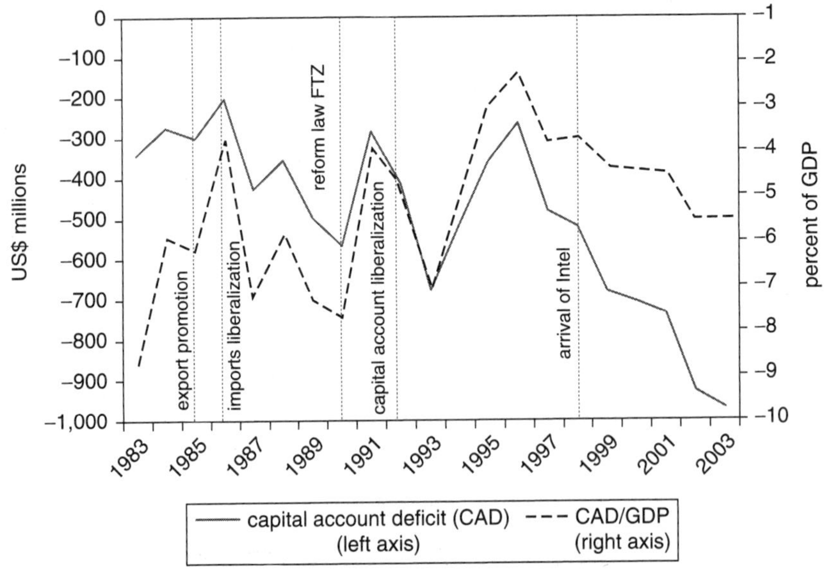

Source: Prepared by the authors using data from Banco Central de Costa Rica.

Note: "Reform Law FTZ" refers to a comprehensive set of amendments introduced to the law that regulates the operation of free trade zones in the country, while "Arrival of Intel" refers to the establishment of Intel's first two microchip assembly plants located in Costa Rica.

Because of the liberalization process, Costa Rica's economy has succeeded in reducing its extremely high dependency on traditional products such as coffee, bananas, sugar, and beef for foreign exchange earnings. In fact, as shown in figure 6.6, because of the economic liberalization, exports of nontraditional products have substantially increased their relative importance within total exports—from 38.6 percent in 1982 to 64.9 percent in 1992 and to 87 percent in 2003. That increased diversification of exports currently provides Costa Rica with greater economic stability and a more stable source of foreign exchange, thus avoiding the recurrent problems of the past when good economic performance depended on whether the price of coffee increased as a consequence of external effects—for example, sleet in Brazil. Moreover, one might wonder what the condition of Costa Rica's economy would be under the current crisis of the coffee sector if this major diversification of exports had not taken place.

Equally important, it should be stressed that the sustained growth of Costa Rica's exports has been linked with an increase in the number of exporting firms, as well as with an important share of microenterprises, including almost 1,000 SMEs. Approximately 250 microenterprises were among the 1,744 Costa Rican firms that

FIGURE 6.4 Costa Rica: Evolution of Inflation and Real Effective Exchange Rate, 1983–2003

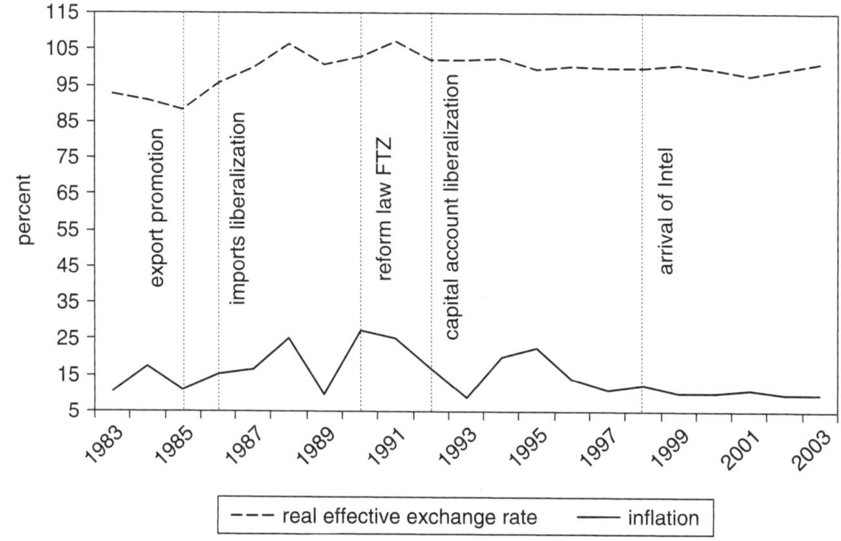

Source: Prepared by the authors using data from Banco Central de Costa Rica.

Note: "Reform Law FTZ" refers to a comprehensive set of amendments introduced to the law that regulates the operation of free trade zones in the country, while "Arrival of Intel" refers to the establishment of Intel's first two microchip assembly plants located in Costa Rica.

enjoyed export sales in 2003 (see figure 6.7).[5] Of the firms that currently export from Costa Rica, almost 15 percent are microenterprises and 58 percent are SMEs. Equally important, the number of products exported by Costa Rica also rose to 3,565 in 2003, according to official data from the Foreign Trade Promotion Bureau.

Finally, note that Costa Rica's economic performance following trade liberalization has had another three major successes. First, trade liberalization facilitated a reduction of the high levels of unemployment and underemployment that resulted from the foreign debt crisis at the end of the 1970s and beginning of the 1980s. Second, trade liberalization has made it possible to create jobs for the large expansion in the number of nonskilled workers, a consequence of the important migration flows of people from Central America, mainly Nicaragua, that occurred in the past few years. Finally, trade liberalization has managed to bring down the level of poverty from 29 percent in 1987 (one year after the liberalization process began) to 18.5 percent in 2003 (see figure 6.8).[6]

In addition to the positive effects of the economic liberalization model on trade flows, foreign investment, employment, and poverty, a point to note is that

FIGURE 6.5 Costa Rica: Direct Foreign Investment Flows, 1970–2003

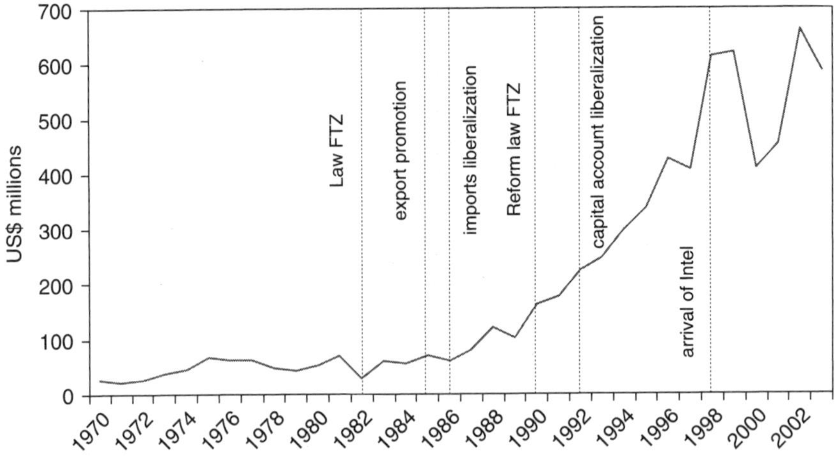

Source: Prepared by the authors using data from Banco Central de Costa Rica.

Note: "Reform Law FTZ" refers to a comprehensive set of amendments introduced to the law that regulates the operation of free trade zones in the country, while "Arrival of Intel" refers to the establishment of Intel's first two microchip assembly plants located in Costa Rica.

FIGURE 6.6 Costa Rica: Relative Importance of Nontraditional Exports, 1982–2003 (by percent of total exports)

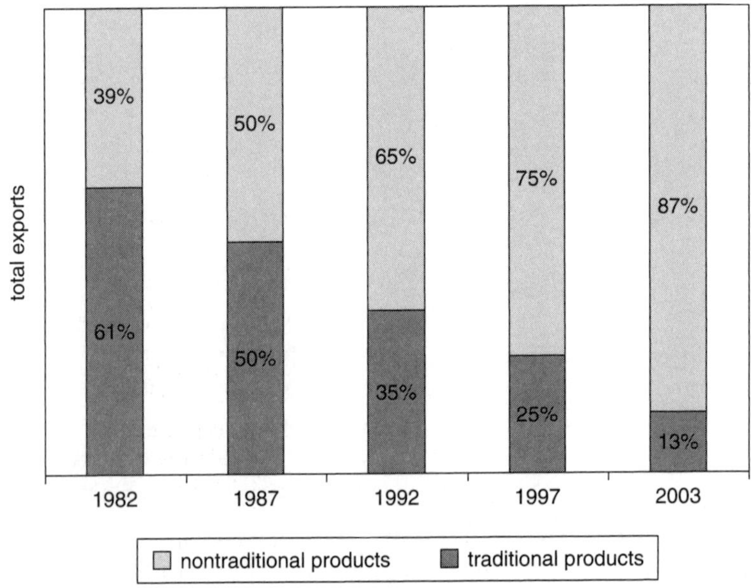

Source: Prepared by the authors using data from Banco Central de Costa Rica.

FIGURE 6.7 Costa Rica: Composition of Exporting Firms, by Size of Firm, 2003

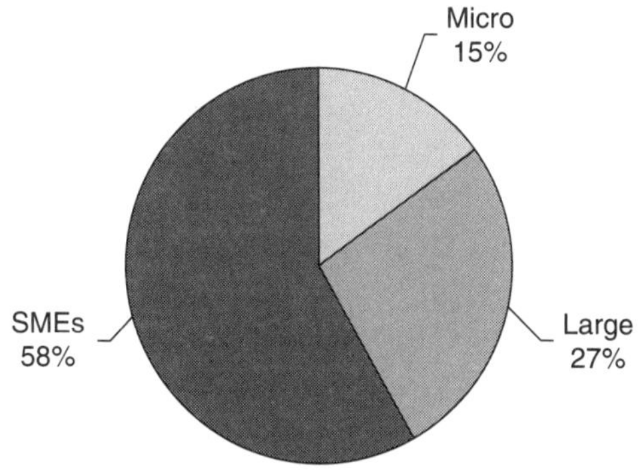

Source: Prepared by the authors using data from PROCOMER.

FIGURE 6.8 Costa Rica: Per Capita GDP, Open Unemployment, Underemployment, and Percentage of Households below Poverty Line, 1982–2003

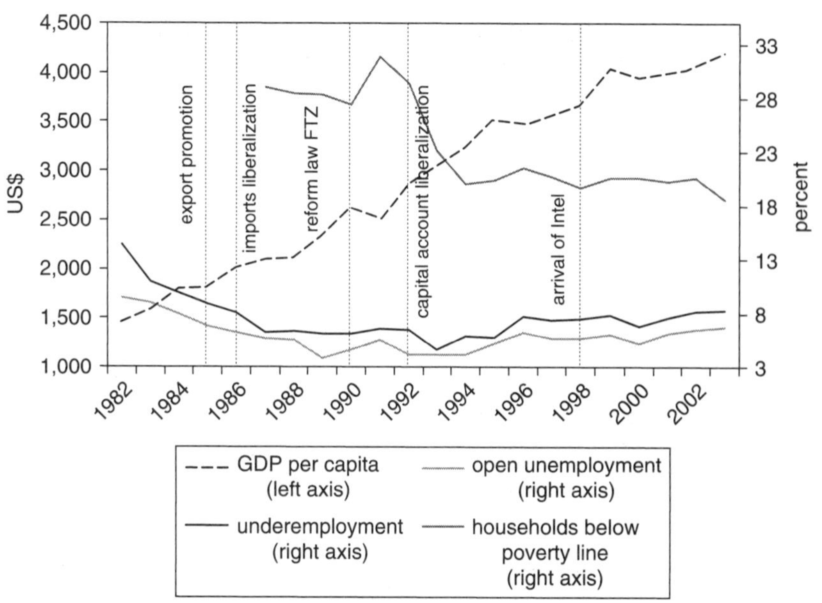

Source: Prepared by the authors using data from Banco Central de Costa Rica.

Note: "Reform Law FTZ" refers to a comprehensive set of amendments introduced to the law that regulates the operation of free trade zones in the country, while "Arrival of Intel" refers to the establishment of Intel's first two microchip assembly plants located in Costa Rica.

although Costa Rica's income distribution did not improve during the liberalization period, neither did it worsen. In fact, according to the family distribution based on per capita income, the Gini coefficient did not change much between 1987 (0.401) and 2003 (0.425), with an average of 0.395 for the period and a variation coefficient of only 4.9 percent.[7]

The evolution experienced by Costa Rica's per capita production shows that the new development model has given greater robustness to the country's economy because it was not seriously affected by significant external events such as the tequila crisis (1995), the Asian crisis (1999), the Argentine crisis (2001), and the most recent recession in the developed economies, notably the United States (2002).

In sum, Costa Rica has managed to attain a positive economic performance over the last two decades by changing the development model from one based on import substitution to another based on economic liberalization. In fact, as cited by numerous academics and international organizations, Costa Rica is a successful example of reform, albeit incomplete, for which no crisis episodes have occurred due to the country's high degree of integration with world markets (see figure 6.9), while there have been significant improvements in poverty reduction.

FIGURE 6.9 Costa Rica: Degree of Liberalization and Per Capita GDP

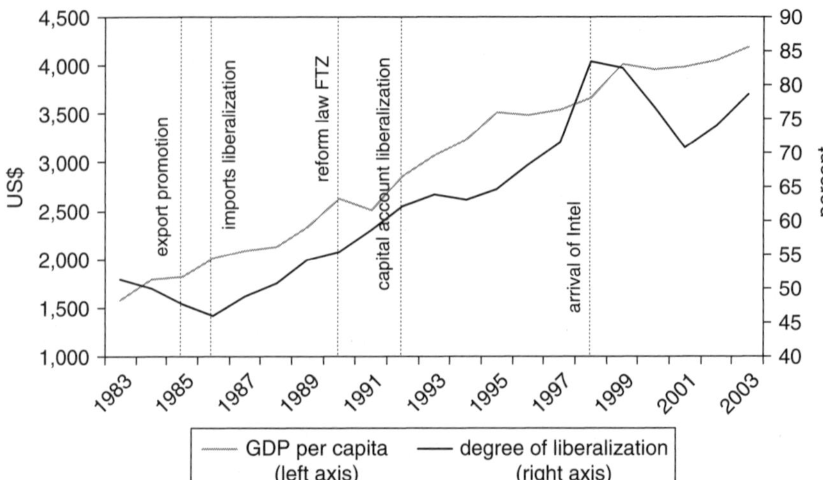

Source: Prepared by the authors using data from Banco Central de Costa Rica.

Note: Degree of liberalization is defined as (exports + imports)/GDP. "Reform Law FTZ" refers to a comprehensive set of amendments introduced to the law that regulates the operation of free trade zones in the country, while "Arrival of Intel" refers to the establishment of Intel's first two microchip assembly plants located in Costa Rica.

Legal Framework

The Uruguay Round agreements on antidumping and on safeguards are the cornerstones of the legal framework that determines the parameters to identify and penalize dumping practices that involve imports into Costa Rica from any WTO member country. Consequently, the agreements regulate dumping practices and the application of safeguard measures within the context of multilateral trade.

Costa Rica adopted these WTO agreements by enacting Law 7475 in April 1994. In addition, the country has established bilateral rules to regulate dumping practices and the application of safeguards in the various free trade agreements it has signed and ratified to date, specifically with Central America, Mexico, Chile, the Dominican Republic, and Canada.[8]

The purpose of this section is to summarize the basic rules established in the above agreements to clarify the way in which the issues of safeguards and antidumping are regulated at the multilateral and bilateral levels.

Antidumping Measures

Costa Rica has in place several different antidumping regulations: those based on the multilateral rules of the WTO and several other regulations that implement the antidumping provisions of bilateral or regional agreements.

Antidumping Measures at the Multilateral Level As mentioned before, the identification and penalization of dumping practices at the multilateral level is regulated by the WTO agreement on antidumping measures of the Uruguay Round, signed and ratified by Costa Rica in 1994. For the purposes of the agreement, a product is considered as being dumped if it is being sold into another country's market at a price that is less than the normal value for that product or an equivalent product (that is, a close substitute). The key to determine dumping from the Uruguay Round's respective agreement lies in the definition of *normal value* because that value is the parameter with which the price of the imported product is being compared. The normal value is defined in three alternative and mutually excluding ways that will be applied in the following order, according to the circumstances:

- If the product under consideration is being sold in the exporting country's domestic market, the normal value is the selling price in said market.
- If the product is not sold in the domestic market of the exporting country, the normal value is the price at which said product (or the equivalent product, as may be the case, that is, a product that either is identical in every respect or has at least very similar characteristics to those of the product

under consideration) is sold in a third country, provided that said price is representative.

- If the product is sold neither in the domestic market of the exporting country nor in third markets (or when there is a special market situation or if the low volume of sales in the domestic market of the exporting country does not make an appropriate comparison feasible), the normal value will be determined as the summation of the per-unit production cost at the country of origin plus a reasonable amount for administrative, selling, and general costs, as well as for profits.

Likewise, the agreement provides that, when the export price is not reliable because there is an association or a compensatory arrangement between the exporter and the importer or a third party, the export price may be constructed on the basis of the price at which the imported products are first resold to an independent buyer.

Another relevant aspect is that the price comparison must be fair, in the sense that the comparison must be made at the same level of trade, preferably at the post-factory level and on the basis of sales made on, as nearly as possible, the same date.

After the authorities determine whether there is dumping, and the amount thereof, the next step involves determining injury to domestic production. In this respect, the agreement provides that, in determining injury[9] to domestic producers, the investigating authority shall examine both the volume of the dumped imports and the effect of the dumped imports on the prices in the domestic market for equivalent products, as well as the consequent effect of those imports on domestic producers of equivalent products.

Two important elements in the WTO antidumping agreement are the possibility of imposing (a) provisional measures and (b) price undertakings. Provisional measures are duties that are applied on a strictly transitory basis and for a defined term. Imposing a provisional measure requires a preliminary determination to confirm the existence of dumping and the consequent injury to domestic production. Provisional measures are applied no sooner than 60 days from the initiation of the investigation and for a period not exceeding six months. The rate shall not exceed the margin of dumping estimated on a preliminary basis.

Price undertakings are voluntary agreements whereby the exporter of the product being dumped revises its prices or ceases exports to the market in question to satisfy the authorities that the injurious effect of the dumping is eliminated. Price increases under such undertaking need not be equivalent to the estimated margin of dumping, but simply sufficient to eliminate the injury caused to domestic production. The application of an undertaking requires, as in the case of provisional measures, a previous preliminary determination of the existence of dumping and of injury resulting from that dumping.

When the investigating authority completes the investigation by determining the existence of dumping and the consequent injury to domestic production—and in the absence of a price undertaking with the exporter—it will proceed to impose a definitive measure, that is, a duty sufficient to eliminate the injury caused by the exporter's selling at prices below normal value. The agreement is clear in the sense that the definitive measure will remain in effect only while it is strictly necessary up to a maximum of five years from the date it is imposed, unless the investigating authority determines that the measure's absence would lead to a continuation or recurrence of injury.

Antidumping Measures in the Central American Common Market At the level of bilateral trade with Central America, the application of antidumping measures is properly regulated by the Central American Rules on Unfair Trade Practices, approved on December 12, 1995, by the Central American Economic Council, in the framework of the Central American Common Market and as a response to the commitments stemming from the Uruguay Round made by each of the countries in the region within the context of the creation of the WTO.

Before joining the General Agreement on Tariffs and Trade (GATT), Costa Rica had enacted the Industrial Protection and Development Act (Ley de Protección y Desarrollo Industrial), which covered dumping in articles 10, 11, and 12.[10] However, the legislation was never enforced, given the high duties that existed and the scant opening of the economy to external competition. Furthermore, there was no specific institutional framework for the enforcement of that legislation.

The Central American Regulations on Unfair Trade Practices established an investigating authority that reports to the general directorate of the Ministry of Economy, Industry, and Trade (MEIC) or, in its absence, either the directorate responsible for regional integration affairs in each country in the isthmus or the investigating unit on unfair trade practices. However, in the case of a regional procedure (that is, a joint application of all the countries in the region against an outside country), the Economic Secretariat of Central American Integration (Secretaría Económica de Integración Centroamericana) will be responsible for the investigation.

The investigating authority will examine, analyze, and evaluate the alleged unfair trade practices and decide whether to recommend the application of duties or antidumping measures, either provisional or definitive. The application to initiate the investigation is most often made by the domestic industry representatives corresponding to the product affected by the imports, but it also can be the result of an administrative initiative, as allowed under WTO rules.

If an application for investigation is accepted by the investigating authority, that authority will notify the government of the country of origin and the authority will give that country the opportunity to carry out consultations to clarify the facts raised.

If the investigating authority rejects an application for an investigation, the party that submitted it is allowed a period in which it may correct and resubmit the application.

Investigations must be completed within 12 months of their initiation and can be extended for 6 more months only under exceptional circumstances. However, within 60 days, the investigating authority shall issue a positive or negative preliminary determination on the case. Figure 6.10 summarizes the process, according to the Central American Rules on Unfair Trade Practices, of a dumping complaint in Costa Rica against imports originating in Central America.

Antidumping in the Free Trade Agreement with Mexico In the case of the free trade agreement with Mexico, chapter VIII of that agreement defines the guidelines relating to the application of antidumping measures under the guise of countervailing quotas, and not duties, as is the typical case. However, it is important to mention that, according to the provisions of the same chapter VIII, those countervailing quotas also can be used to neutralize not only dumping practices but also export subsidies.

With respect to the conditions required to impose an antidumping measure, chapter VII of the free trade agreement with Mexico refers to GATT provisions, that is, the Agreement on Antidumping and Safeguard Measures of the Uruguay Round. The only special specifications made in chapter VII have to do with the conditions required for the accumulation and establishment of "regional injury," as well as some aspects of the process connected with resolutions, notifications, retroactive application, hearings, review, and elimination of the definitive measures.

Treatment of Dumping in Other Free Trade Agreements Chapter VII of the free trade agreements with Chile, the Dominican Republic, and Canada contains provisions related to the application of antidumping measures, if the parties can establish the application of antidumping duties in response to dumping practices pursuant to the WTO agreement on antidumping.

However, the free trade agreement with Canada goes a bit further by noting the interest of the parties to promote improvements and clarifications in the GATT and WTO provisions, as well as their desire to establish a procedure at the domestic level that incorporates broader issues of public interest. Also contemplated is the possibility of applying minor duties (within WTO bound rates). A transparent and predictable method is recommended for the imposition of such duties so that the final determinations of duties can be more easily reviewed.

FIGURE 6.10 Stages in the Process of a Dumping Complaint in Costa Rica, Pursuant to the Central American Rules

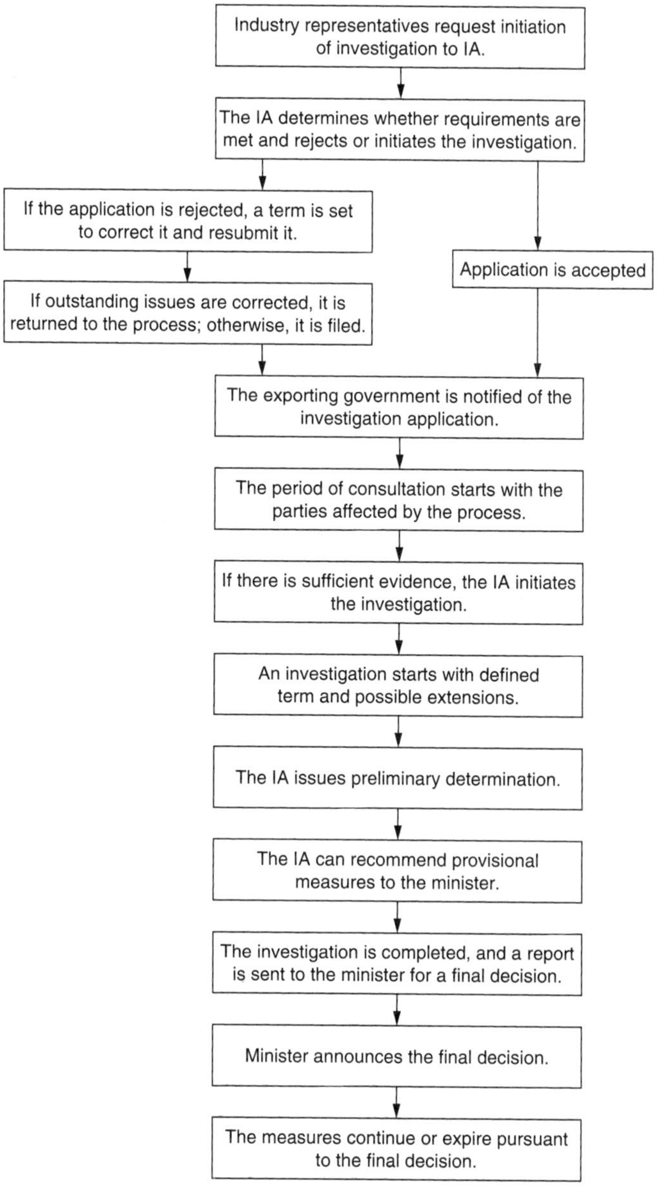

Source: Prepared by the authors using information from Central American Rules on Unfair Trade Practices.

Note: The Minister has powers to terminate the proceedings at any stage. The IA is the Investigating Authority, an agency reporting to the Ministry of Finance, Trade, and Industry.

Safeguard Measures

As it has with antidumping measures, Costa Rica has in place safeguard procedures that follow from bilateral, regional, and multilateral agreements.

Safeguard Measures at the Multilateral Level Safeguard measures at the multilateral level are governed by the WTO agreement on safeguard measures signed and ratified by Costa Rica in 1994.

The basic requirement for the imposition of safeguard measures is that the imports of a certain product must have increased to such an extent—be it in absolute terms or in relation to domestic production—that they cause or threaten to cause a material injury to the domestic industry that produces like products or directly competing ones. The key for the application of safeguard measures is determining the existence of injury. According to the agreement, material injury is understood as a general, significant deterioration in the situation of an industry of domestic production. It is further clearly established that the threat of material injury must necessarily be based on concrete facts and not merely allegations, estimations, or remote likelihood. The measure to be applied can be a duty or a quantitative restriction (quota), in which case the amount of the same cannot be less than the average of the product's imports over the three years before the beginning of the investigation. The WTO agreement also establishes provisional safeguards that may be applied if the investigating authority determines that delay would imply an injury to domestic production that would be difficult to repair.

The duration of provisional safeguard measures is limited to a maximum of 200 days, and they can take only the form of duties, which are to be reimbursed to importers should the investigation conclude that there is no evidence of a causal link of material injury to the domestic industry. Also, the terms of the provisional measures will be discounted from the initial duration of a definitive safeguard measure, should it be imposed as a result of the investigation.

The agreement provides that countries will be able to apply definitive safeguard measures only for the time necessary to prevent or repair the material injury and facilitate a readjustment. However, the duration of that period is limited to a maximum of four years, at the conclusion of which it is possible to extend the restriction if it is demonstrated that the measure continues to be necessary to prevent or repair the injury or complete the period of readjustment of the domestic industry. The extensions of a safeguard are limited; the agreement provides that the total period of application of a definitive safeguard measure—including the period of initial application, the period of definitive application, and the extensions—cannot exceed a total of eight years. Moreover, a product to which a safeguard has been previously applied cannot be the subject of a new safeguard until a period equal to that during which the measure was previously applied has elapsed, and that exempt period will not be less than two years.

One last relevant aspect of the WTO agreement on safeguards is that it prohibits the application of such measures against imports of a product originating in a developing country that is a WTO member when those imports represent less than 3 percent of the total imports of that product by the country supposedly affected by the increased imports.

Safeguards in the Central American Common Market In the Central American Region, Costa Rica's legislation on safeguard measures is governed by the Central American Rules on Safeguard Measures, approved on May 22, 1996, by the Central American Economic Council in the Tegucigalpa Protocol, and intended to bring the regional rules in line with the agreements adopted in the framework of the Uruguay Round.

In general, the investigation procedures and time frames are similar to those applied in the case of antidumping measures. The investigation process can be initiated at the request of a party or, exceptionally, by administrative initiative. The technical study must be completed within 6 months, except under exceptional circumstances where it can be extended to a maximum of 12 months.

It is feasible to apply provisional measures, but they shall be guaranteed by means of securities, which will be promptly returned if the investigation later shows that the increased imports did not cause or threaten to cause a material injury to a domestic industry. Furthermore, before the adoption of any provisional measure, the member country will notify WTO's safeguards committee. Once the measures are imposed, the authorities of the member country are required to hold consultations with WTO member countries that have a particular interest in the measure.

Safeguards in the Free Trade Agreement with Mexico In the case of the free trade agreement with Mexico, the application of safeguard measures is authorized both at the bilateral (against imports from Mexico) and global (imports from Mexico and other countries) level. The application of bilateral safeguards is restricted after 24 months have elapsed from the date that the duty on the product in question reached zero percent. Additionally, the bilateral safeguards establish that the measures will consist of duties.

An interesting aspect in which the bilateral safeguard rules contained in the free trade agreement with Mexico deviate from WTO's bilateral rules refers to the period of application of the safeguard. In effect, the safeguard can be for a single instance and for a maximum of one year with a single possibility of extension for a like period. Moreover, the level of that measure shall not be higher than the duty in force for third countries or the duty that was applied before the entering into force of the duty reduction typified in the treaty.

Another distinctive element of the application of safeguards under the free trade agreement with Mexico is the fact that the party applying the safeguard must give the affected party a compensation that is mutually agreed during the consultations. Such compensation will consist of additional duty concessions (reductions), the positive effects of which (for the trade of the party causing the injury) are equivalent to the effect of the safeguard.

Alternatively, the application of global safeguards to imports of a specific product originating in Mexico applies only when those products are part of the exports of the main supplying countries and when they represent less than 80 percent of the total imports of the product under consideration by the affected country. Application also applies when the rate of increase of the imports from Mexico of the product in question, during the year when their damaging increase occurred, is slightly lower, equal to, or higher than the rate of increase of the imports of the same product from all origins during the same period. The procedure for applying global safeguards in the free trade agreement with Mexico maintains the aspects relating to investigation, notification, and consultations, but not those linked to the tariff compensations for the party receiving the effects of the safeguard.

Safeguards in the Free Trade Agreement with Chile The free trade agreement with Chile regulates the application of safeguard measures both in the case of bilateral measures (that is, only for imports from Chile) and global ones (against imports originating in a group of countries, including Chile).

The period during which the parties may impose and maintain effective the safeguard measures (namely, for the purposes of the treaty, the transition period), is restricted to that period required for the reduction of the duties of a product plus an additional two-year period, counted from the date on which the product becomes completely duty free, identical to the provision of the free trade agreement with Mexico.

In the free trade agreement with Chile, the only applicable safeguards are duties, and their imposition can be suspension of the duty reduction agreed under the treaty or by means of an increase of the rate of duty to a level that may, in no case, exceed the most-favored-nation duty consolidated at WTO.[11]

An element that the application of bilateral safeguards has in common with the free trade agreements with Mexico and with Chile is the obligation to offer a duty compensation (duty reduction) in exchange for the imposition of a safeguard measure with effects equivalent to those of the safeguard. What is new in the free trade agreement with Chile is that this obligation to offer compensation to the other party extends to global safeguards.

Safeguards in the Free Trade Agreement with the Dominican Republic The free trade agreement with the Dominican Republic requires that the domestic producers who request safeguard protection must account for at least 25 percent of the total domestic production of that type of product. The way the agreement treats the duration of the transition period and the application of the measure, however, is identical to that of the free trade agreement with Mexico. That said, an unusual aspect in the treatment of bilateral safeguards in the free trade agreement with the Dominican Republic is that the duty compensations for the imposition of safeguards—which are obligatory in the treaties with Mexico and Chile—are optional in this case and are at the discretion of the party imposing the safeguard measure. In case the parties fail to agree on the compensation being offered in exchange for the safeguard (duty reduction on other products), the requesting party can impose it unilaterally, and the party to which the safeguard applies can unilaterally impose the compensation considered pertinent.

Safeguards in the Free Trade Agreement with Canada In the Canada–Costa Rica Free Trade Agreement, the treatment of safeguards is much briefer; it deals only with the application of bilateral measures (that is, solely against imports originating in Canada). A transition period is established, the duration of which is restricted to the period of the duty exemption time schedule. The maximum duration of safeguard measures is limited to three years without the possibility of a renewal. A measure can be extended only one time and only after a period has passed that is no less than half the length of the first application period. During the second application, the duty cannot be higher than the first time the safeguard was effective. During this second application, it is mandatory to establish a time schedule for the gradual reduction of the duty so that, at the date of final expiration of the measure, the duty will remain at the level contemplated for the product in question in the duty reduction schedule under the treaty.

No safeguards will be applicable after the expiration of the transition period—except where accepted by the other party. The party imposing a safeguard is obliged to negotiate and agree on the respective compensation with the other party, and the party affected by the safeguard can adopt a unilateral retaliation in the absence of an agreement between the parties.

Institutional Framework

As indicated in the previous section, the application of antidumping and safeguard measures in Costa Rica uses the pertinent agreements of the Uruguay Round as a framework at the multilateral level and the pertinent agreements of the various free trade agreements signed by the country at the bilateral trade level.

Within this context, Resolution DM-822-95, dated September 4, 1995, by the Ministry of National Planning and Economic Policy, authorized the creation of the Office of Unfair Trade Practices and Safeguard Measures, which reports to MEIC and is responsible for investigating, analyzing, and assessing those cases, as well as recommending to MEIC the application of antidumping duties, safeguards, and countervailing measures.

The Office of Unfair Trade Practices and Safeguard Measures operated between 1995 and 2000, when the Ministry of National Planning and Economic Policy issued Resolution DM-23-00 whereby the above responsibilities were transferred to the legal unit of said ministry. On December 6, 2000, MEIC published a decree in this sense, although it had argued that transferring the work of the Office of Unfair Trade Practices and Safeguard Measures to the legal unit generated an inconvenient combination of functions.

The authors of this chapter held interviews and conversations with government officials whose work related to the subject and with advisers of domestic companies involved in investigation processes. These interactions revealed major restrictions that MEIC's Office of Unfair Trade Practices and Safeguard Measures experienced during its life, some of which are listed here:

- Financing restrictions
- Limited staff and lack of a consolidated continuity
- Lack of staff specializing in economic and international trade matters
- Lack of training and updating of specialized knowledge on the subject
- Processes that tend to become delayed, partly because of applicant companies' reluctance to provide information and because of personnel limitations and the lack of an adequate budget

Although the Office of Unfair Trade Practices and Safeguard Measures had operated under financial and staff constraints since the time it was set up, Douglas Alvarado, who is currently responsible for processing the applications on these matters, was of the opinion that the authorities justified disbanding the office based on the few investigation applications that were being received.

The legal unit, in turn, continues applying the same procedures prescribed in the pertinent legislation, but does not have a dedicated work team for that purpose. Instead, within the legal unit, the person responsible for processing applications with respect to antidumping, safeguards, and countervailing measures is not exclusively dedicated to this work but also carries out tasks related to specific work the Ministry of Finance, Trade, and Industry issued for MEIC's legal unit. However, while the legal unit carries out work of a legal nature, MEIC's economic department handles the technical investigation in addition to the rest of its duties.[12]

Although the Office of Unfair Trade Practices and Safeguard Measures stopped operating in 2000, a new decree on August 23, 2002, established the mandate to set it up as a legal entity. After that decree, the plan was to have it report to the Office of the Minister and be given exclusive responsibility over unfair trade practices and safeguard measures, except in those cases where international treaties grant powers to other departments, but even in those cases, the other departments would work in coordination with the legal office.

Pursuant to this new decree, several tasks and duties were assigned to the Office of the Minister:

- Receiving and processing complaints related to dumping and subsidies, as well as applications for safeguard measures
- Conducting studies or investigations to determine the validity of the complaints and the need to impose measures
- Advising the minister and other areas of the ministry on those matters
- Advising industry sectors on the operation of the Office of the Minister
- Providing orientation to interested parties on the adequate use of the international protection instruments of reference
- Advising interested parties on the proper filing of an application and the submittal of the pertinent evidence

Although the institutional arrangements for the new Office of Unfair Trade Practices and Safeguard Measures are clearly defined in the above decree, it has not yet been created. Still, today, investigation processes are carried out by the legal unit of the Ministry of Finance, Trade, and Industry.

According to Mr. Alvarado, although the mandate for the reestablishment of the Office of Unfair Trade Practices and Safeguard Measures dates to 2002, the financial resources required are not available, there is a lack of skilled staff, and there is little support for domestic industries because of the lack of professionals who specialize in international trade matters in the market and who are capable of advising businesses during the complaint process. Those limitations represent an enormous challenge for Costa Rica because the various free trade agreements have given rise to multiple rules and different regulations, demanding a more robust and efficient institutional structure that is capable of properly managing their enforcement.

Mr. Alvarado pointed out that it would be advisable to consider the option of creating this investigating office by law, rather than by decree, which would reduce to a minimum the involvement of political interests. Lucrecia Brenes, a specialized private adviser, agreed with the above.

However, it should be noted that, apart from MEIC, the country's institutional framework also relies on the Foreign Trade Ministry, which is responsible for notifying WTO about cases, and relies on the Treasury, through the General Customs Directorate, which is responsible for the implementation of the measures on imports. Although Costa Rica's experience with the application of safeguard and antidumping measures is limited to a single case (burlap bags), the performance of the General Customs Directorate in the case raises doubts on the quality of inter-institutional coordination in the country to implement this type of measure adequately.[13]

Although the imposition of safeguards and antidumping measures is part of the enforcement of the trade agreements to which the country is a party and although the Foreign Trade Ministry has an office to this end, it would seem that, to guarantee better enforcement of such measures by Customs, it would be necessary to strengthen the inter-institutional coordination role to be performed by the Foreign Trade Ministry.

Costa Rica's Experience with Antidumping and Safeguard Cases

Although Costa Rica has processed only a few antidumping and safeguard cases, this experience provides considerable information on how management of these instruments is managed as a part of the liberalization process.

An Analysis of Cases of Applications for Alleged Dumping Practices

From 1995 to 2004, MEIC's investigating authority received six complaints for alleged dumping practices, which are detailed in table 6.1.[14] Out of those six complaints, four corresponded to manufacturing products (chapters 25 to 99 of the Central American Tariff System, or SAC), and only two of the cases involved the agricultural and agroindustrial sectors (chapters 1 to 24 of the SAC).[15] This distribution is consistent with Costa Rica's import structure, which—as a consequence of the high tariff protection prevailing over the agricultural products that are more important for domestic consumption—is mostly concentrated in manufacturing products.

All of the antidumping complaints have involved imports from countries of the Americas: three involving Mexico, two involving South American countries, and one jointly relating to the United States and two countries in Central America. Although Mexico is not a preponderant trade partner with Costa Rica, the free trade agreement signed by the two nations in 1995 revitalized trade links enough for Costa Rica's producers who focus on the domestic market to pay much more attention to the prices offered by Mexican suppliers.

TABLE 6.1 Costa Rica: Dumping Cases

Year	Product	Sector	Related countries	Requester or applicant
1995	Acrylic plates	Manufacturing	Mexico	Acrílicos de Centroamérica S.A.
1996	Refrigerators	Manufacturing	Mexico	Atlas Industrial S.A.
1996	Fresh yellow onions	Agriculture	Guatemala, Nicaragua, and United States	National Association of Onion Producers
1996	Fiber cement plates	Manufacturing	Mexico	Ricalit S.A.
1997	Pasta	Agroindustry	Chile	Pastas Roma S.A.
1998	Sanitaryware	Manufacturing	Venezuela	Incesa Standard S.A.

Source: Prepared by the authors using data drawn from resolutions of dumping cases dealt with by MEIC.

Of the six dumping applications received by the investigating authority, two ended with a finding of no injury, two were dropped because the information required was not submitted, one ended with no measure being applied because it was not confirmed that the injury was directly attributable to dumped imports, and only one case involved a decision to apply a duty, which ended up being 0 percent because the imports practically disappeared (see table 6.2). Space limitations allow only one of the six cases of dumping reported in Costa Rica to be presented as an illustration in the following section.

The Refrigerators Case In October 1996, the company Atlas Industrial S.A. applied for a dumping investigation against imports of refrigerators (classified under item 84.18.21.00 of the SAC) from Mexico. The applicant company argued that from May to September 1996 these imports had entered Costa Rica under dumping conditions (see table 6.3), which—together with the fact that domestic and imported models are homogenous and are accounted for under the same tariff heading—led, in its judgment, to the conditions required to initiate an investigation. The applicant company further added that they represented 100 percent of domestic production and were, therefore, representative of the domestic industry involved.

In March 1997, Atlas Industrial S.A. filed to drop the case, alleging that they had arrived at an agreement with the importers. However, a few days later when MEIC required documents showing that agreement, Atlas did not provide any

TABLE 6.2 Costa Rica: Summary of the Outcome of Dumping Cases Dealt with by Investigating Authority

Product	Firms failed to submit information	Case dropped by applicant	Start of investigation	Withdrawal[a]	No injury found	Preventive measure	Final resolution	
							Measure applied	No measure applied[b]
Acrylic plates	X	X	X		X[c]			
Refrigerators			X	X[d]	X			
Fresh yellow onion			X					X
Fiber cement plates	X	X						
Pasta	X	X						
Sanitaryware			X				X[e]	

Source: Prepared by the authors using data drawn from resolutions of dumping cases dealt with by the MEIC.

a. The firm decided to withdraw the investigation application.

b. In cases where injury was found but no measure applied, the existence of other factors, beyond imports, that contributed to the injury was determined.

c. No injury was found because of lack of evidence demonstrating injury or threat of injury.

d. The firm withdrew the application; however, it continued by administrative initiative.

e. The measure applied amounted to 0 percent because imports had decreased to almost nil.

TABLE 6.3 Costa Rica: Refrigerator Imports, 1995–96

Date	Total imported units
Aug.–Dec. 1995	422
Jan.–Apr. 1996	356
May–Sept. 1996	2,561

Source: Prepared by the authors using MEIC resolution published in the *Official Gazette* of October 17, 1997.

documents, indicating that the agreement had been informal. Therefore, MEIC considered it appropriate to continue the investigation under its own initiative.[16] Interestingly, both the Mexican exporter (Mabe S.A. de C.V.) and its importer counterpart in Costa Rica (Mabeca, the sole importer of refrigerators from Mexico at the time of the investigation) submitted all the documentation required by the investigating authority.

The investigating authority determined that refrigerator imports from Mexico represented 35.5 percent of the total imports of that product in 1996. Nevertheless, it found evidence of the existence of dumping of the imports below the product's normal value. This result is not apparent in the figures contained in table 6.4, which show that in 1996, the year on which the complaint was based, the value in dollars per unit of weight (kilograms) of imported refrigerators from Mexico and from around the world significantly increased, with the increase in the value of the imported unit being greater in the case of Mexico (32 percent) than worldwide (4 percent).

Reviewing the available information, the investigating authority concluded that there was no evidence to believe that the increase of imports under dumping conditions was causing an injury to domestic production because, in its judgment, the reduced profits of Atlas were primarily caused by the reduction of "other income" that dropped by 68 percent during the period in question. That is, the erosion of the company's profits was caused by a reduction of income different from that derived from the sale of refrigerators in the domestic market and could not, therefore, be linked to the entry of imports under conditions of dumping.

Consequently, MEIC concluded the investigation in 1997 without imposing antidumping duties on the imports of refrigerators from Mexico. Furthermore, the investigating authority proceeded to notify the commission to promote competition so that the commission would investigate the arrangements between the parties involved, under the assumption that the two companies might be colluding to implement uncompetitive practices in detriment of free trade.

TABLE 6.4 Costa Rica: Refrigerator Imports, 1994–2002

Year	Mexico			Rest of world		
	Value (US$)	Volume (kg)	Import value per kg	Value (US$)	Volume (kg)	Import value per kg
1994	562,756	138,409	4.07	9,317,673	2,156,017	4.32
1995	638,105	168,393	3.79	6,846,208	1,533,760	4.46
1996	1,777,664	355,587	5.00	6,640,731	1,426,152	4.66
1997	2,376,751	548,106	4.34	7,525,276	1,718,870	4.38
1998	2,101,208	609,683	3.45	8,688,999	2,056,394	4.23
1999	2,850,069	904,441	3.15	9,068,508	2,372,896	3.82
2000	2,610,767	780,547	3.34	8,624,939	2,385,894	3.61
2001	2,588,674	727,741	3.56	12,773,567	3,128,140	4.08
2002	4,245,819	1,185,072	3.58	16,877,366	4,491,867	3.76
2003	5,358,228	1,500,316	3.57	13,356,334	3,657,160	3.65

Source: Prepared by the authors using statistics from SIECA's System of Trade Statistics of Central America (http://www.sieca.org.gt).

An Analysis of the Applications for Safeguard Measures

Between 1995 and 2004, MEIC's investigating authority received a total of five applications for the imposition of safeguard measures, of which four corresponded to manufactured products (classified under chapters 25 to 99 of SAC) and one corresponded to the agricultural sector, specifically, milled and paddy rice (see table 6.5).[17] This structure is approximately consistent with Costa Rica's import structure. As a result of the high tariff protection prevailing over the agricultural products that are more important for domestic consumption, imports tend to concentrate on manufactured products.

Of the five safeguard applications, one was filed against imports from Asian countries, four against imports from countries in the Americas, and one against imports from Europe.[18] This structure is consistent with the structure of Costa Rica's imports by source because practically two-thirds of imports come from North and Central America.

In only one of the cases (ceramic tiles and plates), the investigating authority failed to initiate. In that instance, the applicants dropped the case and did not submit the information required by the investigating authority (see table 6.6). In only two of the five applications, the finding was one of injury to domestic production caused by imports and, although in both of those cases it was decided to apply a provisional measure, in only one (coarse fiber bags) was the measure finally enforced; in the case of rice, the application of the measure was not considered

TABLE 6.5 Costa Rica: Safeguard Cases

Year	Product	Sector	Related countries	Requester or applicant
1995	Coarse fiber bags	Manufacturing	Bangladesh, India, and Nicaragua	National Cabuya Board
1996	Used apparel	Manufacturing	United States	Textile and Apparel Industry Association
1996	Ceramic tiles and plates	Manufacturing	Brazil, Italy, Mexico, and Spain	Productos de Concreto S.A. and Firenze Industrial S.A.
1996	Sanitaryware	Manufacturing	Mexico	Incesa Standard S.A.
2000	Paddy and milled rice	Agriculture	United States	National Rice Board

Source: Prepared by the authors using data drawn from resolutions of dumping cases dealt with by MEIC.

necessary because of the increase of international prices that made imports less attractive. Space restrictions allow only one of the five cases in which an application for safeguards was filed in Costa Rica to be presented as an illustration in the following section.

The Burlap Bags Case In September 1995, the National Cabuya Board filed an application for an investigation to impose a safeguard measure against imports of coarse fiber (burlap) bags[19] originating in Bangladesh, Nicaragua, and India.

The National Cabuya Board requested this measure owing to the massive increase in the number of imports of burlap bags, mainly from Bangladesh. The board alleged that this situation directly affected both the domestic production of cabuya bags and the marketing of coffee because burlap and cabuya bags are used to package coffee for export. In the application, the applicant mentioned that Bangladesh is the source of 55 percent of the world's exports of burlap, whereas Costa Rica's production represents less than 0.2 percent of the production of Bangladesh, for which reason, Bangladesh has the ability to cause material injury to the domestic production of cabuya bags. Furthermore, the National Cabuya Board noted that Bangladesh granted its exporters subsidies covered under WTO agreements.[20]

During the investigation of this case, the investigating authority discovered that most of the import flows (of the bags) affecting the sector originated in Nicaragua, but that in 1995, Bangladesh had supplied approximately 40 percent of Costa Rica's total imports of this product, a figure that is significant because, in 1994, Bangladesh had not exported a single bag to Costa Rica.

TABLE 6.6 Costa Rica: Summary of the Outcome of Safeguard Cases Dealt with by Investigating Authority

Product	Firms failed to submit information	Case dropped by applicant	Start of investigation	Withdrawal	No injury found	Preventive measure	Final resolution	
							Measure applied	No measure applied[a]
Coarse fiber bags			X			X		X
Used apparel			X					X[b]
Ceramic tiles and plates	X	X						
Sanitaryware					X[c]			
Paddy and milled rice					X[d]			

Source: Prepared by the authors using data drawn from resolutions of dumping cases dealt with by MEIC.

a. In cases where injury was found but no measure applied, the existence of other factors, beyond imports, that contributed to the injury was determined.

b. No measure applied because of other causes such as subinvoicing and smuggling.

c. The authority did not consider it necessary to impose any temporary protective measure because the firm was internationally competitive.

d. No measure applied because the increase of international prices made it unnecessary.

TABLE 6.7 Costa Rica: Origin of Imports of Cabuya Bags, 1992–95

Year (Jan.–Aug.)	Total imported bags	Imported bags from Nicaragua	Imported bags from Bangladesh and other countries
1992	371,490	332,409	39,081
1993	286,582	253,596	32,986
1994	209,218	209,218	0
1995	816,683	489,609	330,074

Source: Prepared by the authors using data from MEIC resolution published in the *Official Gazette* of May 13, 1998.

The data in table 6.7 show that in 1995 Nicaragua increased its exports to Costa Rica more than twofold over the previous year. This increase, together with the large increase of imports from other countries (including Bangladesh), meant an aggregate increase of 290 percent in the total imports of cabuya bags to Costa Rica in the same year.

These figures confirm the significant increase of imports that would derive in the eventual injury to the domestic production of burlap bags. Unfortunately, the case's file and the respective MEIC resolution fail to provide any information or analysis of the impact (if any) of the increased imports on the domestic production of burlap bags.

Likewise, no data are available on the sector's evolution or its share in production and employment. However, because one of the main uses of burlap bags is to package coffee for export, the behavior of coffee exports could shed some light on the potential impact of the increased imports of cabuya bags on domestic production.

According to data from the Central Bank of Costa Rica, the volume of coffee exported (in 46-kilogram bags) fell 3 percent in 1995, which is consistent with most of the years in that decade, with the exception of 1996, when the volume of coffee exported recorded a 23 percent increase. Taking into account that burlap bags are not a perishable product and that coffee is a product that is usually traded in futures markets, it makes sense to conclude that the increase in the volume of coffee exported in 1996 would explain part of the increment in the imports of burlap bags in 1995.

That conclusion means that approximately one-tenth of the increased cabuya bag imports recorded in 1995 had no direct effect on domestic production because the increase in bags was simply covering an increase in the demand for the product to be used to package export coffee.[21] However, even though no information is available on the behavior of the other activities that use burlap bags, it is reasonable to assume that the remaining percentage points of increase in the imports of burlap bags did cause an important crowding out of domestic production in the local market.

After analyzing the investigation, MEIC finally decided to apply a provisional measure that would increase the customs duty from 54 percent to 140 percent for a period no longer than 30 days. The implementation of the measure implied that the National Cabuya Board committed to improving the installed capacity and production so the situation would be better once the measure expired, an aspiration that does not seem reasonable because it entails long-term aspects that require a period much longer than 30 days. Interestingly, the investigating authority also determined that, although a substantial increase in the imports of cabuya bags had actually occurred in 1995, to a good extent, this increase was a response to the lack of supply in the domestic market because, since 1992, domestic production failed to meet domestic demand.

In 1997, MEIC lifted the provisional measure that had been imposed after realizing that its application had continued for longer than six months when it actually should have been applied for only 30 days. Therefore, and after verifying that the domestic industry had carried out no adjustment or improvement, MEIC decided to close the investigation in April 1998 and not impose a definitive measure. This case confirms that, although the imposition of the safeguard does not seem to have stemmed from protectionist goals, its incorrect implementation did provide a margin of protection beyond what was contemplated.

Summary of Cases

The figures in table 6.8 show that the applications for safeguard and antidumping measures have mostly focused on manufactured goods, which is not surprising because Costa Rica still retains a high protection rate for basic agricultural products.

TABLE 6.8 Costa Rica: Summary of Cases Dealt with by Investigating Authority

	Sectors		
Measures	Manufacturing	Agriculture	Total
Safeguards	4	1	5
Antidumping	4	2	6
Total	8	3	11

Source: Prepared by the authors using data drawn from resolutions of dumping cases dealt with by MEIC.

TABLE 6.9 Costa Rica: Summary of Cases Dealt with by Investigating Authority

Year	Type of case	
	Safeguards	Antidumping
1995	1	1
1996	3	3
1997	0	1
1998	0	1
1999	0	0
2000	1	0
2001	0	0

Source: Prepared by the authors using data drawn from resolutions of dumping cases dealt with by the MEIC.

By the same token, table 6.9 shows that the applications for the imposition of measures not only have been balanced between safeguard and antidumping measures but also have lagged between the date of entry into force of the rules (1995) and the year when the last case was submitted (2000).

Although elements such as the failure to provide information on the part of the applicant companies and the results shown by some of the statistics reported in this chapter suggest that several of the applications for the imposition of safeguard or antidumping measures seem to have responded to merely protectionist interests, the case of paddy rice is the only one where there appears to have been a political economy scenario that influenced the final imposition of measures. In that case, the technical criterion of the investigating authority pointed out that a measure was not warranted; even so, MEIC's authorities decided to impose a provisional safeguard. The decision was influenced by the strong pressure that local producers put on the competent authorities.[22] In fact, in a later review of the case by the General Controllership of the Republic, serious deficiencies were found in the procedure for the adoption of the final resolution issued by MEIC.

Another important element to be emphasized is that, in those cases in which the investigating authority carried out the investigation process, the contents of the files show little depth to the economic analysis of the cases. In fact, this made it necessary for the authors of this chapter to search for statistics that could at least provide an approximate idea of the relevant economic environment in which each of the applications occurred because the file generally lack figures and analysis.

In sum, the evidence does not support the conclusion that Costa Rica's institutional structure to process applications for safeguard and antidumping measures is working perfectly. Furthermore, a detailed analysis of several cases leads to the conclusion that there have been attempts, albeit failed ones, to use safeguard and antidumping measures in Costa Rica with protectionist purposes. Nevertheless, one can generally conclude that Costa Rica has made a reasonable use of those instruments to date.

Conclusions

The process of economic liberalization that was initiated by Costa Rica in the second half of the 1980s has not yet been completed. Even though there persist sectors that enjoy protection against foreign competition (mainly telecommunication services, insurance, and some agricultural products), one can say that at the beginning of the 21st century, Costa Rica is very different economically from the Costa Rica of the beginning of the 1980s. At that time in the 1980s, the economy was characterized by the preponderance of two export crops (coffee and bananas) as major sources of export earnings, a limited flow of foreign investment, and the participation of the government in diverse production activities. All of those characteristics were results of an import-substitution development model, which also generated rent-seeking activities that were not directly productive and, therefore, were important losses of well-being for the majority of Costa Ricans (Monge and González-Vega 1995).

Twenty years later, Costa Rica is characterized by the diversification of the products it exports, the businesses that export, and the markets in which Costa Rica sells. Liberalization has also led to the growth in supply of a cluster of products and services that are linked to tourism, to the attraction of important flows of foreign investment (mainly in technology), and to a decrease in the direct participation of the government in many economic activities.[23] All those results can be attributed largely to the economic liberalization process that Costa Rica began in the 1980s, a process that was designed and implemented under a rule of law within a democratic regime.

The performance of Costa Rica's economy over the period from 1986 to 2003 can be considered satisfactory. The economy has exhibited important transformations in its production base, as well as progress in the fight against poverty and in the generation of new sources of employment. All this change has been achieved with no increase in income inequality.

The empirical evidence on unfair competition policies and safeguards shows that the country has had to respond to few complaints in this field (11 in total). After an analysis of each complaint, it can be argued that some companies and business organizations have made attempts to seek new forms of protection against imports during the economic liberalization period. However, Costa Rica's government has been careful in handling those applications and has acted in accordance with the standards established in the corresponding legal instruments, thus avoiding an undue application of those instruments. The exception to the rule has been the case of rice, where the result of the application apparently did respond to political pressures, which according to political economy theory results from the direct search for unproductive rent-seeking activities on the part of the companies involved.

Although several manufacturing companies that sought the application of safeguard or antidumping measures had settled in Costa Rica under the umbrella of the previous import-substitution model, in large part they have succeeded in completing an important transformation and have become successful exporters (for example, Atlas Industrial and Pastas Roma). The opposite has been the case with the agricultural activities that brought complaints about unfair practices or safeguards, many of which are still highly protected in Costa Rica (for example, onions, which even succeeded in gaining an exclusion from the free trade agreement between Central America and the United States).

With respect to the evolution of the legal norms in force in Costa Rica on dumping and safeguards, the review conducted in this chapter clearly shows that, in the process of negotiation of bilateral free trade agreements, Costa Rica has improved its rules on those matters, specifically by providing more transparent and faster mechanisms to process applications and by reducing the terms for which dumping and safeguard measures can be effective.

The new safeguard rules have been shaped to minimize any incentive for domestic companies to seek safeguard applications merely for protectionist purposes. Particularly important here have been (a) the requirement within the framework of the Central American Rules that security has to be deposited by the applicant when provisional measures are applied and (b) the compensation to the other party that the bilateral free trade agreements to which Costa Rica is party provide for when a safeguard measure is applied. Moreover, the analysis of the institutional arrangements and the procedures that applicant businesses must follow confirms that the forms they have to complete are not so complex as to be inaccessible for the companies. The need for expertise is, however, important. Following the prescribed processes does require time and knowledge of the subject. Interviews with MEIC officials and representatives of Costa Rica's business sector made clear that the country lacks sufficient skilled human resources to provide adequate coverage of the private sector's requirements for support when preparing and presenting applications for antidumping and safeguard measures.

Furthermore, an important institutional gap apparently still exists, specifically in MEIC, which prevents dealing appropriately with this type of complaint. There is no specialized office to administer such applications because so few complaints have been filed. Consequently, cases are managed by MEIC's legal unit. This limitation is being studied by Costa Rica's authorities, who are trying to strike a balance between the private sector's needs and the opportunity cost of making specialized resources available at the ministry to discharge such responsibilities.

In that respect, authorities might explore the possibility of transferring the responsibility for processing unfair practices complaints and safeguard applications to the Foreign Trade Ministry because that ministry is the agency responsible for managing trade agreements (multilateral and bilateral) signed by Costa Rica, both with reference to free trade agreements and to the country's obligations under WTO. In addition, it has a budget for those purposes.

In sum, Costa Rica has succeeded in making progress toward economic liberalization during the past 20 years, without having had to face economic crises. The country has effectively reduced its levels of poverty and has confronted important flows of immigration, thereby maintaining low and stable levels of unemployment and underemployment, all without income distribution deterioration. Moreover, the country has responded to complaints for unfair trade practices and substantial increases in imports that can affect domestic production; it has differentiated appropriately true cases from those that would seem to be new protectionist endeavors. However, because Costa Rica lacks appropriate institutional arrangements, the country still faces an important challenge linked to the efficient management of its commitments and responsibilities in terms of antidumping and safeguard policies.

Notes

1. There are still important reforms pending: for example, the liberalization of the areas of services, telecommunications, and insurance; tax exceptions for some agricultural products; and government modernization.

2. Using Lerner's Theorem (Lerner 1936/1968), Monge (1994) estimated that out of each percentage point of protection granted to Costa Rica's manufacturing sector during the import-substitution period, 0.66 was transferred as an implicit tax to the country's export efforts.

3. See Corrales and Monge (1990), Lizano (1992), Céspedes and Jiménez (1997), and Monge and Lizano (1997).

4. For a detailed report on the positive effects of the companies included in Costa Rica's free trade zones, see Monge, Rosales, and Arce (2004).

5. According to the records of Costa Rica's Foreign Trade Ministry.

6. In fact, according to figures of the last population census (taken in 2000), immigrants make up one-fourth of Costa Rica's population.

7. Because of a change in the methodology for the household census in 1987, the figures for previous years are not comparable. For that reason, the income distribution and poverty figures used in this document are from 1987 on. However, for the purposes of our analysis, that restriction is not a serious one because Costa Rica's liberalization period began in 1986.

8. In spite of the fact that the Free Trade Agreement with the United States has already been signed by the two executive powers, it is still pending ratification by Congress in both countries. Consequently, the antidumping and safeguards provisions in that agreement are not yet part of the legal framework governing these matters in Costa Rica. For that reason, they have not been included in this chapter. To review the provisions of the Central American Free Trade Agreement (CAFTA) that are relevant to this chapter, see the text of the agreement, at http://www.comex.go.cr.

9. The term injury means material injury or threat of material injury to a domestic industry or material retardation of the establishment of a domestic industry.

10. The Industrial Protection and Development Act, approved on May 18, 1960, authorized the MEIC to take the necessary measures to counteract unfair trade practices.

11. The lowest of the following will apply: (a) the most-favored-nation duty, (b) the duty in force at the time the measure is adopted, or (c) the duty in force on the day before the date of effectiveness of the treaty.

12. Information about this process is based on the interview with Douglas Alvarado, currently responsible for processing applications related to antidumping, safeguard, and countervailing measures.

13. In the case of the burlap bags, although the measure had to be implemented for only 30 days, it was enforced by customs for six months.

14. No complaints for alleged dumping practices or applications for countervailing measures were filed in Costa Rica before 1995.

15. The Central American Tariff System is derived from the Harmonized System and, therefore, it coincides with the Harmonized System for headings with six or fewer digits.

16. Agreements between the parties have to involve the government and the importing or exporting company, wherefore the "deal" between the domestic producer and the exporting company outside the legal framework governing such arrangements was considered illegal. For that reason, the MEIC decided to continue the investigation under its own initiative because it considered that national interests could be compromised. MEIC also sent the case to the Commission on the Promotion of Competition.

17. No application of this type was submitted before 1995.

18. The total number of cases classified by regions is six because, in the case of ceramic plates and tiles, countries from the Americas (Mexico and Brazil) and European countries (Italy and Spain) are involved.

19. Classified under heading 63.05.10.00 of the SAC.

20. MEIC indicated that, where the unfair trade results from the granting of a subsidy in the exporting country, the proper measure is a countervailing duty and not a safeguard.

21. Certainly, the good expectations generated by increased sales of coffee abroad could have induced coffee businesses to increase their stock of packaging material.

22. A review of the press for 2000 makes evident the pressure exerted on the government by the producers of this grain.

23. The government of Costa Rica ended participation in activities such as production of cement and of ethyl alcohol by privatizing the respective government-run companies. For a detailed analysis, see Meléndez and Meza (1993).

References

Bhagwati, Jagdish. 1982. "Directly Unproductive: Profit Seeking (DUP) Activities." *Journal of Political Economy* 88 (August): 409–33.

______. 1991. *Political Economy and International Economics.* Cambridge, MA: MIT Press.

Céspedes, Víctor, and Ronulfo Jiménez. 1997. *Costa Rica, una economía en recesión: Informe sobre la economía en 1996.* San José, Costa Rica: Academia de Centroamérica.

Corrales, Jorge, and Ricardo Monge. 1990. *Exportaciones no tradicionales en Costa Rica.* San José, Costa Rica: Econofín.

Edwards, Sebastian. 1990. "Ajuste cambiario y equilibrio macroeconómico en Costa Rica: Lecciones y perspectivas." In *Políticas Económicas en Costa Rica,* ed. Claudio González Vega and Edna Camacho, 106–21. Tomo II. San José, Costa Rica: Academia de Centroamérica and Ohio State University.

González Vega, Claudio. 1984. "Fear of Adjusting: The Social Costs of Economic Policies in Costa Rica in the 1970s." In *Revolution and Counterrevolution in Central America and the Caribbean,* eds. Donald Shutz and Douglas Graham, 234–52. Boulder, CO: Westview Press.

______. 1989. "Debt Stabilization and Liberalization in Costa Rica: Political Economy Responses to a Fiscal Crisis." In *Latin America Debt and Adjustment,* compiled by Philip L. Brock, Michael Connolly, and Claudio González Vega, 164–78. New York: Praeger.

International Monetary Fund (IMF). 1998. *Costa Rica: Recent Economic Developments.* IMF Staff Country Report 98/45. Washington, DC: International Monetary Fund.

Lerner, Abba P. 1968. "The Symmetry between Import and Export Taxes." *Económica* 3, no. 11 (August): 306–13. Reprinted and revised in *Readings in International Economics,* compiled by Richard Caves and Harry Jonson, Homewood, IL: Richard D. Irwin.

Lizano Fait, Eduardo. 1992. "Estado y Economía en América Central." Paper presented at Asociación Alemana de Investigación en América Latina, Congreso Internacional sobre Estado en América Latina: Orden Democrático, "Cambio Sistemático y Perspectivas," San José, Costa Rica, May 23–24.

Meléndez, Dennis H., and Mauricio R. Meza. 1993. *CODESA: Origen y Consecuencias.* San José: Fiduciaria de Inversiones Transitorias (FINTRA).

Mesalles, Luis. 1998. "Condiciones macroeconómicas de la economía costarricense." In *Estabilidad y desarrollo en Costa Rica. las reformas pendientes,* ed. Ronulfo Jiménez, 81–106. San José, Costa Rica: Academia de Centroamérica.

Monge, Ricardo. 1994. "The Political Economy of Trade Reform in Costa Rica." Doctoral dissertation, The Ohio State University, Columbus.

Monge, Ricardo, and Jorge Corrales. 1988. *Políticas dep protección e incentivos a las manufactura: Agroindustria y algunos sectores agrícolas en Costa Rica.* San José, Costa Rica: Econofín.

Monge, Ricardo, and Claudio González Vega. 1995. *Economía política: Proteccionismo y apertura en Costa Rica.* San José, Costa Rica: Academia de Centroamérica and Centro Internacional para el Desarrollo Económico.

Monge, Ricardo, and Eduardo Lizano. 1997. *Apertura económica e industrialización en Costa Rica.* San José, Costa Rica: Academia de Centroamérica.

Monge, Ricardo, Julio Rosales, and Gilberto Arce. 2005. "Cost-Benefit Analysis of the Free Trade Zone System: The Impact of Foreign Direct Investment in Costa Rica." OAS Trade, Growth and Competitiveness Studies, Washington, DC: Organization of American States.

Oficina de Prácticas de Comercio Desleal y Medidas de Salvaguardia. "Resoluciones de los casos *antidumping* y de imposición de medidas de salvaguardias." Archivo Central, Unidad de Asuntos Jurídicos Ministerio de Economía, Industria y Comercio de Costa Rica. Available from PROCOMER or Banco Central de Costa Rica at http://servicios.procomer.go.cr/estadisticas/Estadisticas.jsp?val=Panel and http://indicadoreseconomicos.bccr.fi.cr/indicadoreseconomicos/.

Rhee, Yung Whee. 1984. "Framework for Export Policy and Administration: Lessons from the East Asian Experience." Industry and Finance Paper 10, World Bank, Washington, DC.

Taylor, Marvin. 1984. *Estructura de la protección al sector industrial en Costa Rica.* San José, Costa Rica: Prodesarrollo.

7

ANTIDUMPING AND SAFEGUARD MEASURES IN THE POLITICAL ECONOMY OF LIBERALIZATION: THE MEXICAN CASE

Luz Elena Reyes de la Torre
and Jorge G. González

From 1986, when Mexico joined the General Agreement on Tariffs and Trade (GATT), until 1994, when the North American Free Trade Agreement (NAFTA) came into effect, the country created new mechanisms and institutions concerned with administering antidumping and safeguard proceedings and it strengthened existing ones.

At first glance, the history of contingent protection mechanisms in Mexico appears to contradict the actions adopted by Mexico to liberalize its trade and economy. Nevertheless, when the country's political economy is analyzed in depth, what is found is not only an indisputably logical connection but also an indissoluble link between the goals of trade liberalization and the strengthening of contingent trade protection institutions and mechanisms. In fact, the undersecretary responsible for the legal and institutional reform that led to the full implementation of antidumping mechanisms in Mexico stated on several occasions that the monster was born only to protect the liberalization process.[1]

The authors acknowledge the valuable support and assistance given to this research by Emiliano Zubieta Medina, Jorge Sentíes Guerrero, and Daniel Reyes Torres.

This chapter is divided into five sections that analyze the political and economic context in which Mexico adopted contingent trade-protection instruments, the ensuing institutional reform, and the economic history of the creation of the institutions in charge of the administration of such instruments, as well as the driving forces that played a relevant role in their development. In addition, this chapter reviews and analyzes the investigations carried out by Mexican authorities, together with their determinations, and concludes by presenting case studies to draw lessons from this process.

Trade Liberalization and Contingent Trade-Protection Instruments

> *Mexico's accession to the GATT in 1986 meant the beginning of a gradual reduction of a highly protected trade system, which was, for 40 years, one of the pillars of industrial development. This first step toward trade liberalization consisted in the lowering of tariffs and the elimination of import licenses, accompanied by the creation of a system against unfair foreign trade practices.*[2]
>
> —Dr. Raúl Ramos Tercero (1995)

Trade Liberalization and Economic Reform in Mexico

In the early 1980s, the limitations of the import-substitution model became evident. This model, based on a protectionist policy, had given rise to an inefficient production structure, combined with monopolistic behavior and technological backwardness. State intervention was a constant feature to counteract the economy's inefficiencies that very often led to widespread, indiscriminate subsidies, exerting a heavy burden on public finances.

As shown in table 7.1, in 1982, Mexico underwent the worst economic crisis of the model period: the GDP dropped by 0.5 percent, and inflation rates rose from 28.7 percent in 1981 to 98.8 percent only one year later. Also in 1982, Mexico had such a severe balance of payments crisis that the country became insolvent in the international financial markets. In the face of that crisis, the government decided to nationalize the banking system and impose strict exchange control. Likewise, the balance of payments crisis obliged the government to maintain, and even reinforce, a highly protectionist trade policy to restrain imports and encourage a trade surplus in the shortest possible run to pay the foreign debt service; in fact, all imports were subject to import licenses. When external financing sources were no longer available, the country entered into a vicious circle of inflation and stagnation with severe implications for Mexico's competitiveness and growth (Serra Puche 1994).

TABLE 7.1 Mexican Macroeconomic Indicators during Economic Liberalization

Year	GDP growth (% per year)	Inflation (% per year)	Observed nominal exchange rate (pesos per US$)[a]	CETES 28-day interest rate (average annual rate)[b]
1981	8.5	28.7	0.0262	—
1982	–0.5	98.8	0.0963	44.408
1983	–3.5	80.8	0.1436	58.741
1984	3.4	59.2	0.1920	—
1985	2.2	63.8	0.3683	61.590
1986	–3.1	105.8	0.9151	87.372
1987	1.7	159.2	2.2097	96.048
1988	1.3	51.7	2.2810	69.534
1989	4.1	19.7	2.6410	44.993
1990	5.2	29.9	2.9454	34.759
1991	4.2	18.8	3.0710	19.278
1992	3.5	11.9	3.1154	15.622
1993	1.9	8.0	3.1059	14.931
1994	4.5	7.1	5.3250	14.098

Sources: INEGI; Banco de México.

Note: — = not available.

a. Nominal exchange rate to face foreign currency obligations (end of period).

b. CETES (Certificados de la Tesoreria de la Federación) 28-day interest rate for 1982 was based only on the September–December average; in the case of 1983, the January–July average was taken into account; and for 1985, the February–December average was considered.

It was in this context that the Mexican government decided to unilaterally liberalize its economy in 1983 as the only way to increase its competitiveness and thus break the vicious circle of inflation and stagnation. The trade liberalization process was strengthened from 1985 onward; maximum tariffs, representing 100 percent, were lowered to 20 percent in only three years. The weighted average tariff dropped from 13.3 percent to 6.2 percent (see table 7.2).[3] In 1985, of a total 5,219 tariff items subject to import permits, 3,064 were exempted from permit requirements. The value of imported goods subject to licenses dropped from 83 percent to 37 percent. The effect of such phasing out of trade-protection mechanisms during the period was mitigated by an exchange policy that significantly devalued the exchange rate—from 368 pesos to 915 pesos per U.S. dollar—from the end of 1985 to the end of 1986 (Zabludovsky 1989).

At that time, the Mexican government realized that, given the significant trade liberalization process it had unilaterally undertaken, remaining outside the GATT was no longer reasonable because that prevented the country from taking advantage of

TABLE 7.2 Mexican Comparative Tariff Structures in Selected Years

Concept	1982	1985	1992
Maximum tariff	100.0	100.0	20.0
Weighted average tariff	16.4	13.3	11.4
Water in the tariff, weighted	24.8	18.8	4.5

Source: SECOFI (1993).

the commercial benefits granted to GATT members through tariff preferences.[4] Thus, Mexico joined the GATT in 1986.[5]

Within the GATT, Mexico stated its commitment to further eliminate import licenses[6] and to reduce maximum tariff levels but was authorized to put in place a system of antidumping and countervailing duties.

Mexico's First Antidumping Legislation and Its Adherence to the Antidumping Code as a Contracting Party

In line with its decision to join the GATT, Mexico began the legal and institutional reforms required at the domestic level to support governmental actions adopted as a result of the new development model and the country's recent international commitments. In this context, in January 1986, the first antidumping legislation was enacted: the Law Regulating Article 131 of the Political Constitution of the United Mexican States on Matters of Foreign Trade (hereinafter, the Law Regulating Article 131) (SECOFI 1990a). In November 1986, the regulations against unfair trade practices in international trade (hereinafter, the Regulations) (SECOFI 1990b) were promulgated, and in 1987, the first request to initiate an antidumping proceeding was filed. It involved the case of caustic soda imported from the United States.[7]

The application of antidumping and safeguard instruments in Mexico was initially within the purview of administrative areas having other responsibilities; in fact, the first investigations were conducted by the agency concerned with exchange control in the General Trade Bureau (Dirección General de Comercio), under the Secretariat of Commerce and Industrial Development (Secretaría de Comercio y Fomento Industrial, or SECOFI).[8]

The antidumping proceedings provided for in the Law Regulating Article 131 and its Regulations were both elementary and limited. By the end of the 1980s, Mexican authorities deemed it necessary to amend the antidumping-related provisions.

One of the most controversial issues of the Law Regulating Article 131 was the possibility for antidumping duties to be applied only five days after a request was filed with the relevant authorities.[9] The time frame granted to respondents was very short, and provisions related to proceedings were not clear enough. All of these factors combined to give rise to a high degree of uncertainty among the parties to the proceedings, allowing room for authorities to act on a discretionary basis. In fact, during the April to July 1986 meetings held by Mexico with the working party appointed under the GATT to analyze its application for accession, one of the first questions posed was how Mexico could possibly reach provisional affirmative determinations of unfair international trade practices within only five working days of the filing of a request for investigation (Gabinete de Comercio Exterior 1986).

Another aspect of the Law Regulating Article 131 that some within the GATT working party objected to was that evidence of injury was not compulsory.[10] The GATT working party concluded that some of the law's provisions were not completely in line with GATT principles and recommended that Mexico subscribe to the Antidumping Code (ADC) (Gabinete de Comercio Exterior 1986). Mexico decided to become a signatory of the Tokyo Round Antidumping Code in 1988.

Contingent Trade-Protection Instruments during NAFTA Negotiations

The Negotiation Context In 1988, immediately after the inaugural speech delivered by the newly elected president of the Republic of Mexico, a modernizing project began to take shape for the furthering of the economic and trade liberalization process.

In 1988, 65 percent of Mexican trade was with the United States; sectoral agreements, mainly those reached in the textile and steel industries, as well as the Generalized System of Preferences, represented only limited trade and investment mechanisms between both countries because the time frames of sectoral agreements and the uncertainty as to their extension were no guarantee of permanent access of Mexican products to the U.S. market (Arriola 1994a).[11]

In June 1990, the Mexican and U.S. presidents issued a joint communiqué stating that the best vehicle for increasing trade and investment flows between both countries was the signing of a Free Trade Agreement (George H. W. Bush and Carlos Salinas de Gortrari 1990). On June 12, 1991, formal negotiations began with a view to concluding NAFTA among Mexico, the United States, and Canada.[12]

Bilateral Panels and Agreements on Domestic Legal Reforms At the beginning of NAFTA negotiations, Canada proposed that antidumping laws should no longer be applied among the countries that would be part of the new North American market. Although Mexico supported Canada's proposal, the United States rejected it categorically (Leycegui 2000, 579). The Mexican and Canadian positions were in full agreement because exporting industries in both countries had been adversely affected by antidumping instruments applied by the United States, a world leader in their use.

The United States was inflexible in its determination not to amend its antidumping legislation and practice as long as the Uruguay Round was not concluded. Even though it agreed to appoint two working groups[13] to analyze the possibility of implementing a substitute system during the transition, in practice, no concrete results have been reached 10 years after NAFTA's implementation.

In this context, the core of the trilateral negotiation on unfair international trade practices was the incorporation of a system of binational panels specifically engaged in reviewing final determinations on antidumping and countervailing duties made by competent authorities in each member country, as it was later established in NAFTA, chapter XIX.

For Mexico, another important aspect of NAFTA negotiations was related to its commitment to amend its domestic statutes and regulations (SECOFI 1993 [Annex 1904.15, Schedule of Mexico]).[14] Mexico had already made the decision to introduce the amendments agreed on in early 1991; therefore, it would be wrong to conclude that Mexico was forced by its NAFTA trade partners to set up transparent procedures to apply antidumping and safeguard measures. Actually, the decision to set up those procedures was adopted at the domestic level as a key component of Mexico's economic liberalization process.

Bilateral and Global Safeguards Unlike antidumping measures—an issue about which, to a certain degree, all three member countries possessed a legal framework common to the ADC—in the field of safeguards, no specific multilateral agreement existed, nor did any proceeding guide their application in Mexico. The only reference in common was the provisions of article XIX of the GATT.

In parallel with NAFTA negotiations, negotiators of the Uruguay Round were reaching consensus on which provisions to include in one of the new agreements of the World Trade Organization (WTO), the Safeguards Agreement. However, at that time, more disagreements than agreements still existed over safeguard actions at the multilateral level; consequently, no final results could yet be foreseen at the trilateral negotiations. Hence, the partners needed a detailed administrative procedure to govern their actions to avoid any inconsistency with the Uruguay Round's final conclusions.

Under NAFTA, two kinds of safeguard measures were negotiated: bilateral and global. Bilateral actions were those applied exclusively between two NAFTA partners. Emergency global actions were those taken pursuant to GATT article XIX. With respect to global actions, "exclusion" clauses among trade partners and compensation for the affected party were included. The agreement reached on these topics is reflected in NAFTA, chapter VIII.

The Amendment of the Antidumping Legal Framework in 1993 and Its Ensuing Institutional Reform

The 1993 Foreign Trade Act

During 1992 and the first months of 1993, Mexico conducted a comprehensive public survey on the draft of the future Foreign Trade Act (Ley de Comercio Exterior), published in the official gazette of the federation (*Diario Oficial de la Federación,* or DOF) in July 1993, before NAFTA's approval[15] and the conclusion of the Uruguay Round's final agreements. The anticipation driving this action was caused by Mexico's urgency to have a foreign trade legal framework in place to provide support to the new proceedings and institutions that were being applied and created since 1991 in line with its new economic and trade policy model. The Regulations of the Foreign Trade Act were published in the DOF on December 12, 1993.

This new law introduced substantial changes in the first Mexican antidumping legal framework, the institutional structure, and the administrative proceedings, incorporating substantive provisions in conformity with the latest progress in this area. The peculiarities of the new proceedings, as well as the complexity of investigations on unfair practices and safeguard actions posed a real challenge for the Mexican procedural tradition.

Among the modifications introduced in domestic laws, WTO-Plus provisions should be highlighted. These provisions, resulting from NAFTA negotiations, were intended to bring transparency to proceedings and to offer equal access to information and defense to all of the parties concerned. The following can be mentioned: (a) technical information meetings are to be held, (b) confidential information shall be made available to the accredited legal representatives of the parties, (c) the parties shall be notified of all documents submitted to the competent authority, and (d) transcriptions and records shall be kept of meetings or hearings before the relevant authority and of any external consultancy requested by such authority in relation to the proceedings.

With respect to proceedings, the Foreign Trade Act and its Regulations explained in detail the methodology to be applied in compliance with the ADC, the progress made in the Uruguay Round, the commitments made by Mexico under NAFTA, and the experience gained by the new administrative body specializing in antidumping measures. Under the Foreign Trade Act, no antidumping duties were allowed to be imposed on the initiation of an investigation,[16] and the time limit for the parties to appear was set at 30 working days, a term that could be extended on justified grounds. The new time frames were consistent with those set forth in the ADC, and proceedings were thus extended from a maximum term of six months to almost one year (260 working days).

Additionally, the act specified that the authority's decisions were to be transmitted to all parties concerned on the same day they were made (article 53, Foreign Trade Act) and that communications between competent authorities and interested parties could be made by any direct means, for example, personally at their domicile, by registered mail with acknowledgment of receipt, by specialized messenger service, or by electronic means such as by fax.[17]

The Foreign Trade Act formalized the searches for the purpose of verification established with the new administrative practice. An innovative aspect of the Mexican practice was that from 1991 onward, verification visits, besides those conducted to investigated exporters, could be conducted to investigate domestic producers or to determine injury in all antidumping investigations initiated by the authority.[18] Determinations of injury had a twofold purpose: to make domestic producers aware of the fact that the new antidumping institutions created in the country were to be taken seriously and to show countries under investigation that determinations by authorities would be both impartial and supported by evidence.

The Foreign Trade Act instituted technical information meetings (as required by Mexico's NAFTA commitments). Under the new act, the parties were to have access to details not included in the authorities' public resolutions about the method used in determining the margins of dumping, injury or threat of injury, and the arguments concerning causality.[19]

Under the new act, public hearings were to be held in all antidumping and safeguard proceedings (article 81, Foreign Trade Act). Mexican authorities were convinced that public hearings would introduce greater transparency and objectivity; therefore, even though the obligation under NAFTA explicitly focused on safeguard proceedings, it was extended to all types of proceedings related to contingent trade protection.

In particular, modification to the nature of antidumping duties stands out.[20] According to the Foreign Trade Act, countervailing duties were to be considered revenue within the meaning of article 30 of the Federal Tax Code. In the previous law (the Law Regulating Article 131), countervailing duties were regarded as taxes, which is why they were often challenged on the grounds of unconstitutionality.

Another reform to which Mexico committed itself during NAFTA negotiations involved ensuring access to confidential information related to the proceedings. This reform was also intended to increase transparency and objectivity in the proceedings, by giving the parties better opportunities for defense.

For the first time in the history of Mexican legislation, the Foreign Trade Act incorporated a procedure specifically designed to apply safeguard measures.

Because the act was drafted before the conclusion of the Uruguay Round, those final agreements on this issue were not yet known; therefore, the act adopted various provisions taken from the drafts of the Safeguards Agreement and others derived from NAFTA negotiations. However, the final draft of the Safeguards Agreement underwent modifications, and several of its final provisions turned out to be less stringent than the ones incorporated in the Foreign Trade Act.

Institutional Reform: Creation of the Unit on International Trade Practices

By the end of 1990, SECOFI submitted for the consideration of the president an initiative to create an administrative body specialized in examining requests for applying contingent trade-protection measures. The reason for its creation and strengthening was to ensure a technical, professional, nondiscretionary, and disciplined administration of these mechanisms "so that they should neither interfere with nor revert the trade liberalization process."[21]

In January 1991, the Mexican government created the first body specifically concerned with antidumping issues, the International Trade Practice General Bureau (Dirección General de Prácticas Comerciales Internacionales, or DGPCI).[22] It was commissioned with the task of strictly applying antidumping instruments, when justified, while preventing the antidumping system from becoming an obstacle to the trade liberalization efforts undertaken by Mexico.

The DGPCI's capacity was reinforced when a practically new staff of highly qualified professionals was hired. Intensive training was given to new members engaged in investigations. As soon as the DGPCI was created, its staff conducted a broad comparative study of the antidumping systems in force in the United States and Canada, countries with which the first contacts on this topic would soon be established in the context of a potential trilateral trade negotiation.

This new entity signed cooperation agreements with the agencies responsible for administering antidumping systems in the United States and Canada, which enabled DGPCI staff members to receive technical training by visiting those countries on several occasions to become more acquainted with their procedures and methodologies. European and Australian models were also studied, and preliminary actions were taken to design a new regulatory framework, leading to the enactment of the Foreign Trade Act and its Regulations in 1993.

Furthermore, an intensive dissemination campaign was launched, targeting Mexican production sectors. Its goal was to inform those sectors about the existence of the new contingent protection instruments, while stressing the strict analysis and methodology to be applied by the authorities. The campaign sought to raise the credibility of the new institutions, whose activities relied on their highly qualified professionals and on the transparency of the proceedings (SECOFI 1995a). As part of this process, SECOFI decided to hire the services of an accountancy bureau, which was selected from among the most important ones in Mexico, to assist its new antidumping officials in their verification visits and thus to validate the information gathered for the proceedings.

The institutional strengthening was furthered in 1993 when the Unit on International Trade Practices (Unidad de Prácticas Comerciales Internacionales, or UPCI) was created to replace the DGPCI. The UPCI was the administrative unit responsible for determining dumping margins, injury or threat of injury, the causal relation between dumping and any injury, as well as antidumping or countervailing duty rates. Its structure, composition, and size were substantially different from those of any other federal government agency of the time. The DGPCI had 18 staff members at the time of its creation whereas the UPCI was established with 120 highly qualified professionals. Many operational and support positions were dismantled while field management areas were enlarged. Additionally, five associated management agencies were created—the Technical-Legal Management Agency, the Dumping and Subsidies Investigation Management Agency, the Injury and Safeguards Investigation Management Agency, the Accounting and Financial Analysis Management Agency, and the International Legal Proceedings Management Agency. The UPCI's budget allocation was substantially larger than that of the DGPCI, and it soon became the administrative unit with the largest qualified staff, outperforming any other department of SECOFI in terms of both personnel and budget allocation.

The role of the competent authorities was both strengthened and diversified. In addition to conducting investigations, the UPCI would act as a technical advisory unit, cooperate in drafting any amendment to the Foreign Trade Act, support SECOFI's determinations submitted before dispute settlement bodies, and offer technical and legal assistance to Mexican exporters who were under investigation in a foreign country for unfair practices or safeguard measures (SECOFI 1997).

As can be inferred from officials' communications and from governmental programs of that period, many persons inside and outside the government were ambivalent about the activities of the new entity; even viewed these activities as contradictory to the transformation the government wanted to achieve.[23] This view is not surprising, considering that the UPCI was administering an instrument that was distrusted in many important countries of the world because of its protectionist use at a time when Mexico was committed to reforms and institutional policies that were intended to reinforce its trade and economic liberalization process.

In this context, the Program for Industrial and Foreign Trade Policy (Programa de Política Industrial y Comercio Exterior, or PROPICE) clearly shows the government's continuing concern arising out of the conflict between the greater use of antidumping instruments and the trade policy objectives. Because the liberalization process had been undertaken with the key objective of increasing the manufacturing sector's competitiveness, the government feared the negative impact that antidumping measures might have on capital and intermediate goods.

Nonetheless, as in 1991, when it was decided that the best alternative was to create a strong institution engaged in the administration of those measures, the new government decided that strengthening its institutions and mechanisms was the best way to guarantee the protection of the trade liberalization process.[24] The main guidelines can be summarized in the following notions of procedural transparency and operational capacity:

> Owing to the inevitable complexity that investigations on unfair practices entail, *the precise enforcement of relevant legislation depends most especially on the resources available to the investigation unit.* This leads to the need to prevent turnover [of personnel] and encourage the specialized training of its management, technicians, and administrative staff, as well as to strengthen its power to take action. (SECOFI 1995a, 87; emphasis added.)

Attempts to Create a National Foreign Trade Commission

In 1994, the UPCI's structure and role were reinforced again through a greater resource allocation. In that year, the Secretariat for Finance and Public Credit (Secretaría de Hacienda y Crédito Público, or SHCP) approved the new budget and structure for the UPCI, even though those changes meant a deviation from applicable federal rules. This exception was accepted by the SHCP, provided it was a transition to get past the elections so that, when the new administration came into office, this body could become an independent agency. Thus, the government had set the administrative and budgetary conditions to create in 1995 a body that would be known as the National Foreign Trade Commission (Comisión Nacional de Comercio Exterior, or CNCE).

The CNCE was conceived as an independent agency, with its own budget appropriation and a decision-making team. In addition to taking on the UPCI's role in proceedings related to contingent trade measures,[25] this commission would perform duties similar to those of the U.S. International Trade Commission—for example, conduct studies on industrial competitiveness relative to the international market, monitor products sensitive to international competition, and do research on the economic effect of trade agreements.

The purpose for creating the CNCE was to ensure that proceedings against unfair international trade practices would be technically based and not subject to political pressure.[26] This institutional and decision-making framework was thought to be the only way to ensure an accurate, transparent, and objective application of contingent protection instruments and to avoid their discretionary or protectionist-based use. Another purpose was to foster a career path for civil servants, thus preventing highly qualified human resources from becoming vulnerable to the political fluctuations inherent to the federal public administration.

The private sector supported and promoted the creation of the CNCE for very different reasons from those of the federal government. Local industry believed that UPCI's decisions were strongly influenced by the liberalization policy and the international trade agenda; consequently, if decisions on contingent trade policies were to become independent from SECOFI, protection measures would be applied more frequently and effectively for the benefit of the local manufacturing sector.

The crisis that was precipitated by the change of government in 1994, the devaluation of the local currency, and the serious problems affecting the Mexican economy in that period prompted a radical change of priorities; in that context, the CNCE lost its precedence. The new secretary of trade thought it was a danger to trade liberalization to strengthen and remove from the sphere of SECOFI—the secretariat most committed to trade liberalization—any decision related to contingent trade protection; consequently, he refused to support the project.[27]

Antidumping and Safeguard Investigations and Their Final Determinations (1987–2003)

Requests, Initiations, and Types of Investigations

Between 1987 and 2003, the Mexican government initiated 262 investigations, of which 92 percent were caused by dumping practices, 7 percent by subsidies, and only 1 percent by safeguard measures (see table 7.3).[28] These data take into

TABLE 7.3 Antidumping, Antisubsidy, and Safeguard Proceedings Initiated in Mexico, 1987–2003

Type of investigation	Number of investigations	Relative to the total number of investigations (percent)	Number of concluded cases in 2002	Number of concluded cases with measures in force in 2002	Concluded cases, with measures in effect (percent) in 2002
Dumping	240	91.60	216	74	34.26
Subsidies	19	7.20	18	7	38.89
Safeguards	3	1.10	3	1	33.33
All types listed above	262	100.00	237	82	34.18

Source: UPCI; DOF.

account only initiations of new investigations and exclude proceedings derived from original investigations, for example, reviews of final determinations or sunset reviews. Proceedings are quantified by product-country pairs following the WTO criterion; that is, a resolution to initiate an investigation on corrugated rods against imports from Brazil and Spain is taken as two investigations. The only exception to the rule is the so-called "China Package." (The China Package is taken up in a later section.)

According to the information available, 73 percent of the requests for investigation filed are admitted by the competent authority.[29] Of the investigations initiated, 86 percent led to the application of provisional duties, and 58 percent concluded with the imposition of antidumping or countervailing duties. These percentages have apparently increased with the passing of time: within the period of 1987–95, only 46 percent of investigations resulted in antidumping or countervailing duties (Miranda 1997).

The last column in table 7.3 shows that 34 percent of concluded cases had antidumping or countervailing duties in force in 2002. This percentage, far lower than the 58 percent previously mentioned, results from elimination of some duties after annual administrative or sunset reviews. Because a number of years have passed since the system's implementation, a great part of its current activity focuses on proceedings other than new investigations, as shown by the UPCI's statistics on resolutions (last two columns in table 7.4).

Fifty-five percent of initiations in Mexico took place in only four years, from 1991 to 1994, the most intense period of trade negotiations and economic reform. In that period, Mexico became one of the five most active countries in the world in the use of antidumping instruments, together with the United States, Australia, Canada, and the European Union.

Figure 7.1 shows that antidumping proceedings in 1993 reached an unprecedented number, never again recorded in the country. Of the 83 initiations reported in that year, 53 percent corresponded to two investigation groups or packages: the first one, against imported goods from China, the so-called China Package; the second one, against steel products from several countries, proceedings known as "Multicountry–Multiproduct Steel Cases."

Between 1992 and 1993, the pressure exerted on the Mexican government by sectors significantly affected by the trade liberalization process was so strong that it began to jeopardize the credibility of the new trade defense institutions and to shake the national consensus reached for the conclusion and approval of NAFTA, other international negotiations, and several economic reforms already under way.

In its first activity report, the UPCI explained that the behavior of the economy had a direct effect on the evolution and development of the system. "The most active years were those in which the reduction of the real exchange rate of the

TABLE 7.4 Resolutions Regarding Unfair Practices and Safeguards, 1987–2002

Year	Rejections	Investigations initiated	Special proceedings[a]	Other[b]
1987	n.a.	18	0	0
1988	n.a.	11	0	0
1989	n.a.	7	0	0
1990	n.a.	12	0	0
1991	n.a.	9	0	0
1992	8	26	0	0
1993	12	83	0	0
1994	16	26	0	0
1995	2	4	8	1
1996	6	4	16	5
1997	5	7	7	1
1998	0	11	6	16
1999	10	11	4	13
2000	5	5	10	22
2001	7	5	13	16
2002	0	12	10	9
2003	n.a.	11	n.a.	n.a.
Total	71	262	74	83

Source: Secretaría de Economía (2003).

Note: n.a. = not available.

a. Special proceedings include product coverage, benefit extension, new exporters, and anticircumvention.

b. Reference price and duty elimination and review.

peso, as well as the economic growth led to an increase in the volume of imports" (SECOFI 1997, 19). Figure 7.2 shows two patterns, one representing the behavior of the number of initiations and the other, the margins of overvaluation or undervaluation of the Mexican peso.

Even though figure 7.2 seems to indicate that the antidumping activity increase in Mexico during 1991–97 could be largely explained by the behavior of the real exchange rate, other political and economic events or circumstances taking place in the country contributed to the expansion of this activity.

According to reports by SECOFI and PROPICE,[30] the increase in antidumping investigations resulted from other economic events taking place at the time that Mexican trade was further liberalized, events such as fluctuation of prices of some goods in international markets, recession periods in industrial countries, and

FIGURE 7.1 Investigations Initiated in Mexico, 1987–2003

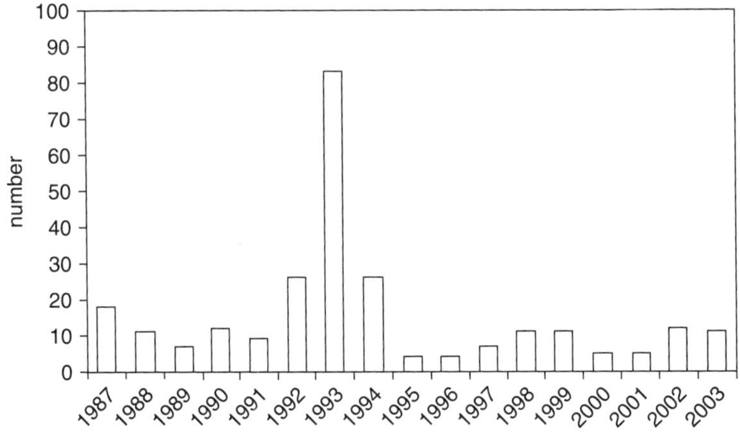

Source: UPCI (1986–2002); DOF (2003).

other events that led to the restructuring of world trade, all of which forced some countries to look for new export markets and to compete under unfair trade conditions (SECOFI 1997). Figure 7.3 illustrates the timing of major economic and political events in Mexico in relation to the peak of antidumping activity.

FIGURE 7.2 Investigations Initiated and Over- and Undervaluation Margins of the Exchange Rate in Mexico, 1987–2003

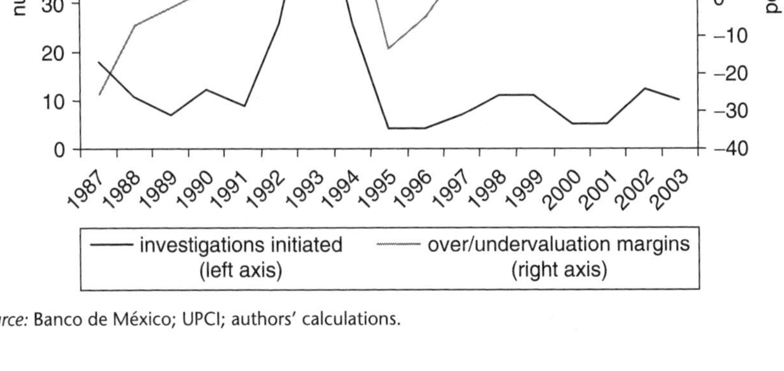

Source: Banco de México; UPCI; authors' calculations.

FIGURE 7.3 Investigations Initiated in Mexico in Relation to Major Economic and Political Events, 1987–2003

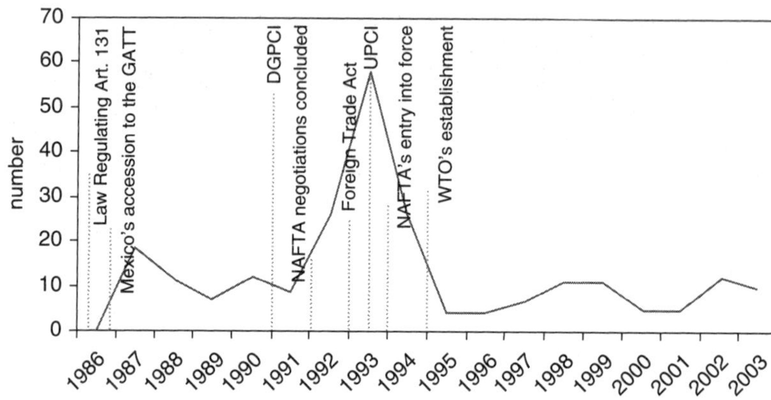

Source: DOF; UPCI.

Breakdown of Investigations by Country and Sector

Mexico has filed proceedings against 49 countries (Secretaría de Economía 2003), three of which account for 55.3 percent of all the investigations (see table 7.5): the United States (27 percent of all initiated cases), China (18.3 percent), and Brazil (10 percent). This ranking changes when the analysis focuses on the main countries affected by antidumping or countervailing duties. Until 2003, duties were still imposed on products from 10 countries. The country on which the highest number of duties has been imposed is China (34.2 percent of total duties), followed by the United States (28.0 percent), the Republic of Korea (8.1 percent), and the Russian Federation (6.3 percent).

It is interesting to compare the number of duties in effect with the number of investigations concluded for each country. Although the greatest number of investigations was initiated against products of U.S. origin, only 19 percent of concluded cases involving the United States have duties in force. By contrast, the percentage of duties in force relative to the investigations concluded is 78 percent for China and 83 percent for Russia (see table 7.5). This asymmetry also stems from the different standards applied by the UPCI to market-oriented or closed economies.

If analyzed from the sectoral point of view, investigations follow clear-cut international patterns. First come basic metals, particularly steel products; second, chemicals; and third, textiles and clothing (see figure 7.4).

TABLE 7.5 Initiated Investigations, Antidumping and Countervailing Duties, by Country and Region, 1987–2002

Country/region	Number of investigations	Percent of Total investigations	Number of duties in effect in 2002	Duties vis-à-vis the number of investigations (percent)
United States	68	27.09	13	19.12
China	46	18.33	36	78.26
Brazil	25	9.96	4	16.00
Venezuela, R.B. de	10	3.98	1	10.00
Korea, Rep. of	9	3.59	2	22.22
Germany	7	2.79	0	0
Russian Federation	6	2.39	5	83.33
Spain	7	2.79	0	0
Taiwan (China)	6	2.39	2	33.33
Ukraine	6	2.39	3	50.00
Canada	5	1.99	0	0
European Union	4	1.59	2	50.00
Colombia	4	1.59	1	25.00
Japan	3	1.20	1	33.33
Indonesia	2	0.80	1	50.00
Other countries	43	18.40	8	18.60
All countries	251	100.00	79	31.47

Source: WTO (2004); also in sources available at http://www.wto.org/english/tratop_e/adp_e/adp_stattab2_e.xls; http://www.wto.org/english/tratop_e/adp_e/adp_stattab7_e.xls (accessed April 2005).

FIGURE 7.4 Investigations in Mexico, by Sector, 1987–2002

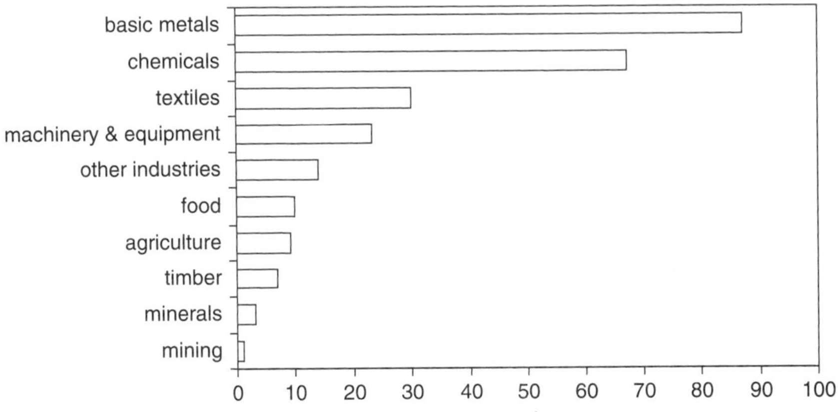

Source: UPCI (2002).

TABLE 7.6 Investigations and Duties by Type of Good Imported to Mexico

	Number of investigations	Percentage of total number of investigations	Number of duties in force	Average duty in force percentage ad valorem
Consumer goods	56	22.31	14	25.00
Intermediate goods	187	74.50	63	33.69
Capital goods	8	3.19	2	25.00
All goods above	251	100.00	79	31.47

Sources: Secretaría de Economía 2003; DOF (several years).

Table 7.6 shows how investigations are distributed per type of good. Intermediate products recorded the highest number of investigations (75 percent), followed by consumer goods (22 percent) and capital goods (3 percent). With respect to the number of duties in force, intermediate goods rank first.

This sectoral breakdown of investigations has changed over time. Between 1987 and 1992, 95 percent of all investigations concerned industrial supplies (Reyes de la Torre 1995). Hence, antidumping investigations need to be conducted with the greatest possible objectivity because duties could affect the competitiveness of other domestic industries using such products.

This concern led the UPCI to create new administrative mechanisms to mitigate the effect of antidumping duties on some industries or prevent too great an effect on the consumer. This particular issue is discussed in the section "Lessons: Case Studies."

Safeguard Cases: Almost Nonexistent?

To date, the UPCI has conducted only three safeguard investigations and has applied (bilateral) safeguard measures on only one occasion. For quite a long time, analysts have been suspicious of this absence of safeguard investigations in Mexico, assuming that, in some cases, the Mexican government was resorting to antidumping measures when safeguards should have been applied. Mexican authorities systematically dismissed all safeguard requests filed before them on the grounds that such measures might introduce distortions in the manufacturing sector and, most especially, because of the compensation Mexico would have to pay its trade partners.

The *Informe de Labores de la UPCI 1991-1996* (UPCI Work Report 1991–1996) indicates that several safeguard consultations were requested but in only three cases were investigations formally filed: pork products, shoes, and fish flour. The report states that many of the safeguard cases filed "were settled by resorting to other types of measures" (SECOFI 1997, 93).

In 1993, the National Commission of Hog Farming filed the first formal request for safeguard measures, but it was dismissed on the grounds that it did not provide sufficient evidence. In 1994, the National Chamber of the Shoe Industry and the Chambers of the Shoe Industries in the states of Guanajuato and Jalisco filed the second formal request—for safeguard measures against imports of all types of shoes (excluding parts not manufactured in Mexico) from all countries, except the United States and Canada. The request was also dismissed for noncompliance with the main substantive provisions laid down in the Foreign Trade Act.

The first safeguard investigation in Mexico was initiated in November 1993. It involved a bilateral safeguard against fish flour imports pursuant to the Mexico-Chile Free Trade Agreement. The investigation was initiated ex officio one month after the conclusion of the antidumping investigation against the same product, as a result of which no antidumping duties were imposed despite the existence of evidence of dumping margins and serious injury to the domestic industry. However, no causal link was proved.

The decision to initiate ex officio safeguard proceedings was strongly influenced by the prevailing political circumstances; it was almost a given that the Mexican authority would take safeguard actions. Moreover, a process of consultation with Chilean authorities had already started and a preliminary agreement had even been reached on the characteristics of the action and the amount of the compensation. This decision was radically changed when the 1994 crisis developed—the peso was devalued by 50 percent in relation to the U.S. dollar, and the ensuing change in market conditions made all imports shrink substantially because of the high increase in their relative prices. Thus, safeguard measures were no longer necessary.

Only in 2002 did the UPCI accept and initiate the second and third safeguard claims. The first one was a request for taking global measures against timber products, and the second one involved bilateral measures against imports of U.S. chicken legs and thigh meat. This case was conducted in conformity with NAFTA chapter VIII and concluded with a tariff increase and a duty-free quota on the border. The measures taken, as well as the compensation, were accepted by the chicken industries in both countries almost before the investigation was initiated; nevertheless, the private sectors pushed their respective governments to carry out this proceeding. In the timber case, no final determination had been issued as of August 2004.

Lessons: Case Studies

Preceding sections have analyzed the antidumping system's history, focusing on its cases, institutions, and legal framework. This section now presents cases illustrating broader relevance or distinctive aspects of the contingent trade defense system in Mexico. As of 2003, 262 new country-product investigations—excluding review proceedings, product coverage, and five-year reviews, among others—had been initiated. These cases offer a wide scope from which we can draw interesting lessons for many sectors and countries.

The China Package and Multicountry-Multiproduct Steel Cases

The cases identified as the China Package and Multicountry–Multiproduct Steel illustrate the history of contingent protection mechanisms in Mexico. These cases are indissolubly linked to the deepening of the Mexican trade liberalization process and constitute clear evidence of the role played by such mechanisms in supporting economic opening processes in countries like Mexico.

Between 1992 and 1993, the government of Mexico was strongly pressured by sectors that were adversely affected by the opening of the economy, mainly the Mexican steel manufacturers and other manufacturing sectors—shoes, textiles, clothing and toy industries, among others—thus jeopardizing the credibility of the newly created institutions concerned with trade defense mechanisms.

The steel industry filed a series of requests for antidumping investigations against almost all basic steel products and international supply sources. Resulting antidumping duties, if applied, would have had an extremely negative effect on the main local manufacturing industries and on the competitiveness of Mexican exporters, thus reversing many of the benefits accomplished so far with the liberalization process.

The Mexican authority delayed the decision-making process to initiate investigations and, later on, to issue provisional or final determinations in the steel cases, for which requests were filed in the first half of 1993. However, it had to take immediate contingent measures in other manufacturing sectors involving final products that also exerted firm pressure on the government, pressure based on what those sectors regarded as an extreme liberalization policy and on the inefficient trade defense instruments. Both the extent of the liberalization process and the capacity of the trade defense mechanisms were beginning to be strongly questioned all over the country.

One of the ways in which the Mexican government responded to these questions was by filing an ex officio antidumping investigation package against products of Chinese origin for which high antidumping duties were applied (see table 7.7). Because the initiation of the investigation was published in conformity with the

TABLE 7.7 The "China Package" and Other Cases against Chinese Products during 1993

Product	Country	Date of initiation	Date of final determination	Duty applied upon initiation (percent)	Final duty applied (percent)
The China Package					
Toys	China	Apr. 14, 1993	Nov. 25, 1994	351	351
Shoes	China	Apr. 15, 1993	Dec. 30, 2003	1,105	1,105
Tools	China	Apr. 15, 1993	Nov. 11, 1994	312	312
Clothing	China	Apr. 15, 1993	Oct. 18, 1994	533	533
Chemicals	China	Apr. 15, 1993	Oct. 18, 1994	673	209
Textiles	China	Apr. 15, 1993	Oct. 18, 1994	501	501
Electrical machines and equipment	China	Apr. 15, 1993	Nov. 18, 1994	129	129
Other cases against Chinese products					
Bicycles	China	Apr. 15, 1993	Sept. 22, 1994	594	279
Pencils	China	Aug. 9, 1993	Oct. 18, 1994	451	451
Valves	China	Nov. 1, 1993	Oct. 18, 1994	0	105
Pencil sharpeners	China	Nov. 19, 1993	Oct. 18, 1994	0	145
Baggage and bags	China	Nov. 29, 1993	Nov. 25, 1994	0	0

Sources: U.S. Census Bureau and Global Trade Information Services (1993–2002); DOF (various dates).

Law Regulating Article 131 (two months before the publication of the new Foreign Trade Act), provisional duties were applied to about 3,000 tariff items.

The decision to initiate investigations and impose high antidumping duties against Chinese products was important from the political perspective. However, its effect from the commercial point of view had been carefully considered. Mexico did not breach any international trade agreement because these investigations involved products from a non-WTO member. Additionally, most antidumping duties were applied to consumer goods, thus avoiding any effect on Mexican exports' competitiveness.

Table 7.8 illustrates—through the multicountry-multiproduct steel cases filed in the same year the China Package was published—some aspects of the ambivalent

TABLE 7.8 Multicountry–Multiproduct Steel Package, 1992–93

Product	Country	Date of initiation	Date of final determination	Antidumping duty at initiation	Final antidumping duty (percent)
Lined flat steel	United States	June 30, 1993	Nov. 11, 1994	0	0
Hot-rolled sheet	Germany	Oct. 27, 1993	Dec. 30, 1995	0	0
Hot-rolled sheet	Brazil	Oct. 27, 1993	Dec. 30, 1995	0	31.41
Hot-rolled sheet	Canada	Oct. 27, 1993	Dec. 30, 1995	0	45.86
Hot-rolled sheet	Korea, Rep. of	Oct. 27, 1993	Dec. 30, 1995	0	0
Hot-rolled sheet	Netherlands	Oct. 27, 1993	Dec. 30, 1995	0	56.54
Hot-rolled sheet	Venezuela, R. B. de	Oct. 27, 1993	Dec. 30, 1995	0	80.95
Cold-rolled sheet	Germany	Oct. 28, 1993	Dec. 27, 1995	0	185.76
Cold-rolled sheet	Australia	Oct. 28, 1993	Dec. 27, 1995	0	0
Cold-rolled sheet	Canada	Oct. 28, 1993	Dec. 27, 1995	0	0
Cold-rolled sheet	Korea, Rep. of	Oct. 28, 1993	Dec. 27, 1995	0	0
Cold-rolled sheet	Brazil	Oct. 28, 1993	Dec. 27, 1995	0	31.57
Cold-rolled sheet	United States	Oct. 28, 1993	Dec. 27, 1995	0	0
Cold-rolled sheet	Venezuela, R. B. de	Oct. 28, 1993	Dec. 27, 1995	0	55.75
Steel plate	Brazil	Oct. 27, 1993	Dec. 29, 1995	0	37.32
Steel plate	Canada	Oct. 27, 1993	Dec. 29, 1995	0	0
Steel plate	United States	Oct. 27, 1993	Dec. 29, 1995	0	0
Rolled steel plate	Brazil	Oct. 28, 1993	Dec. 28, 1995	0	23.95
Rolled steel plate	Canada	Oct. 28, 1993	Dec. 28, 1995	0	31.08
Rolled steel plate	Korea, Rep. of	Oct. 28, 1993	Dec. 28, 1995	0	0

TABLE 7.8 (*Continued*)

Product	Country	Date of initiation	Date of final determination	Antidumping duty at initiation	Final antidumping duty (percent)
Rolled steel plate	United States	Oct. 28, 1993	Dec. 28, 1995	0	0
Rolled steel plate	South Africa	Oct. 28, 1993	Dec. 28, 1995	0	0
Rolled steel plate	Venezuela, R. B. de	Oct. 28, 1993	Dec. 28, 1995	0	84.05
Corrugated rod	Brazil	Nov. 29, 1993	Aug. 11, 1995	0	57.69
Corrugated rod	Spain	Nov. 29, 1993	Oct. 10, 1994	0	0

Source: Based on data from Secretaría de Economía (2003) and Resolutions published in the DOF (various dates).

and apparently contradictory behavior of the federal government with respect to the contingent trade-protection system. Unlike claims against China, here, with the steel cases, no duties were imposed at the initiation of the investigation; some countries were excluded from duty coverage. Most investigations did not conclude until December 1995; in fact, collectively, these cases were the lengthiest in the history of antidumping proceedings in Mexico. In addition, in an effort to mitigate the negative effect that antidumping duties might have on some steel-using industries, the end-use certificate was created. This instrument would allow the importing of some products on duty-free conditions provided that importers could prove that those products were intended for certain end uses.

In 1993, as another response to the pressure from several sectors on the new trade defense system, the federal government created the Advisory Council on International Trade Practices (Consejo Consultivo de Prácticas Comerciales Internacionales, or CCPCI), made up of representatives from the leading sectors using the new contingent protection instruments. With this advisory body for the private sector, the trade secretary pushed the unsatisfied business sector to meet once a month with representatives from the secretariat and UPCI's management to discuss the technical and methodological issues with respect to application of antidumping instruments and to consult on alternative solutions to such issues.

Participation in this forum was on a personal basis, not as a representative of a company or association. Experts in the field, as well as company officials familiar with the UPCI investigation process by virtue of having filed petitions, were summoned to participate. It was agreed that officials of lobbies would not be included. Thus, the federal government managed to channel dissatisfaction and found a mechanism to raise awareness among business representatives and authorities of the problems faced by both in relation to these proceedings.[31]

Mechanisms to Mitigate the Negative Effects of Antidumping Duties

This section analyzes different kinds of mechanisms applied by the UPCI to soften the effect of antidumping duties applied between 1991 and 1996, a distinctive feature of the UPCI's administrative practice during that period.

Lesser Duty Rule Several provisions of applicable laws empowered the investigating authority to determine antidumping or countervailing duties for an amount less than the margins found, provided that the duties were sufficient to eliminate the injury or threat of injury caused by the imports involved.

In 1991, the UPCI tried to develop a methodology that would draw a clearer line between the effect of dumping and the effect of other factors on the industry so that it could apply antidumping duties for less than the margin of dumping found. The European Community applied lesser duties in its investigations on a regular basis; however, its methodology did not suit the UPCI's authorities. The European Community methodology was based on the prices of domestic manufacturers; UPCI officials worried that the extrapolation of this methodology to Mexico would be too supportive of high tariffs. That is why the UPCI developed a methodology of its own, which was first applied in 1991 in the diiodohydroxyquinoline case (see table 7.9).

The Diiodohydroxyquinoline Case The diiodohydroxyquinoline case features three interesting aspects: (a) it was the first case in which the Mexican authority applied a lesser duty than the dumping margin; (b) its determination explicitly revealed the new authorities' concerns about, and conception of, the administration of contingent trade-protection mechanisms in a context of consolidating and reinforcing the Mexican trade liberalization process; and (c) it represented the first use of a method different than any other used until 1991 by the few antidumping systems in force that applied lesser duties in the world.

In its final determination, the authority stated that, according to its view,

> [T]he *dumping margin is excessive* to be taken as a reference, since it would encourage the prohibition of importing goods under investigation, market concentration and monopoly practices, *to the detriment of free competition*. (Final determination on diiodohydroxyquinoline, Finding II; emphasis added)[32]

TABLE 7.9 Cases in Which the Lesser Duty Rule Was Applied, 1991–96

Date of the final determination	Product	Country	Final dumping margin	Lesser duty (less than the margin found)
Oct. 17, 1990	Diiodohydroxyquinoline	India	$15.56 per kg[a]	$4.09 per kg
Nov. 27, 1992	Telephone connectors	United States	$35.34 per kg	$4.59 per kg
Dec. 8, 1992	Tripolyphosphate	Spain	50.0%	36.0%
Dec. 23, 1993	Hydrogen peroxide	United States	72.0%	34.5%
May 27, 1996	Sulfuric acid	Japan	2,484.0%	91.1%[b]

Source: DOF (various dates).

Note: All dollar amounts are U.S. dollars.

a. In the provisional determination, a margin of $12.34 per kg (equal to the dumping margin) was applied.

b. In the provisional determination, a lesser duty than the margin of 166.67 percent was applied.

The decision to lower the final antidumping duty was adopted by the competent authority even though no request was filed by either the importers or the exporters of the product, neither of whom appeared during the proceedings. The decision was also independent of the findings in the injury determination proceeding, during which a substantial injury to the industry was proven.[33]

Instead, the decision to apply the lesser duty rule resulted from the competent authority's analysis of the structure of the international market for the product and from the potential market concentration and market power that the domestic manufacturer would gain if a duty amount equal to the calculated margin were applied. According to the information analyzed, diiodohydroxyquinoline was an active ingredient in a medicine for amoebic-related illness, and was manufactured in only three countries: Germany, India, and Mexico. The Mexican company filing the request was commercially linked with the German manufacturers and exporters. If provisional antidumping duties were applied to the Indian product, imports from India would drop to zero and the only alternative source of supply would be the German company associated with the domestic company that had submitted the request for investigation. The authority feared this result would give the Mexican company too much power over the market and, consequently, over prices.

Taking these elements into account, the authority analyzed the domestic price of the investigated product prior to the significant market penetration of Indian imports and found that the price was equivalent to that of the German product.

The Mexican authority reached the conclusion that the price differential between the Mexican and the Indian product could be corrected by applying a lesser duty of US$4.09 per kilogram rather than the margin of US$15.56 per kilogram. In this way, the injury to the industry would be eliminated, and the Mexican and German business association would be prevented from increasing its prices above fair or market competitive prices.[34]

This case gave rise to a novel methodology—a unitary approach that is based on international prices—that would enable Mexican authorities to apply antidumping duties that were less than dumping margins and to additionally determine the existence of a causal link, which was a key aspect in drawing a distinction between the protectionist and nonprotectionist use of antidumping instruments.

The Connectors, Tripolyphosphate, and Hydrogen Peroxide Cases In the three cases filed after the diiododydroxyquinoline case in which the lesser duty rule was applied, the unitary approach to international prices method, which had been developed after the diiododydroxyquinoline case, was used. The key goal of this approach was to find a relevant fair, or undistorted, price on the basis of which to determine a price as a sort of "injury margin" and to adjust the antidumping duty accordingly. A peculiar aspect of the connector, tripolyphosphate, and hydrogen peroxide cases was the important market concentration revealed by the domestic industry, amounting to 100 percent, 77 percent, and 100 percent, respectively.

In the case of telephone connectors,[35] the Mexican antidumping authority concluded that the prices resulting from imposing a duty amount equal to the dumping margin "would exceed the highest historical levels ever recorded and would even exceed those observed in monopoly situations"[36] and determined, therefore, that the final antidumping duty amount would be less than the dumping margin because the new rate was sufficient "to eliminate the injury caused as a direct result of unfair practices."[37]

In the investigation on connectors, the price evolution of the requesting company was examined and it was observed that the Mexican product had experienced a drop in its domestic prices before competing with dumped prices, for which reason the authority concluded that "such price reduction cannot be attributed to dumping practices"[38]; however, the other part of the price squeeze was attributed to the importers' dumping prices. Therefore, a duty was applied on the basis of that part of the price reduction.

In the case of tripolyphosphate, the Mexican authority explained that it had used an international reference price to determine the lesser duty. Specifically, it stated that "all the injury caused to the domestic industry cannot be attributed to the full dumping margin, since the ceiling price that the domestic industry could feasibly expect would be that of the U.S. product placed in the Mexican market."[39]

In the case of hydrogen peroxide, the authority also applied the unitary approach to international prices; it considered that a duty equal to the dumping margin found "would result in the overprotection of the domestic industry if import prices were brought to higher levels than necessary to avoid a drop in domestic prices."[40] Thus, the nondistorted international price adopted as the reference for the antidumping duty was the average price of the U.S. imports that the requesting company had introduced into the country under fair conditions, according to its statement.[41]

The Sulfuric Acid Case and the "Public Interest" Clause Several years went by before the Mexican authority applied the lesser duty rule again. The pressure exerted by the domestic industry on the new authorities limited the application of the new approach for injury determination purposes, because after dumping was proved the domestic industry could not prevent Mexican authorities from imposing duties nor could it make them lower those duties if the industry had negative indicators. Not until 1996 was a lesser duty applied again.

In the sulfuric acid case, the UPCI applied the lesser duty rule making reference to the "public interest clause," the name under which article 88 of the Foreign Trade Act came to be known. This article indicated that "when imposing a countervailing duty ... the Secretariat shall ensure as far as possible that such measure, in addition to providing timely defense for the domestic industry, avoids any negative impact on other production processes or on consumers." In this case, the decision was based on the idea that the fertilizer manufacturing industry—the main user of sulfuric acid—should not be affected more than necessary.[42]

The dumping margin determined during the proceeding was 2.483 percent for Japanese sulfuric acid. The lesser duty was imposed on the basis of the indifference price of producing sulfuric acid by burning sulfur. For the requesting company, sulfuric acid was an accessory product; it was a by-product manufactured involuntarily from the gas emissions of its copper smelters as a result of environmental regulations that imposed the obligation to process emissions to avoid air pollution.

Because of the sulfuric acid's status as a by-product, as the world's copper production increased, so did the production of sulfuric acid, thus lowering its price. At that stage, the fertilizer industry stopped burning sulfur to produce sulfuric acid and resumed its production as soon as the price of the sulfuric acid rose again. In this context, the Mexican authority decided that "even in the absence of imports, the sulfuric acid price in the domestic market is determined by the reference price of the main domestic consumers,"[43] who are the fertilizer manufacturers. Thus, the authority estimated the indifference price of sulfuric acid on the basis of how much it cost to produce the acid in Mexico by burning sulfur.

Changes in the Application of the Lesser Duty Rule Between 1993 and 2001, lesser duties were applied only on one occasion. Since 2002, this mechanism has been applied in Mexico with renewed intensity and under a different approach. Unlike the 1991–93 period, during which use of the unitary approach to international prices was attempted more systematically, the application of lesser duties in recent cases is based on what is known as market "non-injury price." To estimate the final duty amount, one must compare import prices against non-injury prices, which are usually the domestic prices during a period previous to the one being investigated.

The new Mexican rule is closer to the one used by the European Commission but has a stronger methodological foundation. The European rule also differs from the approach used in Mexico in the early 1990s, although the rules are similar in the sense that they are based on an endogenous reference to domestic production and ignore current international prices or the prices relevant to fair competition. Table 7.10 shows the cases in which a duty less than the margin has been recently applied.

TABLE 7.10 Cases in Which a Duty below the Dumping Margin Was Applied, 2001–4

Date of final determination	Product	Country	Final dumping margin	Lesser duty
June 22, 2001	Polyester filament fabrics	Korea, Rep. of	31.61%	16.03%
		Taiwan (China)	11.69%	11.00%
Oct. 2, 2002	Steel beams	Brazil	80.00%	42.49%
Jan. 13, 2003	Standard tubing	Guatemala	29.93%	25.87%
June 10, 2003	Monobutyl ether	United States	54.25%	32.56%
July 17, 2003	Steel chains	China	$0.80 per kg	$0.72 per kg
Sept. 24, 2003	Ferrosilicomanganese	Ukraine	95.74%	51.28%
Apr. 21, 2004	Seamless steel pipes	Russian Federation	111.37%	79.65%
		Romania	42.00%	42.00%
May 13, 2004	Tubular goods	Venezuela, R. B. de	54.69%	49.94%
Aug. 3, 2004	Sodium hexametaphosphate	China	124.96%	102.22%
Aug. 4, 2004	Steel connections	China	111.41%	81.04%

Source: DOF (various dates).

Note: All dollar amounts are U.S. dollars

The diverse ways in which the lesser duty rule has been applied result from the different criteria used by officials engaged in administering antidumping instruments. This situation also reveals the broad discretion that prevails in the administration of the antidumping system, despite all past attempts to make the system more objective.

End-Use Certificates End-use certificates were the result of deep controversy between the parties, which led to a dispute because of the differences in the technical specifications of the product under investigation, the several uses of the product depending on the industry involved, and the domestic industry's capacity to supply each specific type of product.[44]

In some cases related to steel, imported goods were usually replaceable by other domestically manufactured products, but that strategy was not possible in the case of some specific end uses. Therefore, the Mexican authority sought to prevent these inputs—so essential for important manufacturing and exporting sectors in Mexico such as the automotive, electrical household goods, and engineering industries—from becoming unjustifiably expensive. The case of cold-rolled sheet illustrates the rationale for these end-use certificates and how they were applied.[45]

The clearest example showing the origin of this measure was that of cold-rolled sheets thicker than 52 inches. According to exporters' allegations, domestic manufacturers were incapable of manufacturing cold-rolled sheets thicker than 52 inches—a fact that was entirely taken for granted by the requesting parties because local production facilities had technical limitations preventing manufacture of product in this thickness range, although they could produce all other specifications of the product. Domestic manufacturers, in turn, insisted that practically no demand existed from the market to produce cold-rolled sheets thicker than 52 inches and that imported sheets of those dimensions were acquired by distribution and service centers simply to be cut and sold in the sizes that were manufactured at the domestic level. Thus, manufacturers asked the authority not to exclude sheets thicker than 52 inches from the antidumping duty.[46]

Some users such as the car and tubing industries proved that sheets thicker than 52 inches were required for several production processes. The investigating authority also admitted that, by making a longitudinal cut, sheets thicker than those locally manufactured could be turned into narrower sheets like those manufactured by the domestic industry in the period under investigation. Therefore, the authority concluded that declaring the nonexistence of an equivalent domestic product—a sheet thicker than 52 inches—would require specifying an end use not allowing thinner substitutes.[47]

The same conclusion was drawn for sheets having different carbon content. In this case, it was determined that for some end uses, particularly demanding cutting processes, differences in carbon content were not relevant to ensure the malleability required by the sheet to resist such processes. Consequently, the authority excluded some types of steel sheets from the application of antidumping duties that had been established according to their end use. This determination required a mechanism that would enable the authority to exempt relevant products from the corresponding antidumping duty. Thus, the end-use certificate was created. This certificate was a free-format instrument that had to comply with certain features. In addition, a monitoring procedure was created.[48]

Statement of Exclusiveness The statement of exclusiveness, the third mechanism to mitigate the effects of antidumping duties, was created at the time when Chinese toys were investigated. Its purpose was to exempt from antidumping duties those imported toys that, albeit similar to those manufactured in Mexico, could not cause any injury to the domestic industry because of their price and some distinct characteristics that turned them into unique products. This market situation is typically exemplified by Barbie dolls.

The Mexican authority drafted the following definition of *exclusive products* specific to its final determination:

> toys from China imported under tariff items subject to countervailing duties which ... do not cause any injury to the domestic industry for two main reasons: (1) because they have been so clearly differentiated by their designer that there cannot possibly be an identical local product, being additionally protected by copyright or patents of characters, mechanisms, designs or any other specific feature, that make them exclusive vis-à-vis the toys manufactured in the Mexican market, and (2) because, given their highly differentiated character, they are sold at high prices in the Mexican market, for which reason the price of these products cannot possibly be the cause of any negative impact on the production or price of other locally manufactured toys that may have similarities with these exclusive products imported from the ... Republic of China.[49]

As was the case with end-use certificates, the statement of exclusiveness was a free-format instrument in which the importer had to state the net unit price of the exclusive product; the name of the copyright holder or owner of the patent of characters, mechanisms, designs, or any other distinct feature; and other data. A monitoring system was also devised.

Another interesting aspect of this determination concerning toys was that the investigating authority committed itself to review how effectively the mechanism worked after six months "and at any time, when so justified."[50] In the determination no explanation was given why it was deemed necessary to review this mechanism in such a short time, but the reason was that, in the Foreign Trade Commission, the representatives of the Federal Commission of Economic Competition conditioned their favorable vote on a review to be carried out after six months of implementation, based on their fears that this mechanism might confer strong market power to some economic agents.

However, the review was not conducted in six months' time as prescribed; not until 1998, when relevant modifications introduced to the statement of exclusiveness mechanism were published, was the review made.[51] At that time, the review's objective was far removed from the spirit that originally inspired the idea in 1994. The 1998 determination explicitly observed that the mechanism would be revised because of the breaches and abuses committed by importers with the statement of exclusiveness. Therefore, the investigating authority eliminated the free-format instrument and instead set a compulsory procedure involving import permits to introduce the so-called exclusive products without paying antidumping duties. The permit procedure was under the control of the Secretariat of Economy, which had the power to either grant or reject requests for permits.

The Unitary Approach to International Prices and the Causal Link: The Bond Paper Case

The unitary approach to international prices consists of establishing a causal link between domestic price levels and behavior, export prices under dumping conditions, and fair or undistorted international prices.[52] Dumped export prices may affect domestic production prices, either lowering or anchoring them at a level that might not necessarily be equal to the dumping margin determined for exporters who have been investigated. If, during the dumping period, domestic production prices are lower than an undistorted international price relevant to an importing market and if this difference is caused by competition with like or identical products at dumped prices, it can be concluded that a causal link exists between dumped prices and domestic production prices and, if applicable, in relation to the prices in the production sector involved.

Conversely, if dumped prices of imported goods are the direct cause of a reduction in domestic prices, but the new price levels match undistorted international prices relevant to the importing country, it may be inferred that no causal link exists between the amount of the dumping margin determined and the domestic price reduction. In line with this approach, the Mexican antidumping authority applied the lesser duty rule to the margin of dumping in the first cases because this method enabled the authority to quantify the amount necessary to set the export price of the dumped product higher than the international price relevant to the domestic market.

Some basic rules can be identified in the application of this approach to estimate a duty amount less than the dumping margin that should be sufficient to correct the injury caused by dumped prices: (a) if the relevant international price is equal to the normal value, the duty should be equivalent to the dumping margin; (b) if the relevant international price is between the normal value and the export price, the duty amount should be such that it may position the dumped export price higher than the international price; and (c) if the relevant international price is equal to the dumped export price, the dumping practice does not cause any injury, dumping exporters trade their products in the world market at the same prices as nondumping exporters, and as a consequence, domestic producers face fair competition prices so that no antidumping duties need to be imposed.

The main limitation of this approach is the difficulty in identifying the international price relevant to each case.[53] In addition, other equally important limitations are involved, for example, obtaining accurate information from domestic and international markets and adopting a suitable method to determine the market power of the different actors, their price-fixing arrangements, and their influence on the market prices analyzed.

The first investigation—on bond paper—initiated in Mexico in October 1993, constitutes a clear example of how the unitary approach to international prices is used to establish the causal link between the dumping margin amount and the injury to the domestic productive sector involved. The underlying principle of the unitary approach to international prices implies that, even if an antidumping duty equivalent to the dumping margin is determined for each investigated exporter, the domestic industry will not be able to increase its prices—the situation being the same as if no duties were applied.

In the final determination concerning bond paper imported from the United States,[54] the authority explained that it had access to information furnished by U.S. exporters accounting for 95 percent of the export volume to Mexico during the period subject to investigation. Sixty-one percent of such exports were made by Georgia Pacific Corporation (GPC), an exporter whose dumping margin was 8 percent negative—that is, its selling price in the Mexican market was higher than the normal value.[55]

Because the representative of U.S. bond paper exports to Mexico was a nondumping exporter, the Mexican authority analyzed its selling prices in the Mexican market[56] compared with prices of other competitors and those of domestic producers. As a result of this analysis, GPC's prices were found to be the lowest in the Mexican market during the investigated period, which accounted for the increase in the demand by Mexican customers for this exporter's products.

In addition, the price level in the Mexican market of other dumping exporters was, on average, 2 percent higher than GPC's. The authority concluded that dumping exporters behaved as price followers. Besides, fair prices (that is, those of GPC), "were, on average, 15 percent lower than the domestic prices of bond paper, for which reason the fair price was considerably lower than the domestic industry price in the investigated period; therefore, the fair price exerted a strong downward pressure on the domestic market, since it represented the largest share of the imported product in Mexico."[57]

Given these factors, the investigating authority concluded that the dumped prices of some U.S. exporters were not the direct reason for the deterioration of some indicators of the domestic industry. The lowest price in the domestic market during the period under investigation was neither a distorted nor an unfair price; it was this price that caused a widespread drop of domestic prices, which reached fair price levels. Therefore, no antidumping duties[58] were imposed on exporters resorting to dumping practices.

The unitary approach to international prices may be both useful and interesting, but more analytically rigorous and formal rules need to be developed. Otherwise, the approach might lead to a dangerous and excessive oversimplification and trivialization of the complex relations operating in the markets.

Final Considerations

From the history of the creation and strengthening of mechanisms and institutions engaged in the administration of contingent trade-protection measures in Mexico, we can draw some conclusions that might be of interest to both public officials and academic analysts. Economic liberalization in Mexico took place in an extremely complicated macroeconomic context. In the early 1980s, Mexico underwent a severe economic crisis as a result of the economic model that had been applied in the country for 30 years. It was thought then that the only way for the country to join the global economic community was through an accelerated trade liberalization process. Even though the political system in force gave public officials a wider scope of action than in other parts of the world, domestic industrialists—who were used to operating under a protectionist system—were determined to exert all their political power to stop the liberalization process. Within this context, the contingent trade-protection institutions were born.

The analysis offered in this chapter clearly reveals that the creation of institutions related to contingent trade-protection mechanisms served the fundamental purpose of supporting the new economic model of trade opening. Mexican public officials were fully aware of protectionist abuses often committed by institutions of this kind in other countries and were determined not to create "a back door to protectionism" in Mexico. Therefore, they established new administrative units whose distinct feature was their highly professional culture, which sought clearly unbiased conduct. Systems in other parts of the world were studied, and sound methodologies were applied. The future of the trade liberalization process depended partly on how successful the government could be in convincing domestic producers that serious institutions would defend them against unfair international competitors.

However, local manufacturers also had to understand that the newly created institutions were not meant to provide unjustified protection.

The strengthening of institutions, as well as of the legal structure of the contingent protection system, took place at the time NAFTA was being negotiated. It is important to underscore that most procedures and methods adopted by Mexican institutions resulted from the public officials' interest in creating sound and reliable structures for administering these protection policies. The pressure exerted by Mexico's trade partners was not the key reason for the legal and institutional reforms introduced in that period.

The figures in tables 7.11 and 7.12 serve to assess the actual effect of contingent protection mechanisms on current trade flows in Mexico. Most products affected

TABLE 7.11 Number of Tariff Items Subject to Antidumping Duties in 2002

Investigated country/economy	Number of tariff items investigated	Tariff items covered by investigations as a percentage of the total number of tariff items from which Mexico had imports (from investigated country or countries)
China	1,317	96.27
United States	19	1.39
Russian Federation	10	0.73
Korea, Rep. of	9	0.66
Brazil	7	0.51
Ukraine	7	0.51
Denmark	5	0.37
Taiwan (China)	5	0.37
France	4	0.29
10 countries (an investigation that covered 3 tariff items involved imports from 10 countries)	3	2.19
3 countries (an investigation that covered 2 tariff items involved imports from 3 countries)	2	0.44
4 countries (an investigation that covered 1 tariff item involved imports from 4 countries)	1	0.29
Total tariff items subject to duties	1,368	n.a.

Source: U.S. Census Bureau and Global Trade Information Services (1993–2002); Secretaría de Economía (2003).
Note: n.a. = not applicable.

TABLE 7.12 Estimation of Mexican Total Trade Affected by Antidumping or Safeguard Measures, 2002

Countries	Total Mexican imports per country of origin (US$ millions)	Import of items subject to antidumping duties (US$ millions)	Percentage of imports from the country of origin subject to anti-dumping (percent)
China	6,274	600.44	9.5697
Ukraine	83	1.68	2.0078
Hong Kong	509	7.74	1.5201
Russian Federation	236	2.18	0.9239
United States	106,557	890.25	0.8355
Denmark	177	0.74	0.4155
Taiwan (China)	4,250	8.07	0.1899
Korea, Rep. of	3,910	0.97	0.0248
Brazil	2,565	0.05	0.0018
Japan	9,349	0.12	0.0013
All countries	168,679	34,769	0.8965

Source: U.S. Census Bureau and Global Trade Information Services (1993–2002); Secretaría de Economía (2003).

by antidumping duties come from China; 96 percent of tariff items currently subject to antidumping duties are of Chinese origin (see table 7.11). Nevertheless, when assessing the global effect of such duties on Mexican imports, it is worth noting that Mexican authorities have succeeded in not using these mechanisms as indiscriminate protection tools because their application has affected less than 1 percent of the country's total imports (see table 7.12).

One concern that usually arises out of the Mexican context is the adverse effect that antidumping duties and safeguard measures may have on the country's manufacturing structure. Trade liberalization had been too difficult a process to risk losing its benefits as a result of an excessive use of antidumping duties. Consequently, Mexican authorities decided to resort to several mechanisms to mitigate the negative effects of antidumping duties, particularly from 1991 to 1996. Several cases presented in this chapter illustrate how Mexican authorities were able to apply contingent trade-protection laws flexibly to protect manufacturing sectors deserving protection measures while taking other national interests into account.

The discretionary application of laws on contingent trade protection is a double-edged sword. It can be beneficial when it protects certain sectors at critical moments of the trade liberalization process, but it can also degenerate into an indiscriminate protection instrument. The China Package case is a typical example of how antidumping duties can be applied to support the opening of trade while it also unveils the potential for indiscriminate discretionary use. In the spring of 1993, the financial situation of domestic manufacturers was difficult indeed—import volumes were increasing fast and, more and more, voices were being raised against trade liberalization. This turmoil was most untimely because the Mexican government had embarked on defining NAFTA's fate a few months ahead. Mexico needed to reach the end of that process with a widespread consensus in favor of furthering trade liberalization and high credibility for the new contingent protection mechanisms. The China Package case likely contributed to building that consensus. In other words, a certain degree of flexibility in the application of antidumping rules supported the general opening of the Mexican economy.

The Mexican case illustrates another advantage of creating strong institutions against unfair competition. In this field, attack is the best defense. When the government recruits and trains highly qualified staff members to administer laws to protect domestic manufacturers against unfair competition, the government is also training officials to help domestic exporters in proceedings initiated against them in other countries. At the time of the creation of the UPCI, one of its explicitly stated functions was to advise Mexican exporters involved in investigations of unfair practices and safeguard measures in foreign countries. The international experience shows that one of the most effective ways of deterring foreign manufacturers from filing requests for unfair practice investigations in their own countries is by confronting them with the implicit and potential risk of their being involved in such investigations as exporters in another country.

Mexico is one of the emerging economies with the broadest experience in applying contingent trade-protection laws. The success of these laws as tools to support trade liberalization is clear beyond any doubt. Mexican authorities realized that they had only one chance to get these institutions right and deemed it important to provide them with solid foundations from the very start. As the old saying goes, "A child who grows up without discipline can't be straightened out later."

The WTO multilateral agreements on antidumping and safeguard proceedings are still weak. Current regulations allow the abuse of these measures as protectionist tools. Mexico created relatively solid institutions, but the lack of more accurate rules, specific methodologies, and strict procedures in the WTO agreements open up the possibility for Mexico to change the way it has administered these protection mechanisms so far. Changes in staff and priorities that follow any change of government might gravely undermine originally serious institutions. The most effective way to prevent such institutions from degenerating is through a multilateral agreement that imposes strict discipline on all WTO members.

Notes

1. Dr. Pedro Noyola Garagori was undersecretary of foreign trade and investment between 1990 and 1994 at the Secretariat of Commerce and Industrial Development. He was responsible for not only promoting the creation of a specialized, strong, and professional department in Mexico concerned with international best practices on antidumping but also gaining the president's support for creating the International Trade Practices Agency (Dirección General de Prácticas Comerciales Internacionales), which later became the Unit on International Trade Practices (Unidad de Prácticas Comerciales Internacionales, or UPCI), with a substantial budgetary allocation. Additionally, he introduced radical reforms to the Foreign Trade Act (Ley de Comercio Exterior) in 1993. The official in charge of executing these projects was Dr. Álvaro Baillet, an economist and renowned administrator of the antidumping system, head of the UPCI from 1991 to 1996. We are sincerely grateful to both for their support.

2. According to the Mexican antidumping legislation in force, *unfair international trade practices* are defined as "the importation of goods under conditions of price discrimination or subsidization in the country of origin or source which cause or threaten to cause injury to the domestic industry" (article 28 of the Foreign Trade Act). Dr. Raúl Ramos Tercero, undersecretary of industry, is quoted from a speech he delivered to the Secretariat of Commerce and Industrial Development at the opening of the seminar Unfair Foreign Trade Practices and Emergency Measures, held in Mexico City on September 6, 1995.

3. Broadly speaking, five tariff levels were established based on the following criteria: 20 percent for consumer goods, 15 percent for intermediate goods, 10 percent for raw material, and 5 percent or 0 percent for products either insufficiently produced or not manufactured at all at the domestic level or by agreement with the private sector (SECOFI 1993).

4. On November 26, 1985, the GATT director-general was informed of the Mexican government's decision to initiate the process of accession to the GATT (Gabinete de Comercio Exterior [Foreign Trade Department] 1986).

5. Mexico formally acceded to the GATT in August 1986. This accession, ratified by the Senate of the Republic in September 1986, came into force in November 1986.

6. This elimination was not subject to any scheduling or specific date (Gabinete de Comercio Exterior 1986).

7. In a personal interview, April 1, 2004, Héctor Vázquez Tercero, an official commissioned with administering the first antidumping law in Mexico and with conducting the first antidumping investigation in 1987, pointed out that the government was absolutely convinced that, because the country's development model had changed, a system was required to effectively fight unfair international trade practices for the benefit of domestic manufacturers. Furthermore, he said that after the enactment of the law and its regulations, the government itself promoted the use of this system because its instruments were deemed necessary.

8. Héctor Vázquez Tercero, personal interview, April 1, 2004.

9. Article 11 of the Law Regulating Article 131: "Having satisfactorily received the claim to which the preceding article makes reference, the Secretariat of Commerce and Industrial Development shall issue, within a period of five working days, a provisional resolution establishing the countervailing duty to be applied, if appropriate, and shall further investigate the unfair international trade practice subject of said resolution, which shall become effective one day after its publication in the Official Gazette of the Federation."

10. It was deemed compulsory, as an exception, when Mexico signed bilateral agreements including a reciprocity clause.

11. On his official visit to the United States in October 1989, President Salinas stated in his presentation of October 4 before the two Houses of Congress that for Mexico to continue to be "one of the most open economies at the international level, reciprocity is needed. In a framework of understanding and cooperation, there should not be any nontariff barrier either preventing or hindering the flow of goods between the United States and Mexico. Our country has almost eradicated them entirely;

however, we still face them in the United States.... [W]e want a bilateral agreement that should aim at the collapse of trade barriers, sector by sector" (Arriola 1994a).

12. NAFTA negotiations were formally initiated in Toronto, Canada, at a meeting attended by trade representatives of the three countries: the Mexican secretary of commerce and industrial development, Dr. Jaime Serra Puche; the Canadian minister of industry, science, and technology and the minister of international trade, Michael Wilson; and the U.S. trade representative, Carla Hills (Zabludovsky 1994).

13. To that end, a Working Group on Trade and Competition and another on Antidumping and Countervailing Duties were created (Leycegui 2000).

14. The amendments to which the United States and Canada committed themselves were merely adjustments needed for the binational panel system, as prescribed in chapter XIX of NAFTA text.

15. In August 1992, NAFTA negotiations were concluded. Nevertheless, before the legislative bodies in the three signatory countries enacted NAFTA, presidential elections were held in the United States, and as a result, William Clinton took office. The newly elected president conditioned the enactment of NAFTA on the conclusion of parallel agreements on labor and environmental cooperation. Thus, only in November 1993 was legislative approval of NAFTA concluded in the three countries.

16. This amendment is the first item in NAFTA's "Schedule of Mexico."

17. In its first report, the UPCI stated that, thanks to the fact that notifications by electronic means were allowed, the sending of more than 100 notifications to parties interested in the 1993 multicountry-multiproduct steel case had been possible (SECOFI 1997).

18. On the basis of the Mexican experience, this practice was implemented in many countries that were adopting antidumping mechanisms at that time. The experience was disseminated to other countries through the UPCI's training programs offered to officials.

19. In recent years, this obligation has turned into a mere administrative formality, not contributing to the proceedings' transparency. In the early years of the act's implementation, authorities used to give the parties concerned documents that described the specific method used for injury determination by means of approximate figures or indexes to preserve the confidentiality of the information. The agency also supplied, on request, the SAS programs developed by the authorities for the specific estimation of dumping margins in each company. At present, the only information an exporting company receives is that which the company itself has previously submitted; the other companies are denied SAS programs or the information about the method used for injury determination purposes, allegedly for confidentiality reasons. Meetings serve only to repeat the contents of provisional or final determinations.

20. In Mexican legislation, the term *countervailing duties* is used to refer to either antidumping or countervailing duties.

21. Interview with Dr. Pedro Noyola Garagori, April 23, 2004. He had submitted to the consideration of the president of the Republic the project to create a specialized department engaged in contingent protection instruments, and he was responsible for drafting the new Foreign Trade Act. He further explained that assigning contingent protection to a low-profile, nontechnical, discretionary, and unprofessional area was too high a risk for the opening of the economy because that decision might open up the path for antiliberalization or protectionist groups and for the conservative trends within the government.

22. The first antidumping cases were filed with the area concerned with exchange controls, which in 1987 was still under the purview of the Commerce Bureau (Dirección de Comercio), reporting to the Undersecretariat of Foreign Trade (Subsecretaría de Comercio Exterior), which was part of SECOFI. Between 1986 and 1990, antidumping proceedings were initiated in various departments that were busy with other activities also. In 1990, the Bureau of Countervailing Duties (Dirección de Cuotas Compensatorias) was created within the General Bureau of Foreign Trade Services (Dirección General de Servicios al Comercio Exterior) of SECOFI.

23. Although the National Development Plan 1995–2000 set forth as one of its key guidelines on foreign trade to "penalize with utmost rigor and efficiency any unfair trade practice affecting our

manufacturers," (SHCP 1995) the main objectives of the antidumping policy under the Program for Industrial and Foreign Trade Policy (Programa de Política Industrial y Comercio Exterior, or PROPICE) revealed the government's concern over the potential conflict between contingent protection measures and the new development model for the country because of the substantial increase of investigations filed: "... in designing our policy against unfair international trade practices, we should take into account that applying countervailing or antidumping duties may severely affect our manufacturers' competitiveness in the coming years." (SHCP 1995).

24. On many occasions, high-ranking officials stated that the trade defense system was a necessary evil, but that it should be kept under strict control through its professionalization and the development of its methods and regulations.

25. The proposal was to keep a unified system, that is, that the same body should be in charge of determining both dumping and subsidies, as well as injury or threat of injury to the national industry.

26. UPCI itself had yielded to political pressure in making use of this tool. However, given the profile of its officials and the government's commitment to the economic and trade liberalization process, in practice, the objectives of liberalization would not be affected by the discretionary use of those instruments (see 1993 determinations on the China package and the multicountry–multiproduct steel cases in section "Lessons: Case Studies").

27. This attitude clearly reflects the discretionary bias in authorities' decisions. Clearly, this discretionary power was used for the sake of the liberalization process during the years of its consolidation, but it also reflects its inherent risks because such discretionary power can be used for the opposite purpose. A case in point to show its ill use was *Fructosa*, the Mexican antidumping determination most strongly questioned and challenged to date.

28. The statistical annex in the working paper version of this study includes a detailed list of all the investigations initiated in that period.

29. This percentage corresponds to the 1992–2002 period for which records of rejections are available. Before then, only the interested party was notified of any request rejected by the authority on the grounds of noncompliance with formalities or irrelevance.

30. According to PROPICE, three decisive factors accounted for antidumping activity in Mexico during 1991–94: (a) the effect of the international economic cycle on the raw material markets and the generalization in the related industries of surplus exports at very low prices during the world recessive economic cycle lasting from 1990 to 1993; (b) the increasing role played by socialist countries in international trade; and (c) the almost uninterrupted reduction (from 1988 to the end of 1993) of the real exchange rate, when domestic competitiveness dropped and import incentives rose.

31. The CCPCI's creation was formalized later, in August 1994, when the DOF published the agreement creating the Advisory Council on International Trade and establishing its functions.

32. Final determination on the import of diiodohydroxyquinoline, product of Indian origin included in tariff item 2933.40.01 of the General Import Duty Law, *Diario Oficial del la Federación* (DOF), October 17, 1991, Finding II.

33. Final determination of Finding II about diiodohydroxyquinoline.

34. "... the Secretariat considers that the final countervailing duty of US$4.09 is enough to discourage the import of goods flowing into the national territory on unfair trade conditions and to eliminate the injury to the domestic industry, thus ensuring *free competitive prices*." (Final determination in Finding IV about diiodine; emphasis added.)

35. Final determination on imported connectors for telephone cables, goods under tariff item 8536.90.23 of the General Import Duty Law from the USA, *DOF*, November 27, 1992.

36. *Monopoly prices* were defined as those existing when the requesting company was the only supplier in the domestic market. (Final determination on connectors, *DOF*, November 27, 1992, paragraph 44). We assume the authority was making reference to the time in which the market was not open to imports.

37. Final determination on connectors, *DOF*, November 27, 1992, paragraph 44.

38. Final determination on connectors, *DOF*, November 27, 1992, paragraph 50.

39. Final determination on sodium tripolyphosphate imports, *DOF*, June 28, 1993, paragraph 49.

40. Final determination on hydrogen peroxide imports, *DOF*, December 23, 1993, paragraph 68.

41. Final determination on hydrogen peroxide imports, *DOF*, December 23, 1993, paragraph 69.

42. Final determination of the antidumping investigation on sulfuric acid imports, *DOF*, May 25, 1996, paragraph 132.

43. Final determination of the antidumping investigation on sulfuric acid imports, *DOF*, May 25, 1996, paragraph 133.

44. Final determination of the antidumping investigation on sulfuric acid imports, *DOF*, May 25, 1996, paragraph 7.

45. This case is based on information from the final determinations in antidumping and antisubsidy investigations involving cold-rolled sheet imports, merchandise under tariff items 7209.12.01, 7209.13.01, 7209.22.01, and 7209.23.01 of the General Import Duty Law, from Canada, United States of America, Australia, the Republic of Korea, República Bolivariana de Venezuela, Germany, and Brazil, *DOF*, December 27, 1995.

46. Final determinations for cold-rolled sheet imports, *DOF*, December 27, 1995, paragraph 506.

47. Final determinations for cold-rolled sheet imports, *DOF*, December 27, 1995, paragraphs 507, 510.

48. Final determinations for cold-rolled sheet imports, *DOF*, December 27, 1995, subparagraph A, paragraph 674.

49. Final determination in the antidumping investigation involving toy imports, merchandise under tariff items of headings 95.01, 95.02, 95.03, 95.04, 95.05, 95.06, 95.07, and 95.08 of the General Import Duty Law, from China regardless of their country of dispatch, *DOF*, November 25, 1994, subparagraph H, paragraph 196.

50. Final determination in the antidumping investigation involving toy imports, *DOF*, November 25, 1994, subparagraph H, paragraph 196.

51. Final determination in the antidumping case involving imported toys, *DOF*, November 25, 1994, resolution modifying the mechanism for the statement of exclusiveness.

52. The first time this approach was used was in the diiodohydroxyquinoline case in 1991, and the first time it was made public as a new methodological approach was during the International Seminar on Unfair Trade Practices, organized by SECOFI and the Institute for Legal Research, Universidad Nacional de México, held at the Institute from October 27 to 29, 1993 (Reyes de la Torre 1995).

53. It is relatively easier to find an undistorted international reference price in raw materials or commodities, for which arbitrage is relatively common and information is available in international stock markets. In the case of differentiated products, it is far more difficult to identify the international price relevant to a specific market, but alternatively, one can adopt the average export price of the countries exporting representative volumes to the country conducting the investigation, provided those countries are not involved in the investigation or all parties involved explicitly recognize such countries as having undistorted prices.

54. Final determination in the antidumping investigation on imported bond paper, a merchandise under tariff items 4802.52.01 and 4802.52.99 of the General Import Duty Law, from the United States, regardless of the country of dispatch, *DOF*, November 18, 1994.

55. Final determination in the antidumping investigation on imported bond paper, *DOF*, November 18, 1994, paragraphs 189–93.

56. These prices refer to prices in Mexico; paragraph 190 of the determination on bond paper explains the procedure followed by the authority to estimate the price: all expenses, insurance, freight, and tariffs incurred by the Georgia Pacific Corporation to bring the product to the customer's plant in Mexico were added to the selling price of the company's bond paper in the Mexican market.

57. Final determination in the antidumping investigation on imported bond paper, *DOF*, November 18, 1994, paragraph 193.

58. Final determination in the antidumping investigation on imported bond paper, *DOF*, November 18, 1994, paragraphs 221–28.

References

Arriola, Carlos. 1994a. *Documentos básicos del* TLCAN. Mexico: SECOFI.

———. ed. 1994b. *Testimonios sobre el TLC*. Mexico: Editorial Diana, Grupo Editorial Miguel Ángel Porrúa.

Bush, George H. W., and Carlos Salinas de Gortari. 1994. "Comunicado conjunto de los presidentes de México y Estados Unidos, expedido en la Cd. de Washington, 10 de junio de 1990." Documento 43 in *Documentos básicos* del TLCAN, ed. Carlos Arriola. Mexico: SECOFI.

Diario Oficial de la Federación (DOF). 2002. "Acuerdo que identifica las fracciones arancelarias de la Tarifa de la Ley de los Impuestos Generales de Importación y Exportación, en las cuales se clasifican las mercancías cuya importación está sujeta al pago de cuotas compensatorias." March 25 (published daily). Mexico: Diary of the Federation.

———. 2003. "DOF's Resolutions." Various dates (published daily). Mexico: DOF.

Gabinete de Comercio Exterio. 1986. *El proceso de adhesión de México al acuerdo general sobre aranceles aduaneros y comercio (GATT)*. August 7. Mexico.

Leycegui, Beatriz. 2000. "Acordar para disentir: La solución de controversias en el Tratado de Libre Comercio de América del Norte." In *¿Socios Naturales? Cinco años del Tratado de Libre Comercio de América del Norte*, ed. Beatriz Leycegui and Fernández de Castro, 537–633. México, D.F.: Instituto Tecnológico Autónomo de México (ITAM) and Grupo Editorial Miguel Ángel Porúa.

Miranda, Jorge. 1997. 1st Spanish ed. "Análisis económico de la forma en que México ha venido aplicando las leyes de prácticas desleales de comercio internacional de 1987 a 1995." In *Comercio a Golpes: Las prácticas desleales de comercio internacional bajo el TLCAN*, eds. Beatriz Leycegui, William B. P. Robson, and S. Dhalia Stein, 179–206. Mexico: Grupo Editorial Miguel Ángel Porrúa.

Ramos Tercero, Raúl. 1995. "Prácticas desleales de comercio internacional y medidas de emergencia." *El Mercado de Valores* 11 (November): 436–50.

Reyes de la Torre, Luz Elena. 1995. "Metodología para evaluar el impacto de las importaciones en condiciones de dumping sobre la industria nacional: La experiencia Mexicana." In *Prácticas desleales de comercio internacional*, 383–98. Mexico: Instituto de Investigaciones Jurídicas de la Universidad Nacional Autónoma de Mexico.

SECOFI (Secretaría de Comercio y Fomento Industrial). 1990a. "Ley reglamentaria del artículo 131 de la constitución política de los estados unidos mexicanos en materia de comercio exterior." In *Sistema Mexicano de defensa contra prácticas desleales de comercio internacional*. Mexico: Cuadernos SECOFI, Serie Comercio Exterior.

———. 1990b. "Reglamento contra prácticas desleales de comercio internacional." In *Sistema Mexicano de defensa contra prácticas desleales de comercio internacional*. Mexico: Cuadernos SECOFI, Serie Comercio Exterior.

———. 1993. *Tratado de libre comercio con América del Norte* (official text). Mexico: Miguel Ángel Porrúa Grupo Editorial.

———. 1995a. *Política VIII Promoción de la competencia del Programa de Política Industrial y Comercio Exterior*." Mexico: SECOFI.

———. 1995b. *Programa de política industrial y comercio exterior (PROPICE)*. Mexico: SECOFI.

———. 1997. *Informe de labores de la UPCI 1991–1996; El sistema Mexicano de defensa contra prácticas desleales de comercio internacional*. Mexico: SECOFI.

Secretaría de Economía. 2003. *Informe de labores de la UPCI 2002; El sistema Mexicano de defensa contra prácticas desleales de comercio internacional*. Mexico: SECOFI.

Secretaría del GATT. 1994. "Acuerdo relativo a la aplicación del artículo VI del Acuerdo General sobre Aranceles Aduaneros y Comercio de 1994." In *Los Resultados de la Ronda Uruguay de negociaciones comerciales multilaterales*, Los textos jurídicos, 175–274. Geneva, Switzerland: General Agreement on Tariffs and Trade.

Serra Puche, Jaime. 1994. "Informe del secretario de comercio y fomento industrial a la comisión de comercio de la honorable cámara de senadores; Sobre la reciprocidad internacional a la apertura económica de México, 7 de Julio de 1994, Documento 121." In *Documentos Básicos del TLCAN*, ed. Carlos Arriola, 859–83. Mexico: SECOFI.

UPCI (Unidad de Prácticas Comerciales Internacionales). 1997. (published in various years). *Informe de labores de la UPCI 1991–1996; El sistema Mexicano de defensa contra prácticas desleales de comercio internacional.* Mexico: SECOFI.

———. 2003. *Annual Report 2002.* (See Secretaría de Economía 3. 2003. *Informe de Labores de la UPCI 2002; El sistema Mexicano de defensa contra prácticas desleales de comercio internacional.* Mexico: SECOFI.)

Secretaría de Hacienda y Crédito Público (SHCP). 1995. *Plan Nacional de Desarrollo 1995–2000.* Mexico: SHCP.

U.S. Census Bureau and Global Trade Information Services. *World Trade Atlas.* 1993–2002.

Zabludovsky, Jaime. 1989. *Trade Liberalization and Macroeconomic Adjustment in Mexico, 1983–1988.* Unpublished. Mexico.

Zabludovsky, Jaime. 1994. "El proceso de negociación del tratado de libre comercio de América del Norte." In *Testimonios sobre el TLC,* ed. Carlos Arriola, 1123–67. Mexico: Editorial Diana, Grupo Editorial Miguel Ángel Porrúa.

8

ANTIDUMPING MECHANISMS AND SAFEGUARDS IN PERU

Richard Webb, Josefina Camminati, and Raúl León Thorne

Peru's experience with the application of antidumping and safeguard measures is characterized by a radical change in the philosophy and procedures of trade at the beginning of the 1990s and by an increasing use of these mechanisms. Since the reform was launched, a total of 81 trade protection cases have been presented, of which 57 were followed by a dumping investigation. The application of antidumping duties was approved for 29 of the cases investigated. Only two cases of safeguard investigations were recorded, one of which (Chinese textile clothing articles) is still in the negotiation phase.

This chapter describes Peru's experience and examines whether the measures have worked in favor of a free market economy or in favor of protectionist interests. The analysis is set in the context of the foreign trade liberalization and competition reform launched in 1990.

The chapter is divided into two sections. The first section describes the evolution, context, and components of foreign trade policy in Peru. The second describes

The authors would like to acknowledge the assistance of Roberto Abusada, Mercedes Araoz, Carlos Carrillo, José Ezeta, Cristy García Godos, Ludwig Meier, Jorge Muñiz, Gastón Pacheco, Patricia Teullet, and the Technical Secretariat of the National Institute for the Defense of Competition and the Protection of Intellectual Property (Indecopi) for their collaboration in preparing this report. The authors would also like to acknowledge the valuable comments made by their colleagues Diana Tussie, Elías Bacarat, J. Michael Finger, and Julio J. Nogués in May 2004 at the workshop "Uso de Salvaguardias y Antidumping en América Latina" (Use of Safeguards and Antidumping in Latin America) held in Buenos Aires.

the institutional and legal framework of the trade reform and the application of antidumping and safeguard mechanisms since that reform was launched.

Peru's Trade Policy

The history of Peru's trade policy has been characterized by an uninterrupted pendular movement, with cycles that have responded to the macroeconomic context, and increasingly, to the influence of pressure groups and ideologies.

Evolution of Peru's Trade Policy

At the outset of republican history (1820–40), fiscal requirements of the newly installed Peruvian government led to a period of high tariffs. Next came a long liberal period (1840–80) that was characterized by fiscal abundance and a healthy balance of payments made possible by a guano export boom. But when that boom collapsed and when Peru was defeated in the War of the Pacific (1879–84), protectionism again became the predominant policy, with two distinct interruptions.

The first interruption, a return to liberal policies in 1948, was part of an adjustment program supported by the recovery of exports and direct foreign investment. Nevertheless, during the two decades after 1948, the pressure of protectionist ideas and industrial lobbies gradually eroded this liberalization, and the country recorded the period of greatest manufacturing dynamism. In 1959, an Industrial Promotion Law was passed, which contributed to higher protection through subsidy policies and preferential treatment for the business sector.

In 1968, just before the second interruption, a military government came to power and was strongly influenced by the United Nations' Economic Commission for Latin America and the Caribbean. Subsequently, the protectionist trend became radicalized, mainly for ideological reasons. In the following decade, paratariff measures were multiplied; the imports of products manufactured in the country were banned; tariffs rose; and a severe exchange rate control was imposed, producing an extreme degree of protectionism.

Then, the military government itself went back to liberalization as part of the new adjustment program because of the severe macroeconomic and balance of payments crisis. All paratariff measures were removed, and tariffs were reduced. This policy continued in 1980–82 under the new democratic government.

This return to liberalization aborted in 1983 when the external debt crisis and El Niño weather pattern brought new problems to the balance of payments and employment, of which the industrial lobby took advantage. Between 1985 and 1990, the new government, led by Alianza Popular Revolucionaria Americana (APRA), a social democratic party, restored several paratariff and tariff measures and created an additional degree of effective protection through a scheme of multiple exchange rates. In 1990, both a new government and a severe adjustment program—a response to the political crisis generated by inflation, recession, lack of foreign currency, and terrorism—marked the beginning of economic liberalization.

Economic and Political Context of the Liberalization

Antidumping mechanisms and safeguards were part of an exceptionally profound liberal reform imposed by Alberto Fujimori's government since July 1990. Fujimori became president in the context of one of the most severe economic and political crises of the country. The economy had experienced hyperinflation during the two preceding years while domestic production collapsed by 20 percent and public expenditure decreased even more because of the fall in revenue collection and the loss of the government's credit capacity. The presence of the government in the national territory was strongly reduced because of fiscal impoverishment, corruption, and growing terrorism led by Sendero Luminoso (Shining Path) and Túpac Amaru Revolutionary Movement. In general, quantity and quality of education, public health services, justice, police protection, and other government services declined severely.

That collapse was attributed to APRA, the governing party since 1985. By 1990, terrorism had extended to most of Peru's territory and represented a real threat to the survival of democracy. This danger, along with the loss of popularity of interventionist, progovernment ideologies, opened the door to an extreme reaction in favor of liberal ideas.

During the electoral campaign of 1990, candidate Vargas Llosa's liberal message was no longer regarded as a rationalization for big business and became, instead, a legitimate argument in favor of the national interest. Paradoxically, Fujimori was not elected on a liberal platform, but his lack of political ties or debts, his practical way of perceiving things, and the situation of emergency led him into the liberal path.

Immediate Background of the 1990 Reform

The import substitution policy was based on a tariff structure characterized by a high average-tariff level and high dispersion. More than 56 different tariff levels from 10 percent to 84 percent, combined with diverse exonerations, generated a structure providing varied protection. The simple tariff average was 66 percent, and the weighted average was 44 percent. Additionally, 535 items were restricted,

TABLE 8.1 Number of Paratariff Restrictions in Peru

Items	July 1985	Dec. 1988	Dec. 1989	Dec. 1990
Free	4,757	0	4,192	5,269
Restricted	350	4,724	535	0
Banned	196	539	539	0

Source: Central Reserve Bank of Peru.

and about 540—23 percent of the industrial production—were on the banned imports list (see table 8.1).

The tariff structure generated extreme positive and negative levels of effective protection. Effective protection was 261 percent for articles of clothing, 189 percent for dairy products, and 134 percent for shoes. Several primary and export sectors faced negative effective protection.

Sector officials made the decisions on tariffs and on whether to include or exclude products in the lists of banned or restricted imports, and the central bank assigned the exchange rates applicable to each import item. There was no unified, autonomous technical authority to review protection requests and to ensure uniform criteria and minimal political interference. In practice, the high level of official discretion contributed to uncertainty, inefficiency, and corruption.

The New Economic Policy

From its outset, the new government enforced an aggressive structural reform program to liberalize markets. The early measures focused on eliminating hyperinflation. In August 1990, the government made a "shock" adjustment to rapidly set free controlled prices, remove almost all subsidies, launch a programmed reduction in monetary expansion, and establish a managed floating exchange rate. Inflation was substantially reduced in 1991, even though it was not completely eradicated as it had been following hyperinflationary periods of the past. Despite the emphasis on stabilization, structural changes that became the framework for trade reform were launched in 1990 (see table 8.2). The reform was conceived as an organic set of measures that mutually reinforced one another. Long-term institutional changes were required to ensure its sustainability. The main goal of reform was to create and promote a flexible market economy. The following actions were taken: foreign trade and foreign currency were liberalized, financial and labor markets were also liberalized, the internal revenue administration was modernized, institutions for regulation and competition defense

TABLE 8.2 Main Reforms in Peru, 1990–2000

Area of reform	Date	Reforms initiated
Stabilization	1990–93	Price subsidies eliminated Unified floating exchange rate Monetary expansion reduced New Central Bank Law
Tax	1990–92	Tax structure reduced and simplified
Foreign trade	1990–92	Tariff level and dispersion reduced Prohibitions, paratariff measures, and state import monopolies eliminated Exemptions reduced Customs strengthened
Financial	1990–96	Capital flows and foreign currencies freed Stock exchange reforms launched New law for banks, creation of Banking and Insurance Superintendency Deposit Insurance Fund created First-tier banking prohibited for the state Private pension system created
Privatization	1991–92	COPRI[a] and CEPRIs[b] created Auctions launched Autonomous regulating entities and Indecopi[c] created
Labor	1990–97	Labor market deregulated and flexibilized Labor stability partially eliminated, including a change in the constitution Payroll taxes reduced
State deregulation and reduction	1990–96	Regulations and processes streamlined Number of state workers reduced
Social	1991–98	Social programs created Poverty targeted

Source: Authors' tabulations.

a. COPRI = Private Investment Promotion Commission.

b. CEPRIs = Special Privatization Committees.

c. Indecopi = National Institute for the Defense of Competition and the Protection of Intellectual Property.

were created, and state-run enterprises were transferred to private owners or concessionaires.

Government policy was to gradually replace its role as producer and resource allocator with an increasing regulatory role. For this purpose, privatization and concession processes were launched, and regulatory entities were created.

The New Foreign Trade Policy

In 1992, Fujimori carried out a "civil coup" and closed Congress. The legislative void created by this coup and the already existing climate of liberalization created conditions for the government to remove all the pieces of the protectionist scaffold, to subscribe to World Trade Organization (WTO) agreements, to create institutions to regulate free competition, and to decree the necessary rules.

The new foreign trade policy was designed to achieve productive efficiency, but it also was intended to favor the anti-inflationary strategy and to reinforce public finances. In August 1990, the exchange rate was unified, and in September, the first great tariff reduction established only three levels—15 percent, 25 percent, and 50 percent—but maintained the 10 percent surcharge for certain items (Boloña and Illescas 1997). Table 8.3 describes what each tariff level covers. The banned imports list was eliminated, and the items requiring a license were reduced from 285 to 13. The no-competition requirement and the remaining paratariff restrictions, except for those pertaining to sanitary wares, were discontinued.

The average tariff, including a temporary surcharge, went from 66 to 32 percent in July 1990, and the average dispersion went from 25 to 13 points. The maximum rate dropped from 84 to 50 percent, and most exemptions were eliminated. In November, the surcharge was removed, the average tariff fell to 26 percent, and the subsidy for nontraditional exports was also removed. (At this point, the top rate

TABLE 8.3 Proportion of Imports Covered by the New Tariff Rates in Peru, September 1990

Tariff (percent)	Items	Proportion of 1990 tariff lines at the tariff rate (percent)
10	Inputs with no domestic substitutes, iron and steel, capital goods for the industry, metal mechanics, agriculture, medical equipment, some medicines, completely knocked down vehicle packages, parts and pieces, tires	41.3
15	Other capital goods, inputs with domestic substitutes, reduced incidence on production costs and ad valorem rate more than 25%, agricultural products for final consumption	36.9
25	Other consumption goods	21.8 (25 and 50 combined)
50	Inputs that did not represent an important share of the cost of other productive activities, capital goods with domestic substitutes	

Source: Boloña Behr and Illescas (1997).

was still 50 percent.) In December, a schedule for future annual reductions to reach a uniform flat rate of 15 percent was published.

In March 1991, the 50 percent rate was removed, leaving only two tariff levels, 15 percent and 25 percent. The reform also advanced at the institutional level:

- The Prior Import License, the No Competition Ruling, the Unified Import Registry, the Andean Group Import Registry, and other quantitative restrictions were formally eliminated.[1]
- The monopolies of state-run enterprises in food products and inputs were eliminated.
- Indecopi (National Institute for the Defense of Competition and the Protection of Intellectual Property) was created as the entity in charge of overseeing free competition.
- A total reform of Customs was launched with exceptional success. Total revenue, including sales taxes collected at Customs, rose from 23 percent of imports to 35.8 percent in 1999, and the average length of the Customs clearance process was reduced from several weeks to 24–48 hours.

Also, the foreign currency market and the assets account of the balance of payments were freed, and restrictions on foreign currency transactions and holdings were eliminated, including the requirement that exporters sell their foreign currency to the Central Reserve Bank at the unified exchange market rate.[2]

Business pressures channeled through Congress succeeded in abolishing the announced tariff-reduction schedule, which was understood as a setback and generated doubts about the continuity of the reform. In this sense, it is clear that the so-called civil coup of 1992 was a determining factor in deepening the reform. In 1995, the official proposal for a flat tariff and the position of some business groups in favor of a tiered tariff motivated a public debate that indefinitely postponed the new tariff changes. From 1993 to June 1998, the reform became deeper through new changes in the tariff structure, with some setbacks. But in all, the average rate fell from 16.3 percent in June 1993 to 13.5 percent in March 1998.

This ambitious reform sets a milestone in Peruvian trade history. Neither the extent of liberalization nor the speed of the change has antecedents in the history of Peru.

Antidumping and Safeguards

Institutional Reform

A great part of the reform materialized through new laws that regulate aspects of market behavior such as monopoly,[3] foreign investment,[4] consumer protection,[5] unfair competition,[6] competitiveness of economic agents,[7] micro- and small-enterprise development,[8] bankruptcy,[9] ports,[10] industrial and intellectual property,[11] and others. These laws were designed by new technical and professional staff members who either had studied abroad during the 1980s or had graduated from national schools already influenced by market economics. Previously, each of these topics had been the competence of different ministries or state agencies, Itintec (Technical Standards and Industrial Technological Research Institute)[12] being one of them. It became clear that an effective launch of the new policies would be viable only if legal and procedural changes were complemented by drastic change in how policies are administered. The new procedures would require not only technical expertise but also an independence from political power. Likewise, the culture of decision making (the mindset of the responsible officials) would have to change from a culture in which decisions were based on long-standing relationships to one in which decisions would be based on the facts of economic potential. This change came together in November 1992 in the law that created Indecopi, an organization designed to provide the government with a modern and autonomous technical institution whose main mission would be to promote and arbitrate free competition and market access, as well as to protect intellectual property in its different forms.

National Institute for the Defense of Competition and the Protection of Intellectual Property (Indecopi) The military government (1968–80) created Itintec, an agency responsible for trademarks and patents registration, intellectual property protection, and administration of technical quality standards. Its performance was marked by strong bureaucratization,[13] which, in the context of liberalization, led to its dissolution at the end of 1990, paving the way for a new agency, Indecopi, which started operating in March 1993.

The design and operation of Indecopi was a novelty in the country. It was based on autonomous commissions that specialized in different aspects of the free market. The core criteria included the clear differentiation of jurisdictional and administrative functions, the high technical level of its professionals, and a clearly defined vision of institutional objectives—to arbitrate and promote the market economy in Peru, particularly in the areas of competition and intellectual property. The Commission for Control of Dumping and Subsidies (CDS), created in 1991 in the Ministry of Economy, was merged into the new institution. The organizational structure of Indecopi (see figure 8.1) responded to the need to give greater autonomy to the functional organs of the institution, especially to the commissions.

The executive board and its president are appointed by the executive branch, but their activities are independent of it. They establish the general policies of the institution, but they cannot interfere with the decisions of the commissions.

FIGURE 8.1 Organizational Structure of the National Institute for the Defense of Competition and the Protection of Intellectual Property (Indecopi)

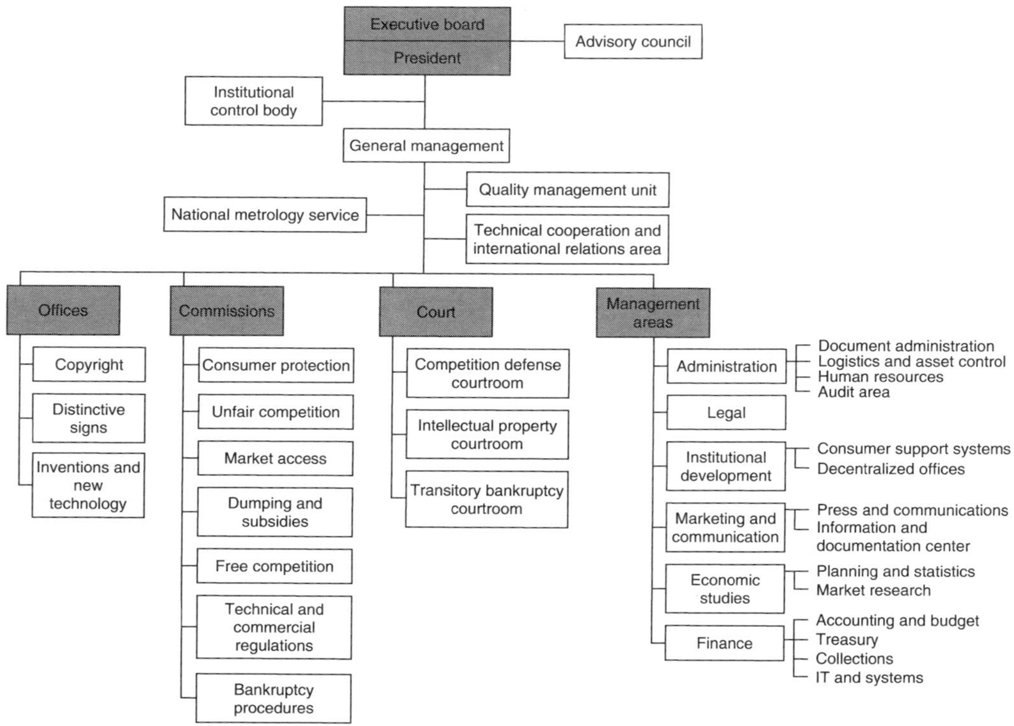

Source: Available at http://www.indecopi.gob.pe.

Each commission has a Technical Secretariat that channels cases for review, conducts studies, and verifies relevant information. They are the technical-economic organs of Indecopi, which are staffed by full-time officials whose analysis is the daily input for the commissions and for the agenda of the institution.

The commissions are collegiate organs. They function as executive boards, and they meet periodically to review and decide on the issues or cases submitted to them. Their members are not officials of the institution, and their remuneration consists of per diems for the meetings they attend.

Commission members are chosen by the executive board of Indecopi and are renowned professionals and technical experts in each field. They are appointed directly through an Indecopi resolution, without government involvement. Commission members do not belong to, nor do they respond to, nor do they represent, any public agency or institution when they give opinions or vote.

Commission members cannot vote or give opinions in the cases where there is a conflict of interest with one of the parties. Members are also not allowed to hold private meetings with other members of the commissions. Interviews are held only with the Technical Secretariat or with the commission in full.

Indecopi has seven commissions, which do not interfere with one another. Its Antidumping and Countervailing Measures Commission, for example, is solely in charge of correcting distortions generated by unfair competition from imported products. However, the reports issued by one commission can be used as reference for investigations conducted by another.

Commission decisions are expressed through resolutions that can be appealed before the Competition Defense courtroom of the Indecopi Tribunal, which is the second administrative instance. The tribunal is a collegiate organ whose members are proposed by the president of the institution and appointed by the Council of Ministers. Members are selected for technical expertise and, in practice, have been chosen for their professional prestige and political independence. Although tribunal judgments are based on the same formal criteria used by any court, they are far more expeditious and also are based on specialized technical analysis carried out by the tribunal secretariat.

Eighty percent of Indecopi's budget is financed by revenue from trademark registrations and renewals as well as other services. The rest is financed by the national budget. Commissions do not have individual budgets. Their expenditure needs are covered by the central administration of the institution.

Although Indecopi's budget is not totally independent, the high degree of independence is crucial for the operation of the agency because it gives it flexibility to hire staff and supports its technical and administrative autonomy. This pattern of technical delegation is part of a general policy that has been evolving in the country.

Institutional life, although an example of effectiveness and modernity, has, nonetheless, been marked by the passage of governments and institutional leaders:

- From Indecopi's creation up to 1994, the institution stood out for its staff of young and highly motivated professionals, who applied technical and market criteria and were conscious of their autonomy and commitment to efficiency.
- Between 1994 and 2001, the institution's leadership and political and public presence stood out; the commissions continued to work autonomously and used each resolution to educate the public about market criteria and consumer rights.
- Since the change of government in 2001, there has been a continuous struggle to lead the country's most prestigious institution. Its new board placed emphasis on enterprise insolvency rather than market regulation. Resources and efforts were focused on issues related to dealing with issues of equity restructuring resulting from the 1997 banking crisis and great number of bankruptcies. The Bankruptcy System Commission was created.
- In 2004, the institution had a lower profile. For several months, the agency operated without a president. This situation was interpreted as an indication of the government's lack of interest in competition and market issues. Some recovery in the technical area was evident, although there was less emphasis on promoting free competition.

It is important to recognize the prestige achieved by this institution inside and outside the country. Throughout the changes in its institutional life, Indecopi has persisted as a service institution, without losing sight of its main goal—the promotion of fair and honest competition. It has become the place for quick resolution of controversies that would otherwise have gone to a judiciary court. Its rulings are respected by the population, which perceives that Indecopi is not part of the traditional bureaucracy. Conciliation meetings are held daily between unsatisfied buyers and vendors, for example, of electric appliances. Several focus groups that held meetings in Lima revealed that this institution is perceived by the population as "the institution that defends people."

Its presence and the respect of the community has spread beyond the country's borders. In fact, Peru chaired the antidumping commission of the Free Trade Area of the Americas.

We stress Indecopi's paradigmatic role because it hosts the CDS. Undoubtedly, Indecopi's prestige and authority play an important role in the acceptance of that commission's decisions.

The Commission for Control of Dumping and Subsidies The creation of the Commission for Control of Dumping and Subsidies (CDS) in 1991 grew out of government negotiations with international organizations to reinsert the country into the international financial system. The commission was born as a collegiate and technical body that reported to the Ministry of Economy and Finance before the WTO agreements on exceptional measures—safeguards and antidumping—contemplated by the General Agreement on Tariffs and Trade (GATT) became effective. It was originally staffed by representatives of the Ministry of Economy and Finance, the Ministry of Industries, the National Society of Industries, and Customs. Only a few cases were submitted, and their resolution was based on the general guidelines of the GATT. However, the commission became the first instance created to oversee the application of trade liberalization criteria in the country.

In 1993, CDS was transferred to the newly created Indecopi, maintaining its technical approach but also adopting a new style. Its members were no longer representatives of ministries or of public or private entities, and its autonomy was highlighted. Its line was clearly centered on economic liberalization. In fact, it was restrictive in approving antidumping duties. It was in favor of stopping damage, but it was against investigation requests that were designed to evade competition or get protectionist support. The lesser duty rule was mandatorily applied from 1997 until 2001.

The distinct zeal for economic liberalization and the delayed resolution of the investigations initiated by the commission, combined with the temporary government of 2000–1,[14] provoked a campaign by the industrial lobby against the "hard" line of the commission, a campaign that advocated for "more flexible time frames" and "better treatment" for national producers. This campaign response was motivated by the number of cases declared inadmissible or unfounded because they did not comply with the necessary requirements.

The commission's pressure achieved its goal at the start of Alejandro Toledo's government. In 2001, he was persuaded by the industrial lobby of the need to fight against contraband, subsidies, and dumping. This fight coincided with the change in the presidency of Indecopi and with the resignation of all CDS members as a sign of their commitment to economic liberalization and of their independence, which were being threatened by political and trade union pressures.

The substitution of all commission members by others who were mainly linked to the business sector had an inevitable cost in terms of expertise and continuity of criteria. The technical or professional level of investigations was not lost, but the commission was more influenced by the industrial sector and, to some extent, this influence affected the institution's image of impartiality.

At present, this countertrend has abated and a new emphasis on the "technical" approach is noticeable, an approach that is halfway between the early proliberalization view and the proindustry approach of recent years. The current negotiation of a free trade agreement (tratado de libre comercio, TLC) with the United States does not seem to be reflected in the proliberalization line of the commission.

Clearly, the institutional design is not sufficient to achieve the goals that motivated the commission's creation, and the influence of interests in one way or other will always be possible. The important thing to stress is that, with clear objectives and technical criteria, together with carefully selected commission members, the existing institution concept can guarantee substantial autonomy from political power and private interests.

Legal Rules and Procedures Peru's legislation for antidumping and for safeguard differs in its basics, its application criteria, and its procedures. Although CDS is the competent authority in cases of dumping—for which it investigates and solves—CDS can conduct only investigations for safeguards, after which it issues a report on the findings of the analysis performed in each case, but it does not decide on them. The competent authority to decide whether to apply safeguards is the Multisector Commission, formed by the Ministry of Economy and Finance, the Ministry of Industry, and the Ministry of Production of the corresponding sector.

This difference is not simply procedural. The reason behind the outlined differences is that dumping cases are regarded as the result of practices that create distortions in the market, and, thus, should be judged on strictly technical criteria. Cases that might justify safeguards, for example, when imports affect domestic industry, are understood as extraordinary situations. These cases require both a technical analysis to determine causes and a political decision. Domestic production, consumers, other economic sectors, and the overall country points of view are taken into account for the application of safeguards.

Antidumping Peruvian legislation establishes the same treatment for cases of dumping and countervailing measures based on subsidies granted by the country of origin. In chronological order, the most important rules are the following:

- **Supreme Decree 133-91-EF, June 1991**—Regulates the criteria and procedures to correct market competition distortions created by cases of dumping and subsidies. This rule takes up the basic concepts of the working groups that designed WTO agreements. It establishes general time frames without indicating specific ones for each instance of the process. It also authorized the application of provisional duties in any stage of the investigation if injury, or threat of injury, was determined. This rule is still in force for cases with countries that have not signed WTO agreements. It was also applied to cases against WTO signatory countries during the period from December 1994, when Peru signed WTO agreements, until April 1997, when those agreements were regulated. The decree was applied as long as it did not contradict the provisions of the agreements.

- **Supreme Decree 043-97-EF, April 1997**—Approves the new Regulation on Dumping and Subsidies for cases against signatory countries of the WTO agreements. In general, it takes up the same guidelines and approach of the agreement. However, the Peruvian rule was more strictly in favor of economic liberalization than the WTO itself. The central criterion was to ensure that the application of duties should not hinder the course of economic liberalization in any way. For example, the minimum dumping margin required to apply duties was raised from 2 percent (by the agreements) to 3 percent, and the lesser duty rule became mandatory (in WTO agreements it is optional). This increase was a clear effort to prevent the possible use of the mechanism as a way to obtain protection against fair competition. When other countries reviewed Peru's regulation, they neither objected to nor found any threat against free market criteria.[15] On the contrary, the fact that the same entity was responsible for competition and dumping issues was understood as a sign of respect for competition criteria in the application of antidumping duties.
- **Supreme Decree 144-2000-EF and Supreme Decree 225-2001-EF, December 2000**—Some points in the original regulation (Supreme Decree 043) are defined. The first point is about time frames, procedures, and qualification criteria for applications. The second one is related to the criteria that qualify a country as a free market economy—to allow the identification of cases in which selling prices in exporting countries cannot be considered normal because they are economies that cannot be qualified as free markets.
- **Supreme Decree 006-2003-PCM, January 2003**—Replaces the regulation contained in Supreme Decree 043 and its modifications with a new regulation that consolidates all antidumping and subsidies rules in force into one single legal body. In general, concerning the application of duties, this new regulation is less strict than the replaced regulation. The new regulation organizes the time frames to submit applications, changes working days for calendar days, and eliminates the mandatory nature of the lesser duty rule.

Figure 8.2 shows the procedure for an antidumping investigation. Applicants request an investigation by the Technical Secretariat of CDS. To do so, they fill out a questionnaire and present supporting documentation on the existence of dumping, the degree to which the applicant represents the domestic industry, the product that is the subject of dumping, the exporting country, the country of origin, producers, known exporters, importers, prices, volumes, the evolution of sales, and all data related to the damage caused. The commission is also entitled to initiate an investigation on its own account.

To submit an application for a dumping or subsidies investigation, the applicant must pay the equivalent of 80 percent of the *unidad impositiva tributaria*,[16]

FIGURE 8.2 Antidumping Procedure

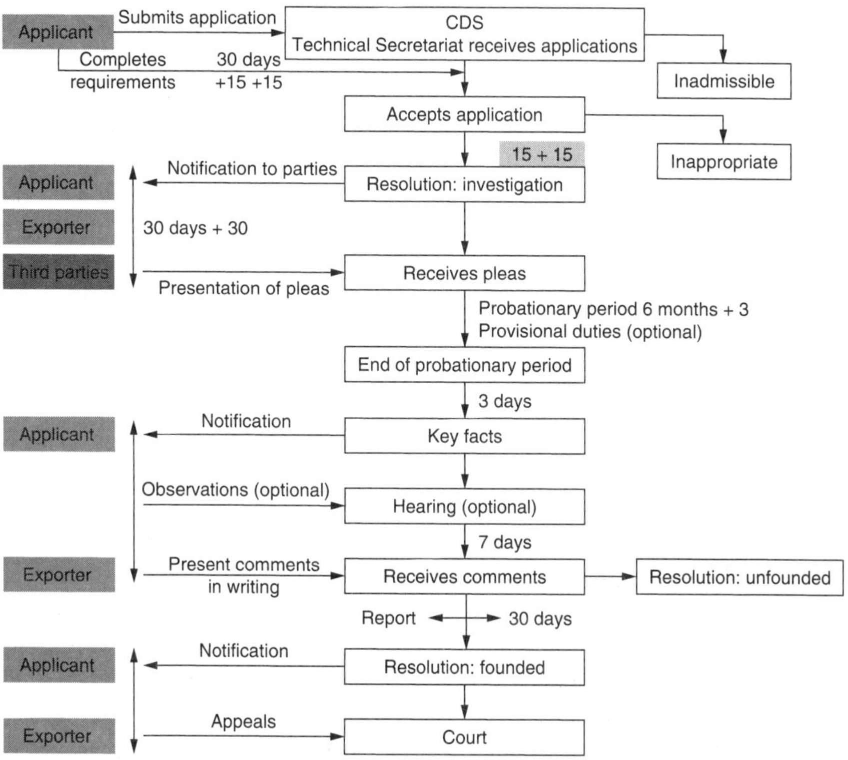

Source: Constructed by authors according to current legislation.

a tax unit that is equivalent to S/.3,200, or approximately US$925. This fee is divided into two payments. The first one is made when the application is submitted, and it is equivalent to 20 percent of the tax unit. The remaining 60 percent is paid only when an investigation is initiated.

In principle, the information submitted is not confidential. The parties can request the confidentiality of certain information, but they have to justify this request and attach a nonconfidential summary of that information.

This stage is followed by a period to complete the preliminary information, after which the competent authority will decide whether the case is accepted for an investigation. The time frames are 30 days and 15 days, respectively, but both time frames can be extended for an equivalent period, so this stage can last up to 90 days.

The data submitted by the applying company are used as the basis to start an investigation and the parties quoted in the application are then notified; these parties are to make their pleas within the next 30-day period, which can be extended to 60 days.

A probationary period of six months, extendable to three more, follows, allowing the Technical Secretariat to gather and analyze the information available. Before a determination is made, the commission issues a document containing the key facts that will support its final decision. The key facts report is sent to the parties so that they can submit their final comments within five days of receiving the notice. When either party responds to the key facts report, a final hearing is convoked so they can expose their allegations in writing within the following seven days.

The time frame for the commission's final assessment and decision either to apply duties or to declare the application unfounded is 30 days. If duties are imposed, they come into effect on the day following the publication of the commission's resolution and remain in effect during subsequent appeals. In sum, the maximum length of the process is nine months, extendable to twelve. All periods are expressed in calendar days.

The detailed written report describing the facts generated and the analysis performed for each case is available to the parties, or anyone interested, at the Indecopi Web site at http://www.indecopi.gob.pe.

The resolutions of the commission can be appealed before the Court of Indecopi, which acts as the second administrative instance. The time frame for the revocation or confirmation of the appeal is six months, extendable to eight. The next option is to take legal action or to make a complaint before WTO.

Safeguards The most important rules with respect to the safeguards procedures are the two that follow:

- **Supreme Decree 020-98-ITINCI**—Supreme Decree 020 is the first device that regulates safeguard agreements in Peru, jointly with the WTO Agreement on Textiles and Clothing. This rule defines the concepts and procedures for the application of safeguard clauses to cases when the increase of imports affects local industry. It establishes that applicable safeguards will preferably be ad valorem tariff levies and, only in exceptional cases, be specific tariff levies or quantitative restrictions. It also establishes the creation of a Multisector Commission, formed by several ministers, as the competent authority to decide on the application of safeguards, its decision being based, in each case, on the investigation conducted and the report prepared by Indecopi's CDS, which behaves as the investigating authority. The decree also establishes a special treatment for the application of safeguards to developing countries that are members of the WTO, demanding that imports of the product reported should represent a minimum 3 percent individually, or 9 percent jointly, with other countries over Peruvian imports. The application of provisional safeguards, which will not exceed 200 days, is authorized for exceptional cases. In general, such limits on the imposition of restrictions seek to discourage the use of the safeguards mechanism, for example, when the transitional safeguards foreseen in the WTO Agreement on Textiles and Clothing are applied, then provisional safeguards under this provision demand the same requirements as definitive safeguards.

- **Supreme Decree 023-2003-MINCETUR, October 2003**—Regulates (a) transitional safeguards foreseen in the WTO Agreement on Textiles and Clothing and (b) transitional safeguards foreseen in China's accession document to WTO. The rule establishes that applicants must justify that the requested measure will favor the public interest. But the trend is toward more flexible requirements. In fact, a provisional transitional safeguard clause is introduced.

Figure 8.3 shows the procedure for a safeguards investigation. The Technical Secretariat of CDS, which acts only as an investigating authority, receives the investigation request submitted by the applicant and prepares a report that is presented

FIGURE 8.3 Safeguards Procedure

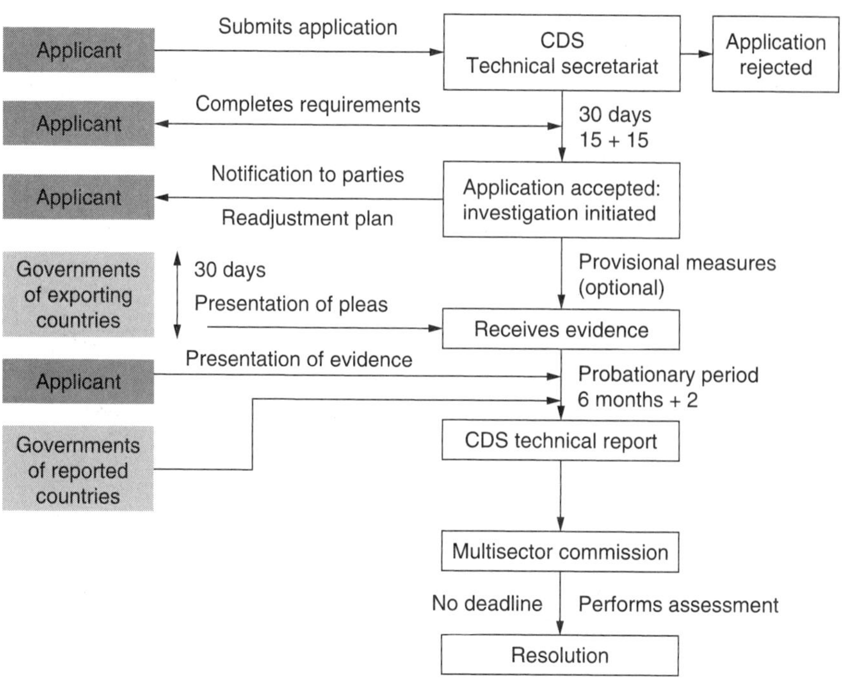

Source: Constructed by authors according to current legislation.

to the Multisector Commission. The application includes information about the product, the volume and the evolution of reported imports, as well as the alleged damage, but it must also include an economic report that quantifies the effect of the measure on final and intermediate consumers and on public interest.[17] In exceptional situations, and when the national interest is involved, the investigating authority is also entitled to initiate investigations.

The first part of the process is similar to dumping investigations. The difference is that the applicant must present a readjustment plan for the domestic industry within 30 days of the start date of investigations. This plan must explain how the domestic industry is going to adjust to competition created by imports in the medium term.

The probationary period lasts six months, and can be extended to eight. It concludes with the technical report issued by CDS. During this time, consultations take place with WTO members whose exports might suffer significant damage by the requested safeguards.

There is no limit to the time that the Multisector Commission may take to reach a resolution after receiving the report from CDS. It also can choose whether to take the recommendations of CDS into account. In principle, CDS must assess the general economic interest of the country; the effects of the measure at the national level; and the implications for trade relations with countries that will eventually be affected, especially if Peru's consolidated tariff level in the WTO of 30 percent is surpassed.

If safeguards are applied, they will be in force for three years, extendable to three more. This time frame is shorter than the eight-year period allowed by GATT rules. In summary, the decision to apply safeguards has much more political room for maneuvering than decisions about antidumping.

Other Aspects of Peru's Experience

Information Available Sources from the investigating authority and from the users of the mechanisms agree that one of the hindrances to the agility of dumping investigations is the unavailability of complete statistical data. Even though Customs statistics are available, information concerning production statistics is less accurate, and in some cases, the data available in ministries of production are incomplete, outdated, and unreliable. Data verification consumes valuable time and effort by the commission, which often must decide on the basis of the best information available.

Application Costs The use of advisers is not a formal requirement to submit an application for a dumping or safeguard investigation. In practice, companies tend to commission the preparation of their cases to law firms or economists specialized in this field, having them not only submit the file but also closely track its evolution. On average, these specialists charge a fee that ranges from US$10,000 to $15,000 per case.

However, there are also companies that do not resort to external services to support their cases. In 1999, a small company managed to get provisional duties applied and, later, definitive duties of 120 percent and 734 percent from China and Taiwan (China), respectively, for dumping caused by imports of bodyboards and fins for surfing and recreation and kickboards for swimming. The company was able to support every point on its application, even opposing China's claim to be treated as a free-market economy.

A particular aspect of Peru's procedure is the fee paid by the company for submitting an investigation application. Compared with other countries where this process is free, charging a fee could be regarded as a barrier to making applications. However, the amount—fixed at 80 percent of a tax unit that is equivalent to S/.3,200 (approximately US$925)—is very low. The businesspeople contacted have said that they agree with the fee, and some even said they were in favor of charging a fee as a way of contributing to the costs of investigation. For example, a businessman who, when interviewed on this topic, said that if he did not win the case, he would at least get a useful study on his product at very low cost.

Representativeness of the Applying Company Both the agreement and the regulation are based on the criteria that applicants should represent at least 25 percent of the domestic industry affected. Peruvian legislators have preferred to keep this minimum level because they understand that raising it would give an advantage to large companies.

Circumvention of Duties Circumvention cases that wrongly specify the tariff item or the origin or other technical description of the product can be reported by the applicant or taken up at the CDS's own initiative. CDS must ensure that the imported product that has been penalized with antidumping duties pays the penalty independently of the tariff item through which it enters the country. However, controlling the right item and collecting its revenue is a Customs task. The new law for Customs crimes establishes imprisonment not only for economic agents who try to elude antidumping duties by faking product information but also for Customs officials who collude in such elusion.

Budget for Commissions Commissions have tight budgets. Although these bodies have been able to conduct investigations in a reasonable way so far, the Technical Secretariat's lack of resources is notorious. The time frames and technical rigor of reports could improve with adequate resources that would, for example, enable the agency to hire specialized studies or, when a neighboring country is involved, enable a member of the Technical Secretariat to travel to conduct in situ investigations.

Public Interest in Peruvian Rules In the specific case of safeguards, point 10 of article 8 of Supreme Decree 020-98-ITINCI requires that applications for safeguard clauses should include an "economic report that quantifies the impact of the measure on final and intermediate consumers and on the public interest." This requirement was modified in 2004 (Supreme Decree 017-2004-MINCETUR). Applicants are no longer required to submit the report as described. Instead, authorities issue a public invitation to all potentially affected parties to submit their points of view, and it is now the responsibility of Indecopi to evaluate the effect on consumers and other parties.

In the case of antidumping measures, when imports come from countries that are not members of WTO, article 17 of Supreme Decree 133-91-EF indicates that, to the extent possible, the commission should gather "opinions from buyers and/or users of the product that is subject of an investigation application." In the case of imports from countries that are WTO members, article 23 of Supreme Decree 006 entitles the commission to initiate self-imposed investigations when the "national interest is involved." However, the consideration of the national interest is not necessary when analyzing the convenience of applying antidumping duties because it is understood that, when correcting distortions generated by unfair practices, the authority is acting in favor of free competition and, therefore, public interest.

Transparency of Information The applications, the questionnaires that the parties fill out, the key facts of a case, the hearings, and the reports of the commission are all open documents. The rule establishes that a company can request that confidential information not be disclosed, provided a nonconfidential summary of that information is attached. The reports prepared by the commission are detailed; they record the facts, the findings of the analyses conducted, and the considerations that are taken into account for the decision that is made. Reports are published on the Indecopi Web site so the public can have access to them. The public nature of the information is meant to be consistent with a free competition scheme, and it is not intended to discourage applications, although in some cases it can have that inevitable effect.

Dissemination of Mechanisms The antidumping and safeguard mechanisms that are available are not as familiar to the business sector as would be desirable. Indecopi, mainly through CDS, has made efforts to disseminate the criteria on which trade defense mechanisms are based, not only to assist companies as possible applicants but also to defend them should claims against their exports be made by other countries. The National Society of Industries also has a department in charge of antidumping and subsidy issues, which coordinates activities for its members, but it is not very active. Other efforts to inform have included meetings, round tables, and conferences, but these have been sporadic. Thus, the mechanism is scarcely used to date; however, the growing flow of cases is directly related to the learning process of the business sector.

So far, the best way to disseminate the mechanisms and their scope has been through the businesspeople who have presented cases, the advisers who have studied the cases, former officials, and other related professionals, all of whom are generating a considerable degree of maturity and knowledge in the private sector.

Interagency Support There is no interagency cooperation in formal or regular terms. During some phases of CDS, there has been informal but close cooperation with Mexico's Secretariat of Commerce and Industrial Development. Authorities say that their needs for cooperation are channeled through Peru's trade delegations abroad, especially in Geneva and in the WTO. A frequent complaint is that formal foreign cooperation does not always reach investigating authorities because the formal channels that should be used constitute a limitation and sometimes cooperation is wrongly channeled.

Peru's Cases

Until 2004, a total of 81 trade defense applications were submitted to CDS since it was created in 1999 (see table 8.4). Most (70) correspond to cases of alleged dumping, 7 were claims for subsidies, and only 4 were requests for safeguard clauses.

TABLE 8.4 Applications and Measures in Peru, 1993–2004

	Total	Subsidies	Safeguard	Dumping
Applications	81	7	4	70
Investigations	64	5	2	57
Provisional duty	30	3	1	26
Provisional and final duty	23	2	0	21
Final duty on all products	28	2	0	26
Final duty on some products but not all	4	1	0	3
Final determination negative	28	2	1	25
Pending resolution	4	0	1	3

Source: Indecopi; authors' calculations.

Note: Two cases that were presented but subsequently withdrawn by the petitioner are included in the total for the final determination of negative cases.

Outcomes of Investigation Applications

Of the 81 applications submitted, 17 (approximately 1 in 5) were considered inappropriate or were withdrawn by the applicant; therefore, no investigation was initiated. Of the 64 applications admitted for an investigation, 2 were later withdrawn by the applicants. Provisional duties were applied in 30 cases, of which 26 were dumping cases. Of the dumping cases, 21 eventually led to definitive duties, and 5 were declared unfounded or received negative determinations.

Of the 70 applications for dumping cases, 29 ended with affirmative final determinations, and definitive duties applied for all or for some of the products covered by the investigation

Investigations undertaken at CDS's initiative have been few. They consist of one case against Indonesia (involving shoes) and three cases against China (involving clothing, shoes, and water meters). As a rule, the commission tends to consider that the damage must be proved by the applicant whenever possible.

Incidence over Time

Figure 8.4 shows a marked increase in the number of investigations initiated from 1993 to 2002, though the numbers have dropped significantly since 2002. The average number of 3.8 cases per year submitted during the first six years, 1993-98,

FIGURE 8.4 Investigations and Antidumping Duties in Peru, 1993 to July 2004

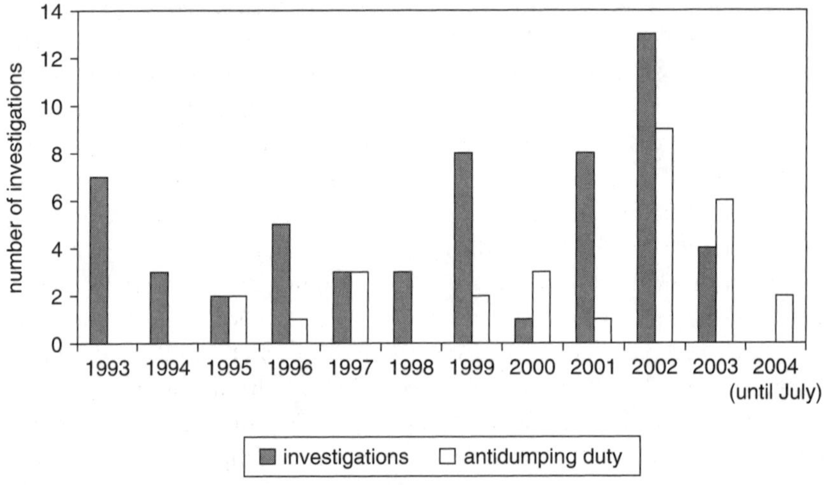

Source: Constructed by authors from data listed in http://www.indecopi.gob.pe.

rose to 6.2 in the following five-and-a-half years (1999 to July 2004). The increase in the number of applications that were declared founded was even more significant—increasing from 1.3 to 4.2 per year (1993 to 1999, a time frame that starts a year later to allow for the time required to decide on each petition).

According to a survey conducted by the National Society of Industries in June 2003, 77 percent of industrial companies that have faced some form of unfair foreign competition consider that they were affected by dumping practices, and 20 percent were affected by subsidies. Surprisingly, fewer than 5 percent of those companies have submitted applications to CDS.

The authors believe that (a) the limited use of these mechanisms registered during the first years and (b) the increasing volume of cases submitted reflects, for the most part, a gradual learning process by companies. Conversely, in countries such as Mexico or Argentina, we see that the number of cases has started to decline. A learning process is also taking place with exporters. In the long term, trade defense measures have the effect of discouraging unfair trade practices.

An increase in the average number of investigations initiated is also observed. It rose from 4.7 cases per year (28 in five years) during the first period to 6.4 per year (32 in five years) in the second period. The increase coincides with the political change that took place beginning in 2000, when Valentín Paniagua was sworn in as interim president and was then succeeded by the government of Alejandro Toledo in 2001. Of these investigations, antidumping duties were applied to 9 cases in the first five years (1.5 per year) whereas, in the second stage, this figure rose to 21 cases in five years (4.2 per year). Investigations that were considered founded grew from 32 percent from 1993 to 2000 and from 66 percent from 2001 to 2003.

Incidence by Sectors In terms of sectors, the use of the antidumping mechanism has been diversified (see table 8.5). Though table 8.5 presents the data in larger categories, sixteen different sectors have requested trade defense measures, eight of which submitted three or more applications. This diversified pattern has not varied significantly between the early period (1993–98) and the most recent period (1999–2003), the most frequent user being the iron and steel sector, with 18 percent of total cases. Likewise, agriculture, textiles, and meters (electricity and water) represent 11 percent each of the total, while chemical products have a 9 percent share.

Only six agricultural cases involved antidumping investigations. This scarce use of defense mechanisms must not be seen as an absence of unfair practices in agriculture but as a result of the composition of the sector in Peru. It is mostly composed of small- and medium-size farms that lack the organizational or management capacity to prepare an antidumping case. A group of cotton producers, for instance, expressed their interest in presenting a dumping case, but they did not submit an application requesting that the commission initiate an investigation

TABLE 8.5 Antidumping Investigations in Peru, by Sector

Sector	1993–98 (number)	1999–2003 (number)	1993–2003 Number	1993–2003 Percentage
Iron and steel	4	6	10	18
Meters	5	3	8	14
Agriculture	2	4	6	11
Textile	3	3	6	11
Chemicals	2	3	5	9
Tires	2	1	3	5
Shoes	1	2	3	5
Others	7	9	16	28
Total	26	31	57	100

Source: Central Reserve Bank of Peru.

on its own account, arguing that they lacked the necessary management capacity. However, commission policy is that affected producers must provide proof of damage themselves and be involved in the process.

Incidence by Country The incidence of antidumping investigations by country of origin of imports shows that the main country reported was China with 28 percent of total cases (see table 8.6). Most imports of Chinese origin are textiles, clothing, and water meters, and to a lesser extent, stainless steel cutlery and pans, tires, zippers, pottery, and iron hinges. Of the total applications against China, only three cases were declared unfounded, one because the product reported was not similar to the product manufactured in the country and another because the cause of damage disappeared. Peru does not apply the most-favored nation clause to imports from China.

Chile has the second highest number of antidumping reports with 15 percent of the total, a frequency that is explained by the existence of the Bilateral Trade Agreement, which does not include dumping clauses. Argentina is third with 13 percent of the total. Likewise, the figures on antidumping investigations that led to definitive duties show a similar pattern of incidence by country; China represents 32 percent of the total, and Chile has a 19 percent share. Most investigations initiated against Argentina did not lead to the application of antidumping duties, and thus, its share is only 4 percent. Nevertheless, of total investigations initiated against those three countries, 64 percent, 56 percent, and 17 percent, respectively, led to the application of antidumping duties.

TABLE 8.6 Antidumping Investigations, by Country and Region

Country/region	Dumping (number)	Subsidies (number)	Safeguards (number)	All three mechanisms Number	Percent
China	19	0	1	20	28
Other Asian countries	7	0	0	7	10
Chile	11	0	0	11	15
Argentina	7	2	0	9	13
Brazil	5	1	0	6	8
Colombia–R. B. de Venezuela–Bolivia	4	0	0	4	6
Mexico	3	0	0	3	4
Europe	1	1	0	2	3
Non-WTO	6	0	1	7	10
Others	1	1	0	2	3
Total	64	5	2	71	100

Source: Indecopi; authors' calculations.

Note: Some cases are recorded in more than one country. Therefore, sums differ from other tables.

Average Length of Processes The average delay for the resolution of cases has varied over time. For safeguard and antidumping duty applications, from presentation of the request to the final resolution, the delay has been 9.5 months on average, without including appeals. This figure increased slightly, from 8.4 months for cases presented between 1993 and 1996 to 10 months for cases presented since 2001, with the exception of those that received provisional duties, in which case the waiting time was shorter.

Although some sources interviewed say that time frames have become shorter, this trend is not reflected in the data. There are still petitions that go through an 8-month decision process and others that delay 12 months. Although a dumping or safeguard investigation requires a certain amount of time to get reliable results, there is no consensus as to the most desirable length for processes. Investigators who are former members of commissions believe that extended processes not only are part of the technical investigation of reported cases but also discourage the unnecessary presentation of applications.

Andean Community Cases WTO agreements state that dumping or safeguard cases between countries that are signatories of bilateral or multilateral agreements may be solved within the context of such agreements. Because Peru is a signatory member of the Andean Community, the applications for investigations against imports from countries that are also members must be presented before the General Secretariat of the Andean Community pursuant to Decision 456.

Five cases have been presented by Peruvian producers before the Andean Community in the past 10 years, 6 percent of total applications received by CDS. The figure might seem low, but it is proportional to the low volume of Peruvian imports from the Andean Community, which in 2002 represented 8 percent of total imports. At present (December 2004), some cases remain unresolved, such as the case of edible vegetable butter presented by Peru against Colombia.

In the Andean Community, the investigation is carried out by the authorities in charge of the integration process within the Andean market. Applications for dumping or safeguards could, therefore, be perceived as an obstacle to the integration process, which is the Andean Community's overriding priority.

Between 1998 and 1999, Peru was invited by its partners to adopt community safeguard and antidumping policies against third parties. Peru chose to keep its individual regime.

Safeguard Cases Only four investigation applications for safeguard duties have been presented in Peru. Two of them were declared inappropriate, and only two deserved an investigation. One of them was initiated on May 11, 1999, by Siderperú, an iron company, which requested the application of safeguards on hot-rolled and cold-rolled steel sheets and coils, and construction steel bars from non-WTO member countries. CDS investigated the case and presented a favorable report to the Multisector Commission. However, this body never met to make a decision, thus, the political decision not to apply these measures became evident by default. Seven months later, the company presented a dumping case for the same products. In December 1999, definitive antidumping duties over the same imports from Ukraine and the Russian Federation were approved at the request of Siderperú.

The other safeguard case concerns clothing from China. It was presented in October 2003 and is covered in the section describing specific cases.

Appeals The Competition Defense Courtroom of Indecopi's court is the second administrative instance, and it hears appeals presented by the parties in the processes followed before any of Indecopi's commissions. Of the 81 cases reviewed by CDS, 7 percent of the total cases received by the court, 34 were appealed, of which 30 corresponded to dumping cases and one to safeguards.

According to the data available, of 30 dumping appeals, the court confirmed the CDS determination in nearly 90 percent of the cases. In three cases, the appeal has been revoked or returned to be modified, and four cases have pending resolutions.

Specific Cases

In the following cases we do not reveal the names of the companies involved. Otherwise the reports are factually correct—real, not hypothetical cases.

Cast Steel Balls: Chile In February 2000, a Peruvian company, called Acme Peru in this discussion, which manufactures 50 percent of the domestic production of cast steel balls for metallic mineral grinding, requested that CDS conduct an investigation into imports from a Chilean company, which we will call Monarch Chile, on the grounds of suspected dumping practices. In July 2000, the company (called Steelco Peru here) that manufactures the remaining 50 percent of the domestic production—in this case, forged steel balls, formally appeared in the process and opposed the investigation request, indicating that it was not affected by Chilean imports.

In 1998, Peru and Chile had signed an Economic Complementation Agreement to form a free trade zone and had established duty free schedules for several products. Steel balls for mineral grinding had been exonerated from tariff payments since the second half of 1998.The volume of Chilean steel balls in the Peruvian market increased from 200 metric tons in 1999 to 7,000–8,000 metric tons in 2000. In March 2001, having completed the investigation and proved the dumping and its relation to the damage caused, CDS imposed definitive ad valorem duties of 11.05 percent.

However, parallel to the Peruvian investigation, in Chile, a local company, called Acme Chile in this discussion, presented a dumping investigation request against Peruvian imports of the same product—steel balls manufactured and exported by Steelco Peru.

The Peruvian and Chilean companies that submitted the applications are business partners with the same name. They have a corporate agreement by which the Peruvian company cannot export to Chile and vice versa. The goal of this joint strategy was to consolidate their positions in the local markets through parallel applications against their main competitors, thus neutralizing the recent trade agreement between both countries, which established mutual tariff exonerations for this product.

The corporate objective of the Peruvian producer and its Chilean partner succeeded only partially. Peru applied an 11 percent antidumping duty and Chile turned down the application against the Peruvian exporter.

Cornstarch and Glucose Syrup: Mexico On May 10, 1996, CDS initiated an investigation of suspected dumping in cornstarch and glucose syrup imports from Mexico. The Mexican company accepted the dumping charges and requested a price undertaking that was refused by the commission. Given the significant increase of imports recorded two months after the investigation was initiated, provisional duties of 9.51 percent were applied for cornstarch and of 14.68 percent for glucose syrup. When the investigation was over, definitive duties were fixed. The Mexican company appealed but the Court confirmed the resolution of the commission in August 1997.

Two years later, the Mexican company requested a new investigation to leave without effect the antidumping duties that had been applied. This action led to the reduction of duties on glucose syrup to 3.32 percent.

This case was the first one in which a revision of duties was requested on the basis of a change of circumstances. The process was favorable to the exporting company in relation to one of its products.

In addition, the case resulted in a commission policy of not accepting price undertakings, considering that the effect, which would be the same as for the application of antidumping duties, would not justify the effort and logistics necessary to track and inspect accordingly. Instead, antidumping duties are controlled by Customs, they are fiscal revenue, and they do not require supervision by the commission.

Although Peruvian law contemplates price undertakings, the commission interpreted it as an option and not as an obligation, choosing to restrict them to inevitable cases, as, for example, when instead of being proposed by the exporter or its government, price undertakings are agreed by the parties as a way to suspend the investigation.

Textile Clothing: China In October 2003, the Society of Industries requested that CDS carry out a safeguard investigation against textile clothing products of Chinese origin because of the extraordinary increase in their volume. The commission conducted a study of 288 items of clothing, towels, bed sheets, and bed linens and identified 106 that represented the main quantity of Chinese imports into Peru at present. Safeguard measures were to be applied to these imports.

China's protocol of accession to WTO established a *Specific Product Transitional Safeguard* mechanism, which contains a clause that allows for the imposition of provisional safeguards. For this mechanism to be applied, it must be proved that the reported imports cause, or threaten to cause, disruption in the domestic industry.

In November 2003, only one month after the investigation was initiated, Indecopi's CDS report concluded that conditions for an immediate application of provisional transitional safeguards to Chinese textile clothing articles had been met and that, if these measures were not taken, the domestic industry that supplies the local market would suffer an injury that would be difficult to repair. The commission also recommended that Customs take adequate control measures to avoid evasion of the possible duties to be applied, through migration of items or contraband. It also recommended that the Ministry of Production and the interested economic agents be alert for any increase in the imported volume of items that were not affected, so they could take new measures as soon as possible.

The report was presented to the Multisector Commission. On December 5, 2003, provisional safeguards to Chinese textile clothing articles were applied for an effective period of 200 days.

The hidden protectionist interests of the liberal period of the past decade had reappeared, taking advantage of the fall in popularity of Fujimori's government, in an attempt to identify the elimination of protectionist barriers in Peru among the excesses of his government. The local textile industry, pressed by massive and frustrating competition from China, served as a scenario for these appearances.

Although they had the option to present a dumping application and they knew that dumping would be easy to prove, some industrial sectors—part of the textile industry joined by small- and medium-size clothing manufacturers—chose the course that offered them the greatest margin of trade union and political pressure, and they pressed the government for the more political and drastic measure of safeguards because they refused to assume the effort and costs of an antidumping investigation.

The pressure on the government that was channeled through the Ministry of Production sought to create the image that all unfair competition in the textile clothing sector came from China. In a highly political context, and with unprecedented swiftness, safeguard measures were imposed.

In June 2004, when the effective period of 200 calendar days was about to expire, an open political battle broke out between prosafeguard groups, textile and clothing companies, and antisafeguard groups, especially exporters with important Chinese clients and the Embassy of China in Peru. The battle involved the media, government sectors, Congress, and public opinion. The debate centered on whether possible retaliation by China on Peruvian exports to that country could be more harmful than the damage caused by Chinese textile clothing imports.

After many years, protectionist interests were again seen to be maneuvering in the media, as well as in street demonstrations, in coordination with textile clothing manufacturers' arguments in front of Congress. And for the first time, there was a debate in which neither the damage nor the right to exercise trade defense was discussed. The argument was between (a) those who opposed safeguards and demanded that the issue should be settled through a technical antidumping investigation, which would not constitute a protectionist measure, and (b) those who insisted on political support for the industry, defending the use of safeguards as a traditional protectionist measure.

At the time of writing this chapter, the government's position on the safeguards was not clear. The most recent decision was to eliminate provisional transitional safeguards to avoid trade retaliation from China, and to adopt provisional general safeguards instead. But the new countries affected by that decision are likely to apply countervailing measures.

Peru's legal and institutional system has worked to the extent that protectionist pressure for the immediate application of general safeguards was avoided. But in the long term, the operation of the system will depend on the capacity of governments to define a course in the face of inevitable pressures.

Conclusions

The creation of the current antidumping and safeguard system between 1990 and 1993 in Peru must be understood within the context of a long historical process in which there have been swings between protection and liberalization. However, the current context of strong globalization and the gradual consolidation of a market culture in the country suggest the probability of an "end of story," and that most of the current system will last.

The rules and institutions of the current antidumping-safeguard system were conceived as part of an ambitious reform package that was applied beginning in 1990 and that focused on liberalization and the promotion of competition. The current system was designed before and independently of the Uruguay Round. Likewise, neither the design nor the application of the system has been influenced by exchange rate fluctuations. Both the design and the staffing of the institutions system have strongly reflected the principles of technical autonomy, low level of political capture, and belief in the market.

There is a clear differentiation between unfair competition and dumping on the one hand, and damage and safeguards on the other hand, applying strict technical criteria to the former and an openly political decision to the latter. Nevertheless, there are various indicators of a partial retreat from the principles of nonpolitical interference and liberalization, especially since 2000. Peru's experience suggests that WTO should place a greater priority on institutional monitoring in countries such as Peru, including the certification of its institutional processes, and an insistence that the operation of the system be adequately financed.

Notes

1. A relation of these restrictions is presented in table 2.10 of Boloña Behr and Illescas (1997, 56).
2. Single Exchange Market, official exchange rate.
3. Legislative Decree 701, (October 1991).
4. Legislative Decree 662, (August 1991).

5. Legislative Decree 716, (October 1991).

6. Law 26122.

7. Law 28032.

8. Law 28015.

9. Law 27809.

10. Law 27943.

11. Law 26017.

12. Itintec is an agency responsible for trademarks and patents registration.

13. An example of the agency's bureaucratic style: A company that imported rubber tires requested a Certificate of Technical Standards from Itintec. The company required this certificate to import a lot of 50 tractor tires with special specifications. Throughout the process, inefficient bureaucracy and duplicity of roles required that 25 tires be delivered for inspection. The tires were cut in slices and made unusable. When the certificate was granted for the 50 units, only 25 were left. This illustration could have become a mere anecdote, but the importing company belonged to the family of the new president's in-laws, and this event occurred precisely some months before the agency was dissolved.

14. The temporary government of Valentín Paniagua, 2000–1.

15. Question-response procedure reported in the WTO Web site after the notification of Peru's antidumping regulation in 1998. The questions came from Canada and the European Union and referred to the lesser duty rule.

16. To date, the tax unit is fixed in S/.4,000, equivalent to US$1,160.

17. Up until the date of the draft of this study, consumers were not recognized as interested parties. However, a subsequent decree, Supreme Decree 017-2004-MINCETUR, has modified the procedure. Possible affected parties are now notified and invited to present their opinion, and the impact report is now prepared, not by the petitioner, but by Indecopi.

References

Boloña Behr, Carlos, and Javier Illescas 1997. *Políticas arancelarias en el Perú, 1980-1997*. Lima: Free Market Economy Institute, University of San Ignacio de Loyola.

Central Reserve Bank of Peru (BCRP).

National Society of Industries. 2003. *Company Experiences with Foreign Competition*, Lima.

INDEX